LATER LANGUAGE DEVELOPMENT
AGES 9 THROUGH 19

LATER LANGUAGE DEVELOPMENT
AGES 9 THROUGH 19

■

Edited by

Marilyn A. Nippold, Ph.D.
Associate Professor
Speech Pathology-Audiology
University of Oregon
Eugene, Oregon

A College-Hill Publication
Little, Brown and Company
Boston/Toronto/San Diego

College-Hill Press
A Division of
Little, Brown and Company (Inc.)
34 Beacon Street
Boston, Massachusetts 02108

Library of Congress Cataloging in Publication Data
Main entry under title:

Later language development.

  "A College-Hill publication."
  Bibliography.
  Includes index.
  1. Language acquisition.   I. Nippold, Marilyn A.,
1951–
P118.L3895   1988   401′.1   88-6866

ISBN 0-316-61115-8

Printed in the United States of America

Contents

■

Acknowledgments		vi
Preface		vii
Contributors		ix
Chapter 1	Introduction *Marilyn A. Nippold*	1
Chapter 2	The Nature of Literacy *Nickola Wolf Nelson*	11
Chapter 3	The Literate Lexicon *Marilyn A. Nippold*	29
Chapter 4	Spoken and Written Syntax *Cheryl M. Scott*	49
Chapter 5	Reading and Writing *Nickola Wolf Nelson*	97
Chapter 6	Cognition *Alan G. Kamhi and René Friemoth Lee*	127
Chapter 7	Verbal Reasoning *Marilyn A. Nippold*	159
Chapter 8	Figurative Language *Marilyn A. Nippold*	179
Chapter 9	Linguistic Ambiguity *Marilyn A. Nippold*	211
Chapter 10	Language and Socialization *Douglas C. Cooper and Lynne Anderson-Inman*	225
Chapter 11	Pragmatics *M. Irene Stephens*	247
Subject Index		263

ACKNOWLEDGMENTS

Appreciation is extended to the following individuals for their editorial assistance with earlier versions of the chapters: Roberta Corrigan, Nancy Creaghead, René Friemoth Lee, Philip J. Levinson, M. Irene Stephens, and Genese Warr-Leeper.

Several people assisted with the research and writing efforts for chapters two and five. During the project, Kathryn Klein served as the author's graduate assistant. In that role, she transcribed and coded written language samples for computer analysis. She also played a major role in the research on narrative structure as part of her graduate research project. Jon Miller and Robin Chapman, University of Wisconsin-Madison, shared the IBM version of the SALT program and the accompanying file management program (SALTFile) for use in this project. Edwardsburg, Michigan, public schools administrators and teachers and Professor Phillip Egan of Western Michigan University assisted with data collection. Constance Weaver, Michael Clark, and Lynne McCauley of Western Michigan University shared their libraries and their ideas. The willingness of the author's son, David, and daughter, Nicki, along with her friends, Monica and Jarrod, to permit the sharing of samples of their writing is also appreciated.

PREFACE

∎

Interest in later language development has escalated in recent years, particularly among speech-language pathologists, educators, psychologists, sociologists, and linguists. Along with this heightened interest has come a burgeoning of research in normal language development in older children and adolescents. This topic should occupy the minds of researchers well into the future as the realization proliferates that language development continues well beyond the preschool years and, in fact, has no clear point of completion.

Despite the recent interest and research in later language development, most textbooks on normal language development focus primarily on young children, thereby giving the impression that later language development is insignificant, particularly during adolescence. Vicki Reed (1986)[1] targeted this problem, stating "there is no cohesive, integrated body of knowledge regarding normal language development during adolescence" (p. 229). The basic purpose of this book is to fill that void. The book attempts to describe what is known about later language development and to point out what is not known, thereby providing direction for future research on this topic. Normal development during the 9 through 19 age range is the focus. Chapters cover development of the lexicon, spoken and written syntax, reading and writing, verbal reasoning, figurative language, linguistic ambiguity, and pragmatics. The nature of literacy, cognition, and socialization are also covered because of their relevance to later language development.

The authors of each chapter assume that the reader has a basic understanding of normal language development, particularly in young children. The chapters are based largely on research contained in well-known journals and books published in the United States or the United Kingdom. To present a cohesive and timely review of the various topics, the results of recent, unpublished research are also included where appropriate. The book is data-based and reflects the view that scientific inquiry should be the basis for educational and clinical activities. In discussing the origins of speech-language pathology as a formal profession, Carol Prutting (1983)[2] pointed out that "the field was founded for the purpose of promoting the scientific

---

[1]Reed, V. A. (1986). Language-disordered adolescents. In V. A. Reed (Ed.), *An introduction to children with language disorders* (pp. 228-249). New York: Macmillan.
[2]Prutting, C. A. (1983). Scientific inquiry and communicative disorders: An emerging paradigm across six decades. In T. M. Gallagher and C. A. Prutting (Eds.), *Pragmatic assessment and intervention issues in language* (pp. 247-266). San Diego, CA: College-Hill Press.

study of speech correction" (p. 262), and that "our earliest leaders prided themselves on being scientists as well as practitioners" (p. 261). Although the profession now encompasses far more than "speech correction," the basic principles set forth in 1925 by Lee Edward Travis, Robert West, and Sara Stinchfield Hawk (1987)[3] are just as relevant today.

It is expected that this book on later language development will serve as a reference for professionals working with older children and adolescents, particularly speech-language pathologists, teachers, and psychologists. However, it must be emphasized that this is not a book on language disorders. Although the content of the book has important implications for the educational or clinical management of language disordered children and adolescents, it was not the authors' intention to discuss those implications in detail, a task that could easily constitute a separate publication.

Marilyn A. Nippold
Editor

---

[3]Douglass, R. (1987). Lee Edward Travis: 1896–1987. *ASHA, 29*, 9.

CONTRIBUTORS

Lynne Anderson-Inman, Ph.D.
Teacher Education
University of Oregon
Eugene, Oregon

Douglas C. Cooper, Ph.D.
Teacher Education
University of Oregon
Eugene, Oregon

Alan G. Kamhi, Ph.D.
Department of Audiology
  and Speech Pathology
Memphis State University
Memphis, Tennessee

René Friemoth Lee, Ph.D.
Charter-Lakeside Hospital
Memphis, Tennessee

Nickola Wolf Nelson, Ph.D.
Department of Speech Pathology
  and Audiology
Western Michigan University
Kalamazoo, Michigan

Marilyn A. Nippold, Ph.D.
Speech Pathology-Audiology
University of Oregon
Eugene, Oregon

Cheryl M. Scott, Ph.D.
Department of Speech and Language
  Pathology and Audiology
Oklahoma State University
Stillwater, Oklahoma

M. Irene Stephens, Ph.D.
Department of Communicative
  Disorders
Northern Illinois University
De Kalb, Illinois

CHAPTER 1

■

INTRODUCTION

■

MARILYN A. NIPPOLD

T his book is about normal language development during the preadolescent and adolescent years. Preadolescence is the period of late childhood
(ages 9 through 12) and adolescence is the period of transition between
childhood and adulthood (ages 13 through 19). It will be shown that significant growth occurs in language development during the 9-through-19 age
range.

Research in language development traditionally has emphasized young
children (Obler, 1985). As a result, most books on language development
contain a great deal of information detailing the early stages of phonologic,
syntactic, morphologic, and semantic development and far less information
on later language development (e.g., Dale, 1976; de Villiers and de Villiers,
1978; Elliot, 1983; Muma, 1986; Owens, 1988). Because of this research
emphasis, some readers may question the possibility of significant language
growth during the preadolescent and adolescent years, particularly if they
subscribe to the popular notion that language development is complete by
the onset of puberty.

The roots of this notion run deep. Over 20 years ago, Lenneberg (1967)
set forth his influential theory concerning the "critical period for language
acquisition." The theory stated that the normal child is maximally ready
to acquire language between the ages of 2 and 12 years due to biological
maturational processes that regulate the onset and timing of language
acquisition. With the onset of puberty, according to the theory, the capacity
for language acquisition is severely restricted. The theory also stated that

the bulk of language is acquired by age four, and that after that time further refinements consist mainly of additions to the lexicon and stylistic improvements in the use of grammar.

Some support for Lenneberg's theory can be found in the study of bilingualism (for example, see de Villiers and de Villiers, 1978). Most normal children can easily learn a second language before puberty, particularly if they are immersed in a foreign culture where their native language is not spoken. After puberty, however, it becomes increasingly difficult to learn a second language (Fromkin and Rodman, 1988; Obler, 1985). This was observed during the mid-1970s when Vietnamese families began immigrating to the United States following the conflict in Southeast Asia. Within months, the young Vietnamese children attending American schools had learned to speak English with little or no formal instruction, while their parents struggled arduously through formal language classes in an effort to master the basics of English phonology, syntax, morphology, and semantics.

However, while adolescents and adults have greater difficulty acquiring a second language, it is possible for them to do so with proper instruction, practice, and motivation (Obler, 1985). This fact alone casts serious doubt on the view that the language acquisition process comes to a halt with the onset of puberty. In addition, as the study of the language of children has broadened to include topics other than lexical and grammatical attainments, further evidence against Lenneberg's theory has accumulated. For example, research reviewed in this book shows that significant growth occurs in the areas of discourse, pragmatics, figurative language, and linguistic ambiguity throughout the preadolescent and adolescent years. Research with older children and adolescents has also generated greater awareness of the linguistic bases of traditional classroom activities such as reading and writing (Wallach and Liebergott, 1984; Wolf and Dickinson, 1985), further dispelling the notion that the bulk of language is acquired by the age of four. Indeed, the evidence suggests that language development has no clear point of completion, and that "language through the life-span" (Obler, 1985) may be a more realistic perspective.

EARLY VERSUS LATER LANGUAGE DEVELOPMENT

It is important to contrast early with later language development. During early childhood, language is acquired rapidly, and the changes that occur from year to year are highly salient. For example, on hearing the taperecorded language samples of two young children, even the lay person should have no difficulty distinguishing the 1-year-old from the 2-year-old. However, the task of distinguishing a 9-year-old from a 10-year-old under similar listening conditions would be far more challenging even for an expert in children's language development. This discrepancy arises because the linguistic changes that occur during later childhood and adolescence are much more subtle, a phenomenon which undoubtedly has reinforced the view that "not much happens in the language department beyond the pre-school years." However, the research suggests that language development during the 9-through-19 age range unfolds in a slow and protracted manner, and that change becomes obvious only when sophisticated linguistic phenomena are analyzed and nonadjacent age groups (e.g., 9-year-olds and 12-year-olds) are compared. Documenting language growth in older children and adolescents also requires that written forms of communication be scrutinized in addition to spoken forms.

This brings up another contrast between early and later language development: the emphasis in growth. During early childhood, the major language goal is the acquisition of spoken communication skills. During the school years, however, the major goal becomes the acquisition of written communication skills (Wolf and Dickinson, 1985). Learning to read and write effectively requires a strong foundation in spoken communication (Reed, 1986; Wallach and Liebergott, 1984). But this fact does not imply that the foundation is complete by the time a child begins school or that the acquisition of spoken communication is no longer important. Throughout the school years, important developments occur in both spoken and written forms of communication.

Another contrast between early and later language development concerns the sources of input. With preschool children, spoken communication is the major source of language stimulation. However, with older children and adolescents both spoken and written forms of communication are significant sources of stimulation. At about the fourth-grade level, a major transition occurs and children begin to use their reading skills to learn advanced vocabulary (Miller and Gildea, 1987), complex syntax, and figurative meanings (see Chapters 4, 5, and 8). Proficiency in reading suddenly frees the child to acquire a great deal of linguistic and cognitive knowledge independently and to pursue personal interests more readily (Reed, 1986). As a result, children become increasingly individualistic in their cognitive and linguistic abilities during later childhood and adolescence (Gallatin, 1975; Kamhi, 1987). For example, a fourth grader's special interest in dinosaurs may inspire her to read many books on this subject. As her interest develops, she may gradually acquire a specialized "dinosaur lexicon" that contains such words as *theropod*, *sauropod*, *cretaceous*, and *triassic*. As her interest in dinosaurs continues, it may eventually expand into related subject areas such as paleontology, archaeology, or volcanology during the high school or college years (see Chapter 3).

As youngsters progress through school, the greater freedom afforded to them in the selection of course work, extracurricular activities, and social contacts also promotes the development of linguistic and cognitive individualism (Kamhi, 1987). Thus, it is not uncommon to find adolescents who, for example, show average performance in algebra but outstanding performance in literary analysis or theatre arts. This phenomenon of increasing individualism makes it difficult for researchers to establish firm guidelines for "normal" linguistic and cognitive performance in adolescents and young adults, a theme that recurs throughout this book.

Another contrast between early and later language development concerns the settings for development and the directness of instruction. Young children learn language primarily from hearing and using it in nondirected, informal settings. In general, adults do not directly teach a young child to talk, although they often simplify their linguistic input to the child and reinforce the child's communicative attempts (Owens, 1988). Although older children and adolescents also learn language in informal settings through indirect modeling and reinforcement, they also acquire a great deal of language through formal instruction, particularly in language arts or English classes where subjects such as grammar, spelling, vocabulary, etymology, literature, and composition are featured (e.g., Coon, Cramer, Fillmer, Lefcourt, Martin, and Thompson, 1980; Welch and Bennett, 1981; see also Chapters 3, 4, and 5).

Related to formal classroom instruction is another point of contrast: the use of metalinguistics. Language development in older children and adolescents often requires metalinguistic competence (Grunwell, 1986; Van Kleeck, 1984). For example, learning to read and write requires the active analysis of certain aspects of language which were largely ignored during the preschool years or experienced passively (see Chapter 5). In first grade, for example, students are asked to perform such tasks as identifying the words in a sentence that sound the same but look different (e.g., "He saw the man's son standing in the sun"), or identifying the word in a sentence that tells how an agent performed some action (e.g., "The pig walked away slowly") (Fay, Ross, and LaPray, 1981). By seventh grade, students are asked to determine the meanings of unfamiliar compound words (e.g., *yachtsman, landfall, breadstuffs*) by analyzing the smaller component words and then examining the linguistic context for additional clues to meaning (Welch and Bennett, 1981). Metalinguistic competence also enables the older child or adolescent to determine the meanings of unfamiliar expressions such as metaphors, proverbs, and idioms (see Chapter 8). As with unfamiliar words, this determination can be accomplished by attending to the linguistic context in which an expression occurs, then generating a temporary interpretation of it that can later be accepted or rejected as more information becomes available.

Another point of contrast concerns the fact that aspects of language that are learned by older children and adolescents are often more abstract than those that are learned by younger children. Whereas young children are quite literal in their interpretations of language, older children show an increasing ability to appreciate nonliteral meanings (see Chapter 8). For example, on hearing Mom and Dad talk about "skeletons in the closet," a 4-year-old girl may think about Halloween and feel frightened. In contrast, her 12-year-old sister will quickly determine from the linguistic context that their parents are talking about old family secrets. A difference in abstractness is also evident in the types of words youngsters acquire (see Chapter 3). For example, as the 4-year-old's lexicon expands, a large number of words having concrete referents (e.g., the names of animals, people, vehicles, clothing, toys) will be added. In contrast, as her 12-year-old sister acquires new words, many of them will represent abstract notions (e.g., *dimension*, *inefficient*, *officialdom*) (Dale and Eichholz, 1960).

Youngsters' reasoning processes also evince this transition from concrete to abstract (see Chapters 6 and 7). For example, the 4-year-old firmly believes that Santa Claus is a man in a red suit with a long white beard who brings toys at Christmas. Several years earlier, however, her 12-year-old sister went through a complex process of weighing the evidence concerning the literal existence of Santa (Scheibe and Condry, 1987) and now believes that he is actually a symbol of the Christmas spirit. This contrast in abstractness is also apparent in youngsters' understanding and appreciation of linguistic ambiguity (see Chapter 9). For example, in the second or third grade, children begin to tell and laugh at jokes and riddles whose humor stems from phonological, lexical, or syntactic ambiguity (e.g., Q: "What animal can jump as high as a tree?" A: "All animals. Trees cannot jump") (McGhee, 1979). By sixth or seventh grade, youngsters can readily appreciate the linguistic ambiguity that occurs in magazine advertisements (e.g., "Introducing the Upper Crusts. Two sensational new entrees from Stouffer's") (Nippold, Cuyler, and Braunbeck-Price, in press). In contrast, preschoolers have little or no appreciation of linguistic ambiguities.

Related to abstractness is the youngster's social ability to take the perspective of another. Compared to young children, preadolescents and adolescents are more aware of the needs of their listeners and adjust the content and style of their speech accordingly (see Chapters 10 and 11). This enhanced sensitivity to the communicative needs of others is also evinced during formal writing tasks (see Chapter 5) and story telling activities (see Chapter 11) where older children and adolescents typically provide greater contextual and background information than young children are able to provide.

CONTENT OF THIS BOOK

In the chapters that follow, these themes of later language development are discussed in detail. In Chapter 2, Nickola Wolf Nelson discusses various social, educational, cultural, and cognitive factors that influence the acquisition of literacy, and the similarities and differences between spoken and written communication. This chapter provides important background information for those that follow, particularly Chapters 3, 4, and 5.

In Chapter 3, Marilyn A. Nippold discusses lexical learning during the 9-through-19 age range, focusing on youngsters' comprehension of particular verbs, adverbs, and connectives closely associated with literacy. She also covers the development of word definition, a metalinguistic process that requires lexical knowledge, semantic organization, and clarity of expression. The development of spoken and written syntax is the topic of Chapter 4, where Cheryl M. Scott discusses issues concerning developmental schedules, expanding contexts, multifunctional structures, the adult model, and the measurement of growth. She also presents quantitative and qualitative data for the development of the production of selected syntactic structures. In Chapter 5, Nelson reviews the developmental shifts that occur in youngsters' reading and writing skills. Her review focuses primarily on research from English speaking countries where formal education is widespread. Included are some original data based on written language samples gathered from fourth-, seventh-, and tenth-grade students, and from college freshmen.

Chapter 6, by Alan G. Kamhi and Rene Friemoth Lee, discusses the development of cognition during the preadolescent and adolescent years. Four different approaches are presented: Piagetian theory, Case's neo-Piagetian theory, Fischer's skill theory, and Sternberg's triarchic theory. The authors also discuss the relationship between language and cognition, and provide insight into mechanisms related to growth in both of those areas. Information contained in their chapter is particularly relevant to the chapters on verbal reasoning, figurative language, and linguistic ambiguity that follow.

The theme of Nippold's Chapter 7 is that verbal reasoning is a mental construct where language and cognition converge. In this chapter, development of two major types of verbal reasoning, analogical and syllogistic, are discussed. It is shown that various internal and external factors are related to youngsters' competence in solving problems of both these types; for example, cognitive development is an important internal factor, whereas semantics is an important external factor. Similarly, in Chapter 8, Nippold shows how cognition and semantics are also related to youngsters' competence with figurative language. Major types of figurative language discussed in this chapter include metaphors, similes, idioms, and proverbs. In Chapter 9, Nippold discusses the development of linguistic ambiguity in three different domains: isolated sentences, humor (jokes and riddles), and advertisements. A distinction is made between ambiguous stimuli occurring in structured versus naturalistic contexts. This chapter also provides information concerning the relationship between cognitive development and competence with linguistic ambiguity.

In Chapter 10, Douglas C. Cooper and Lynne Anderson-Inman discuss the close relationship between language and socialization, and the role that language plays in the socialization process during the 9-through-19 age range. They also discuss linguistic socialization in relation to five issues affecting youngsters of this age range: identity, gender, cross-sex communication, the peer group, and friendship. Information contained in Cooper and Anderson-Inman's chapter is particularly relevant to M. Irene Stephens' chapter on pragmatic development. Stephens' Chapter 11 concludes the book with a review of the literature on classroom discourse, peer instruction, narrative abilities, and special settings. She highlights the contrast between structured versus naturalistic contexts as it relates to the study of pragmatics in older children and adolescents.

IMPLICATIONS

This book has important implications for educational planning of normal youngsters in the 9-through-19 age range, and for assessment and intervention with preadolescents and adolescents with language disorders. It should prove useful to a variety of professionals working with both populations, including teachers, curriculum planners, psychologists, social workers, and communicative disorders specialists. However, this is not a book on language disorders and no extensive efforts have been made to apply the information directly to clinical or educational issues. That is a task that could easily constitute several additional publications. It is hoped that other professionals will carry out that task. Nevertheless, it is important at least to mention some salient implications of the book for populations with language disorders.

In recent years, older children and adolescents with language disorders in the United States have received more attention than previously from teachers, communicative disorders specialists, and other professionals in public school settings. With the passage of Public Law 94-142 in 1975, all handicapped youngsters — including older children and adolescents — were guaranteed the right to a free, appropriate education in the least restrictive environment. As a result of this federal law, it was no longer excusable to ignore the older child or adolescent having language-based academic difficulties, and problems with verbal expression and comprehension of the language spoken by teachers, parents, and peers.

Standardized Tests of Later Language Development

The effort to assist these youngsters resulted in the production of a large number of standardized tests designed to identify language disorders in older children and adolescents. However, many of those tests reflected the "cart before the horse" syndrome: because no solid frame of reference was available for later language development, tests were produced largely under the guidance of clinical intuition and guesswork. Many of the standardized tests for older children and adolescents were reviewed by Stephens and Montgomery (1985) who discussed the psychometric properties of those measures. A major problem with many of the tests is that they often contain subtests that evaluate aspects of language that normally develop at much younger ages. For example, the *Adolescent Language Screening Test* (Morgan and Guilford, 1984) was designed for youngsters ages 11 through 17. However, this test evaluates the production of consonant clusters and Brown's (1973) grammatical morphemes. As another example, the *Fullerton Language Test for Adolescents: Second Edition* (Thorum, 1986) contains subtests that evaluate sound blending, syllable counting, and basic morphology. Standardized tests that evaluate aspects of early language acquisition are likely to identify youngsters having the more severe and obvious problems while bypassing those having less obvious but still troublesome linguistic deficits.

However, this problem could be remedied by the development of psychometrically adequate standardized tests that evaluate later aspects of language development, such as the use and understanding of advanced connectives (e.g., *whereas, although, likewise*), figurative expressions (e.g., proverbs, metaphors, and idioms), and advanced syntactic constructions (e.g., adverbial clauses, appositive constructions, nonfinite clauses). With older children and adolescents, both spoken and written language development should be evaluated. When deficits in any of these areas are identified, individualized intervention programs can be designed to remedy a youngster's specific problems.

On the positive side, test developers are beginning to incorporate research in later language development into their products. For example, the *Test of Language Competence* (Wiig and Secord, 1985) for the ages of 9 through 18 contains subtests that assess the understanding of linguistic ambiguity and figurative expressions. *The Word Test* (Jorgensen, Barrett, Huisingh, and Zachman, 1981) for the ages of 7 through 11 assesses the ability to explain lexical ambiguities (e.g., *rock, duck, bark*) and to define words aloud. The *Fullerton* (Thorum, 1986) contains a subtest that assesses explanations of idioms. It is hoped that this trend will continue as more research is conducted on normal language development during the preadolescent and adolescent years, and the results become available to a wide audience of consumers.

REFERENCES

Brown, R. (1973). *A first language: The early stages.* Cambridge, MA: Harvard University Press.

Coon, G.E., Cramer, B.B., Fillmer, H.T., Lefcourt, A., Martin, J., and Thompson, N.C. (1980). *American book English.* New York: Litton Educational Publishing.

Dale, P.S. (1976). *Language development: Structure and function* (2nd ed.). New York: Holt, Rinehart, and Winston.

Dale, E., and Eichholz, G. (1960). *Children's knowledge of words: An interim report.* Columbus, OH: Bureau of Educational Research and Service, Ohio State University.

de Villiers, J.G., and de Villiers, P.A. (1978). *Language acquisition.* Cambridge, MA: Harvard University Press.

Elliot, A.J. (1983). *Child language.* Cambridge, England: Cambridge University Press.

Fay, L., Ross, R.R., and LaPray, M. (1981). *Rand McNally reading program, Level 6: Red rock ranch.* Chicago: Rand McNally.

Fromkin, V., and Rodman, R. (1988). *An introduction to language* (4th ed.). New York: Holt, Rinehart, and Winston.

Gallatin, J.E. (1975). *Adolescence and individuality: A conceptual approach to adolescent psychology.* New York: Harper and Row.

Grunwell, P. (1986). Aspects of phonological development in later childhood. In K. Durkin (Ed.), *Language development in the school years.* Cambridge, MA: Brookline.

Jorgensen, C., Barrett, M., Huisingh, R., and Zachman, L. (1981). *The Word Test: A Test of Expressive Vocabulary and Semantics.* Moline, IL: LinguiSystems.

Kamhi, A.G. (1987, November). *Normal language development: Ages 9 through 19.* Short course presented at the Annual Convention of the American Speech-Language-Hearing Association, New Orleans, LA.

Lenneberg, E.H. (1967). *Biological foundations of language.* New York: John Wiley.

McGhee, P.E. (1979). *Humor: Its origin and development.* San Francisco: Freeman.

Miller, G.A., and Gildea, P.M. (1987). How children learn words. *Scientific American, 257,* 94-99.

Morgan, D.L., and Guilford, A.M. (1984). *Adolescent language screening test.* Tulsa, OK: Modern Education Corporation.

Muma, J.R. (1986). *Language acquisition: A functionalistic perspective.* Austin, TX: Pro-Ed.

Nippold, M.A., Cuyler, J.S., and Braunbeck-Price, R. (in press). Explanation of ambiguous advertisements: A developmental study with children and adolescents. *Journal of Speech and Hearing Research.*

Obler, L.K. (1985). Language through the life-span. In J. Berko Gleason (Ed.), *The development of language* (pp. 277-305). Columbus, OH: Merrill.

Owens, R.E. (1988). *Language development: An introduction* (2nd ed.). Columbus, OH: Merrill.

Reed, V.A. (1986). An introduction to language. In V.A. Reed (Ed.), *An introduction to children with language disorders* (pp. 3-22). New York: Macmillan.

Scheibe, C., and Condry, J. (1987, April). *Learning to distinguish fantasy from reality: Children's beliefs about Santa Claus and other fantasy figures.* Poster session presented at the Biennial Meeting of the Society for Research in Child Development, Baltimore, MD.

Stephens, M.I., and Montgomery, A.A. (1985). A critique of recent relevant standardized tests. *Topics in Language Disorders, 5*(3), 21-45.

Thorum, A.R. (1986). *The Fullerton language test for adolescents* (2nd ed.). Palo Alto, CA: Consulting Psychologists Press.

Van Kleeck, A. (1984). Metalinguistic skills: Cutting across spoken and written language and problem-solving abilities. In G.P. Wallach and K.G. Butler (Eds.), *Language learning disabilities in school-age children* (pp. 128-153). Baltimore, MD: Williams and Wilkins.

Wallach, G.P., and Liebergott, J.W. (1984). Who shall be called "learning disabled": Some new directions. In G.P. Wallach and K.G. Butler (Eds.), *Language learning disabilities in school-age children* (pp. 1-14). Baltimore, MD: Williams and Wilkins.

Welch, B.Y., and Bennett, R.A. (1981). *Teacher's handbook for introduction to literature: Grade 7.* Lexington, MA: Ginn.

Wiig, E.H., and Secord, W. (1985). *Test of language competence.* Columbus, OH: Merrill.

Wolf, M., and Dickinson, D. (1985). From oral to written language: Transitions in the school years. In J. Berko Gleason (Ed.), *The development of language* (pp. 227-276). Columbus, OH: Merrill.

CHAPTER 2

■

THE NATURE OF LITERACY

■

NICKOLA WOLF NELSON

For people living in literate and technological societies, the ability to read and write is a major factor determining their potential for academic and vocational success (Hirsch, 1987). For societies that are not traditionally literate, increasing the literacy of their members is often viewed as the key to greater power within larger world hierarchies (Whiteman, 1981).

Spoken communication is a universal phenomenon. Most children who have unimpaired cognitive, sensory, and motor capabilities learn to speak with little or no formal teaching. In contrast, written communication is far from universal. To learn to read and write effectively, children must be formally taught (Romaine, 1984). This chapter discusses various social, cultural, and educational factors that influence the acquisition of literacy. Its major topics are (1) the relationships among reading, writing, and literacy, (2) the relationships between orality and literacy, and (3) and relationships among literacy, schooling, and cognition.

RELATIONSHIPS AMONG READING, WRITING, AND LITERACY

General agreement exists in the psychological, educational, and linguistic literature that possessing the ability to read and write does not make a person literate. Yet definitions of reading, writing, and literacy vary, and often blend together.

Consider the desired end product, literacy, first. With all of the attention it has recently received, literacy as a domain does not have well defined boundaries (Szwed, 1981). The concept is defined differently by different people for different purposes. As Resnick and Resnick (1980) pointed out, it has also been defined differently at different points in time. For example, well into the nineteenth century, when few people could sign their own names, the high standards of literacy comparable to those of today were applied only to an elite portion of the population. Education was available only to those with social and economic advantages. The application of higher standards of literacy to an entire population is a relatively recent occurrence. The review by Resnick and Resnick showed that this kind of standard has been applied for at most three generations in the United States. It seems that this relatively recent shift in standards has resulted in the increased perception that America has a literacy problem.

Reading and Literacy

Resnick and Resnick also reported that the standard currently used in America seems to be that literacy "requires, at a minimum, the reading of new material and the gleaning of new information from that material" (p. 397). They indicated that the illiteracy rate would be even higher if readers were expected to draw inferential rather than directly stated information from the text, and higher still if the criteria were to read a complex text with literary allusions and metaphoric expression, to interpret it, and to relate it sensibly to other texts. Yet, from an academic perspective, these latter attainments are highly desirable.

In discussing the relationships between reading and literacy, Sticht (1978) indicated that the acquisition of reading is a more limited concept than the acquisition of literacy. He defined learning to read as learning to comprehend language automatically using the visual modality of written language. Sticht defined the process of becoming literate additionally as "learning the new vocabulary and concepts found in the printed materials one uses in learning to read" (p. 159), and as learning "new skills for processing information from printed displays based on the unique properties of such displays" (p. 160). Sticht thought that the distinction between reading and literacy was important. He was concerned that when reading and literacy are treated as synonymous, the failure to respond correctly to a multiple choice question designed to assess literacy might be attributed to inability to read the material, when the failure could as easily be explained by lack of experience with the concept or context, or by insufficient knowledge of the vocabulary.

Hirsch (1987) emphasized that a literate person has knowledge not only of vocabulary but also of history and culture. He commented that "to be truly literate, citizens must be able to grasp the meaning of any piece of writing addressed to the general reader" (p. 12). He developed the concept of *cultural literacy* as the grasp of background information that writers and speakers assume their listeners already have. Lest anyone assume that cultural literacy is the property of any group or class, Hirsch quoted Harvard historian and sociologist Orlando Patterson as saying:

> To assume that this wider culture is static is an error; in fact it is not. It's not a WASP culture; it doesn't belong to any group. It is essentially and constantly changing, and it is open. . . . The English language no longer belongs to any group or nation. (p. 11)

Hirsch conceived of cultural literacy as a "vocabulary" that a group of people are able to use throughout their land because they share associations with others in their society. Hirsch acknowledged that what one needs to know to be literate in a particular culture or country (e.g., Australia) can be specific to that context. In emphasizing the importance of prior knowledge, Hirsch indicated that although much of that knowledge is fuzzy rather than exact, it provides a schema for understanding what is read. He then provided "The List," a 63-page appendix of vocabulary, dates, abbreviations, names, titles, and sayings comprising the knowledge Hirsch believed an individual needs to exhibit a high-school level of literacy in the United States currently.

In addition to the ability to draw on prior knowledge in understanding what is read, another major feature of literacy seems to be the person's ability to consciously monitor his or her own comprehension process. This aspect of literacy, which is related to the ability to perform metacognitive processing, was examined by Forrest-Pressley and Waller (1984). They studied the skills of 227 poor, average, and good readers in grades 3 and 6 in Ontario, Canada, using a set of performance and verbalization tasks related to reading (decoding, comprehension, and strategies), and to developmental factors related to reading (language, attention, and memory). Stressing the importance of metacognitive strategies of comprehension monitoring, Forrest-Pressley and Waller noted that "only older/better readers know that there is a difference between what a word 'says' and what a word 'means'" (p. 125). Readers who have moved into this developmental phase will be able to recognize that even when words have been accurately decoded according to their sounds, the appropriate meanings may not have been constructed or accessed. They also recognize that they may need to use other strategies, such as asking someone or consulting a dictionary, when their decoding skills and existing knowledge alone are insufficient to obtain the full meaning. Forrest-Pressley and Waller took the position that both the availability of prior knowledge about the world (cognition), and the control of flexible strategies for obtaining meaning from written language (metacognition) are important determinants of mature reading ability. Although they did not identify these traits as distinguishing the person who is literate from the one who simply can read, the skills involved are parallel to those identified by

Sticht (1978), and they are consistent with extension of the concept of literacy beyond the concept of the ability to read.

The question of when a reader can be considered literate has been addressed operationally in many parts of the United States in which English competency testing has been introduced (Cooper, 1981). Purves (1981) questioned the validity of many of the currently used instruments for measuring reading competency as being based on too limited a construct. He offered the following elements towards a definition of competence that should be attained by the end of high school by a fluent and flexible reader.

> So far we have seen that the competent reader has a fairly large vocabulary; a working knowledge of a variety of phenomena in the world; a capacity to deal with a variety of syntactic constructions—both to supply connections and to disentangle complexities; and a capacity to determine meaning, purpose, and intended tone and to separate these from personal significance. We have seen, too, that a competent reader approaches a text with a set of preconceptions and a sense of the context in which reading occurs. In general, one doesn't just read; one has a purpose for one's reading, and one reads for many purposes. (p. 77)

Literacy and Writing

Definitions of literacy are consistently tied to developing competence in reading such that meaning can be obtained from a variety of kinds of written language in a variety of contexts (Purves, 1981). Definitions of literacy are less consistent in the degree to which importance is assigned to the role of learning to write as well as learning to read. Whiteman and Hall (1981) lamented the fact that the ongoing national concern about the condition of literacy in the United States is focused almost entirely on reading and often does not include writing. They pointed out that when functional literacy tests do not test writing, even though they often test math and consumer skills, "we lose sight of the lack of writing abilities as a central part of the 'illiteracy problem'" (p. 2).

Complementary to definitions of competence in reading, definitions of competence in writing go beyond the learning of handwriting and spelling skills that are sufficient to transform spoken language into its written counterpart. Odell (1981) indicated that definitions of mature writing by literate individuals should go beyond those that "equate competence with the ability to follow the practice of 'educated people,' to observe the conventions of formal written English, to write clearly, correctly, and concisely" (p. 102). The problem with such definitions, Odell added, is that they do not acknowledge that effective writing requires that writers have something to communicate and that they can determine what they wish to say and how they should say it, given the wide variety of available choices. Odell suggested that the definition of competence in writing should mean "the ability to discover what one wishes to say and to convey one's message through language, syntax, and content that are appropriate for one's audience and purpose" (p. 103).

Definitions of writing must consider both *process* and *product* (Cooper and Odell, 1977). In a more elaborate description of the writing process, Cooper and Odell included the following:

> Composing involves exploring and mulling over a subject; planning the particular piece (with or without notes or outline); getting started; making discoveries about feelings, values, or ideas, even while in the process of writing a draft; making continuous decisions about diction, syntax, and rhetoric in relation to the intended meaning and to the meaning taking shape; reviewing what has accumulated, and anticipating and rehearsing what comes next; tinkering and reformulating; stopping; contemplating the finished piece and perhaps, finally, revising. (p. xi)

A list of the products that might be expected to be written by high school students includes dramatic writing, sensory recording, reporting, generalizing and theorizing, research, personal writing, poetry, prose fiction, and business/practical writing (Cooper and Odell, 1977). In preparing this list, Cooper and Odell emphasized the importance of evaluating a variety of kinds of writing, including those that are produced "out there in the world" (p. x), and not just those that are traditionally evaluated in academic settings.

Summary

Although agreement exists in the psychological, educational, and linguistic literature that definitions of literacy should go beyond definitions of the simple ability to read and write, the boundaries of the definitions are not clearly established. It is generally agreed that in learning to read and write, children must first learn that marks on paper have meaning (e.g., Purves, 1981; Smith, 1971). They must also learn to make the marks and to interpret them so that they make sense. This is the beginning of a continuum that extends through various levels of literacy in which children develop sources of knowledge, and cognitive and metacognitive strategies for comprehending and producing texts of a variety of types, involving both literal meanings and meanings that must be inferred.

In the process of making these developmental shifts, children learn to use written language in ways that differ from their uses of spoken language. Such differences are the topic of the next section.

RELATIONSHIPS BETWEEN ORALITY AND LITERACY

Considerable disagreement can be found among psycholinguists, socio-linguists, and other reading specialists about the degree to which a *great divide* (Goody, 1977; Scribner and Cole, 1980; Street, 1986) separates oral and literate uses of language, and the degree to which oral and literate uses of language rely on, and influence, general cognitive abilities. The great divide argument takes on particular social significance when it is extended to examining differences between the intellectual competencies of people living in oral versus literate cultures, and then attributing those differences to literacy (Scribner and Cole, 1980).

Romaine (1984) identified the orality–literacy debate as one between linguists who believe that written language is heavily dependent on spoken language and those who maintain that writing is essentially distinct. She took the position that speech and writing are coexistent, autonomous systems, and that written language and spoken language are used, for the most part, for different purposes in different situations.

Emig (1977) compiled a list of ways that written language differs from spoken language. Her list included two characteristics that are consistently mentioned in discussions of the differences between the two forms of communication: (1) differences in the *contextualization* of written language compared with spoken language; and (2) differences in the immediacy of *audience* or author when using written language compared with spoken language.

Contextualization

Emphasis on the distinction in contextualization between spoken and written language (and resulting differential effect on cognition) is generally credited to Greenfield and Bruner (1966). Their position was that because spoken language relies on context for the communication of messages, it is context-dependent language. This contrasts with written language, which requires that meaning be clarified independently of the immediate reference (Greenfield, 1972). Written language also differs from spoken language in that it requires language users to be able to glean meaning almost exclusively from texts (and from their own prior understandings) when reading, and to encode meaning into text when writing. This is because a nonverbal context cannot be relied on to provide significant portions of the meaning in written communication to the extent that it can in spoken communication, even when pictorial illustrations are provided.

Such differences in contextualization are said to be intertwined with critical differences in the types of meaning expressed in spoken and written communication. They also are related to variation in both vocabulary and syntactic complexity. However, authors who wish to minimize the existence of the great divide between orality and literacy (e.g., Blank, 1982; Cooper, 1982; Street, 1986; Tannen, 1982) have pointed out that contextualization differences, and related differences in vocabulary and sentence-structure choices, also characterize different types of spoken communication events that vary in degree of formality. Even so, part of becoming competent as a reader and a writer is developing the ability to use decontextualized language (Cooper, 1982).

A number of terms have appeared in the literature for labeling the ends of the contexualization continuum (see Table 2-1). For example, Cook-Gumperz (1977) labeled the type of meaning associated with heavy reliance on nonverbal context as *situated* meaning. She described situated meaning as being common in spoken communication events, particularly those in which the participants are intimately familiar with each other. Cook-Gumperz differentiated situated meaning from *lexicalized* meaning, which is common in written language and in more formal spoken communication events shared by unfamiliar participants. Lexicalized meaning is not available from the nonverbal contexts, but is encoded in the words and phrases themselves. Bernstein (1972) differentiated meaning into similar types. He termed these (1) *particularistic* or *restricted* meaning, in which meaning is implicit in the text and heavy reliance is placed on context to provide part of the meaning, and (2) *universalistic* or *elaborated* meaning, in which meaning is explicit in the language of the text itself apart from nonverbal context. A related set of terms, which has been used by linguists (e.g., Gregory and Carroll, 1978), describes meaning as being *exophoric* or *endophoric*. Exophoric meaning is that in which the context is clear to both parties so that the language of the message can be less explicit. In contrast, endophoric meaning is that in which little shared context is available so that the message must be expressed in a more explicit and self-contextualizing way within the text. Although written language is usually viewed as relying more heavily on endophoric meaning, both spoken and written communication can involve

Table 2-1.
Terms used to represent ends of the contextualization continuum.

Heavy reliance on nonverbal context	Heavy reliance on linguistically encoded meaning
Situated meaning (Cook-Gumperz, 1977)	Lexicalized meaning
Particularistic (restricted) meaning implicit in text (Bernstein, 1972)	Universalistic (elaborated) meaning explicit in text
Exophoric meaning (Gregory & Carroll, 1978)	Endophoric meaning

varying uses of endophoric and exophoric meaning, depending on the functions of the language (Nystrand, 1982a).

Audience

The concept of audience also plays a role in both spoken and written communication, but a different one in each modality (Nystrand, 1982b). In spoken communication, the audience is generally physically present, or can take conversational turns over a telephone. However, in written communication the audience often has to be imagined by the writer. This difference shifts the responsibility for the development of meaning among the participants using the two modalities. In spoken communication, the responsibility among mature communicators is usually a temporally shared joint effort on the part of both participants (alternating roles as speaker and listener). Furthermore, spoken communication participants are generally aware that, in many cases, they can rely heavily on shared knowledge of old information (especially if they know each other well), or they can augment their verbal messages with nonverbal context. This contrasts with the situation in written communication, in which writers must assume the responsibility to keep in mind the needs of their audience without immediate feedback and to anticipate the degree to which information should be made explicit. Conversely, readers must assume the responsibility of reconstructing the writer's purpose and plan in writing, and of understanding the text in the context of wider sources of shared meaning. As expressed by Schleusener (1980), for authors and readers, "their only common ground is the text, and they share nothing but the words that pass between them" (p. 669).

The Intention of Communication

But what of formal oral presentations, such as lectures or sermons? What of informal writing, such as notes to oneself, to peers, or to family members? What of writers of technical reports who assume that their readers have much of the background information necessary to understand the report and only need detail regarding newly reported data? The boundaries of the great divide become fuzzy when different kinds of spoken and written communication are considered.

Romaine (1984) resolved the apparent discrepancies among views of the relationship of orality and literacy by concluding that literate modes of expression should not be associated solely with writing, but should be viewed as part of an orality–literacy continuum. Romaine pointed out that, for most cultures, both oral and literate traditions exist in which "literate modes centre on decontextualized, non-participant presentation of material, whereas oral modes of expression whether spoken or written, focus on contextualized participant interaction" (p. 202). As examples, she cited a lecture, which is delivered orally, but in the literate mode, with little assumption of shared knowledge and high focus on thematic progressions, and many personal letters, which are delivered in written form, but focus on interpersonal relationships and shared knowledge.

Britton (1970, 1979) also tied the differences in style of audience involvement more to the function of the communication event, and to the resulting type of text, than to its modality. He distinguished between texts that were primarily *pragmatic* (i.e., texts used for social interaction, to get and give information, and to share feelings) and those that were primarily *mathetic* (i.e., texts used to narrate, explain, hypothesize, or predict). Britton pointed out that the roles speakers, listeners, readers, and writers play in constructing the discourse they are processing is determined by the function of the discourse. In pragmatic discourse, a participant role is assumed and communicative interactants work together to make sense of bits and pieces of information about a current situation. Consider, for example, the pragmatic discourse exchange between two fourth graders that appears in Figure 2-1. The primary function in this exchange is social interaction, with information exchange and the expression of feeling being used as part of the interaction. Because of the high level of shared information among the participants, phrases like "bring or buy" communicate clearly without explanation. However, in mathetic discourse, a spectator role is assumed and communicators who are removed in time and space use language to represent experiences in which they are not participating so that the text forms a coherent unit. The following poem, which was written in response to a ninth-grade composition course assignment, demonstrates the mathetic role of spectator discourse:

Dandelion

You brighten many fields.
Are you friend or foe?
You are the nemesis of every gardner [sic].
Are you friend or foe?
You embellish the ever boring grass.
Are you friend or foe?
Your long roots have caused many
Agonizing moments!
Are you friend or foe?
Dandelion, like a stone you go on,
You are friend and foe.

—David Nelson, 9th Grade

The importance of the similarities between spoken and written language

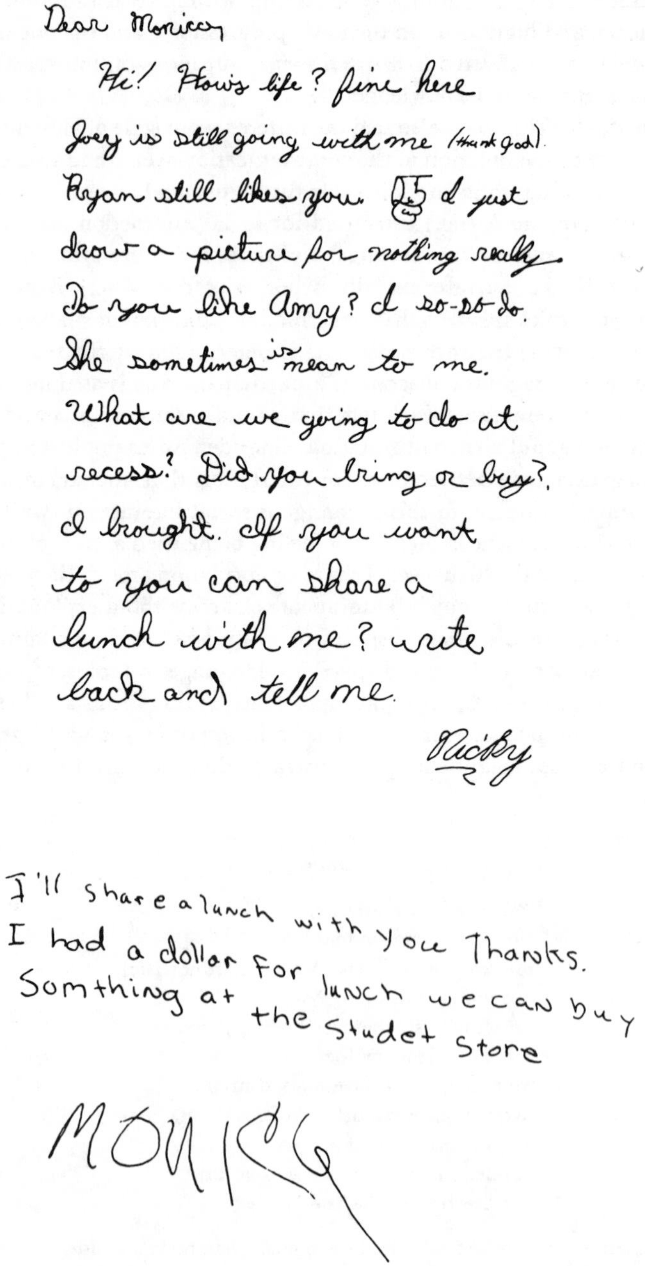

Dear Monica,

Hi! How's life? fine here

Joey is still going with me (thank god).

Ryan still likes you 🙂 I just

draw a picture for nothing really.

Do you like Amy? I so-so do.

She sometimes is mean to me.

What are we going to do at

recess? Did you bring or buy?

I brought. If you want

to you can share a

lunch with me? write

back and tell me.

Ricky

I'll share a lunch with you Thanks.
I had a dollar for lunch we can buy
Somthing at the Studet Store

MONICA

Figure 2-1. Spontaneous pragmatic discourse exchange written by two fourth-grade girls.

has been stressed by a number of recent authors (e.g., Nystrand, 1982a, 1982b; Street, 1986) including Steinman (1982), who emphasized the similar requirements for managing speech acts in spoken and written communication. Speakers and writers both become more effective when they can phrase their speech acts to achieve not only desired illocutionary effects (i.e., speaking or writing information so clearly that listeners or readers easily experience the effect of understanding the discourse), but also the desired perlocutionary effects (i.e., speaking or writing discourse so persuasively that listeners or readers experience other intended effects beyond the mere receipt of information) (Steinman, 1982).

Furthermore, the most effective discourse is that in which the speaker or writer has communicated so well that the message is *transparent*, and the listener or reader can get directly to the meaning (Nystrand, 1982c). Messages that become *opaque*, requiring listeners or readers to focus on their surface structure, and to consciously analyze it in order to get to the meaning, are less effective. Yet writers do not have complete responsibility for constructing meaning any more than speakers do. Readers add a critical factor to the meaning of any text, and Nystrand (1982c) commented that

> Comprehension is never a case of the reader passively "absorbing the text's meaning," but rather the active business of bringing knowledge to the text. This knowledge is visual, lexical, syntactical, personal and cultural. (p. 76)

In each method of communication, the listeners, speakers, readers, and writers must also observe the rules of *implicature* (Cooper, 1982). These are the unspoken but generally operational rules of communication, as Grice (1975) described them for discourse: (1) to be clear and organized; (2) to be informative (but not overly so); (3) to be relevant; and (4) to be truthful and accurate. Rules of implicature have to do with managing the degree of clarity, the degree of informativeness or contextualization (as discussed previously), the degree of relevance, and the degree of truthfulness of discourse, whether it is spoken, heard, written, or read. This is why Cooper (1982) commented

> I have insisted on the similarities between communication in writing and communication in speaking because the widespread tendency to dwell on differences between the two obscures the fact that the fundamental communicative process remains the same. (p. 109)

Summary

Although spoken and written language are not entirely different systems, they vary in important ways. The two factors most often mentioned are (1) *contextualization*, which refers to the degree to which meaning is available in nonverbal context (high in spoken language) or must be encoded in words (high in written language), and (2) *audience*, which refers to the distance between the sender and receiver of information. In written language, more information must be lexicalized, which often results in adjustments in vocabulary and sentence structure. However, differences in contextualization and audience are not just related to differences between orality and literacy; they can also be attributed to the degree of formality of communicative events. The general rules of language are similar for both spoken and written communication. In fact, as the following section shows, teachers have used variations in contextualization and audience in spoken communication to help students improve their skills in written communication (Elsasser and John-Steiner, 1980).

RELATIONSHIPS AMONG LITERACY, SCHOOLING, AND COGNITION

To what degree do outside influences such as cultural and parental factors affect the development of literacy during the 9-through-19 age range? Partial answers to this question and to related questions can be found in the psychological and sociolinguistic literature. As Collins (1984) commented, "Writing development is a hybrid; it combines development in the sense of genetic maturity with development in the sense of learning from instruction and socialization" (p. 202). But questions arise concerning the nature of the interaction. To what degree is learning to read and write dependent on home factors? To what degree is it dependent on schooling? To what degree is it dependent on the development of general cognitive abilities? To what degree does learning to read and write influence the development of general cognitive abilities? These questions are addressed in this final section of the chapter.

A problem that has plagued educators and developmental specialists in the United States for years is that children in varied segments of the heterogeneous American culture do not learn to read and write with the same level of proficiency (Whiteman, 1981), and that gaps between those with low and high abilities widen from year to year (Loban, 1963). Maxwell (1977) found similar discrepancies among good and poor readers in Scotland. Following analysis of a wide variety of school programs and teaching techniques, Maxwell concluded that the differences observed in children's performance were based more on inherent differences in children than on differences in the way they were schooled. He commented that differences in reading attainment were influenced mainly by factors beyond the control of teachers.

Differences in reading and writing ability associated with socioeconomic status (Loban, 1963) have been attributed to the kinds of language that children have experienced in their homes (Bernstein, 1972), particularly their experiences with written language, such as being read to (Chomsky, 1980). The argument has been that hearing language spoken or read that is less contextualized and more lexicalized, as it is in homes where parents are educated and where literacy is practiced, influences children's ability to learn to read and write well.

Based on the assumption that knowledge of strategies for varied contextual and audience expectations is associated with written language, and that such variations must be learned through experiences that contribute to cognitive shifts, strategies have been developed for increasing literacy among groups of people who have traditionally shown high rates of illiteracy. For example, Elsasser and John-Steiner (1980) emphasized that "mastery of written communication requires a difficult but critical shift in the consciousness of the learner, a shift of attention from an immediate audience that shares the learner's experiences and frame of reference to a larger, abstract, and unfamiliar audience" (p. 454). To facilitate this shift, the authors recommended that people be taught to modify the skills of competent spoken communication they have typically developed within their linguistic communities to provide a base for more decontextualized and elaborated communication using written language.

As a part of the program reported by Elsasser and John-Steiner, Chicano and Native American students in the southwestern United States were given practice learning to use elaborated language to communicate to different kinds of audiences. For example, in one exercise, students were shown pictures of mountains and mesas and were asked to select one picture and to list a series of words that described the picture in such a way that the other members of the class could easily identify it. In another exercise, they wrote grocery lists first as they would write them for themselves, and then as they would write them for several different buyers (audiences) who were decreasingly familiar with the shopper and the shopper's store (requiring further elaboration). In a third exercise, they learned the importance of elaboration in a task in which they had to describe a geometric design in such detail that their classmates could reproduce it, first facing the class and with verbal and visual interaction allowed, and then with their backs turned and no interaction allowed with the audience (the usual distinction between spoken and written communication audience relationships). Speakers practiced with their backs turned until their classmates could achieve accuracy in reproduction from the speakers' descriptions alone. Then they wrote descriptions using similar strategies.

Efforts to increase literacy skills by providing experience with increasingly abstract and decontextualized forms are based on the assumption that literacy, schooling, and cognition are interrelated. Yet controversy continues to surround the questions of whether the advances in learners' general cognitive abilities, which have been consistently observed in literate cultures (Olson, 1977a), are associated specifically with learning to read and write or whether they are simply associated with schooling in general. The ability to obtain answers has been obscured by the fact that, as Scribner and Cole (1980) commented, "In most discussions of schooling and literacy, the two are so closely intertwined that they are virtually indistinguishable" (p. 382).

However, Scribner and Cole addressed the questions by studying a group of people for whom schooling and the acquisition of literacy were separate activities. Their intention was to test the thesis adopted by others (e.g., Greenfield and Bruner, 1966; Olson, 1977a, 1977b) that writing promotes cognitive development. Such a thesis, which is known as the *developmental perspective*, is defined by its specification of "literacy's effects as the emergence of general mental capacities — abstract thinking, for example, or logical operations — rather than specific skills" (Scribner and Cole, 1980, p. 385).

To test the developmental thesis, Scribner and Cole studied the Vai people, who are a traditional society living on the northwest coast of Liberia in Africa. The Vai invented a syllabic writing system to represent their own language approximately 150 years ago. It has since been transmitted from generation to generation without schooling or professional teachers, and it continues to be used for daily activities that do not require a person to master large bodies of information that are unavailable from spoken sources (e.g., letter writing regarding family business and recording the names of donors and gifts at funerals). Scribner and Cole tested the literate and nonliterate, schooled and unschooled Vai people using cognitive tasks (e.g., sorting and verbal reasoning tasks) similar to those that had been used earlier by Greenfield and Bruner (1966) and by Olson (1977a, 1977b) to demonstrate the association of increased cognitive abilities with literacy and schooling. Although Scribner and Cole found that the Vai people showed the expected association of improvement in cognitive performance with years of formal schooling, they found that literacy in the Vai script did not substitute for schooling. In subsequent experiments they also found that acquisition of literacy was not associated with increased metalinguistic skills for specifying the nature of grammatical rules in the Vai language either. This was surprising, and it is inconsistent with hypotheses such as those advanced by Forrest-Pressley and Waller (1984) discussed previously regarding the association of increases in literacy with increases in metacognition in individuals in schooled western societies.

Scribner and Cole's (1980) research suggested that there was little support for the thesis that becoming literate has any effect on generalized cognitive abilities. However, when those researchers redesigned their cognitive tasks to relate more closely to the skills required for reading and writing in Vai script, their results were different. For example, when tested for knowledge of the syllabic structure of Vai oral language (recall that the Vai written language system is based on syllabic encoding), the Vai literates did score significantly higher than the nonliterates. They also scored higher on both written and spoken explanations of how to play a game, indicating that increased ability to use decontextualized language is associated with literacy and not just with schooling.

Scribner and Cole cautioned that the Vai used a restricted sort of literacy. However, they interpreted their results as providing evidence that literacy alone, without schooling, can promote specific skills that are available to support other behaviors, but they "did not find that literacy in the Vai script was associated in any way with generalized competencies such as abstraction, verbal reasoning, or metalinguistic skills" (p. 391). They further concluded that "terms that refer to oral and literate modes of thought, although historically significant, are not useful characterizations of the mental abilities of nonliterate and literate adults in American society," and further that "research does not support designing literacy programs on the assumption that nonliterates do not think abstractly, do not reason logically, or lack other basic mental processes" (p. 393). If such cognitive skills need to be assessed and encouraged, Scribner and Cole suggested that other communicative contexts used by nonliterates (e.g., disputation, hypothetical reasoning, or oral narration) be used for doing so.

Olson and Astington (1986) interpreted both Scribner and Cole's findings with the Vai culture, and the results of their own earlier research regarding the metalinguistic skills of children measured both before and immediately after they learned to read, as follows:

> Contrary to our expectations, we found that important metalinguistic distinctions, specifically that between what was said (or written) and what was meant by it, were neither immediate consequences of learning to read and write nor were they pre-requisites for the acquisition of those competences. We now suspect that such metalinguistic distinctions are part of the language in any literate culture and children will acquire such distinctions if they encounter them in speech *whether they learn to read and write or not* [italics in the original]. In other words, the cognitive consequences of literacy are tied to involvement in a literate culture and not directly to the skills of reading and writing. (p. 10)

Summary

It appears that answers to questions regarding the degree to which literacy, schooling, and cognition are causally related depend on the specific circumstances. Literacy can be acquired without schooling (Scribner and Cole, 1980), but usually it is not (Romaine, 1984). Schooling appears to have a greater effect on the development of general cognitive abilities than does the acquisition of literacy per se (Scribner and Cole, 1980). However, becoming literate does result in stronger evidence of particular, closely related cognitive skills, such as the ability to analyze the phonologic or syllabic structure of language (depending on the nature of the language's written language system), or the ability to use decontextualized language (Olson and Astington, 1986; Scribner and Cole, 1980). The studies reviewed here have used cultural variation to address the questions about the relationships among literacy, schooling, and cognition in cultures.

CONCLUSIONS

For youngsters growing up in technological societies, schools place considerable emphasis on the acquisition of literacy. During the 9-through-19 age range, expectations for literacy move from the simple ability to read and write to sophisticated levels of inference, generalization, and flexibility while reading, writing, speaking, and listening. The extent to which a particular child becomes a literate adult depends on a combination of intrinsic and extrinsic factors. Literacy involves the development of both spoken and written communication skills and represents a blend of linguistic, cognitive, and world knowledge.

REFERENCES

Bernstein, B.B. (1972). A critique of the concept of compensatory education. In C.B. Cazden, V.P. John, and D. Hymes (Eds.), *Functions of language in the classroom* (pp. 135-154). New York: Columbia University Teachers College Press.

Blank, M. (1982). Language and school failure: Some speculations on the relationship between oral and written language. In L. Feagans and D. Farran (Eds.), *The language of children reared in poverty* (pp. 75-93). New York: Academic Press.

Britton, J.N. (1970). *Language and learning*. London: Penguin Press.

Britton, J.N. (1979). Learning to use language in two modes. In N.R. Smith and M.B. Franklin (Eds.), *Symbolic functioning in childhood* (pp. 185-197). Hillsdale, NJ: Erlbaum.

Chomsky, C. (1980). Stages in language development and reading exposure. In M. Wolf, M.K. McQuillan, and E. Radwin (Eds.), *Thought and language/Language and reading* (pp. 382-395). Reprint series No. 14. Cambridge: Harvard Educational Review. (Reprinted from *Harvard Educational Review*, 1972, *42*, 1-33).

Collins, J.A. (1984). The development of writing abilities during the school years. In A.D. Pellegrini and T.D. Yawkey (Eds.), *The development of oral and written language in social contexts* (pp. 201-212). Norwood, NJ: Ablex.

Cook-Gumperz, J. (1977). Situated instructions. In S. Ervin-Tripp and C. Mitchell-Kernan (Eds.), *Child discourse* (pp. 103-124). New York: Academic Press.

Cooper, C.R. (1981). Competency testing: Issues and overview. In C.R. Cooper (Ed.),

The nature and measurement of competency in English (pp. 1-20). Urbana, IL: National Council of Teachers of English.

Cooper, M.M. (1982). Context as vehicle: Implicature in writing. In M. Nystrand (Ed.), *What writers know: The language, process, and structure of written discourse* (pp. 106-129). New York: Academic Press.

Cooper, C.R., and Odell, L. (1977). Introduction. In C.R. Cooper and L. Odell (Eds.), *Evaluating writing: Describing, measuring, judging* (pp. vii-xii). Urbana, IL: National Council of Teachers of English.

Elsasser, N., and John-Steiner, V.P. (1980). An interactionist approach to advancing literacy. In M. Wolf, M.K. McQuillan, and E. Radwin (Eds.), *Thought and language/Language and reading* (pp. 451-465). Reprint series No. 14. Cambridge: Harvard Educational Review. (Reprinted from *Harvard Educational Review*, 1977, *47*, 355-369).

Emig, J. (1977). Writing as a mode of learning. *College Composition and Communication*, *28*, 122-127.

Forrest-Pressley, D.L., and Waller, T.G. (1984). *Cognition, metacognition, and reading*. New York: Springer-Verlag.

Goody, J. (1977). *The domestication of the savage mind*. Cambridge, England: Cambridge University Press.

Greenfield, P. (1972). Oral or written language: The consequences for cognitive development in Africa, the United States and England. *Language and Speech*, *15*, 169-178.

Greenfield, P., and Bruner, J. (1966). Culture and cognitive growth. *International Journal of Psychology*, *1*, 89-107.

Gregory, M., and Carroll, S. (1978). *Language and situation: Language varieties and their social contexts*. London: Routledge and Kegan Paul.

Grice, H.P. (1975). Logic and conversation. In P. Cole and J. Morgan (Eds.), *Studies in syntax and semantics: Speech acts* (Vol. 3), (pp. 64-75). New York: Academic Press.

Hirsch, E.D. (1987). *Cultural literacy: What every American needs to know*. Boston: Houghton Mifflin.

Loban, W.D. (1963). *The language of elementary school children*. No. 1 in a series of research reports sponsored by the NCTE Committee on Research. Urbana, IL: National Council of Teachers of English.

Maxwell, J. (1977). *Reading progress from 8 to 15*. Windsor, Great Britain: NFER Publishing.

Nystrand, M. (Ed.). (1982a). *What writers know: The language, process, and structure of written discourse*. New York: Academic Press.

Nystrand, M. (1982b). Rhetoric's "audience" and linguistics' "speech community": Implications for understanding writing, reading, and text. In M. Nystrand (Ed.), *What writers know: The language, process, and structure of written discourse* (pp. 1-28). New York: Academic Press.

Nystrand, M. (1982c). The structure of textual space. In M. Nystrand (Ed.), *What writers know: The language, process, and structure of written discourse* (pp. 75-86). New York: Academic Press.

Odell, L. (1981). Defining and assessing competence in writing. In C.R. Cooper (Ed.), *The nature and measurement of competency in English* (pp. 95-138). Urbana, IL: National Council of Teachers of English.

Olson, D. (1977a). From utterance to text: The bias of language in speech and writing. *Harvard Educational Review, 47,* 257-281.

Olson, D. (1977b). The languages of instruction: The literate bias of schooling. In R. Anderson, R. Spiro, and W. Montague (Eds.), *Schooling and the acquisition of knowledge* (pp. 65-89). Hillsdale, NJ: Erlbaum.

Olson, D.R., and Astington, J.W. (1986, October). *Talking about text: How literacy contributes to thought.* Paper presented at the Boston University Conference on Language Development, Boston, MA.

Purves, A. (1981). Competence in reading. In C.R. Cooper (Ed.), *The nature and measurement of competency in English* (pp. 65-94). Urbana, IL: National Council of Teachers of English.

Resnick, D.P., and Resnick, L.B. (1980). The nature of literacy: An historical exploration. In M. Wolf, M.K. McQuillan, and E. Radwin (Eds.), *Thought and language/Language and reading* (pp. 396-411). Reprint series No. 14. Cambridge: Harvard Educational Review. (Reprinted from *Harvard Educational Review,* 1977, *47,* 370-385).

Romaine, S. (1984). *The language of children and adolescents: The acquisition of communicative competence.* Oxford, England: Blackwell.

Schleusener, J. (1980). Convention and the context of reading. *Critical Inquiry, 6,* 669-680.

Scribner, S., and Cole, M. (1980). Literacy without schooling: Testing for intellectual effects. In M. Wolf, M.K. McQuillan, and E. Radwin (Eds.), *Thought and language/Language and reading* (pp. 382-395). Reprint series No. 14. Cambridge: Harvard Educational Review. (Reprinted from *Harvard Educational Review,* 1978, *48,* 448-461.)

Smith, F. (1971). *Understanding reading: A psycholinguistic analysis of reading and learning to read.* New York: Holt, Rinehart and Winston.

Steinman, M. (1982). Speech-act theory and writing. In M. Nystrand (Ed.), *What writers know: The language, process, and structure of written discourse* (pp. 291-323). New York: Academic Press.

Sticht, T.G. (1978). The acquisition of literacy by children and adults. In F.B. Murray and J.J. Pikulski (Eds.), *The acquisition of reading: Cognitive, linguistic, and perceptual prerequisites* (pp. 131-162). Baltimore, MD: University Park Press.

Street, B.V. (1986, October). *Literacy practices and literacy myths.* Paper presented at the Boston University Conference on Language Development, Boston, MA.

Szwed, J.F. (1981). The ethnography of literacy. In M.F. Whiteman (Ed.), *Writing: The nature, development, and teaching of written communication: Volume 1, Variations in writing: Functional and linguistic-cultural differences* (pp. 13-24). Hillsdale, NJ: Erlbaum.

Tannen, D. (1982). *Spoken and written language: Exploring orality and literacy.* Norwood, NJ: Ablex.

Whiteman, M.F. (Ed.). (1981). *Writing: The nature, development, and teaching of written communication: Volume 1, Variation in writing: Functional and linguistic-cultural differences.* Hillsdale, NJ: Erlbaum.

Whiteman, M.F., and Hall, W.S. (1981). Introduction. In M.F. Whiteman (Ed.), *Writing: The nature, development, and teaching of written communication: Volume 1, Variation in writing: Functional and linguistic-cultural differences* (pp. 1-10). Hillsdale, NJ: Erlbaum.

CHAPTER 3

■

THE LITERATE LEXICON

■

MARILYN A. NIPPOLD

On graduating from high school, the average adolescent has learned the meanings of at least 80,000 different words (Miller and Gildea, 1987). Words are learned primarily through two different methods: (1) *direct teaching*, where a parent or teacher provides a definition or labels an unfamiliar stimulus; or (2) *contextual abstraction*, where a word occurs repeatedly in spoken or written language and the youngster infers its meaning from the context (Werner and Kaplan, 1950).

At about the second grade, dictionary usage is introduced, a direct and scholarly method of lexical learning (Coon, Cramer, Fillmer, Lefcourt, Martin, and Thompson, 1980). An important study skill, the use of a dictionary is encouraged throughout the elementary, middle, and high school years (Bennett, 1981; Coon et al., 1980; McDonnell, Nakadate, Pfordresher, and Shoemate, 1979; Welch and Bennett, 1981). The use of contextual clues to determine the meanings of unfamiliar words is also encouraged throughout the elementary, middle, and high school years (e.g., Bennett, 1981; Duffy and Roehler, 1981; Welch and Bennett, 1981). Both of these strategies, dictionary usage and contextual abstraction, enable independent lexical learning to occur. However, contextual abstraction seems to be the more common source of lexical learning with older children and adolescents because new words are acquired at a faster rate than would be possible through more direct teaching methods (Miller and Gildea, 1987).

Literacy and lexical learning enjoy a symbiotic relationship during the 9-through-19 age range: whereas literacy requires knowledge and use of a wide variety of words, the process of lexical growth itself is facilitated by literate activities. At about the fourth-grade level, written language becomes a major source of lexical learning and students who read widely develop larger vocabularies (Miller and Gildea, 1987). As youngsters progress through school, the types of words introduced in the classroom become more abstract and occur increasingly more often in written- rather than in spoken-language contexts. These qualitative changes are reflected in Table 3-1, which contains examples of words that are understood by 75 percent of students in each of the fourth, sixth, eighth, tenth, and twelfth grades (Dale and Eichholz, 1960).

Lexical learning, however, continues well beyond the high school years and new words are acquired throughout the lifespan (Palermo and Molfese, 1972; Riegel, Riegel, Quarterman, and Smith, 1968). The vocabulary of a particular language constantly changes because of cultural, historical, and regional influences in addition to scientific and technological advances (Langacker, 1973). Therefore, lexical learning must include not only the acquisition of longstanding words but also of those that are new to the language. For example, *concede, assert*, and *remark* are words that entered the English language during the early part of the seventeenth century (Olson and Astington, 1986a) whereas *callaloo, edutainment*, and *intrapreneur* are quite recent additions to the language (Flexner and Hauck, 1987).

Growth in vocabulary, however, involves more than the addition of words to the lexicon. For example, growth occurs also through the development of an organized network where semantically related words become more closely associated (Entwisle, Forsyth, and Muuss, 1964; Nelson, 1977; Riegel et al., 1968). The syntagmatic-paradigmatic shift, which occurs most dramatically between the ages of five and nine years (Lippman, 1971), seems

Table 3-1.
Examples of words understood by 75 percent of students in various grade levels.

Grade Four:	bulldog, camper, cigar, crocodile, distance, dizzy, dodge, locket, sheriff, sniff, tangle, thirst, widow, weedy, wives
Grade Six:	adhesive, alto, appetite, bacteria, berth, bridal, campus, davenport, fatherless, fishery, gadget, grit, midst, pardon
Grade Eight:	amend, archeology, byway, dimension, fluorescent, horoscope, inefficient, laughingstock, lingerie, officialdom, salutation
Grade Ten:	circumstantial, deface, diversion, enshrine, gallows, hinder, implication, negligent, orthodox, pollination, proton, refrain
Grade Twelve:	acetylene, aft, buxom, condone, curlew, fascism, heresy, indicative, opportune, oppression, prophetic, secretariat

Adapted from Dale and Eichholz, 1960.

to reflect this type of semantic reorganization. This shift can be observed during word-association tasks where a word is presented (e.g., *dog*) and the subject is asked to say the first word that comes to mind; whereas a 5-year-old is likely to respond *syntagmatically* with a word that might follow in a sentence (e.g., *runs*), a 9-year-old is likely to respond *paradigmatically* with a semantically related word (e.g., *cat*) that is often an antonym, coordinate, subordinate, or superordinate of the target word (Israel, 1984).

Vocabulary growth also occurs through changes in the meanings of particular words for the individual (Palermo and Molfese, 1972). As McNeil (1970) pointed out, simple vocabulary counts give a misleading picture of lexical development because "words can be in a child's vocabulary but have different semantic properties from the same words in the vocabulary of an older child or an adult" (p. 116). For example, preschoolers often use the words *because* and *before* even though a complete understanding of those words as intrasentential connectives may not be reached until adolescence (Flores d'Arcais, 1978). Double function terms such as *cold, bright,* and *crooked* also illustrate this phenomenon because their physical meanings are understood by the age of six, but their psychological meanings may not be understood until the age of nine (Asch and Nerlove, 1960). Similarly (as will be discussed in Chapter 8), a youngster's understanding of the figurative meanings of metaphors and idioms often lags behind a literal understanding of those same words and phrases by several years.

It is also important to note that the speech errors of children aptly illustrate the phenomenon of partial lexical knowledge. For example, during the early 1970s, investigators such as Bloom (1973) and Clark (1973) studied semantic development in young children and reported that toddlers used overextensions (e.g., calling all small furry animals *kitty*) which were inconsistent with adults' usage of those same words until the child had developed a more complete understanding of the concepts involved. It is interesting that investigators are now beginning to study the speech errors of older children to gain insight into their conceptions of word meanings. For example, Miller and Gildea (1987) reported that fifth- and sixth-grade students, having only a partial understanding of words such as *meticulous, relegate,* and *redress*, wrote the following revealing sentences:

I was meticulous about falling off the cliff.
I relegated my pen pal's letter to her house.
The redress for getting well when you're sick is to stay in bed. (p. 99)

As with toddlers, the speech errors of older children indicate that lexical learning is a gradual rather than "all or none" process.

This chapter focuses on the development of the lexicon during the 9-through-19 age range. It covers particular classes of words, including verbs, adverbs, and connectives, that are important for the literate activities of reading and writing, and talking about language and thought. The chapter also covers the development of word definitions during this age range because this ability offers some insight into youngsters' changing conceptions of word meanings and reflects the adoption of a literate, scholarly convention (Watson, 1985).

WORD CLASSES

Verbs

Astington and Olson (1987) studied comprehension of *literate verbs* in sixth, eighth, tenth, and twelfth graders ($n = 99$) and in college students ($n = 77$). Literate verbs are words such as *assert, concede, predict,* and *contradict* that are used in discussions of spoken and written language interpretation, particularly in literature, science, and philosophy classes at the high-school and college levels. Literate verbs were reported to have been borrowed from Latin during the sixteenth and seventeenth centuries when attempts were made to improve the quality of the English language as it became the standard for law, government, science, theology, and philosophy (Olson and Astington, 1986b).

In Astington and Olson's (1987) study, the literate verbs included a metacognitive set (*remember, doubt, infer, hypothesize, conclude, assume*) and a metalinguistic set (*assert, concede, imply, predict, interpret, confirm*). Metacognitive verbs refer to various acts of thinking, whereas metalinguistic verbs refer to acts of speaking. To assess comprehension of the verbs, the subjects were presented with a written multiple-choice task that consisted of 12 short stories—one for each of the 12 different verbs. In each story, the simple verb *think* or *say* was used to mark what a character thought or said; given the story context, however, the simple verb could be replaced by a more complex literate verb. Each story was followed by a choice of four sentences, one of which would best replace the last sentence in the story; the students were instructed to choose the best alternative. Two examples from Astington and Olson's study are presented, the first for the metacognitive verb *remember,* and the second for the metalinguistic verb *predict*:

1. Last week in science class, Mr. Jones showed Dave that acid solution turns litmus paper pink. This week there's a test. The first question says, "What color will litmus paper be when you dip it in acid solution?" *Dave thinks that it will be pink.*
   A. Dave *remembers* that it will be pink.
   B. Dave *hypothesizes* that it will be pink.

    C. Dave *infers* that it will be pink.

    D. Dave *observes* that it will be pink.

2. Susan and Eva are planning to go on a picnic. They want to choose a nice day. One morning they wake up early. Eva says, "Shall we go today?" Susan looks out of the window and *she says, "It will be sunny all day."*

    A. Susan *predicts* that it will be sunny all day.

    B. Susan *knows* that it will be sunny all day.

    C. Susan *interprets* that it will be sunny all day.

    D. Susan *implies* that it will be sunny all day.

Results indicated that comprehension of the verbs increased with age: mean accuracy scores of 45, 42, 59, 71, and 92 percent were obtained by the students in the sixth, eighth, tenth and twelfth grades and college, respectively. Although the task was not completely mastered until the college level, this was not surprising in view of the subtle and scholarly nature of the terms involved. In fact, it is possible that a large segment of the adult population never masters these and other literate verbs, particularly if their educational experiences are restricted to the high-school level or below. This issue of incomplete or gradual mastery is discussed in Chapter 4 in relation to syntax (where Scott emphasizes the importance of recognizing a variety of adult levels of competence). It is also discussed in Chapter 6 in relation to cognition, and in Chapter 10 in relation to communicative competence. The point is equally valid for lexical development.

    Another purpose of the Astington and Olson study was to examine the relationship between students' comprehension of the literate verbs and their general vocabulary development and critical thinking ability. Therefore, the students in the eighth and twelfth grades were also administered the reading vocabulary subtest of the Canadian Achievement Tests, and the Cornell Critical Thinking Test. Controlling for age effects, results indicated that performance on the literate verbs task was positively correlated to both of those measures.

    Youngsters' comprehension of *factive* and *nonfactive* verbs was examined by Scoville and Gordon (1980). Factive verbs (e.g., *know, notice*) presuppose the truth of the complement clause that follows. For example, in the sentence *Bill knows that the ball is red*, the ball's color is a certainty. However, with nonfactive verbs (e.g., *think, believe*), the truth of the complement clause is uncertain as in the sentence *Bill thinks that the ball is red*. Students of ages 12, 14, and 20 years ($n = 52$) were included in the study. Comprehension of five factive verbs (*know, forget, be sorry, be happy, be surprised*) and five nonfactive verbs (*be sure, think, figure, say, believe*) was assessed using a task where subjects were asked to judge the truth of the complement clause in a sentence. For each of the 10 verbs, three sentences

were presented, each representing a different combination of positive and
negative values. These variations were described as + + (e.g., *Bill knows
that the ball is red*), − + (e.g., *Bill does not know that the ball is red*),
and + − (e.g., *Bill knows that the ball is not red*). The complement clauses
were of the form *the ball is (red/green/blue/yellow)*, and each color was
paired randomly with a main verb. The sentences were presented in the context of a television quiz show. Subjects viewed a black and white videotape
which showed a blindfolded "Dr. Fact" whose job it was to guess the color
of a series of pingpong balls drawn randomly from a box by an assistant,
"Miss Fancy." On the videotape, all of the balls appeared to be the same
shade of gray but it was emphasized to the subject that Miss Fancy always
knew the color of the balls. After a ball was drawn, Dr. Fact whispered its
color to Miss Fancy, who then produced each stimulus sentence; for example, *Dr. Fact is not sure that the ball is yellow*. The subject then repeated
the stimulus sentence and was asked by an announcer, *Is the ball (color)?*.
The subject answered the question *Yes, No,* or *Don't know* by pushing an
appropriate button. For the three sentence variations, + +, − +, and
+ −, the predicted "adult" response pattern for the factive verbs was *Yes,
Yes, No,* respectively, and *Don't know, Don't know, Don't know,* respectively,
for the nonfactive verbs. Results showed that neither verb type proved more
difficult than the other, and that comprehension of both types steadily
improved with increasing subject age; most of the 20-year-olds displayed
the predicted adult patterns and, as a group, outperformed the 14-year-
olds, who outperformed the 12-year-olds. This study therefore indicated that
comprehension of factive and nonfactive verbs gradually improves during
the adolescent years.

Adverbs

Youngsters' comprehension of adverbs has also been studied, and there
is evidence that subtle differences in meaning are gradually learned during
the 9-through-19 age range. For example, Bashaw and Anderson (1968)
designed a paired-comparisons judgment task involving a set of nine adverbs
of magnitude. Previous research (Cliff, 1959) indicated that a group of
college-educated adults had ranked the adverbs in the following order of
increasing magnitude: *slightly, somewhat, rather, pretty, quite, decidedly,
unusually, very,* and *extremely*. In Bashaw and Anderson's study, the subjects included students in fourth, fifth, sixth, eighth, tenth, and twelfth
grades, and a group of college sophomores (*n* = 999). In constructing the
task, each adverb was combined with the adjective *large* (e.g., *slightly large*),
and each of the resulting combinations was paired with each of the others
(e.g., *slightly large–extremely large, slightly large–quite large*). For each pair,
the subject was to decide which combination expressed a greater degree of

largeness. Immediately after the paired-comparisons task, the subject was presented with a randomly ordered list of all of the adverb-adjective combinations and asked to rank them in order from low to high. Results showed that as subject age increased, accuracy on both the paired-comparisons and ranking tasks steadily improved, and finer distinctions could be made between semantically adjacent combinations (e.g., *somewhat large–rather large*). However, even the oldest subjects did not consistently distinguish between all of the adjacent pairs (e.g., *quite large–decidedly large*) and presumably viewed them as synonymous.

Connectives

Youngsters' use and understanding of various connectives has also been studied during the preadolescent and adolescent years. Development in the use of connectives is discussed in Chapters 4 and 5, and understanding of them is discussed here.

Connectives are relational words, such as conjunctions or relative pronouns, that join sentences, clauses, or other words in spoken and written language (Robertson, 1968). Although the speech of young children often contains connectives, the process of acquiring a full understanding of these words is a gradual one that extends into adulthood (Flores d'Arcais, 1978; McClure and Geva, 1983; Neimark and Slotnick, 1970). Connectives frequently occur in reading material for upper grade students and are particularly important to the development of literacy.

> Conjunctions act as clues drawing attention to and making explicit the logical relationship between propositions. In ongoing discourse these relationships may be made clear by context. However, in the written mode, conjunctions are extremely important. Readers who fail to note a conjunction or who misunderstand it may interpret the proposition it connects as either unrelated or related in ways unintended by the author. . . . Conversely, authors who fail to make judicious use of conjunctions leave their readers guessing about the connections between the ideas they have presented. (McClure and Steffensen, 1985, p. 218)

To study youngsters' understanding of the adversative conjunctions *but* and *although*, Katz and Brent (1968) constructed a paired-sentences task where a correct and an incorrect usage of each conjunction was presented. For the conjunction *but*, the sentences were *Jimmie went to school, but he felt sick* and *Jimmie went to school, but he felt fine*; for the conjunction *although*, the sentences were *The meal was good, although the pie was bad* and *The meal was good, although the pie was good*. For both pairs of sentences, subjects were asked to select the one that seemed better. Groups of sixth graders (ages 11 and 12; $n = 22$) and college sophomores (approximately ages 19 and 20; $n = 41$) were included in the study. Results indicated that 98 percent of the college students selected the correct usage of *but* and that 100 percent did so for *although*; in contrast, only 68 percent of the sixth graders made the correct selections for both of these conjunctions. This implies that an understanding of the conjunctions *but* and *although* improves considerably during the adolescent years.

Robertson (1968) examined youngsters' understanding of connectives that frequently occurred in fourth- through sixth-grade reading textbooks. The intersentential connectives *thus* and *however* were examined, in addition to the following intrasentential connectives: the coordinate conjunctions *and, but, for,* and *yet*; the subordinate conjunctions *although, because, if, so, that, when, where,* and the "absent" *that* (e.g., *The horse the boy was riding won the race*); and the relative pronouns *that, which,* and *who*. Students in the fourth, fifth, and sixth grades ($n = 402$) were given a task called the "Connectives Reading Test" that consisted of 150 multiple-choice items. Test items were sentences taken directly from the students' reading textbooks. Each item was presented in the form of an incomplete sentence containing a connective (e.g., *He held the rod and. . . .*) followed by four choices of ways to complete the sentence; only one choice was grammatically correct and expressed an appropriate meaning (e.g., *the horse jumped over it*). The students were asked to choose the best alternative. Performance on the Connectives Reading Test steadily improved as a function of age, with mean accuracy scores of 57, 66, and 75 percent obtained by the fourth, fifth, and sixth graders, respectively. However, because the sentences had been considered "grade appropriate," Robertson interpreted these results as poor, and suggested that the failure to understand connectives could contribute to reading problems among upper elementary grade students. The study also showed that six of the connectives were substantially more difficult than the others; these included the intrasentential connectives *although, which, and, yet,* and the intersentential connectives *thus* and *however*. Robertson therefore suggested that textbook writers consider more closely the comprehension skills of students at various grade levels, and that teachers systematically teach the meanings of connectives in written language.

Also in the Robertson study, a standardized measure of academic achievement, the Sequential Tests of Educational Progress, was administered. Scores in the areas of reading, writing, and listening were available. Correlation coefficients calculated between each of these subtests and the Connectives Reading Test were signficant and positive. These findings further supported the view that knowledge of connectives is important for the development of literacy and, therefore, that educators should pay closer attention to youngsters' understanding of connectives. This view was also expressed more recently by McClure and Geva (1983), who reported that even eighth grade students lacked a full understanding of the cohesive properties of the adversative connectives *but* and *although*. In addition to teaching directly the meanings of connectives, Geva and Ryan (1985) emphasized the importance of training students to attend more closely to connectives as they occur in written expository texts. Support for their view was based on research they had conducted with fifth and seventh graders, which showed that comprehension of intrasentential and intersentential information was enhanced when connectives were underlined and capitalized in the written text.

Other investigators have also shown that the acquisition of connectives is a gradual process. For example, Flores d'Arcais (1978) examined Dutch children's understanding of various connectives. In one experiment, the connectives *because (omdat)*, *since (doordat)*, *so that (zodat)*, and *before (voordat)* were tested using a judgment task where subjects were asked to decide if pairs of sentences were equivalent in meaning. Groups of 10- and 12-year-olds (*n* = 40) were included in the study. The task consisted of 12 pairs of complex sentences where the words of each pair were identical except for the connective, (e.g., *The dog barks because the cat approaches. The dog barks so that the cat approaches*). Each of the four connectives was paired with each of the other three, and an additional four pairs of sentences ("dummy pairs") were presented as foils, for a total of 32 sentences in the task. The subject read each pair of sentences aloud and was asked to decide if the second sentence could be used "to tell another child about the event described in the first sentence" (p. 138). Results indicated that the 10-year-olds made significantly more incorrect judgments than the 12-year-olds, particularly in distinguishing the following pairs of connectives: *because–before*, *because–so that*, and *before–since*. However, even the 12-year-olds could not completely master the task.

In a second experiment, Flores d'Arcais examined youngsters' understanding of the connectives *because*, *before*, and *so that* using a written multiple choice task. As in the first experiment, groups of 10- and 12-year-olds (*n* = 40) participated. The task consisted of nine short stories. Each was followed by a choice of three sentences, one of which best paraphrased the story. Three stories were presented in random order for each of the three connectives. The examiner read each test item aloud and then asked the subject to choose the sentence that best expressed the meaning of the story. An example of a test item for the connective *because* was as follows:

> The dog is sitting in the garden. At a certain moment, a cat arrives.
> The dog sees the cat. He then begins to bark.
> 1. The dog barks *because* the cat arrives.
> 2. The dog barks *before* the cat arrives.
> 3. The dog barks *so that* the cat arrives. (p. 143)

As with the first experiment, the 12-year-olds outperformed the 10-year-olds, but not even the 12-year-olds could completely master the task. It was also shown that the connective *so that* was the most difficult, *because* was easiest, and *before* was intermediate in difficulty.

To further examine the development of comprehension of connectives, Flores d'Arcais designed a sorting task that involved 20 common Dutch connectives. Children of the ages of 10 and 12 and a control group of adults (*n* = 60) were tested. Each subject was given a stack of 20 cards, randomly ordered. A different connective had been typed on each card, and the subject was asked to sort the cards into different piles having similar meanings. The underlying assumption of this experiment was that greater semantic knowledge of the connectives would be reflected in a greater tendency to sort the words into three distinct clusters: causal (e.g., *because, since, so that*), temporal (e.g., *after, before, until*), and conditional (e.g., *provided that, unless, although, in case*). Although the adults could do this accurately, the 10-year-olds showed little awareness of the semantic clusters, and the 12-year-olds performed only slightly better than the 10-year-olds. Thus, it was concluded that a full understanding of connectives is acquired gradually and continues to develop beyond the age of 12. However, because of the metalinguistic demands of the three experiments just described, Flores d'Arcais cautioned that poor performance on such tasks does not necessarily imply that a youngster will fail to understand or use connectives correctly in other situations where contextual information may facilitate meaning.

Wing and Scholnick (1981) examined children's understanding of concepts expressed by five different subordinating conjunctions: *because, although, if* with indicative, *if* with subjunctive, and *unless*. *Because* and *although* express belief about a proposition, *if* with indicative and *unless* express uncertainty, and *if* with subjunctive expresses disbelief. These researchers had predicted that conjunctions expressing uncertainty would be more difficult to understand than those expressing belief or disbelief. Subjects included third and fifth grade students (*n* = 60). Understanding of the concepts was assessed using a judgment task that involved a set of 25 sentences, with five containing each of the conjunctions under investigation. The following examples were provided:

1. This is a monkey *because* it has two hands.
2. This is a monkey *although* it has a trunk.
3. This is a monkey *if* it has two hands.
4. These would be monkeys *if* they had two hands.
5. This is a monkey *unless* it has a trunk. (p. 352)

The child was told that an astronaut was studying some animals on a new planet and was reporting his observations back to Earth; however, because the animals were unfamiliar and the atmosphere was cloudy, the astronaut was not always sure of his observations. Thus, it was the child's job to determine if the astronaut was expressing belief, disbelief, or uncertainty in his statements about the animals. Immediately after the astronaut produced a statement (e.g., "This is a monkey if it has two hands"), the child was questioned about the astronaut's beliefs concerning three things: the truth of the main clause (e.g., "Does he believe this is a monkey?"), the truth of the subordinate clause (e.g., "Does he believe it has two hands?"), and the entailment relation between the clauses (e.g., "Does he believe most monkeys have two hands?"). The child was to answer *Yes, No,* or *He's not sure* to each question. Correct responses to the first two questions were each worth one-half point, whereas a correct response to the third question was worth one point. Thus, it was possible to earn a maximum of 50 points for the entire task. Results indicated that overall accuracy was greater for the fifth graders than for the third graders, with mean raw scores of 33.35 and 37.02 obtained by the two groups, respectively. From easiest to most difficult, the five conjunctions were ordered as follows: *because, although, if* with subjunctive, *if* with indicative, and *unless.* It was also found that for both grade levels, statements expressing uncertainty (*if* with indicative, *unless*) were most difficult, those expressing belief (*because, although*) were easiest, and those expressing disbelief (*if* with subjunctive) were intermediate in difficulty.

Summary

Developmental studies of word classes have shown convincingly that the subtle meanings of various types of verbs, adverbs, and connectives are acquired gradually during the 9-through-19 age range. Although preschool children use many of those words correctly in their spontaneous speech (e.g., *but, know, remember, for, yet, think, believe, say, very*), a full understanding of such words may not be reached until late adolescence or early adulthood, and seems closely tied to educational experience and performance. For example, studies indicate that literacy as measured by performance on various academic achievement tests is closely related to students' understanding of metacognitive and metalinguistic verbs, and of intrasentential and intersentential connectives. Therefore, researchers have cautioned that educators should not assume that older children and adolescents have an adequate grasp of these words. In addition, researchers have advocated that words of this nature be taught directly in the classroom because of their importance for the development of literacy.

WORD DEFINITION

Word definition is a metalinguistic process requiring the youngster to reflect on the meaning and use of words, and to state explicitly what is known implicitly (Watson, 1985). In its advanced Aristotelian form, a definition contains a superordinate category term (Nelson, 1978) and an informative phrase that is predicated about the word in question (Watson, 1985; Wehren, De Lisi, and Arnold, 1981); for example, *A bed is a piece of furniture used for sleeping*.

Word definition tasks have long been used as indices of intelligence and verbal ability. For example, an early edition of the *Stanford-Binet Intelligence Scale* (Terman, 1916) contained a task requiring youngsters to explain the meanings of words, and the most recent edition of that test (Thorndike, Hagen, and Sattler, 1986) also contains a word definition section which is positively correlated to both verbal and nonverbal sections of the test. Other intelligence tests that assess word definition skills include the *Wechsler Intelligence Scale for Children—Revised* (Wechsler, 1974), the *Wechsler Adult Intelligence Scale* (Wechsler, 1955), the *Wechsler Preschool and Primary Scale of Intelligence* (Wechsler, 1967), and the *McCarthy Scales of Children's Abilities* (McCarthy, 1972).

Developmental studies of word definition have shown consistently that growth in this area is a gradual process and that both quantitative and qualitative changes occur during childhood and adolescence; not only are youngsters increasingly able to define more words, but the nature of their definitions change as they get older. Normative data reflecting quantitative improvements during preadolescence and adolescence are available in the *Stanford-Binet* (Thorndike et al., 1986) and WISC-R (Wechsler, 1974) manuals. In addition, a number of published studies provide both quantitative and qualitative data on word definition.

For example, Feifel and Lorge (1950) asked youngsters to define a series of 45 words from the 1937 Stanford-Binet (Form L) and analyzed their responses using the classification system shown in Table 3-2. Subjects included groups of youngsters of the ages of 9 through 14 ($n = 600$). Quantitatively, the results showed that the number of correct responses steadily increased as a function of age; mean accuracy scores of 22, 26, 31, 34, 39, and 39 percent were obtained by the groups of 9-, 10-, 11-, 12-, 13- and 14-year-olds, respectively. Qualitatively, it was found that for all six age groups, the Error response was the most common of the five types, followed by the Synonym response; however, the Error response steadily declined and the Synonym response steadily increased with age. The other three response types were low at all age levels, although the Explanation response rose slightly with age, and the Use-Description and Demonstration-Repetition-Illustration-Inferior Explanation types both declined as age increased. The study also found that as age increased, the definitions reflected a greater tendency to place objects into superordinate categories (e.g., defining an orange as *a fruit which grows in California or Florida*, p. 16).

This categorical tendency was also observed by Storck and Looft (1973), who not only replicated the Feifel and Lorge (1950) study, but also extended

Table 3-2.
Qualitative classification system.

Synonym Category
   a. Synonym unmodified: *Orange* = a fruit
   b. Synonym modified by use: *Straw* = hay that cattle eat
   c. Synonym modified by description: *Gown* = long dress
   d. Synonym modified by use and   *Eyelash* = ha.. over the eye that
      description: protects you
   e. Synonym qualified as to degree: *Tap* = touch lightly

Use, Description, and Use and Description Category
   a. Use: *Orange* = you eat it
   b. Description: *Straw* = it's yellow
   c. Use and description: *Orange* = you eat it and it's round

Explanation Category
   a. Explanation: *Priceless* = it's worth a lot of money
                     Skill = being able to do something
                     well

Demonstration, Repetition, Illustration, and Inferior Explanation Category
   a. Demonstration: For words like *tap, eyelash*, etc.
   b. Repetition: *Puddle* = a puddle of water
   c. Illustration: *Priceless* = a gem
   d. Inferior explanation: *Scorch* = hot

Error Category
   a. Incorrect demonstration: *Eyelash* = points to eyebrow
   b. Misinterpretation: *Regard* = protects something
   c. Wrong definition: *Orange* = a vegetable
   d. Clang association: *Roar* = raw; *skill* = skillet
   e. Repetition without explanation: *Puddle* = puddle
   f. Omits: When the word is left out

From H. Feifel and I. Lorge (1950). Qualitative differences in the vocabulary responses of children. *Journal of Educational Psychology, 41*, 1–18.

it to subjects older than the age of 14. Relevant subject groups in the replication study were of the ages of 10 through 13, 14 through 17, and 18 through 25. The results were essentially the same as Feifel and Lorge's for the overlapping ages, but Storck and Looft also found that the Synonym response, which was often categorical (e.g., defining an orange as *a fruit with an orange-colored skin*, p. 194), continued to increase, and the Error response continued to decrease throughout the adolescent years and into young adulthood.

A developmental increase in the categorical response was also observed by Al-Issa (1969) in a word definition study that included 9- and 10-year-olds ($n = 61$). Each child was asked to define 30 common words (e.g., *soldier, dog, chair, orange*), and the responses were classified as either Descriptive (e.g., Orange: *it's round*), Functional (*you eat it*), or Categorical (*it's a fruit*). Results showed that for the 9-year-olds, the responses were 11 percent Descriptive, 45 percent Functional, and 41 percent Categorical; however, for the 10-year-olds, the responses were 11 percent Descriptive, 28 percent Functional, and 61 percent Categorical. Thus, it was found that Descriptive responses were low for both age groups, but that Functional responses decreased and Categorical responses increased as a function of age.

Other word definition studies using similar procedures (e.g., Swartz and Hall, 1972; Wehren et al., 1981; Watson, 1985; Wolman and Barker, 1965) have supported the findings of those just reported. Andersen (1975), using a different type of task, made additional findings. The purpose of her study was to examine children's understanding of the vagueness of boundaries between semantically related categories. Children of the ages of 9 and 12 ($n = 11$) were included in her study. At the outset, each child was shown an array of 25 different drinking vessels that varied widely in shape, size, color, composition, and function (e.g., blue plastic cup, brown ceramic coffee mug, clear wine glass). The prototypicality of the vessels ranged from those that were unequivocally cups (e.g., made of china with a handle) or glasses (tall, made of clear glass) to those whose category membership was equivocal (e.g., tall, made of red metal). The child was asked to name each vessel independently, and then to sort the vessels into categories—"cup," "glass," or "neither." The child was then asked to provide definitions for the words *cup* and *glass* as part of a role-playing task. For example, to elicit a definition of *cup*, the examiner said the following:

> Suppose you had a friend from another country and that friend didn't speak English very well. And one day he/she said to you. "My mother told me to go to the store and buy some cups, but I'm not sure what a *cup* is. Can you tell me what it is/what it looks like"? What would you tell him/her? (p. 85)

In naming the 25 different vessels, the 12-year-olds used a greater number of functional modifiers than the 9-year-olds (e.g., *martini glass, beer mug, coffee cup*), reflecting greater cultural knowledge and "real world" experience. In sorting the vessels, the 12-year-olds assigned more items to the "neither" category than the 9-year-olds, reflecting greater awareness of the vagueness of boundaries between cups and glasses. Finally, the definitions of the 12-year-olds were "much closer to actual dictionary entries" (p. 97) than those of the 9-year-olds. However, the definitions of both the 9- and 12-year-olds reflected an awareness of vagueness through the use of hedges (e.g., *sometimes, usually, could have*). In addition, the definitions of both groups were quite detailed, mentioning material, size, shape, and function. For example, one 9-year-old explained that a cup "holds things to drink, sometimes has a handle. . . is like cylinder shape, and sometimes has a stand on the bottom" (p. 96).

In interpreting the developmental studies of word definition, it is important to remember that this is a literate metalinguistic task where words are used to talk about other words. It also requires the meaning of a word to be abstracted from a lexical knowledge base and thereby reflects the youngster's conception of the word (Litowitz, 1977). Further, performance on word definition tasks reflects a youngster's cultural knowledge, world experience, knowledge of what a definition is (Wehren et al., 1981), and previous exposure to definition tasks in school (Watson, 1985). Thus, it should not be assumed that performance is solely a measure of lexical knowledge: youngsters often know more about words than they can actually explain. For example, it is clear that preschoolers know that cats and dogs are animals, that apples and cookies are food, and that boys and girls are children. However, when asked to define the words *cat, dog, apple, cookie, boy*, and *girl*, the appropriate categorical terms—*animal, food*, and *children*—are typically omitted from their responses (Nelson, 1978). Older children also show limitations in the extent to which they display their knowledge of word meanings on definition tasks. For example, Watson (1985) asked a group of 10-year-olds ($n = 40$) to define a series of eight nouns that were very familiar to preschoolers (e.g., *cat, horse, flower*). After the definitions were elicited, a series of yes or no questions were asked about each word (e.g., "Is a cat an animal?") and it was found that the children knew a great deal more about the words than was reflected in their spontaneous definitions.

Summary

When word difficulty is kept to a low level, youngsters' performance on definition tasks reflects their ability to organize their knowledge about word meanings and to state that knowledge in a succinct, conventional form that is modeled on their experiences in educational settings. Definition tasks that employ word lists of increasing complexity (e.g., Feifel and Lorge, 1950; Storck and Looft, 1973) also call on metalinguistic ability. However, they also place significant demands on the youngster's lexical knowledge base. The differential contribution of metalinguistic ability and lexical knowledge to overall performance on word definition tasks has not yet been determined, and represents an important issue for future research.

When asked to define words aloud, young children typically respond by stating a function of the named stimulus (Al-Issa, 1969; Wehren et al., 1981) or by producing an idiosyncratic response (e.g., Diamond: *people steal diamonds*) (Litowitz, 1977). With development, however, the tendency to produce a synonymous or categorical response steadily increases well into the adult years (Storck and Looft, 1973) and reflects an advanced conception of a word's socially shared meaning (Litowitz, 1977). However, it is interesting that when children are asked to define words from semantically related categories, older children show a greater tendency to mention functional characteristics than younger children, and also show greater awareness that the boundaries between semantically related categories are vague (Andersen, 1975).

CONCLUSIONS

Developmental studies of word classes and of word definition are consistent in finding that competence in these two areas is related to academic achievement, verbal ability, and general intelligence. Both areas of research show that quantitative and qualitative improvements occur in lexical development during the 9-through-19 age range, and that youngsters are capable of increasing levels of abstraction: new words are added to the lexicon, old words take on new and subtle meanings, and it becomes easier to organize and reflect on the content of the lexicon and to articulate that knowledge.

Future research should investigate youngsters' comprehension of additional verbs, adverbs, and connectives necessary for literacy, as well as other classes of words such as adjectives and prepositions as they develop during the 9-through-19 age range. Such information could then be used by teachers and curriculum planners to faciliate the acquisition of literacy during this important period of language development.

REFERENCES

Al-Issa, I. (1969). The development of word definition in children. *Journal of Genetic Psychology, 114*, 25–28.

Andersen, E.S. (1975). Cups and glasses: Learning that boundaries are vague. *Journal of Child Language, 2*, 79–103.

Asch, S.E., and Nerlove, H. (1960). The development of double function terms in children: An exploratory investigation. In B. Kaplan and S. Wapner (Eds.), *Perspectives in psychological theory: Essays in honor of Heinz Werner* (pp. 47–60). New York: International Universities Press.

Astington, J.W., and Olson, D.R. (1987, April). *Literacy and schooling: Learning to talk about thought.* Paper presented at the Annual Meeting of the American Educational Research Association, Washington, DC.

Bashaw, W.L., and Anderson, H.E. (1968). Developmental study of the meaning of adverbial modifiers. *Journal of Educational Psychology, 59*, 111–118.

Bennett, R.A. (1981). *Types of literature.* Lexington, MA: Ginn.

Bloom, L. (1973). *One word at a time: The use of single-word utterances before syntax.* The Hague, Netherlands: Mouton.

Clark, E. (1973). What's in a word? On the child's acquisition of semantics in his first language. In T. Moore (Ed.), *Cognitive development and the acquisition of language* (pp. 65-110). New York: Academic Press.

Cliff, N. (1959). Adverbs as multipliers. *Psychological Review, 66,* 26-44.

Coon, G.E., Cramer, B.B., Fillmer, H.T., Lefcourt, A., Martin, J., and Thompson, N.C. (1980). *American book English.* New York: Litton Educational Publishing.

Dale, E., and Eichholz, G. (1960). *Children's knowledge of words: An interim report.* Columbus, OH: Bureau of Educational Research and Service, Ohio State University.

Duffy, G.G., and Roehler, L.R. (1981). *Building reading skills: Level 4.* Evanston, IL: McDougal, Littel, and Company.

Entwisle, D.R., Forsyth, D.F., and Muuss, R. (1964). the syntactic-paradigmatic shift in children's word associations. *Journal of Verbal Learning and Verbal Behavior, 3,* 19-29.

Feifel, H., and Lorge, I. (1950). Qualitative differences in the vocabulary responses of children. *Journal of Educational Psychology, 41,* 1-18.

Flexner, S.B., and Hauck, L.C. (1987). *Random House Dictionary of the English Language* (Second Edition—Unabridged). New York: Random House.

Flores d'Arcais, G.B. (1978). Levels of semantic knowledge in children's use of connectives. In A. Sinclair, R.J. Jarvella, and W.J.M. Levelt (Eds.), *The child's conception of language* (pp. 133-153). New York: Springer-Verlag.

Geva, E., and Ryan, E.B. (1985). Use of conjunctions in expository texts by skilled and less skilled readers. *Journal of Reading Behavior, 17,* 331-346.

Israel, L. (1984). Word knowledge and word retrieval: Phonological and semantic strategies. In G.P. Wallach and K.G. Butler (Eds.), *Language learning disabilities in school-age children* (pp. 230-250). Baltimore, MD: Williams & Wilkins.

Katz, E.W., and Brent, S.B. (1968). Understanding connectives. *Journal of Verbal Learning and Verbal Behavior, 7,* 501-509.

Langacker, R.W. (1973). *Language and its structure: Some fundamental linguistic concepts* (Second Edition). New York: Harcourt Brace Jovanovich.

Lippman, M.Z. (1971). Correlates of contrast word associations: Developmental trends. *Journal of Verbal Learning and Verbal Behavior, 10,* 392-399.

Litowitz, B. (1977). Learning to make definitions. *Journal of Child Language, 4,* 289-304.

McCarthy, D. (1972). *McCarthy Scales of Children's Abilities.* New York: Psychological Corporation.

McClure, E.F., and Geva, E. (1983). The development of the cohesive use of adversative conjunctions in discourse. *Discourse Processes, 6,* 411-432.

McClure, E.F., and Steffensen, M.S. (1985). A study of the use of conjunctions across grades and ethnic groups. *Research in the Teaching of English, 19,* 217-236.

McDonnell, H., Nakadate, N.E., Pfordresher, J., and Shoemate, T.E. (1979). *England in literature.* Glenview, IL: Scott, Foresman and Company.

McNeil, D. (1970). *The acquisition of language: The study of developmental psycholinguistics.* New York: Harper and Row.

Miller, G.A., and Gildea, P.M. (1987). How children learn words. *Scientific American*, *257*, 94-99.

Nelson, K. (1977). The syntagmatic-paradigmatic shift revisited: A review of research and theory. *Psychological Bulletin*, *84*, 93-116.

Nelson, K. (1978). Semantic development and the development of semantic memory. In K. Nelson (Ed.), *Children's language, Volume I* (pp. 39-80). New York: Gardner Press.

Niemark, E.D., and Slotnick, N.S. (1970). Development of the understanding of logical connectives. *Journal of Educational Psychology*, *61*, 451-460.

Olson, D.R., and Astington, J.W. (1986a). Children's acquisition of metalinguistic and metacognitive verbs. In W. Demopoulos and A. Marras (Eds.), *Language learning and concept acquisition: Foundational issues* (pp. 184-199). Norwood, NJ: Ablex.

Olson, D.R., and Astington, J.W. (1986b, October). *Talking about text: How literacy contributes to thought*. Paper presented at the Boston University Conference on Language Development, Boston, MA.

Palermo, D.S., and Molfese, D.L. (1972). Language acquisition from age five onward. *Psychological Bulletin*, *78*, 409-428.

Riegel, K.F., Riegel, R.M., Quarterman, C.J., and Smith, H.E. (1968). Developmental differences in word meaning and semantic structure. *Human Development*, *11*, 92-106.

Robertson, J.E. (1968). Pupil understanding of connectives in reading. *Reading Research Quarterly*, *3*, 387-417.

Scoville, R.P., and Gordon, A.M. (1980). Children's understanding of factive presuppositions: An experiment and a review. *Journal of Child Language*, *7*, 381-399.

Storck, P.A., and Looft, W.R. (1973). Qualitative analysis of vocabulary responses from persons aged six to sixty-six plus. *Journal of Educational Psychology*, *65*, 192-197.

Swartz, K., and Hall, A.E. (1972). Development of relational concepts and word definition in children five through eleven. *Child Development*, *43*, 239-244.

Terman, L.M. (1916). *The measurement of intelligence*. Boston: Houghton Mifflin.

Thorndike, R.L., Hagen, E.P., and Sattler, J.M. (1986). *Stanford-Binet Intelligence Scale* (Fourth Edition). Chicago, IL: Riverside.

Watson, R. (1985). Towards a theory of definition. *Journal of Child Language*, *12*, 181-197.

Wechsler, D. (1955). *Wechsler Adult Intelligence Scale*. New York: Psychological Corporation.

Wechsler, D. (1967). *Wechsler Preschool and Primary Scale of Intelligence*. New York: Psychological Corporation.

Wechsler, D. (1974). *Wechsler Intelligence Scale for Children—Revised*. New York: Psychological Corporation.

Wehren, A., De Lisi, R., and Arnold, M. (1981). The development of noun definition. *Journal of Child Language*, *8*, 165-175.

Welch, B.Y., and Bennett, R.A. (1981). *Introduction to Literature*. Lexington, MA: Ginn.

Werner, H., and Kaplan, E. (1950). The acquisition of word meanings: A developmental study. *Monographs of the Society for Research in Child Development*, *15*, Serial No. 51.

Wing, C.S., and Scholnick, E.K. (1981). Children's comprehension of pragmatic concepts expressed in "because," "although," "if," and "unless." *Journal of Child Language*, *8*, 347-365.

Wolman, R.N., and Barker, E.N. (1965). A developmental study of word definitions. *Journal of Genetic Psychology*, *107*, 159-166.

CHAPTER 4

■

SPOKEN AND WRITTEN SYNTAX

■

CHERYL M. SCOTT

Readers might question the inclusion of a chapter on syntax in a book about language development in the 9-through-19 age range. Perhaps they have taken to heart McNeill's (1966) forceful statement that by the age of four, children are producing sentences of "every conceivable syntactic type" (p. 99). Or perhaps they have adopted the more tempered view expressed by Rees (1974) that children have "basically" mastered syntax by the age of five.

The paucity of research on later syntactic development might suggest that growth in this area is relatively minor and unimportant. However, this chapter will show that important and interesting syntactic developments do occur during the 9-through-19 age range, and that the syntax of older children and adolescents is indeed different from that of younger children. Contrary to what some readers may have thought during the recent emphasis on pragmatic and metalinguistic development, the yoke of syntax cannot be shaken off quite so easily.

This chapter is divided into four major sections. The first section contrasts the study of syntax in the 9-through-19 age range with syntactic study of younger children. Issues raised in this section affect the interpretation of the data that follow. The second section discusses several measures devised over the years to characterize developmental changes in syntactic complexity. These include sentence length, clause length, the subordination index, and multistructural indices. The third section charts changes in structures at the phrase, clause, and discourse levels, and changes in major types of subordination. Structures highlighted in this section were chosen because of their prominence in the literature or because of the author's intuitive notion of their importance. Production studies employing naturalistic or semistructured tasks are featured rather than experimenter-generated comprehension tasks (e.g., Chomsky, 1969) or highly metalinguistic tasks. The fourth section discusses syntactic development within the broader context of discourse and shows how discourse affects the types of syntactic structures produced. Due to the technical nature of the chapter, terms and structures in need of further explanation are numbered consecutively in the text. Definitions and examples are then provided by corresponding number in the Appendix.

ISSUES IN THE STUDY OF SYNTAX

The study of syntax in the 9-through-19 age range shares several theoretical and methodological problems with research focusing on younger children. Issues relevant to all ages include acquisition criteria for structures (cf. Bloom and Lahey, 1978; Brown, 1973; Wells, 1985), differences between naturalistic and contrived or experimenter-generated tasks (cf. Karmiloff-Smith, 1979), sampling variability (e.g., Scott and Taylor, 1978), and comprehension versus production knowledge. However, the study of later syntactic development is unique in that different theoretical issues come to light and additional methodological problems are encountered. These issues and problems are discussed throughout the chapter.

Developmental Schedules

One major outcome for syntactic studies of younger children has been the establishment of developmental schedules for the acquisition of specific syntactic structures. For example, most students of children's language can recite an order of acquisition for grammatical morphemes (Brown, 1973), an age range when children begin to produce four-element clauses (Crystal, Fletcher, and Garman, 1976), or an age when various connectives first appear (Bloom, Lahey, Hood, Lifter, and Fiess, 1980). As preschoolers move from absence to presence of basic syntactic structures, developmental schedules can be constructed with relative ease. However, it is much more difficult to construct comparable syntactic schedules for the 9-through-19 age range because the concern now is not with the presence or absence of high-frequency structures, but with the gradual acquisition of low-frequency structures and the ability to form unique combinations of structures. To uncover later syntactic developments, finer grained methods of analysis are needed. Thus, the developmental schedules for the 9-through-19 age range, when they can be constructed, will be of a different nature than those for younger children.

Expanding Contexts for Language

The contexts for language use pose a second point of contrast for the study of early versus later syntactic development. Whereas most data for preschool children have come from dyadic adult–child play settings, the study of syntax in the 9-through-19 age range is complicated by rapidly expanding contexts for language use and the well-documented influence of these contexts on language structure (Crowhurst, 1979; Perera, 1986a; Scott, 1987). Context includes the setting and occasion of language use (e.g., a school report), the channel (spoken or written), and the discourse genre (e.g., narrative, persuasive, expository). Throughout this chapter, a major theme will be that syntactic structure is greatly affected by language context. Whereas studies of younger children have implied a more unitary type of syntactic competence (e.g., a single level of syntactic competence per se, irrespective of context), a major focus of inquiry with older children and adolescents is that of syntactic adaptability across a wide range of spoken and written language contexts. For example, a high school student rarely uses the passive voice when talking with peers but frequently uses it in writing reports of science experiments (e.g., *The bunson burner was lit* . . . .) (D. Crystal, personal communication, April, 1982).

Multifunctional Structures

With continuing development, many syntactic structures begin to serve more than one functional master, further complicating the study of syntax in older children and adolescents. This can be observed in the progression of *because* adverbial clauses from semantic contexts of admonition in the preschooler (e.g, *You can't have that 'cause it's mine*) to contexts of logical justification in the preadolescent (e.g., *He used a compass because that's all he had*). Another example is the preschooler's use of *if* clauses encoding real situations (e.g., *If I bring my bat, do you want to play?*) and the preadolescent's use of *if* in hypothetical situations (e.g., *If we were spacemen, we could fix this*) (Perera, 1984). Much of the recent work of Karmiloff-Smith (1979, 1983, 1986) with French noun markers, pronominal reference, and subordination has also demonstrated the gradual pattern of acquisition for these multifunctional structures through the preadolescent years. Forms first appear selectively, and it is only across a considerable time span that the full range of adult usage can be found. Thus, the study of syntactic development in older children and adolescents requires sensitivity to the range of possible meanings encoded by any one structure.

The Adult Model

One additional contrast when studying early versus later syntactic development becomes increasingly obvious as late adolescence is approached. As the adolescent of 19 becomes the adult of 20, the implication is that an "adult" level of syntactic competence is attained. To appreciate this accomplishment, it is important to specify what constitutes an adult level of competence. Two issues seem particularly relevant. The first concerns the necessity of having a realistic (rather than idealistic) adult standard, and the second concerns the possibility of having several adult standards.

Students of children's language sometimes operate with putative notions about the way adults actually talk and write. These notions may take the form of negative interpretations imposed on a number of structural characteristics of children's language, and seem to imply that such characteristics will decrease with age or that they are more typical of children with language disorders. Several examples of this can be found in the clinical literature. For example, Wiig and Semel (1984) reported that children with language learning disorders frequently used the coordinating conjunction *and* as the connective device when telling stories. In a preadolescent narrative which they cited as an illustration, 60 percent of the utterances began with *and* or *and then*. However, this figure conforms closely to comparable stories told by normally developing children between the ages of 6 and 12 (Martin, 1983; Scott, 1984b). Adult stories also contain comparably high percentages of *and* connectives (Scott, 1987). Other structures often cited as problems are low-information words like *stuff* (McKinley and Lord-Larson, 1985; Simon, 1979) and verbal mazes (Simon, 1979). However, Scott (1983) reported that the frequency of phrases like *and everything, and stuff*, and *or something* increased threefold between the ages of 8 and 12 in normal children. In addition, Miller (1987) found that verbal mazes in children's speech increased with age (through 13, the oldest age studied) and discourse demands. Verbal mazes increased for all ages in narrative discourse (versus conversational discourse) and in long utterances (versus short utterances). The distinction between normal and abnormal use of mazes is particularly elusive, as demonstrated by the following excerpt of an interview aired over National Public Radio. The speaker was an educated adult who was discussing a legal issue:

> Well ... there's ... there's no ... uh ... the only limit I see to this type of ... first of all ... uh you have to understand ev ... even in this court in this ... uh urban area ... about 65 percent of the

defendents uh . . . go to probation . . . uh . . . the others generally go
to jail.*

Accurate information concerning adult syntactic competence is
necessary before judgments can be made concerning the relative competence
of older children and adolescents. It is therefore recommended that adults
be included as subjects in studies of later syntactic development.

However, it is also important to realize that adults, like children, display
a wide range of competency levels. Hunt's research (1970) illustrated the
importance of allowing for several levels of adult syntactic competence. He
asked whether the written language skills of graduating high school seniors
would differ significantly from those of average and skilled adult writers.
Hunt's skilled adult writers had published essays in *The Atlantic Monthly*
or *The New Yorker*, whereas his average adult writers were high school
graduates employed as firemen. On a writing task which required the subjects to combine simple sentences, the twelfth graders and the average adults
performed similarly, but the skilled adults outperformed both of those
groups. Hunt offered the tentative conclusion that the average twelfth-grade
writer has achieved full syntactic maturity unless that student continues on
a path requiring educational and occupational practice in text writing. The
implication for this discussion of later syntactic development is clear: the
adult model should be expanded to include a variety of adult language levels.
This is true not just for the study of syntax but also for other aspects of later
language development such as the literate lexicon (Chapter 3), reading and
writing (Chapter 5), figurative expressions (Chapter 8), ambiguities (Chapter
9), and pragmatics (Chapter 11). It is also true for cognitive development
(Chapter 6) and verbal reasoning (Chapter 7). Literate students of language
development may have unrealistic expectations for some adolescents, particularly if their own language level has been internalized as the adult model
of comparison.

QUANTITATIVE MEASURES OF SYNTACTIC GROWTH

The Data Sources

A number of large-scale projects within the field of education were
begun in the 1950s, with reports continuing through the mid 1970s (Hunt,
1965, 1970; Loban, 1963, 1976; O'Donnell, Griffin, and Norris, 1967). A
major goal of each of those projects was to find an educationally useful quantitative index of grammatical development during the school years. Across

---

*From the author's files.

these studies, youngsters' spoken and written language in kindergarten through the twelfth grade was sampled and analyzed. The Hunt and O'Donnell studies were cross-sectional with large numbers of subjects ($n = 54$ in Hunt, 1965; $n = 250$ in Hunt, 1970; $n = 180$ in O'Donnell et al., 1967), whereas the Loban work was a longitudinal study of 211 children over a 13-year period from kindergarten through the twelfth grade. The Hunt studies were concerned exclusively with written language, whereas the Loban and O'Donnell studies compared spoken and written language. In addition to the search for quantitative measures of language growth, the projects tallied frequencies of particular syntactic structures. Subordination was a focus in each of the projects.

Although the projects just mentioned are often cited as major sources of information on later syntactic development, it must be emphasized that their data are relevant only within the confines of their discourse contexts. Hunt's (1965) writing samples were described as "whatever he [the student] normally writes about in school" (p.3), whereas O'Donnell and colleagues (1967) employed a contrived narrative task in which children were asked to tell and write about a silent animated fable. Loban's (1976) spoken data were based on adult-child conversational interviews, and his written data were described only as school compositions. During the past 10 years, additional projects (e.g., Perera, 1986a; Rubin, 1982; Scott, 1984a, 1984b, 1987) have contributed to the data base on later syntactic development. These more recent projects, which sometimes involved fewer subjects, are also discussed in this chapter.

The Unit of Analysis

Language produced by older children and adolescents sometimes poses special segmentation problems. For example, it is difficult to segment productions involving the coordination of main clauses with *and*, and productions such as *the more the merrier, pardon me,* and *thanks,* which do not have full clausal status. Advanced syntactic productions are often characterized by elliptical units, single-word *yes* and *no* responses to questions, and other types of units that also lack clausal status. Even written language can be difficult to segment when the writer either fails to use capitals and periods consistently or uses them in unconventional ways. Preadolescents frequently produce written texts that are syntactically well structured but imperfectly punctuated (cf. Scott, 1988a).

The sentence has long been the relevant unit of syntactic analysis in studies of young children. Sentences contain other smaller units that can be identified, ordered, and further dissected. However, when studying advanced syntactic productions, more precise methods of analysis must be employed. All of the studies to be reviewed in this section employed the *terminable unit* (T-unit) as the method for segmenting discourse. First proposed by Hunt (1965), the T-unit consists of a main clause with all subordinate clauses or nonclausal structures attached to or embedded within. All main clauses that begin with coordinating conjunctions (*and, but, or*) initiate a new T-unit unless there is co-referential subject deletion in the second clause. For example, the sentence *Jane went to the store and bought some Coke* would be one T-unit, but the sentence *Jane went to the store and she bought some Coke* would be two T-units. The C-unit, devised by Loban (1976) to analyze spoken language, is identical to the T-unit, but includes units that do not have clausal status. For example, a two-word response (e.g., *Yes, please*) to a question (e.g., *Would you like some dessert?*) would be a C-unit. Most investigators who analyzed the spoken and written language samples of adolescents used the T-unit as the basis for segmentation and for calculating average length in words. However, few investigators specified the way nonclausal units were analyzed.

In this section, the terms *T-unit* and *sentence* are used interchangeably, but with the understanding that a sentence is defined as a T-unit. Some studies (e.g., Scott, 1984a) used the term *utterance* for spoken T-units, thus recognizing that only some spoken units have clausal status (a characteristic associated more with sentences). It could be argued that the term *sentence* should be reserved for written language where clausal status is usually the rule. However, for the sake of simplicity, this discussion uses the term *sentence* for both spoken and written units.

Sentence Length

There is now a sizeable literature documenting a slow but steady increase in T-unit length during the preadolescent and adolescent years in both spoken and written language (Hunt, 1965, 1970; Klecan-Aker and Hedrick, 1985; Loban, 1976; Morris and Crump, 1982; O'Donnell et al., 1967; Scott, 1984b). The data from several projects are summarized in Table 4-1. Arranged by grade level, the table shows data for spoken (S) and written (W) language. The type of discourse sampled in each project is also indicated. With the exception of the data for Hunt's sentence-combining study (column f), there was considerable agreement in T-unit mean lengths across studies despite methodological differences. For example, at the third-grade level, most studies showed a T-unit length of approximately 7.6 words for spoken and written language. T-unit length increased to 11.7 words by twelfth grade for spoken language (Loban, 1967), and was only slightly higher (14.4 words) in the written compositions of twelfth-grade students (Hunt, 1965). On a controlled writing task, where students were asked to rewrite a list of related simple sentences, T-unit length increased from 5.2 to 11.5 words between fourth and twelfth grades (Hunt, 1970). Two studies compared T-unit length in

TABLE 4-1.
Average T-unit length for youngsters in third through twelfth grades.

						Research Project					
	a*	a	b	b	c	d	e	f	g	h
Grade	s†	W	S	W	S	S	W	W	W	W
3	7.62	7.60	8.73	7.67					7.45	
4	9.00	8.02	8.90	9.34		8.52	8.60	5.21		
5	8.82	8.76							8.81	10.70
6	9.82	9.04	9.80	9.99	9.03	8.10				11.40
7	9.72	8.98						7.32	8.53	
8	10.71	10.37					11.50	10.34	11.68	
9	10.96	10.05								
10	10.68	11.79			10.15			10.46		
11	11.17	10.67								
12	11.70	13.27					14.40	11.45		

*(a) Loban (1976): $N = 35$ at each grade. Data also available for high and low language ability groups. Ages unavailable. Spoken: adult–child informal interview. Written: school compositions.

(b) O'Donnell and colleagues (1967): $N = 30$ at each grade. Ages available. Spoken and written: retelling/rewriting of silent fable (narrative).

(c) Klecan-Acker and Hedrick (1985). $N = 24$ at each grade. Retelling of a favorite film (narrative).

(d) Scott (1984b). $N = 25$ 10-year-olds, 29 12-year-olds. Retelling of a favorite book, TV episode, film (narrative).

(e) Hunt (1965). $N = 18$ at each grade. School compositions.

(f) Hunt (1970). $N = 50$ at each grade. Sentence combining exercise.

(g) Morris and Crump (1982). $N = 18$ at each age (9.6, 11.25, 12.54, 14.08 years). Rewriting of silent film (narrative).

(h) Richardson and colleagues (1976). $N = 257$ 11-year-old boys, 264 11-year-old girls. School compositions.

†S = spoken; W = written. The d, f, and g projects reported data for age only. The data were entered in the table using the following formula: Grade = Age – 6 Years.

spoken and written language for the same children: O'Donnell and colleagues (1967) found that written T-units were slightly shorter than spoken T-units until fifth grade, whereas Loban (1976) found that written units were shorter than spoken units until tenth grade. However, with the exception of Loban's twelfth grade students, differences in spoken and written T-unit length in those two studies were minimal.

Although it is clear that T-unit length steadily increases as a function of age, the interpretation of this knowledge is problematic because of the T-unit's slow rate of growth and its susceptibility to contextual factors. In fact, length increases so slowly that it is rare to find statistically significant differences between grade or age levels of one or two years difference. This complicates the use of T-unit length as a measuring device in educational settings where fine distinctions between ability levels are often desired. In addition, it has been known for some time that T-unit length can vary dramatically within the same individual as a function of the particular discourse type, an effect that has been reported for both normal students (e.g., Crowhurst, 1979) and those with learning disablities (e.g., Blair and Crump, 1984). Crowhurst (1979), for example, reported a difference of 3.11 words on mean T-unit length between tenth graders' written narrative and argument texts, with the argument texts containing longer sentences. Interestingly, the effects of discourse context (one subject sampled in two different discourse contexts) frequently exceed developmental effects (two subjects of different ages sampled in the same context).

Although the data show convincingly that sentence length gradually increases during the 9-through-19 age range, longer does not always mean better, particularly if conciseness is valued. This point is illustrated by the following unwieldy sentence written by an adolescent (Crowhurst, 1979):

> If someone is found doing something wrong he should be told and then punished in a way that would convince him to pay attention instead of goofing off, such as calling and notifying the parents and telling them what a bad little boy they have. (p. 95)

Clause Length

Clause length (mean number of words per clause) is a second type of quantitative measure of syntactic development. Because some T-units contain more than one clause, this measure differs from T-unit length. For a given sample, assuming there is some subordination, clause length will always be a lower number (i.e., fewer words per clause than words per T-unit). Clauses become longer by many different syntactic operations (e.g., more expansion of noun phrases and verb phrases), but T-units become longer by the same mechanisms that increase clause length plus the addition of clauses by subordination. Clause length, therefore, allows for a measure of complexity without the effects of subordination operations.

Clause length has been reported more often in studies of written language than of spoken language development (e.g., Hunt, 1965, 1970; Rubin, 1982). In written language, clause length increases monotonically from approximately five words per clause in fourth grade to eight words per clause by twelfth grade. Hunt (1970) demonstrated significant increases in clause length as a function of ability grouping (high, medium, and low). In the Hunt writing task, students were given short sentences and asked to rewrite the "short and choppy" sentences "in a better way." The resulting clauses of the older students and of the high-ability students were longer because they reduced the simple sentences to less than clausal units. For example, the sentence *They grind the bauxite* became an element of a larger clause such as *Grinding the bauxite* . . . , or the sentence *Bauxite is an ore* became *Bauxite, an ore* . . . . Studying the same age range as Hunt but using a persuasive writing task, Rubin (1982) found that clause length changed significantly as a function of the writer's sense of audience. Clauses were longer when the students were writing for a more remote audience as opposed to a more intimate audience.

The Subordination Index

Degree of subordination is a measure of the average number of clauses (main and subordinate) per T-unit. For a given sample, the subordination index is expressed as a ratio of the number of total clauses over total T-units (see Appendix, item #1). Table 4-2 shows that mean figures range from 1.22 for the spoken language of third graders (transformed data from Loban, 1976) to 1.73 for the written language of twelfth graders (Rubin, 1982). In practical terms, this indicates that the spoken sentences of a third grader contain a subordinate clause 22 percent of the time, or about one in every five sentences; the written sentences of a twelfth grader will have a subordinate clause approximately 67 percent of the time. Comparing spoken and written language, Loban (1976) found few differences for this measure. However, O'Donnell and colleagues (1967) found that by the seventh grade, written language contained greater subordination than spoken language. It is noteworthy that the type of task was controlled across channels in the O'Donnell study; the children both spoke and wrote about a silent fable. (The O'Donnell data were not included in Table 4-2 because they were calculated in a manner that was not comparable to other projects). Compared to T-unit length, the growth of the subordination index is less monotonic, with several short plateau periods (Loban, 1976) and a general leveling off by eighth grade (Hunt, 1970; Rubin, 1982).

TABLE 4-2.

Average subordination index for youngsters in third through twelfth grades.

	Research Project						
Grade	a* S†	a W	b S	c S	d W	e W	f W
3	1.22						
4	1.30	1.19		1.33	1.30	1.00	1.32 (int) 1.30 (imm) 1.24 (rem)
5	1.29	1.21					
6	1.37	1.29	1.28	1.39		1.24	
7	1.35	1.28					
8	1.39	1.50			1.42	1.46	1.67 1.34 1.52
9	1.45	1.47	1.31				
10	1.48	1.52				1.41	
11	1.52	1.45					
12	1.58	1.60			1.68	1.48	1.73 1.68 1.52

*(a) Loban (1976): Loban reported this ratio as the number of subordinate clauses/sentence. The figures have been converted to number subordinate plus main clauses/sentence for purposes of comparison with other projects.

(b) Klecan-Aker (1985): See Table 4-1.

(c) Scott (1984b): See Table 4-1.

(d) Hunt (1965): See Table 4-1.

(e) Hunt (1970): See Table 4-1.

(f) Rubin (1982): $N = 18$ at each grade. Persuasive writing task. Data are reported separately for intimate (int), immediate (imm), and remote (rem) audience tasks.

†S = spoken; W = written. The subordination index is the number of subordinate and main clauses per T-unit.

A recurring methodological problem with the subordination index has been the lack of agreement concerning the types of structures that should be included as subordinate clauses. Although Loban (1976) criticized Hunt's definition of subordination because it included only clauses with finite verbs (see Appendix, item #2), it is not clear whether his own method included nonfinite constructions. Scott (1988b) discussed the implications of considering nonfinite object nominal clauses (e.g., *She tried to correct the error*) as instances of subordination.

The Multistructural Index

The demonstrated increase in degree of subordination complies with the generally held notion that sentences become more complex with multiple degrees and types of subordination (clause-adding complexity). However, it has long been recognized that other types of syntactic structures also undergo significant advances during later childhood and adolescence. For example, noun phrases and verb phrases become more complex, and discourse-structuring devices (adverbial connectives such as *therefore*) are added. Several attempts have been made to develop quantitative measures that reflect a cumulative account of various structures. Golub and Frederick (1971) devised the Syntactic Density Score (SDS), which summed and assigned weights to variables shown a priori to correlate with teacher's judgments of children's language. Loban (1976) also devised a list of later-developing structures, the Elaboration Index, which listed 22 variables with weights from 1/2 (adjectives, adverbs, auxiliaries) to 7 (a third-order infinitive clause). Loban's strategy was to credit anything beyond basic subjects and predicates, as shown in Table 4-3. For any particular sample, those numbers were tallied and expressed as an average number of points per sentence.

Loban's findings for students in kindergarten through twelfth grade were revealing. The Elaboration Index yielded results for spoken language that were almost identical to the C-unit length measure, showing a slow but steady growth rate. The growth rate was strongest for the written language of high-ability students. From the fourth grade on, measures of written language were consistently higher than measures of spoken language for this group. This spoken–written discrepancy was slower to develop for the randomly selected group, and became evident only by the eighth grade for the low-ability group. Moreover, the discrepancy was smallest for the low-ability group, indicating that these students wrote much like they talked. Loban stressed the importance of examining all of the variables in the Elaboration Index, arguing that differences in syntactic competence would not show up unless variables other than dependent clauses are considered. However, Loban did not report which particular variables in the Elaboration Index were most discriminatory. Perhaps this issue could be addressed in future research. Information presented in the the third section of this chapter on selected later-developing structures could be used toward that end.

The Use of Quantitative Data

Questions arise concerning the application of the data just presented. For example, should the data be used in a normative sense? Is it appropriate to believe that one number accurately represents a 12-year-old's average T-unit length (or clause length or subordination index)? Should this number

TABLE 4-3.
Loban's elaboration index weights.

Language Variable	Points
Adjective	1/2
Adverb	1/2
Compounding	1/2
Auxiliary	1/2
Possessive	1
Determiner	1
Topic*	1
Frozen Language[†]	1
Parenthetical**	2
Nominative Absolute	2
Prepositional Phrase	2
Modal	2
Participle	2
Gerund	2
Infinitive	2
Objective Complement	3
Appositive	3
First-order Dependent Clause[‡]	4
First-order Participial Phrase[‡]	5
First-order Gerund Phrase[‡]	5
First-order Infinitive Phrase[‡]	5
First-order Infinitive Clause[‡]	5

*Topic: instances of repeated subjects such as *The boy, he was in the street* or *I knew that the girl, she was my friend.*

[†]Frozen language: idiomatic expressions such as *once upon a time, in other words, a couple of weeks ago, more or less, back and forth, a long time ago.* This was a vague category but, fortunately, few instances occurred.

**Parenthetical: structures inserted within a communication unit such as *I guess, I suppose, you might say, as it were, generally speaking.*

[‡]Some subjects produce more complicated constructions, for instance, a dependent clause within a dependent clause. All dependent clauses and verbal phrases beyond first-order (second-order, third-order, etc.) received one additional point as the order of embedding increased. For example, a second-order dependent clause received five points; a second-order participial phrase received six points; a third-order infinitive clause received seven points, etc. These occurred very seldom.

From W. Loban (1976). *Language development: Kindergarten through grade twelve* (Research Report No. 18). Champaign, IL: Copyright © (1976) by the National Council of Teachers of English. Reprinted with permission.

then be compared to a number representing a larger sample of 12-year-olds? The influence of discourse context, and the relatively slow growth rate over a broad age range, are factors that seem to mitigate the normative applications of the data to older children and adolescents. However, there may be normative applications of a more selective type, such as the comparison with a sample collected in nearly identical contexts (e.g., a conversational interview in school could be compared to Loban's figures) or the comparison of two similar samples for a particular youngster at intervals of two or more years. The data might also be helpful in providing some quantitative evidence of a youngster's structural adaptability across several different discourse contexts.

Although the data provide firm evidence of syntactic development during the 9-through-19 age range, they reveal very little about the nature of the syntactic changes that take place during those years. For example, knowing that sentences gradually become more subordinated reveals nothing about the specific types of subordination that become more prominent as a function of age. This problem makes it difficult to apply the information during language evaluations or curriculum-planning activities. In addition, attention to quantitative measures alone implies that development is a simple matter of incremental tallies of structures. However, evidence for selected structures discussed in the third section of this chapter demonstrates otherwise.

Finally, confusion arises from the tendency to equate measured increases in syntactic complexity with increases in syntactic maturity, and then to conclude that language so characterized is somehow qualitatively superior (Crowhurst, 1979). As previously discussed regarding measurement of sentence length, longer T-units do not necessarily mean better writing. The literature is equivocal and sometimes contradictory in the search for positive associations between measures of syntactic complexity and ratings of quality. Perera (1984) also stressed that grammatical form by itself cannot account for more holistic judgments about the "goodness" of a piece of discourse. Nonlinguistic variables including truthfulness, vigor, and the speaker's (or writer's) commitment also enter into such evaluations.

Crowhurst (1979) made two suggestions that help to clarify the issues of complexity, maturity, and quality. First, she promoted an alternative view of maturity as the possession of greater syntactic resources which can be called upon according to the particular discourse demands. Second, in relation to writing, she stressed the importance of examining a large volume of language data, stating that "over a substantial body of writing, these greater syntactic resources are manifested in a higher average level of syntactic complexity than is the case for younger or less able writers" (p. 95). Issues surrounding the relationship between form and quality have a long history, particularly with regard to written language, and cannot be addressed in depth in this chapter.

THE DEVELOPMENT OF SELECTED SYNTACTIC STRUCTURES

The data in this section are presented in a variety of formats, depending on the original source. Relative frequencies are sometimes reported, such as the proportion of all subordination taken up by relative clauses. Another format is to report the occurrence of a particular structure normalized for a certain volume of language, usually 100 T-units. A third format is to report the relative increase in frequency with age, such as a threefold increase in the use of a structure between two ages. Because this chapter will serve as a reference for later syntactic development, frequency measures are important to report. Nevertheless, some structures are discussed without any type of quantitative information because such information was not available in the original sources. The lack of such data does not diminish the importance of those structures in the overall development of syntax.

The examples of syntactic structures were taken from a variety of sources. Most were taken from the author's files and published works, and from the published works of Perera (1984, 1986a, 1986b). The Perera references and several Scott references (1984a, 1984b) drew many of their examples from the British corpus of spoken language covering the ages of 6 through 12 published by Fawcett and Perkins (1980).*

Structures at the Phrase Level

Noun Phrases

Noun phrases undergo considerable change in specific contexts during the 9-through-19 age range. Noun phrase postmodification via prepositional phrases, relative clauses, nonfinite clauses (see Appendix, item #3), and appositive contructions (see Appendix, item #4) are particularly active growth areas. Examples of those structures are shown in Table 4-4. O'Donnell and colleagues (1967) reported an increase in postmodification via prepositional phrases though the age of 13 (the oldest age studied), and Perera (1984) reported that an adult level of competence in spoken language, with a full range of pre- and postmodifying constructions, was not reached until the age of 15 or 16. Hunt (1965) provided an example of "highly complicated" noun phrase postmodification in the writing of a twelfth-grade student. In his example, shown below, *fear* postmodifies *display*, *ghost* postmodifies *fear*, and *ghost* itself is postmodifed by two additional pieces of information:

---

*In the examples, italics were added by this author to highlight structures under discussion. In keeping with common linguistic conventions, samples of spoken language do not contain punctuation or capitalization except for personal names and the pronoun *I*, whereas samples of written language preserve the original form except for the correction of spelling errors. For spoken language, slashes are used to indicate T-unit boundaries.

TABLE 4-4.
Examples of noun phrase postmodification.

Noun phrase postmodification via prepositional phrase:
1. I saw that the air *in the mountains* goes down and heats off / (*age 11*)*
2. and the plant life *of the desert* is mainly the cactus / (*age 11*)*
3. and then they show when it rains the buds *on them* they bloom and hurry and spread their seeds real fast / (*age 11*)*
4. and they talked about the food chains *in the desert* / (*age 11*)*
5. The leather made him think of a sail *on a ship.* (*age 11*)*

Noun phrase postmodification via nonfinite clause:
1. The desert has one main tree *called the soursos* [saguaro]. (*age 11*)*
2. Commercials make the actor really look like a pirate like the fake wooden leg and the hat and his clothes and the patch over his eye and the paper *stuffed in his shirt.* (*age 11*)*
3. and he taught him the way *to fish.* (*age 11*)*
4. and he had a machine *controlling his brain* / (*age 12*)†

Noun phrase postmodification via appositive constructions:
1. Mr. Spoon *the village policeman* he's not very pleased with them finding out mysteries and always trying to interfere / (*age 10*)†
2. and he took this vase thing *it was like an ornament* as proof and these papers from the safe / (*age 12*)†
3. it's about Jennifer *the girl* she starts a recycling project / (*age 11*)*

*From Scott, 1987.
†From Scott, 1984b.

> Macbeth breaks up the feast with his remarks and his display *of fear of a ghost of Banquo visible only to him.* (p. 118)

Most instances of noun phrase expansion, both pre- and postmodification, occur in noun phrases that function as postverbal elements. In other words, they occur in grammatical roles other than preverbal subjects. Subjects, particularly in spoken language, are almost always pronouns (90 percent of the time in adult speech; Perera, 1986b). Compared to spoken language, however, written language is characterized by higher percentages of complex noun phrases that function as grammatical subjects. Perera (1986b) studied the distribution of complex subject noun phrases in youngsters' speaking and writing. She defined a complex noun phrase as any noun phrase that consists of more than a determiner plus a noun. Of considerable interest was the fact that the writing of 9-year-olds contained higher percentages of complex subject noun phrases (9 percent of all subject noun phrases) than did the informal speech of adults (7 percent). By the age of 12, 12 percent of subject noun phrases in writing were complex.

By comparison, adult scientific writing contains complex noun phrases as subjects 38 percent of the time (Quirk, Greenbaum, Leech, and Svartvik, 1985). Two examples of complex noun phrases functioning as grammatical subjects (Scott, 1987) are:

> *One example of the exaggeration shown in this film* was when they show a close-up of something (mainly food items) to make it look bigger than it really is. (*age 14*)
> *Animals such as lizards, snakes, birds, and some mammals* live there. (*age 14*)

The tracking of complex noun phrases functioning as subjects in youngsters' written language exemplifies the necessity of using fine grained analyses when studying syntactic development in the 9-through-19 age range. The grammatical role of the noun phrase seems to be the critical variable. Complex noun phrases also illustrate the importance of tracking low-frequency linguistic phenomena because of their sensitivity to syntactic growth (Perera, 1986b).

Although noun phrase errors in preadolescents are rare, they are usually one of two types. One error type is the failure to observe co-occurrence restrictions between determiners and nouns (e.g., *much bricks*; age 10, spoken; Perera, 1984, p. 102), and the other type is the inappropriate use of a definite reference for an as yet unspecifed noun. In the following example (Perera, 1984), the indefinite article *a* is more appropriate than the definite article *the* for the first-mentioned nouns *dial* and *lap*:

> **Interviewer:** what's Willy Wheelers?
> **Youngster:** it's a game you put some batteries in / and you turn *the dial* for *the lap* / and little men on motorcycles pedal round / (*age 12*) (p. 103)

Verb Phrases

Verb phrase development was addressed in the Hunt (1965) and Loban (1976) projects. Loban was convinced that the verb phrase was a sensitive indicator of syntactic growth, but failed to uncover any strong evidence of this in his measure of verb density (the number of verb words, main and auxiliary, as a percentage of total words). By way of explanation, he acknowledged that the sampling context for oral language, informal conversational interviews, may not have been conducive to using a variety of verb forms. Loban also counted instances of nonfinite verbs and discovered an increase that went from 6 percent (of total verbs) in first grade to 10 percent in twelfth grade. Although the numbers were small, language ability, a composite rating of a number of language-related skills made by teachers, was strongly associated with the use of nonfinite verbs in written language. Loban maintained that nonfinite verb forms (which, by definition, occur only in subordinate clauses) are important indicators of syntactic growth. He argued that nonfinite verbs allow for a more direct expression of subordinate thought because subjects are optionally deleted and auxiliary verbs carrying tense and number are always deleted. The following example (Scott, 1987) illustrates a nonfinite verb phrase in a subordinate adverbial clause:

> After continually *being turned down* Yanis tries to make his own fishing pole. (*age 14*)

Hunt (1965) reported on specific types of verb phrase expansion in the written language samples of fourth-, eighth-, and twelfth-grade students. He found a doubling of modal auxiliaries between fourth and twelfth grades, with the largest relative growth period occurring between eighth and twelfth grades. The modals *will, would, shall, should, may*, and *might* showed significant levels of change. Scott (1984b) noted increased use of *could* and *would* between the ages of 8 and 12 in spoken narratives that recounted the plots of favorite films, books, or television shows. Through the use of modals, the children were able to talk about the possibilities for action as well as the facts of action, as indicated in the following example (Scott, 1984b):

> they said *they'd* give a million pounds reward for the first one that *could* find the ring because it was hidden in an ice cream / (*age 10*)

Studying the same corpus used by Scott, Perera (1984) found an occasional error in the use of the modal *would* for hypothetical reference at the age of 10. In the first example that follows, the auxiliary is omitted in a context that calls for future hypothetical reference; in the second example, the wrong form of the modal is used:

> **Interviewer:** why would you like to be an air hostess?
> **Youngster:** 'cos I go all over the world in a plane / (*age 10*)
>
> the rain'*ll* get in if it was a real house wouldn't it / (*age 10*) (p. 111)

Perera reported that the occasional modal error persisted in written language until the age of 14.

Other verb phrase developments include greater use of the perfect aspect (*have* + past participle) and the passive voice (*be* + past participle), both of which increased threefold in children's written language between the fourth and twelfth grades (Hunt, 1965). At the same time, the progressive aspect (*be* + ing) decreased in writing to the point that twelfth graders used less than half the number produced by fourth- and eighth-grade students (Hunt, 1965). Surprisingly, there is little information available about the patterns of development for the perfect aspect in the 9-through-19 age range, although

Johnson (1985) studied the development of perfect verbs in younger children. It is noteworthy that the perfect aspect marks a subtle semantic distinction in the time framework of discourse, the phenomenon of the current relevance of a piece of information (Quirk et al., 1985). For example, in the following sentence, Claire's decision to quit took place while she was still dancing: *Although she had danced with the ballet for three years, Claire decided to quit.* Presumably, the appreciation of this phenomenon is a later linguistic attainment. The semantic significance of the perfect aspect suggests that these forms occur more frequently in subordinate clauses than in main clauses (Scott, 1984b):

about a week after it *had come back* it died / (*age 10*)

Perera (1984) cited the following examples of perfect aspect that occurred in the written verb phrases of 12- and 13-year-olds:

We *must have looked* like a row of rheumatic cancan girls.
This *would have been* an encouragement.
I *have decided to put together* all the general facts.
He *had been longing* to go.
(*ages 12 and 13*)   (p. 228)

There is a sizeable literature on the development of passive constructions in older children and adolescents which deals with production and comprehension. Recent reviews of this literature are contained in Perera (1984) and Romaine (1984). Variations of passives with relatively late developmental schedules include full passives (i.e., passives that state the agent, as in *She was taken to the hospital by her mother*) and passives with inanimate subjects and animate agents (e.g., *The window was broken by the child*). Passives rarely occur in spoken language, and O'Donnell and colleagues (1967) reported a frequency rate of only one for every 120 utterances in narrative discourse at the age of 13. Passive constructions aptly illustrate an issue raised earlier about multifunctional structures: these constructions may be well formed syntactically by preadolescents, but they are rarely used with the same range of meaning that the adult demonstrates. For example, Horgan (1978) found that it was not until the age of 11 that youngsters produced both reversible (e.g., *The car was hit by the truck*) and nonreversible (e.g., *The pedestrian was hit by the truck*) passives. Before that age, they produced one or the other type, but not both.

In discourse, verb tense and aspect must be coordinated from sentence to sentence. In the Fawcett and Perkins (1980) transcripts of children of the ages of 6 through 12, Perera (1984) found occasional errors of verb phrase tense or aspect maintenance in spoken language before the age of 10. However, such errors were often more frequent and persistent in written than in spoken language. The following example (Perera, 1984) demonstrates difficulty within the same sentence:

The Africans *are getting* tired of continually thatching their houses, every time a drip *came* through the roof. (*age 10*)   (p. 228)

These types of problems can persist in written language well into the high-school years. For example, the following passage was written by an adolescent who was summarizing a film about television commercials (Scott, 1987):

It explained that something that you see on a commercial can be, and probably is, exaggerated. One example of the exaggeration *shown* on this film *was* when they *show* a close-up of something (mainly food items) to make it look bigger than it really is. Another example is when some sound effects *are added* to make the toy sound like it's the real thing. They also *showed* where in commericals they put important things in small print. (*age 14*)

In the example above, even adults might disagree about the propriety of the successive forms of the italicized verbs.

Structures at the Clause Level

By the time children enter school, they are already using a wide variety of clause types (variations of the basic five sentence elements—subject [S], verb [V], object [O], complement [C], and adverbial [A]), but only a few of these clauses occur frequently. Two studies (O'Donnell et al., 1967; Strickland, 1962) reported clause type frequencies through the seventh grade for spoken language. In those studies, the following clause types, listed in order of decreasing frequency, accounted for approximately 90 percent of all clauses: SVO, SVOA, SVA, SVC, and SV (see Appendix, item #5). In English, there are constraints on the number and order of all elements except adverbials. Therefore, it is reasonable to expect that further development in clause types (both in terms of number of elements within the clause, and order of elements) will center on adverbial elements. However, Hunt's (1965) data for written language did not show that students increased their use of adverbial elements (see Appendix, item #6) as they got older. A closer analysis of the adverbial type, however, indicated that time and place adverbials decrease but that manner adverbials doubled in frequency between fourth and twelfth grades. Riling (1965) noted a similar pattern when analyzing the spoken and written language samples of students in the fourth and sixth grades.

Loban (1963) contended that syntactic development during the school years is concentrated at the phrase level rather than at the clause level. In other words, the youngster develops an increasing repertoire of ways to "fill the slots" of clause elements. However, Loban may have overstated the case in view of the limited research on older children's clause patterns in various discourse contexts. Further research is required to determine the developmental patterns for low-frequency clause types, such as SVOO (direct and indirect objects) (see Appendix, item #7) and SVOC (see Appendix, item #8). Presumably, these clause types would become more available to the older student as the demands for discourse flexibility increase.

Subordination: Nominal, Adverbial, and Relative Clauses

Approximately two or three out of every 10 sentences spoken by a 9-year-old contain a subordinate clause (Loban, 1976). The corresponding subordination index, as discussed previously, is 1.22 (Table 4-2). Over 90 percent of all subordination will be one of the three major clause types discussed in this section—nominal, adverbial, or relative (see Appendix, item #9) (Hunt, 1965; O'Donnell et al., 1967; Scott, 1984b). Nominal and adverbial clauses are nearly equally represented, together accounting for 80 percent of the subordination (O'Donnell et al., 1967). Relative clauses comprise a smaller proportion of total subordination, with frequencies in the range of 6 to 20 percent in narratives (O'Donnell et al., 1967; Scott, 1984b) or 24 to 34 percent in a conversational interview (Loban, 1976). Whereas an 8-year-old produces relatively more subordination in spoken than in written language, by the age of 10, written language is more subordinated than spoken language. The differences between spoken and written language are small when discourse type is controlled (O'Donnell et al., 1967).

Nominal Clauses

Nominal clauses serve various grammatical functions (e.g., as object, complement, or subject) and contain either finite or nonfinite verbs. Most nominal clauses function as direct objects as in *that* clauses (*I know that he likes me*) and *to*-infinitive clauses (*She started to walk home*). These types of clauses are very common from early childhood (Wells, 1985) through the adult years in interactive, face-to-face forms of spoken discourse when statements and opinions are offered (e.g., *I know that. . . , I think that. . .*) (Biber, 1986). They are also common in narrative discourse. In the following example (Scott, 1987), an adolescent was retelling an episode from the television program "Family Ties." Note that a *to*-infinitive nominal clause is functioning as the object in a *that* nominal clause, which itself is the object of the main clause verb *realize*:

and she realized *that the girls wouldn't want to invite the boys* / (*age 14*)

Grammatical function is a major determinant of production frequencies. In both spoken and written discourse, nominal clauses that function in preverbal positions as grammatical subjects are rare. Hunt (1965) found that only 3.6 percent of the nominals in the writing samples of 13-year-olds functioned as grammatical subjects. One reason why nominal clauses infrequently serve as subjects is the strong tendency for important information to occur at the end of the sentence, a principle called *end-weight* by Quirk and colleagues (1985). In the example that follows (Perera, 1984), the subject nominal clause is shifted to the end of the sentence and the pronoun *it* surfaces to fill the subject slot:

it doesn't really matter *what color we do* / (*age 8*)

Written language functions without the assistance of prosody to indicate the new and important information. Consequently, in writing, when several bits of new information compete for the end position, subject nominals are more likely to remain in preverbal position. This has occurred in the following text, a write-up of a peer interview for a school newspaper. The second and third sentences each contain subject nominal clauses before the main verb, thereby allowing the new information (great teachers, switching for classes, and short recesses) to occur at the end of each sentence:

We asked Erin Henderson a few questions about school.
What she likes most about Will Rogers is our great teachers.
What Erin dislikes is having to switch for classes and short recesses. (*age 10*)*

Adverbial Clauses

When adverbial clauses are categorized according to relational meaning (e.g., time, reason, condition, purpose), an uneven picture emerges for the 9-through-19 age range in terms of frequency of occurrence. Throughout this developmental period, a small group of high-frequency adverbials, which include time (usually *when*) and reason (usually *because*), account for approximately 75 percent of all adverbial clauses (Loban, 1976). There is also a group of mid-frequency adverbials that occur at much lower rates. These include the conditional *if*, the nonfinite purpose *to*, and the resultant *so (that)*. Developmental increases in the use of high- and mid-frequency adverbial clauses reach a ceiling by the late elementary grades (fourth through sixth). After that point, the use of such adverbials is influenced more by the particular discourse context and topic than by syntactic development (Hunt, 1965).

In spoken narratives of children of the ages of 6 through 12, Scott (1984b) found that clauses of time (*when*), reason (*because*), and purpose (*to*)

---

*From the author's files.

accounted for most of the adverbial subordination, and that the conditional *if* was practically nonexistent. Citing the work of Kroll, Kroll, and Wells (1980), Perera (1984) discussed the use of adverbial clauses in narrative versus game-instruction writing. She reported that *if* occurred frequently when children wrote about games but that it rarely occurred in narratives. The following spoken version of how to play the game *Monopoly* demonstrates the conditional nature of game instruction:

> well / see / there's this little man you can get / and there's spaces around the board / and you roll the dice / and *if* you get six spaces and *if* it says community chest you pick up community chest cards / and *if* it says pay money you pay some kind of money / and *if* it says get out of jail and you land in jail you can get out of jail on your next turn free / (*age 8*)[†]

During the preadolescent and adolescent years, the use of common adverbials may actually decrease, as Rubin (1982) demonstrated using a persuasive writing task. He asked students in fourth, eighth, and twelfth grades, and a group of adults ($n = 72$), to write about the necessity of recycling glass bottles. The older subjects (eighth grade and above) used fewer common adverbials such as *because* and *if*, which accounted for the overall decrease in adverbial clauses. However, the twelfth graders and adults used a greater variety of adverbials, including some of the lower frequency subordinate conjunctions such as *although* and *unless*. Rubin considered some of the common adverbial clauses produced by the fourth and eighth graders to be rhetorically "heavy-handed," and provided the following example to illustrate this point:

> You should save your glass bottles and jars up to give to a recycling center *if you can*. (*grade 8*) (p. 506)

There is also a third low-frequency group of adverbials that should be mentioned. This group includes adverbials of concession (e.g., *though, although, even if*) and manner (*as*), and some of the less common conditional subordinators (e.g., *unless, provided that*). These particular adverbials tend to be used more often by high-ability groups than by low-ability groups of students (Loban, 1976), and therefore may be more sensitive indicators of syntactic development during the 9-through-19 age range than some of the more common adverbials. Another sensitive indicator of syntactic development, according to Perera (1984), may be the use of nonfinite forms (forms in addition to purpose *to*, which develops early). Table 4-5 contains examples of adverbial clauses in this low-frequency but developmentally important group.

[†]From the author's files.

TABLE 4-5.
Examples of later-developing types of adverbial clauses.

1. She was so excited that she shook the grab-bag puppy box, *forgetting what was in it.* (*age 10*)*
2. She can't think of her least favorite book *even though she has books she really did not like.* (*age 10*)*
3. Jennifer got real mad at her mom *for inviting the boys.* (*age 11*)*
4. and finally *as soon as she did that* all her friends went over and asked the boys to dance / (*age 14*)†
5. he tied a string to it and hook and just tried to catch fish like that and never caught anything *until he met this old man* / (*age 14*)†
6. *since nobody let him have a job* he went out and started to sea / (*age 14*)†

*From the author's files.
†From Scott, 1987.

Relative Clauses

Even though relative clauses occur less frequently overall than nominals and adverbials, both Loban (1976) and Hunt (1965) emphasized their significance for syntactic development. Greater use of relative clauses characterized the high-ability language group in Loban's spoken samples, and a steady increase in the use of relative clauses through twelfth grade characterized Hunt's written samples. In the O'Donnell project (1967), relative clause frequency increased from 1.0 to 3.4 to 4.5 per 100 T-units in the written language samples of third-, fifth-, and seventh-grade students; comparable figures for spoken language samples were 2.6, 3.3, and 3.9.

The details of relative clause development have been studied extensively in young children, perhaps because these clauses afford so many opportunities for comparison based on structural variation (e.g., center versus right embedded, grammatical function of the replacing relative pronoun, and the particular relative pronoun used). Some studies of relative clauses in spoken language included children in the early adolescent years (e.g., Scott, 1984b). One of the most complete reviews of relative clause development in child language is available in Romaine (1984) whose own studies of relative clause development included youngsters through the age of 10. Several studies indicated that center-embedded relative clauses following subjects rarely occurred (e.g., Scott, 1984b; Strickland, 1962). By far, most relatives postmodify the object, complement, or adverbial nouns that follow the verb. The most frequent type of relative clauses are those that postmodify object nouns and in which the relative pronoun serves as the subject of the embedded clause (e.g., *He asked his friend who lives in Ohio*). Romaine speculated that this distributional imbalance results from a discourse-motivated system in which most new information in need of expansion (via relative clauses) is located at the end of the sentence. These types of relative clauses are also structurally similar to the early developmental strategy whereby new information is added through coordination (e.g., *He asked his friend and his friend lives in Ohio*) rather than embedding. Romaine found that some center-embedded relatives appeared in spoken language by the age of 10 and suggested that by that age children have better control of true embedding operations as opposed to conjunction operations (see Appendix, item #10). However, Perera (1984), citing Strickland (1962), reported that only 40 percent of a group of 9-year-olds used relatives in center-embedded positions in spoken samples.

Perera (1984) proposed that the most mature types of relative clauses contain nonfinite forms of verbs and postmodify main clause subjects, as in the following example:

One colt, *lying down on the hay*, was trembling. (p. 238)

In Perera's system, another late-developing relative clause structure in written language is the nonrestrictive form (see Appendix, item #11) which postmodifies the subject:

Harold, *whose army had just marched across England after fighting an invading group of Norwegians back*, was tired and sore. (*age 11*)*

Another example of a nonrestrictive, center-embedded relative is the following (Scott, 1987):

...and all the other boys and girls, *who had wanted to dance the whole time, but were just too embarrassed to admit it*, got together and danced. (*age 14*)

The Syntax of Discourse

A number of structures in English are intersentential in nature, that is, their semantic and syntactic domains span several sentences. These structures serve to organize sentences into a coherent discourse. There are several methods for achieving a well-organized discourse. One method is to add structures, usually at the beginning or end of an utterance (e.g., adverbial conjuncts and discourse particles such as *you know* and *or something*). Such structures function outside of the clause structure per se. A second method is to substitute structures (e.g., pronominal reference), and a third method is to reorder clause elements (e.g., word order variations for theme and focus).

---

*From the author's files.

Developmental data on selected aspects of discourse grammar in older children and adolescents are discussed next.

Adverbial Conjuncts

Explicit encoding of logical relations between segments of discourse is signaled with a group of structures called *adverbial conjuncts* by Quirk and colleagues (1985), *conjunctions* by Halliday and Hasan (1976), and *sentence adverbials* elsewhere (e.g., Hunt, 1965). Youngsters' comprehension of such structures is discussed in Chapter 3. Using the Fawcett and Perkins (1980) corpus of 120 British school children of the ages 6 through 12, Scott (1984a) studied adverbial conjunct use in peer interactions and adult-child informal interviews. Results indicated that by the age of 10, children were using conjuncts at a rate of 4 per 100 utterances, and that only a small subset of possible conjuncts were used. These included inferential *then*, transitional *now*, concessive *though* and *anyway*, and resultant *so*. Interestingly, conjunct use was more frequent during the context of peer interaction than during the adult-child interview context. In the portions of the interviews where the children told about a favorite film or book (i.e., narrative discourse), conjunct use was almost nonexistent. Thus, in discourse contexts where temporal rather than logical relations predominate (as during narratives as opposed to negotiated peer interactions), adverbial conjuncts are underrepresented. The following example (Scott, 1984a) illustrates both inferential *then* and concessive *though* in a dialogue where two youngsters were talking about building a house using Legos:

Child A: we haven't got enough bricks *though* I don't think /
Child B: we start using another color *then* / (*both age 12*) (p. 440)

By the age of 12, a few additional conjuncts were used by some children. These included *otherwise, instead, after all, only,* and *still.* This is illustrated in the following example (Scott, 1984a), where a youngster was commenting on the film *Jaws:*

well only the part where he jumps out of the sea onto the boat / that's all / *otherwise* it's like any other shark attack you get in a film / (*age 12*) (p. 442)

Other examples of adverbial conjuncts are contained in Table 4-6. When comparing children's conjunct use with a spoken corpus of British adults, Scott (1984a) found that the adults used a greater variety, and three times as many, of these structures as did the children. By inference, then, considerable improvement in the use of adverbial conjuncts takes place beyond the age of 12, the oldest children studied in Scott's project.

The use of adverbial conjuncts in written language has also been examined. For example, Hunt (1965) reported that the frequency of adverbial

TABLE 4-6.
Examples of adverbial conjuncts used as sentence connectives.*

Concessive conjunct:
  a. it's a game with a like a big board / *only* it's not a board / it's like a ring / (*age 8*)[†]
  b. Child A: let's do a road by there /
     Child B: yeh you don't get buses on country roads *though* / (*age 10*)[†]
  c. Child: no I've never had nightmares /
     Adult: no /
     Child: no not as far as I know *anyway* / (*age 12*)[†]

Transitional conjunct:
  well there's this lady / and she had oh how much was it *now* fifty hundred thousand pounds / (*age 10*)[†]

Resultant conjunct:
  the tree in it breaks out when it rains / *so* water would be trapped in it / (*age 11*)**

Inferential conjunct:
  Child A: don't have her /
  Child B: who do you have for English *then* / (*age 12*)[†]

Summation conjunct:
  In all the film showed that there was an environment in the desert with living plants and animals. (*age 14*)**

*See Quirk and colleagues (1985) for semantic classification of conjuncts.
[†]From Scott, 1984a.
**From Scott, 1987.

conjuncts doubled between fourth and eighth grades, but that no changes occurred thereafter. However, Rubin (1982) reported that the frequency of adverbial conjuncts in written language actually declined after the eighth grade, but that the older writers used a greater variety of adverbial conjuncts.

Several studies attempted to tap youngsters' awareness of adverbial conjuncts using contrived tasks involving the cloze procedure, sentence completion, or sentence generation. For example, Bridge and Winograd (1982) asked 20 ninth graders to complete a cloze passage in which the deleted words represented either conjunctive relations (e.g., adverbial conjuncts), referential relations (e.g., pronouns for previously mentioned referents), or lexical relations (e.g., reiteration of the same or a related word) (cf. Halliday and Hasan, 1976). The students had relatively more difficulty supplying conjunctive compared to referential or lexical cohesive relations. When examining the students' "think aloud" reasoning as they attempted to find the appropriate conjuncts, Bridge and Winograd found that students who were good readers used intersentential information significantly more often than poor readers, thereby indicating that the good readers were scanning larger amounts of text in their efforts to respond correctly. Using a variety of tasks that included sorting, sentence generation, judgments of grammaticality, and cloze, Scott and Rush (1985) reported that children younger than the age of 10 had little success generating or judging adverbial conjuncts appropriately (see Appendix, item #12), but that a 13-year-old was much more successful with the tasks. Henderson (1979), cited by Perera (1984), reported that college students sometimes failed to write sentences incorporating adverbial conjuncts such as *moreover, consequently,* and *likewise* when directed to do so. Thus, it appears that difficulty with adverbial conjuncts continues into adulthood.

Word-Order Variations for Theme and Focus

In the absence of prosodic cues, writers learn to rely on structural tactics to highlight important information and to achieve a coherent text. As explained previously, the usual practice in writing is to place the new information at the end of the sentence. Structural tactics used to accomplish this include the clefting construction (see Appendix, item #13), the extraposition construction (see Appendix, item #14), and word-order variations where certain structures are shifted to the beginning of the sentence, thereby leaving the end of the sentence "open" for new information (Quirk et al., 1985). Adverbial fronting is an example of word-order variation:

> The major silversmithing centers were Boston, New York City and Philadelphia. *From these cities* came such silversmiths as Paul Revere, John Coney and John Hull. *(age 13).**

In this example, the adverbial element (*From these cities*) was fronted and the verb (*came*) was moved in front of the grammatical subject (*silversmiths*). These adjustments enabled the important new information to be placed at the end of the sentence while a smooth flow of theme and focus was maintained. Perera (1986a) called such reorderings *discourse structuring constructions* and examined their presence in the spoken and written descriptions of a Lego-building task in 48 children of the ages of 8 through 12. Although the frequency of such constructions showed no change in spoken language, Perrera found a fourfold increase in written language. In the following example from that study (p. 102), a 12-year-old writer successfully employed fronted adverbials so that new information could occur at the ends of sentences:

> We built the house because it was very simple and we had alot of bricks to build it with. *Around the house* we put a fence and three gates in

---

*From the author's files.

it. We built a bus stop outside with three people waiting for a bus. *Inside the fence* we put two trees.

A DISCOURSE-BASED APPROACH TO SYNTAX: GENRE AND CHANNEL

In the previous sections of this chapter, later syntactic development was discussed apart from the larger context of discourse. This approach was used for heuristic purposes only. In this final section of the chapter, syntactic development is discussed in relation to discourse context. It is shown that different syntactic structures are used in different types of discourse. This phenomenon makes syntax an especially interesting and critical component of later language development.

Relevant terminology must first be defined. *Mode* is an important aspect of discourse context. Mode is composed of both *channel* and *genre* (Pellegrini, Galda, and Rubin, 1984). Channel is the particular *method* of communication (e.g., spoken, written, gestural), and genre is the particular *type* of communication (e.g., chat, narration, letter writing, reporting). Each particular genre has a unique set of structural characteristics and is used in similar situations (Himley, 1986). Although the list of possible genres would be very long, Table 4-7 contains a set of genres that have appeared in recent accounts of discourse in the 9-through-19 age range. This set is a modification of one developed by Perera (1984). Two major determinants of syntactic structure are chronological versus nonchronological (logical) organization of subject matter, and personal versus impersonal relatedness between the communicators. Longacre (1983) would include a third determinant: the extent to which the discourse is *agent-focused* (AF) or concerned with the activities of people or animals. Some genres tend to be channel-specific (e.g., chat) whereas others commonly occur in both spoken and written channels (e.g., a report of a personal experience). In Table 4-7, the possible channels are indicated in parentheses as spoken (S) or written (W). If the genre is usually a dialogue (D) or a monologue (M), this is also indicated.

Research concerning discourse context and later syntactic development is in its infancy (Pellegrini et al., 1984) and little information is available on this topic for youngsters in the 9-through-19 age range. What follows is a discussion of how syntax might vary as a function of discourse, focusing on the same structures that were discussed in the third section of the chapter. Many of the points raised in the discussion are offered as topics for future research rather than as statements of fact. The section concludes with a presentation of four texts used to illustrate the possible effects of age and discourse mode on syntax.

TABLE 4-7.
Major discourse genres in preadolescent and adolescent language.

	Organization of Subject Matter	
	Chronological	Nonchronological (logical)
Personal	Chat (S, D, AF)	
	Narratives (S, W, M, AF):	
	Biographical	
	Fictional	
	Historical	
	Personal journals (W, M, AF)	
	Letters (W, M, AF)	Persuasion (S, W, M)
	Procedures (S, W, M)	Reports (S, W, M)
Impersonal		Compositions (W, M):
		Generalization
		Speculation
		Argument

AF = agent focused; S = spoken; W = written; D = dialogue; M = monologue.

Syntactic Variation as a Function of Discourse Mode

At one end of the oral-literate discourse continuum is informal conversation, called *chat* by Brown, Anderson, Shillcock, and Yule (1984). Chat consists of friendly conversation about topics such as the weather and mutual friends, that is done for enjoyment and is not expected to have specific outcomes. Chat is similar to what Danielewicz (1984) called *unplanned* spoken language. Given the characteristics of chat, certain predictions concerning its use can be made. For example, during chat, each speaker takes a short turn. Therefore, syntactic structures used to organize longer turns, such as specific types of adverbial conjuncts (e.g., *further, in conclusion*), would not occur very often. Chat is usually chronologically based (see Table 4-7), particularly when speakers lapse into short narratives. It is also personal and agent-focused, often involving the use of pronouns such as *I, me, we,* and *us.* Complex noun phrases, particularly as subjects, would be rare in chat, as would relative clauses, especially when the speakers know each other well. On the other hand, nominal clauses functioning as grammatical objects after verbs such as *think* and *know* might occur frequently. Other structures that would occur infrequently in chat are nonfinite forms of verb phrases, the passive voice, and logical adverbial clauses other than the common *when* and *because* constructions. Future research should examine the use of chat by older children and adolescents to determine if these predictions are accurate.

At the other end of the continuum from unplanned spoken chat is non-chronological, impersonal, planned written language (see Table 4-7). For older children and adolescents, this would include school reports (other than biographical reports, which resemble narratives and would therefore be chronologically based) and compositions that involve generalization, specula-tion and thesis-argument (cf. Britton, Burgess, Martin, McLeod, and Rosen, 1975). Students engaged in this type of writing are usually expected to be explicit, detached, and logical. Planning time is necessary to meet these expectations and can lead to a "tighter packaging" of information. Such packaging is accomplished, according to Danielewicz (1984), with structures that incorporate additional verbal elements into clauses, including nonfinite relatives (e.g., the point *mentioned* earlier) and nominalization (e.g., the use of *development* instead of *develop*). Attributive adjectives behave similarly (e.g., *the important development* versus *the development was important*). In a pilot study involving 8-year-olds, 12-year-olds, and adults ($n = 6$), Danielewicz (1984) found that the adults used twice the number of these three structures as did the 12-year-olds, who used more than the 8-year-olds. With the exceptions of time adverbial conjuncts (e.g., *afterwards*) and time subordinate clauses (e.g., *when*), which would be more common in chronological genres, most of the selected structures discussed in the third section of this chapter lend themselves to the types of discourse constraints characteristic of planned written genres. Thus, nonfinite verb forms, com-plex noun phrases used as grammatical subjects, the passive voice, and discourse-organizing structures such as adverbial conjuncts and word-order variations are likely to occur more frequently in planned written language than in unplanned spoken language. The Loban (1976) and Hunt (1965) projects could be searched for additional details of syntax in planned writing. However, their written samples were not described according to specific genre type, and they could have included narrative writing. Of course it is in school that preadolescents and adolescents are doing over 90 percent of such planned writing (Applebee, 1984). Britton and colleagues (1975) found that 92 percent of school writing is done for the teacher as the sole audience, and that in half of all pieces of school writing, the students are being for-mally examined. The extent to which these contextual realities would affect syntactic structure is unknown.

Between the two extremes of unplanned spoken language and planned written language, there are many other genres relevant to older children and adolescents. These include several forms of narratives, personal jour-nals, letters, procedures (also called directions and regulative genres), persuasion (also called argument), and reports. Table 4-7 shows the status of these genres in terms of their chronological base and personal involvement. Narratives are fairly well represented in the data base for older children and adolescents (e.g., O'Donnell et al., 1967; Scott, 1984b). Rubin's (1982) work on persuasive writing was described previously. However, detailed syntactic accounts of spoken persuasive and spoken or written procedural genres in the 9-through-19 age range are not available, to this author's knowledge.

Comparison of Four Texts

Four complete texts will now be presented to illustrate the possible effects of age and discourse mode on syntactic structure during later childhood and adolescence. These texts were taken from a project on syntactic development involving fifth and eighth graders and college students (Scott, 1987). All subjects viewed the same stimuli, which consisted of four different 20 minute films (Barr Films). The content of the films varied along the discourse-genre dimensions outlined previously. Two films were chronologically organized. The other two were nonchronological; one was persuasive and the other, expository. After viewing a film, a subject summarized it orally for the experimenter. Following a short distracting activity, the subject then wrote a summary of the same film. The spoken summary took about five minutes whereas the written summary took about 15 minutes. More time was allowed for the written summary if needed.

Text 1 was written by an 11-year-old boy, who was a normally achieving fifth grader, as a written summary of a film about deceptive advertising techniques used in television commercials for children's products (e.g., cereal, dolls, toy cars). The film was persuasive and nonchronological. The discourse structure of the film consisted of a general point supported by examples. Texts 2, 3, and 4 are spoken summaries of a film that dramatized a classic narrative, a tale about a Greek boy who goes against family tradition to become a fisherman rather than a farmer. These texts were produced by an 11-year-old (the same child as Text 1), a 14-year-old normally achieving eighth grader, and a 22-year-old college student, respectively.

The comparison of Texts 1 and 2 provides a mode comparison—written persuasion versus spoken narrative—where age is constant (i.e., 11 years). The comparison of Texts 2, 3, and 4 provides an age comparison—11, 14, and 22 years—where mode is constant (i.e., all three texts are spoken summaries of the same narrative material). The texts are divided into T-units which are numbered consecutively. The written text preserves the punctuation used by the child but spelling errors have been corrected. The spoken texts were edited for repetitions and reformulations.

TEXT 1: PERSUASIVE (*age 11, written*).

1. This story is about this guy who acts like he is a pirate and lies about sailing the seven seas,
2. and he hates his product.
3. So he tells about how commercials make the product look better.
4. How leaving the candy bar in front of the camera with nothing to compare it to makes the product look bigger or holding the product close to camera.
5. How it looks better when you add excitement or background.
6. Read the little print at the end of a commercial like sold, artificial flavors.
7. And adding sound helps alot like if you're trying to sell a car you want make a big roaring sound.
8. And special lenses on the camera make the lights glimmer and look alot better.
9. Commercials make the actor really look like a pirate like the fake wooden leg and the hat and his clothes and the patch over his eye and the paper stuffed in his shirt.
10. The background made it look good like the skeleton, and the chest of jewels.

TEXT 2: NARRATIVE (*age 11, spoken*).

1. the story is about the kid named Yanis /
2. he is a farmer /
3. and he was a real dedicated farmer /
4. and one day he was taking the sheep to the meadow /
5. and the sheep went up on the mountain /
6. and he followed the sheep /
7. and on top of the mountain he saw the ocean /
8. and he thought he was going to be a fisherman from then on /
9. and then his dad finally took him to the elder at the city /
10. and the elder said he should try new things /
11. and first he tried baking /
12. and the water that they baked with just made him think of the ocean /
13. he went to shoe making next /
14. and the leather made him think of the ocean because it was so dry that it needed water or something /
15. and then he went to wood working /
16. and wood working just made him think of building a boat /
17. no the leather made him think of the sail of the boat /
18. and so one day his father decides to let him go /
19. and his father thought that when he went and found out how hard fishing was he'd come back and just forget it /
20. but Yanis he traveled there /
21. and the kids made fun of him /
22. and this lady took pity on him and took him in for a day /
23. and then she told him that he will have to work to stay there /
24. and he built a fishing pole and started fishing there /
25. one day this kind of [name] saw him /
26. and he taught him how to fish /
27. and he learned the ways of fishing /

28. then a fisherman got real real sick /
29. and the [name] talked the fisherman into taking Yanis /
30. and they found out he was a very very good fisherman /

TEXT 3: NARRATIVE (age 14, spoken).

1. it was a Greek kid who lived on an island /
2. I guess he is about twelve years old or something /
3. and I guess everybody on that part of the island would never leave that village /
4. and they just kind of thought that was where they put their farm /
5. that was all they were ever going to do /
6. so his father and mother thought he should never go anywhere /
7. and he went along with that /
8. but deep down he really didn't think that was what he wanted to do /
9. and then one day this goat ran away from their farm /
10. and he chased it up a mountain /
11. and he got to the top of the mountain which he'd never seen before /
12. he saw the ocean /
13. and it just made him determined to be a fisherman and work out on the ocean /
14. and he told his dad /
15. and his dad said that was just a dream /
16. and he should just forget about it because he's supposed to be a farmer /
17. so his dad thought he should probably do something other than farming /
18. he took him to like one of the real smart guys /
19. and this guy said that maybe he should just do something else to help like another craft /
20. maybe he just didn't like that craft /
21. but he knew he shouldn't leave that village and go somewhere else /
22. so he tried /
23. he made shoes /
24. and he didn't like that /
25. but he did /
26. but he didn't like it too much /
27. he was a carpenter and made clothes /
28. and he did something else /
29. but he didn't like any of those /
30. and finally he came back and worked at the farm for a little while /
31. but he still was pretty determined to go down to the ocean and be a fisherman /
32. and finally his mom talked to his dad /
33. and they let him go down there /
34. his dad said that he could stay down there but he's going to come back /
35. he just knew he's gonna come back /
36. and so Yanis traveled all the way down there /
37. when he got down there nobody had any room for him /
38. nobody would want him to work there or anything /
39. and so he met this lady /
40. and she let him stay with her /
41. but she didn't want him to be a fisherman very much because her husband had been killed out at sea I guess in a shipwreck /
42. and so he just went out /

43. since nobody let him have a job he went out and started to sea /
44. built his own pole /
45. tied a string to it and hook and just tried to catch fish like that and never caught anything until he met his old man /
46. he used to be a fisherman /
47. and this guy taught him like the techniques of fishing /
48. how to make a better fishing pole all that stuff /
49. and finally one day this guy and Yanis were fishing /
50. and this fishing boat they said one of the guys was getting sick all of a sudden /
51. and they needed somebody to help /
52. and they didn't want to take this little kid /
53. but finally they took him /
54. when they took him they kind of made fun of him because he was younger and everything /
55. and they didn't have much respect for him /
56. but after a while he kind of proved himself to them /
57. and they kind of gained some respect for him /
58. and he wrote back to his parents and told them that he found his dream /
59. and they thought that now he'd return since he found his dream /
60. but he was not going to return because he just liked that so much /

TEXT 4: NARRATIVE (*age 22, spoken*).

1. the story was about a little Greek boy named Yanis /
2. and he lived on a Greek island /
3. the village was mostly farmers peasants that lived there /
4. and it talked about how strong they were in tradition /
5. and he went to school untill the age of twelve /
6. and he was expected to follow in his father's footsteps going to the field and be a farmer /
7. and the girls were supposed to follow the mothers and do women's work and everything else I guess /
8. and so Yanis he finished his schooling /
9. and he went out in the fields with his father /
10. he was the only son /
11. and so his father was pretty dependent upon him to carry on the land and farming land and carry on the family name and so forth /
12. one day when Yanis was out with the goats and letting them graze or whatever they do one of the goats went up a mountain off too far away from the herd /
13. and he followed him /
14. and it was then that he climbed up a mountain /
15. and he was able to see the sea that surrounded his island /
16. and this is the first time I guess he'd ever seen this /
17. it was really overwhelming to him /
18. and it was then they said that he decided that he wanted to make his life on the sea /
19. and he wanted to be a fisherman /
20. and so after that he progressively lost more interest in his work and his friends /
21. and he shut out everybody in his life /
22. and one day he had a dream about being a fisherman on the sea /

23. and one day his father was getting concerned and talked to him /
24. asked him what was wrong /
25. and he had told him about his dream to be a fisherman /
26. and the father wasn't very encouraging /
27. in fact he discouraged it and told him that he was meant to be a farmer and to follow in his footsteps /
28. and his father even took him to talk to the elder of the village /
29. and the elder told him the same thing that being a fisherman it was hard work and all the dangers of it /
30. but it really didn't discourage Yanis /
31. and he still wanted to do this /
32. and so the elder had told him if he didn't want to farm to find another trade /
33. and so his father sent him out /
34. and he was apprentice to a baker and to a shoe maker and carpenter and various different trades which he was good at /
35. but he still wanted to be a fisherman /
36. his heart was still at the sea /
37. and so his father and mother decided to let him go pursue his dream /
38. his father thought once he was there and he fulfilled his dream he would be back to where he belonged /
39. his mother didn't think so /
40. but they let him go /
41. he had to walk to go to the sea /
42. and he went to the capital of the island where it was along the sea and tried to find work /
43. and nobody would hire him or let him help /
44. he couldn't find anybody that would take time with him /
45. and so he went to another village along the coast /
46. you know he started along the coast trying to find work there with the fisherman /
47. and nobody will hire him because all their sons were helping them /
48. and they didn't have to help a little peasant boy /
49. and kids made fun of him because he wanted to be a fisherman /
50. he met a lady in this village on the coast that took him in /
51. and her husband had died at the sea /
52. and she didn't have a man around to help /
53. so she took him /
54. and he would work for her /
55. and he worked /
56. he still longed to be a fisherman /
57. and so he started to be a fisherman on his own /
58. made his own fishing pole /
59. and one day when he was doing that an old man was there and took an interest in him and saw that he was eager to learn /
60. and he was an old fisherman and taught him all secrets of fishing and worked with him /
61. and they did that for a while /
62. and then one day a fisherman got sick that was going to go out on one of the boats to the sea /
63. and the old man talked the other fisherman into taking Yanis with them /
64. and once he was out there they saw what a natural he was at this and how good he was /

65. so he sent word back to his family that he had found success being a fisherman /
66. and the mom knew that he wouldn't be back then because he was becoming a man /

TABLE 4-8.
Quantitative data and frequency of occurrence for selected structures in four texts.

	Text 1*	Text 2	Text 3	Text 4
Text length (in T-units)	10	30	60	66
Average T-unit length (in words/T-unit)	17.0	9.86	10.37	11.64
Subordination index (in clauses/T-unit)	3.1	1.76	1.97	2.18
Noun phrase postmodification				
via nonfinite clause	1	1 (.033)	—	4 (.060)
via prepositional phrase	4	4 (.133)	3 (.050)	15 (.227)
appositive	—	1 (.033)	—	5 (.075)
Verb phrase				
perfect aspect	—	—	2 (.033)	5 (.075)
modal auxiliary	—	3 (.100)	8 (.133)	7 (.106)
passive	—	—	1 (.016)	2 (.030)
Nominal clause				
as subject	3	—	—	1 (.015)
(*that*) as object	—	6 (.200)	14 (.233)	7 (.106)
other types (as O, C)	12	7 (.233)	14 (.233)	24 (.363)
Adverbial clause				
when, because, to	1	3 (.100)	6 (.100)	8 (.121)
other	2	—	3 (.050)	6 (.090)
Relative clause	1	1 (.033)	2 (.033)	9 (.136)
Discourse form				
temporal conjuncts	—	7 (.233)	7 (.116)	7 (.106)
adverbial conjuncts	1	1 (.033)	6 (.100)	11 (.166)
sentence initial *and*	3	23 (.766)	20 (.483)	45 (.681)
sentence initial *(and) then*	—	4 (.133)	—	1 (.015)
sentence initial *but*	—	1 (.033)	10 (.166)	2 (.030)
and everything, etc.	—	1 (.033)	4 (.066)	3 (.045)
clefting	—	—	—	2 (.030)

Texts taken from Scott, 1987.

*Text 1: written persuasive (age 11). Text 2: spoken narrative (age 11). Text 3: spoken narrative (age 14). Text 4: spoken narrative (age 22).

Quantitative data include text length, average T-unit length, and subordination index. Proportional frequency is shown in parentheses.

Table 4-8 shows the analysis of the texts according to average sentence length, subordination index, and frequency of occurrence for selected structures discussed in this chapter. Because the texts are different lengths (e.g., Texts 3 and 4 contain twice the number of T-units as Text 2), proportional frequencies are shown in parentheses. Text 1, which consists of only 10 T-units, is too short for meaningful proportional frequencies. Therefore, for this text, only the absolute frequency is shown.

A comparison of Texts 1 and 2 dramatically demonstrates the effect of discourse mode on quantitative measures such as sentence length and subordination index. The sentence length and subordination data for the persuasive Text 1 are considerably higher than the figures for any age in Tables 4-1 and 4-2. Whereas the sentence length data for Text 2 (narrative) are close to previously reported narrative data (e.g., O'Donnell et al., 1967; Scott, 1984b in Table 4-1), the subordination data are higher. Text 1 contains several structures, identified as later-developing, which are either absent or infrequent in the narrative Text 2. These include nominal clauses as subject (sentences 4 and 7) and adverbial clauses other than *when* and *because* (e.g., *like* in sentence 1). The nominal *that* clause as object, a frequent construction in all three narrative texts, is absent in the persuasive summary. The nonchronological organization of Text 1 is evident in the absence of sentence initial *(and) then*, other temporal adverbials, and the less frequent use of *and* as a connectivity device.

Texts 2, 3, and 4 were included in this analysis because of their comparability to previous research, much of which is based on narrative text. In addition, narrative texts, particularly classic stories with a well-developed central problem, are relatively constrained forms of discourse from a syntactic standpoint (Scott, 1984b). If age differences in syntactic form are uncovered in narratives, such differences represent a conservative picture of syntactic development. The disadvantage of the narrative texts is that development of several structures discussed in this chapter, such as nonrestrictive relative clauses and nominal clauses as subjects, may not be observed because they are more characteristic of expository texts.

As shown in Table 4-8, the figures for average sentence length and subordination increase with age in a nondramatic but steady manner. Average sentence length is very similar to comparable age figures shown in Table 4-1, but subordination indices for the texts are higher than those shown in Table 4-2. As noted previously, researchers in different projects may have counted slightly different sets of structures for this index.

One prominent structural difference between Texts 2 and 3 compared to Text 4 is the ability to elaborate on nouns with postmodification structures and relative clauses. The adult used postmodifying prepositional phrases, nonfinite clauses, appositives, and relative clauses to a much greater extent than the 11-year-old or the 14-year-old. Summing the frequencies for these structures in Texts 2 and 3, there are 12 instances compared to 33 in

Text 4. Of all the possibilities for noun elaboration, prepositional phrases are most favored in Texts 2 and 3. Verb phrase complexity also seems to increase with age. Perfect aspect verbs are absent in Text 2, but occur in Text 3 and are twice as frequent in the adult text. Modal auxiliaries are slightly more prominent in Text 3 (see proportional frequencies in Table 4-8).

Texts 2 and 3 are almost identical in the use of nominal clauses, which are the dominant subordination strategy in the narrative texts. However, the adult used the common object nominal *that* clause less frequently, and produced proportionally more nominal clauses of different varieties. The adult was the only speaker to use a nominal clause as a subject, and this occurred only once. All three texts are similar in the appearance of the common narrative adverbial clauses *when, because,* and *(in order) to.* Less common and later-developing adverbials are absent in the 11-year-old text. There are three instances in the 14-year-old text (e.g., *since* in sentences #43 and 59; *until* in sentence #45) and six instances in the adult text (*until* in sentence #5; *if* in sentence #32; *once* in sentences #38 and 64; nonfinite forms in sentences #46, 65).

In terms of discourse cohesion, Texts 3 and 4 rely proportionally less on explicit temporal conjuncts (*then* and others) and emphasize the resultant logical relation signalled by *so.* Sentence initial *and* is well-represented in all texts; however, the 14-year-old used *and* less than the others, and used *but* frequently to make contrastive relations. The adult was the only speaker to use the clefting construction (in sentences #14, 18).

These texts illustrate a number of themes that have been developed in this chapter. Quantitative measures such as sentence length and degree of subordination are shown to increase (although slowly) with age when genre and channel are tightly controlled, and to vary widely across discourse types. During the three years between the ages of 11 and 14, increases in frequency occur for a few structures (e.g. verb phrase complexity, later developing adverbial clauses, the conjunct *so*), but the differences are not as pronounced as the comparison of either text with the adult text. The implication is that syntactic development continues well beyond the age of 14. Structural differences with age would probably be more dramatic for nonchronological types of discourse. Preliminary results from Scott (1987) showed that adverbial subordination differences between adolescent and adult texts are greater in persuasive and expository summaries than in narrative summaries.

CONCLUSIONS

Imagine the following scenario. A grandmother is visiting her 9-year-old grandson for the first time in three years. She notices how much the boy has grown, but the thought that his language has changed never enters her mind. The boy could carry on a conversation three years ago just as he can today. Interactions during this visit are limited to casual conversations in the home. The grandmother does not visit the school where she could see the boy give an oral report, nor does she see any of her grandson's writing. She thinks about an earlier visit when the boy was 3-years-old. At that time, she had not seen him for two years and she had been amazed at how much he talked and how "grown up" he sounded. His growth in language had made a big impression on her. Now imagine that ten years have passed, and the 19-year-old grandson sends his grandmother a copy of a composition he has written, a critical analysis of a book by Melville. Once again she is amazed at how "grown up" he sounds in the composition.

This scenario dramatizes the contrast between early and later syntactic development. While advances are obvious in the conversational speech of young children, to see the growth that occurs in older children and adolescents, it is necessary to look beyond conversational contexts and examine, for example, the planned, written texts of such youngsters. It is also necessary to perform a finer grained analysis of their spoken and written syntax because it is the cumulative effect of many subtle changes that make the 19-year-old talk and write differently than the 9-year-old.

The sentence length data in Table 4-1 indicated that sentences "grow" by approximately one word per year, a change that is not likely to be noticed by anyone but the researcher. The number of subordinate clauses increases with age, but these changes also occur gradually. Another contrast is that with older children and adolescents, the structures making their first appearance are not very obvious compared to the structures first used by a younger child. For example, when a toddler suddenly begins to use determiners, that is an obvious change. In contrast, when an adolescent begins to use nonfinite verbs in subordinate clauses (*After being examined, he....*) instead of finite verbs (*After he was examined, he ... .*), the change will probably go unnoticed.

Research in later syntactic development is still in its infancy and the current data base is rather fragmented. Certain structures have not been examined (e.g., low-frequency adjective phrases) and it is difficult to make inferences across the available studies because of methodological differences in segmentation, grammatical analysis techniques, the structures analyzed, and the contexts employed for gathering samples. The research needs in this area are critical. For example, longitudinal studies should be conducted where syntax is sampled at regular intervals in a number of discourse settings, along with concurrent cognitive and social measures. There is also a need for innovative methods of structural analysis. To date, the usual pattern has been to single out particular syntactic structures, count the occurrences of those structures, and determine if frequencies are affected by age, ability, and so forth. However, the rationale for examining particular structures in this manner is often unclear. Finally, there is a need for research that combines naturalistic sampling of language with experimenter-generated tasks so that syntax employed in naturalistic and nonnaturalistic contexts can be compared.

REFERENCES

Applebee, A.N. (1984). *Contexts for learning to write*. Norwood, NJ: Ablex.

Biber, D. (1986). Spoken and written textual dimensions in English: Resolving the contradictory findings. *Language, 62*, 384-414.

Blair, T.K., and Crump, W.D. (1984). Effects of discourse mode on the syntactic complexity of learning disabled student's written expression. *Learning Disability Quarterly, 7*, 19-29.

Bloom, L., and Lahey, M. (1978). *Language development and language disorders*. New York: Wiley.

Bloom, L., Lahey, M., Hood, L. Lifter, K., and Fiess, K. (1980). Complex sentences: Acquisition of syntactic connectives and the semantic relations they encode. *Journal of Child Language, 7*, 235-261.

Bridge, C.A., and Winograd, P.N. (1982). Reader's awareness of cohesive relationships during cloze comprehension. *Journal of Reading Behavior, 14*, 299-312.

Britton, J., Burgess, T., Martin, N., McLeod, N., and Rosen, H. (1975). *The development of writing abilities (11–18)*. Schools Council Research Studies. London: MacMillan Education LTD.

Brown, R. (1973). *A first language*. Cambridge, MA: Harvard University Press.

Brown, G., Anderson, A., Shillcock, R., and Yule, G. (1984). *Teaching talk: Strategies for production and assessment*. Cambridge, England: Cambridge University Press.

Chomsky, C. (1969). *The acquisition of syntax in children from 5 to 10*. Cambridge, MA: MIT Press.

Crowhurst, M. (1979). On the misinterpretation of syntactic complexity data. *English Education, 11*, 91-97.

Crystal, D., Fletcher, P., and Garman, M. (1976). *The grammatical analysis of language disability*. New York: Elsevier.

Danielewicz, J.M. (1984). The interaction between text and context: A study of how adults and children use spoken and written language in four contexts. In A.D. Pellegrini and T.D. Yawkey (Eds.), *The development of oral and written language in social contexts* (pp. 243-260). Norwood, NJ: Ablex.

Fawcett, R., and Perkins, M. (1980). *Child language transcripts 6–12, Volumes 1–4*. Pontypridd, Mid Glamorgan, Wales: Department of Behavioral and Communicative Studies, Polytechnic of Wales.

Golub, L.S., and Frederick, W.C. (1971). *Linguistic structures in the discourse of fourth and sixth graders* (Tech. Rep. No. 166). Madison, WI: Univeristy of Wisconsin, Wisconsin Research and Development Center for Cognitive Learning.

Halliday, M.A.K., and Hasan, R. (1976). *Cohesion in English*. London: Longman.

Henderson, I. (1979). *The use of connectives by fluent and not-so-fluent readers.* Unpublished doctoral dissertation, Columbia University Teachers College, New York, NY.

Himley, M. (1986). Genre as generative: One perspective on one child's early writing growth. In M. Nystrand (Ed.), *The structure of written communication* (pp. 137-157). Orlando, FL: Academic Press.

Horgan, D. (1978). The development of the full passive. *Journal of Child Language,* 5, 65-80.

Hunt, K.W. (1965). *Grammatical structures written at three grade levels* (Research Report No. 3). Champaign, IL: National Council of Teachers of English.

Hunt, K.W. (1970). Syntactic maturity in school children and adults. *Society for Research in Child Development Monographs,* No. 134, 35, No. 1.

Johnson, C. (1985). The emergence of present perfect verb forms: Semantic influences on selective imitation. *Journal of Child Language,* 12, 325-352.

Karmiloff-Smith, A. (1979). Language development after five. In P. Fletcher and M. Garman (Eds.), *Studies in language acquisition* (pp. 307-335). Cambridge, England: Cambridge University Press.

Karmiloff-Smith, A. (1983). Language acquisition as a problem solving process. *Stanford Papers and Reports on Child Development,* 22, 1-22.

Karmiloff-Smith, A. (1986). Some fundamental aspects of language development after age 5. In P. Fletcher and M. Garman (Eds.), *Language acquisition* (Second edition) (pp. 455-474). Cambridge, England: Cambridge University Press.

Klecan-Aker, J.S. and Hedrick, L.D. (1985). A study of the syntactic language skills of normal school-age children. *Language, Speech, and Hearing Services in Schools,* 16, 187-198.

Kroll, B.M., Kroll, D.L., and Wells, C.G. (1980). Researching children's writing development: The "children learn to write" project. *Language for Learning,* 2, 53-81.

Loban, W. (1963). *The language of elementary school children.* (Research Report No. 1). Champaign, IL: National Council of Teachers of English.

Loban, W. (1976). *Language development: Kindergarten through grade twelve.* (Research Report No. 18). Champaign, IL: National Council of Teachers of English.

Longacre, R.E. (1983). *The grammar of discourse.* New York: Plenum Press.

Martin, J.R. (1983). The development of register. In J. Fine and R.O. Freedle (Eds.), *Developmental issues in discourse* (pp. 1-39). Norwood, NJ: Ablex.

McKinley, N.L., and Lord-Larson, V. (1985). Neglected language-disordered adolescent: A delivery model. *Language, Speech and Hearing Services in Schools,* 16, 2-15.

McNeill, D. (1966). The creation of language by children. In J. Lyons and K.J. Wales (Eds.), *Psycholinguistic papers* (pp. 99-132). Edinburgh: Edinburgh University Press.

Miller, J. (1987, April). *The grammatical characterization of language.* Paper presented at the First International Symposium, Specific Language Disorders in Children, University of Reading, England.

Morris, N.T., and Crump, W.D. (1982). Syntactic and vocabulary development in the written language of learning disabled and non-disabled students at four age levels. *Learning Disability Quarterly, 5,* 163-172.

O'Donnell, R.C., Griffin, W.J., and Norris, R.D. (1967). *Syntax of kindergarten and elementary school children: A transformational analysis.* (Research Report No. 8). Champaign, IL: National Council of Teachers of English.

Pellegrini, A.D., Galda, L., and Rubin, D.L. (1984). Context in text: The development of oral and written language in two genres. *Child Development, 55,* 1549-1555.

Perera, K. (1984). *Children's writing and reading.* London: Blackwell.

Perera, K. (1986a). Grammatical differentiation between speech and writing in children aged 8 to 12. In A. Wilkinson (Ed.), *The writing of writing* (pp. 90-108). New York: Open University Press.

Perera, K. (1986b). Language acquisition and writing. In P. Fletcher and M. Garman (Eds.), *Language Acquisition* (Second edition) (pp. 494-533). Cambridge, England: Cambridge University Press.

Quirk, R., Greenbaum, S., Leech, G., and Svartvik, J. (1985). *A comprehensive grammar of the English language.* London: Longman.

Rees, N. (1974). The speech pathologist and the reading process. *ASHA, 16,* 255-158.

Richardson, K., Calnan, M., Essen, J. & Lambert, L. (1976). The linguistic maturity of 11-year-olds: Some analysis of the written composition of children in the National Development Study. *Journal of Child Language, 3,* 99-115.

Riling, M.E. (1965). *Oral and written language of children in grades 4 and 6 compared with the language of their textbooks.* Cooperative Research Project No. 2410, Cooperative Research Program, Office of Education, United States Department of Health, Education, and Welfare.

Romaine, S. (1984). *The language of children and adolescents.* Oxford: Blackwell.

Rubin, D.L. (1982). Adapting syntax in writing to varying audiences as a function of age and social cognitive ability. *Journal of Child Language, 9,* 497-510.

Scott, C.M. (1984a). Adverbial connectivity in conversations of children 6 to 12. *Journal of Child Language, 11,* 423-452.

Scott, C.M. (1984b, November). *What happened in that: Structural characteristics of school children's narratives.* Paper presented at the Annual Convention of the American Speech-Language-Hearing Association, San Francisco, CA.

Scott, C.M. (1983, November). You know and all that stuff: Acquisitioning in school children. Paper presented at the meeting of the American Speech-Language-Hearing Association, Cincinnati, OH.

Scott, C.M. (1987, April). *Summarizing text: Context effects in language disordered children.* Paper presented at the First International Symposium, Specific Language Disorders in Children, University of Reading, England.

Scott, C.M. (1988a). A perspective on the evaluation of school children's narratives. *Language, Speech, and Hearing Services in Schools, 19,* 67-82.

Scott, C.M. (1988b). Producing complex sentences. *Topics in Language Disorders, 8:2,* 44-62.

Scott, C.M., and Rush, D. (1985). Teaching adverbial connectivity: Implications from current research. *Child Language Teaching and Therapy, 1,* 264-280.

Scott, C.M., and Taylor, A. (1978). A comparison of home and clinic gathered language samples. *Journal of Speech and Hearing Disorders, 43,* 482-495.

Simon, C. (1979). *Communication competence: A functional–pragmatic approach to language therapy.* Tucson, AZ: Communication Skill Builders.

Strickland, R.G. (1962). The language of elementary school children: Its relationship to the language of reading textbooks and the quality of reading of selected children. *Bulletin of the School of Education, 38, No. 4.* Bloomington, IN: University of Indiana.

Wells, G. (1985). *Language development in the preschool years.* Cambridge, England: Cambridge University Press.

Wiig, E., and Semel, E. (1984). *Language assessment and intervention for the learning disabled* (Second edition). Columbus, OH: Merrill.

APPENDIX

1. This example demonstrates how the subordination index is calculated. The 10-utterance sample below has a subordination index of 1.20. Two of the 10 utterances (Nos. 4 & 8), or 20 percent, contain a subordinate clause.

Utterance Number	Number of Clauses
1	1
2	1
3	1
4	2 (main + subordinate)
5	1
6	1
7	1
8	2 (main + subordinate)
9	1
10	1
10 T-units	12 clauses

Subordinate Index = 12/10 = 1.20

2. Finite verb phrases are marked for tense, and there is person and number agreement with the subject. Main clause verbs must be finite. Nonfinite verbs include the infinitive form, the *ing* participle, and the *ed* participle. Tense, number, and person are not marked. Nonfinite verb phrases occur only in subordinate clauses. See Quirk and colleagues (1985) for further information. Examples of nonfinite forms of verb phrases contrasted with finite versions include:

He felt better *sitting up* in bed. (NF)

He felt better when he *was sitting up* in bed. (F)

Having tried the new recipe, she entered it in the fair. (NF)

She *had been trying* a new recipe and entered it in the fair. (F)

3. The head noun in a noun phrase may be premodified and postmodified by a variety of structures. In terms of development, premodification precedes postmodification. Major types of postmodification include prepositional phrases (e.g., the girl *in the car*), nonfinite clauses, where the verb phrase is in nonfinite form (e.g., the next bus *to come*, the man *using the telephone*), and relative clauses (the man *who is using the telephone*; the next bus *that will arrive*). See Quirk and colleagues (1985).

4. Appositive structures (phrases or clauses) follow head nouns in situations calling for restatement of the noun in another form:

   John *the fireman* is on the phone.

   The message *he would be late* arrived with Jane.

5. SVO: The cat   chased   the dog.
             S   V   O

   SVOA: They   ate   their dinner   in a hurry.
            S   V   O   A

   SVA: They   came   last night.
            S   V   A

   SVC: She   is   a good student.
            S   V   C

   SV: The baby   is crawling.
            S   V

6. Adverbial elements provide time, place, and manner information within a clause. They may take the form of a noun phrase (e.g., they came *last night*), prepositional phrase (I'm going *to the store*), adverbial phrase (they disappeared *very quickly*), or an adverbial clause (Mary watched TV *when she got home*). Adverbial elements are likely sources of clause pattern growth due to their flexibility. Unlike the other elements, adverbials are frequently optional and movable in terms of order (*very quickly* they disappeared). There may also be more than one adverbial element per clause.

7. SVOO: She   wrote   him   three letters.
            S   V   O   O

          My dad   gave   me   this ring.
            S   V   O   O

8. SVOC: They   voted   him   chair of the meeting.
            S   V   O   C

            That group   made   the concert   a success.
            S   V   O   C

9. Subordinate clauses may be classified according to function. *Nominal clauses* function as noun phrases in the main clause. Because noun phrases may function in the grammatical role of subject, object, or complement, nominal clauses also occur in these roles:

    What made her do it   is   a mystery.
            S   V   C

    He   knew   *he'd made a mistake.*
    S   V   O

    The agreement   is   *that I'll work for a year.*
            S   V   C

Adverbial clauses function as adverbial elements in the main clause. Major semantic categories include clauses of time, condition, result, place, and concession (see Quirk et al., 1985). Position is usually final, but may be initial or medial in the main clause. A wide variety of subordinate conjunctions introduce adverbial clauses:

    She   can't come   *until her parents get home.*
    S   V   A

    If you want to come   you   must get   permission.
            A   S   V   O

Relative clauses postmodify head nouns in noun phrases. They may postmodify nouns serving in any grammatical role (e.g., S,O,C):

    The girl *who lives next door*   is   my best friend.
                    S   V   C

    I   got   the teacher *who gives homework every night.*
    S   V   O

    She   is   a child *who can't sit still.*
    S   V   C

10. Conjunction operations add information by simply adding clauses at the end of other clauses. The clauses joined together (with conjunctions *and, but, or*) have equal syntactic status. Embedding operations add information by insertion of subordinate clauses within the main clause. Relative clauses which postmodify subject nouns literally insert new information between the head noun and the verb that follows.

11. Restrictive relative clauses add information that is essential for identi-
    fying the head noun. For example, the restrictive relative clause in the
    sentence *take the coffee to the lady that's sitting in the corner* identifies
    a particular lady and no other (the relative clause restricts the head
    noun to a particular person). By contrast, nonrestrictive relative clauses
    add information which is not required for identification; for example,
    take the coffee to Mrs. Smith, who is sitting in the corner.

12. Scott and Rush (1985) asked children to generate sentences incorporating
    various conjuncts. For example, a 9-year-old was asked to use the word
    however and produced *I can play today/however today is Saturday.*
    When asked to retell discourse they had just heard which contained par-
    ticular conjuncts, the children seldom used those forms. When asked
    to sort conjuncts with similar meanings into piles (e.g., *consequently,
    so,* and *as a result* would go in the same pile), 9-year-olds grouped only
    about half of the forms correctly.

13. The clefting construction splits a clause into two parts for the purpose
    of making the highlighted information more obvious. Via clefting, the
    first sentence below is transformed into the second:
    She came home from the hospital yesterday.
    It was yesterday that she came home from the hospital.

14. The extraposition construction shifts nominal clauses to the end of the
    sentence, and the pronoun *it* becomes the subject of the sentence. Via
    extraposition, the first sentence is transformed into the second:
    What you do doesn't matter.
    It doesn't matter what you do.

CHAPTER 5

■

READING AND WRITING

■

NICKOLA WOLF NELSON

Dogs,

dogs are cute
dogs are Fluffy
But I really like
GoldenReteivers
they are neat,
they have a long tail.
there cute when
their wet. The have
golden fur. There really
cute when they are
asleep. And if you ever
come to my house you
better be careful
because they lick.

Vicky

4th grade

Refinement in reading and writing ability is a major educational focus during the 9-through-19 age range. Youngsters spend increasing periods of time both in and out of school reading and writing for a variety of academic purposes, such as obtaining and giving information, being creative and appreciating the creativity of others, and assisting memory. But reading and writing are not only activities of the formal educational setting. Older children and adolescents often use reading and writing to perform all kinds of functions outside of school as well. These include personal functions such as reading novels or writing in a diary, interactive functions such as reading love notes or writing party invitations, heuristic functions such as reading statistics in sports magazines or writing for information from others, and memory functions such as reading grocery lists or writing down phone numbers.

Predictable shifts in reading and writing ability during the 9-through-19 age range are discussed in this chapter, emphasizing the following topics: (1) changes in *cognitive strategies* for processing written language and their relation to general cognitive development; (2) changes in *discourse strategies* for processing texts and exhibiting rhetorical sensitivity; (3) changes in *semantic strategies* for relating word meaning and context and for processing abstract meanings; (4) changes in *syntactic strategies* for processing later-developing syntactic structures; and (5) changes in strategies for relating *orthography, pronunciation,* and *punctuation*.

The "top-down" organizational structure of the chapter (i.e., from cognitive strategies to pronunciation and punctuation strategies) is intentional. Although the relative importance of perceptual-level processing in the early stages of learning to read is still somewhat controversial, it is widely agreed that a mark of advanced reading skill in older children, adolescents, and adults is the ability to use cognitive strategies more, to use phrase-by-phrase, word-by-word, and syllable-by-syllable strategies less, and to use sound-by-sound strategies hardly at all.

The decision to discuss reading and writing in tandem also was intentional. It represents the view that, "At no time in our recent history have researchers been so concerned and practitioners so interested in the connections between reading and writing" (Squire, 1987, p. 7). Kucer (1987), reporting on the interface of theories of reading and writing in the 1980s, commented that one of the possible connections between reading and writing is the "notion that comprehending and composing share key cognitive mechanisms" (p. 29), and that these mechanisms are used in both modalities to form mental representations of texts. However, Wittrock (1987) cautioned that "from a cognitive perspective, effective writing is more than putting meaning on the pages, and reading with comprehension involves more than getting meaning off the pages" (p. 374). Although it is appropriate to begin to study reading and writing as "different sides of the same coin" (p. 374), it is also important to remember that differences in teaching reading and writing may be called for even if the basic cognitive processes for reading and writing are closely related or the same (Wittrock, 1987).

In addition to the literature review, this chapter contains some original data on written language samples that were gathered from 22 fourth graders (mean age = 10:7), 19 seventh graders (mean age = 13:1), 28 tenth graders (mean age = 15:10), and 20 college freshmen (mean age = 18:8). Students wrote in their regular classrooms, and were instructed by their teachers to write about "something interesting that has happened to you in the past year or so." The computer program, *Systematic Analysis of Language Transcripts* (SALT; Miller and Chapman, 1986), was used for analyzing the written language samples in this study. Minor adaptations were made because the program originally was designed for analysis of spoken language samples. Full details of the methods used in the study are available in Nelson (1988) and Nelson and Friedman (1988).

Before discussing the development of written language, it must be emphasized that individual differences among youngsters at later developmental levels are great, and that the effects of context must be considered in any quantification efforts. Therefore, the information presented in this chapter should not be used as "normative data." As Rubin (1984) noted, "Research aimed at providing developmental descriptions of children's writing abilities must tread cautiously in formulating age–norm generalizations that fail to provide for the effects of communicative context" (p. 227).

It must also be emphasized that it is difficult to identify appropriate, nontrivial indices of development in reading and writing because the qualities that superficially indicate growth may not necessarily be valid signs of improved written language ability. As an example, Rubin (1984) noted that although composition length often predicts judged quality (Page, 1968), under certain circumstances, mature writers employ strategies that reduce rather than increase verbosity (Rubin, 1982). Hence, greater quantity does not necessarily imply greater quality. Similarly, although syntactic complexity has often been used to reflect composition quality (Cooper, 1976), complex syntax may not be appropriate in certain contexts (Crowhurst, 1980), and it may indicate that the writer has not judged the reader's needs. Both semantic and syntactic growth in child writers is normally accompanied by errors (Weaver, 1982). For example, "when they start adding to or elaborating their ideas, they may produce fragments consisting of compound or explanatory phrases. And when they begin using a variety of subordinate clauses, they may punctuate some of these as if they were complete sentences" (p. 443). In summarizing the research of others, Brannon (1985) also found that "when writers push toward intellectual complexity in their work, their texts may not demonstrate the formal and technical competence of their previous, less complex texts" (p. 20).

Neither is "better reading" necessarily more error free. The presence of errors in children's reading cannot be simply counted in order to determine maturity, since different kinds of errors represent different levels of maturity (Goodman, 1976). Some errors may represent children's development of faster strategies for constructing meaning in the most efficient way, and their ability to ignore insignificant miscues that have no effect on meaning. Goodman (1973) used the term *miscues* rather than *errors* in describing children's reading, stating that "nothing the reader does in reading is accidental" (p. 5). He further argued that miscues during oral reading can serve as "a window on the reading process" (p. 5). As children gain maturity in their reading ability, perhaps the best way to measure their reading skill is to have them write about what they have read in critical and interpretive ways (Petrosky, 1982). However, this process is fraught with all of the increased-error effects of taking greater risks in thinking and writing that were just identified.

The caveat is made not to avoid completely attempts to identify predictable changes in older children and adolescents. Rather, it is made to encourage researchers to choose the measurements carefully, with awareness of the complexity of the later stages of learning to read and write and knowledge of the contexts in which they occur, and to interpret findings regarding individuals and groups of individuals with caution.

COGNITIVE STRATEGY DEVELOPMENTS

Attempts to relate developments in reading and writing to developments in cognition have ranged from those that have stuck closely to reading and writing processes themselves to those that have extended to more global theories of cognitive development. Chall's (1983) work is an example of the first kind of approach. She proposed a comprehensive, stage-development theory of reading similar to Piaget's cognitive development stages, but unique to the process of learning to read. Chall included six stages (Stage 3 has two substages) in her sequence, starting with a kind of pseudoreading and advancing to reading that is highly creative and constructive.

Stage 1

Chall called this stage "Initial Reading or Decoding" (first and second grades; ages six and seven). The essence of this stage is learning the arbitrary set of letters and associating them with the corresponding parts of spoken words. It is also the stage in which children learn to interiorize knowledge about reading, and learn such things as when a mistake was made. In the early part of Stage 1, most children are pseudoreaders in that they "read" by telling a familiar story in a book, mostly from recall, and with the aid of pictures. "They must supply their own words because they do not know enough about how to get the author's words from the printed page" (p. 18). However, to move through this stage, Chall noted that children must be willing "to engage, at least temporarily, in what appears to be less mature reading behavior—becoming glued to the print—in order to achieve real maturity later" (p. 18).

Stage 2

Chall called this stage, "Confirmation, Fluency, Ungluing from Print" (second and third grades; ages seven and eight). It is used to consolidate what was learned in Stage 1, and to engage in reading for the purpose of confirming what is already known to the reader rather than for gaining new information. In Stage 2, readers learn to use their decoding knowledge, the redundancies of the language, and the redundancies of the stories they read. As they gain skill in using context, they gain reading fluency and speed.

Stage 3

This stage, "Reading for Learning the New," consists of two substages, 3A and 3B. During 3A (fourth, fifth, and sixth grades; ages 9, 10, and 11), children develop the ability to read beyond egocentric purposes in order to gain conventional information about the world from sources that do not usually require special prior knowledge. This substage is the beginning of the ability to use reading to acquire new knowledge (rather than just to encounter old knowledge in a new modality, as in prior stages). At the end of this substage, children can read material that is of adult length but does not exhibit the reading difficulty of most popular adult literature. During 3B (seventh, eighth, and ninth grades; ages 12, 13, and 14), readers "grow in their ability to analyze what they read and to react critically to the different viewpoints they meet" (p. 22). Chall reported that by the end of this substage, children can read local newspapers, popular adult fiction, and popular magazines such as *The Reader's Digest*, but that they still have difficulty with news magazines such as *Newsweek* and *Time*.

Stage 4

Called "Multiple Viewpoints" (ninth, tenth, eleventh, and twelfth grades; ages 14, 15, 16, 17, and 18), the essential characteristic of this stage is the development of the ability to deal with more than one point of view. Recognition of this ability is reflected in textbooks, which provide greater depth and more varied viewpoints in treating topics at the high school level than they do at earlier levels. Chall reported that youngsters reach Stage 4 mostly through formal education; that is, through "the assignments in the various school textbooks, original and other sources, and reference works in the physical, biological, and social sciences; through reading of more mature fiction; and through the free reading of books, newspapers, and magazines" (p. 23).

Stage 5

This is the most mature stage of reading, "Construction and Reconstruction—A World View" (college; ages 18 and above). At this stage, readers have learned to read books and articles with the degree of detail and completeness they need for particular purposes, and they can start at the end, middle, or beginning. In Stage 5, reading is essentially constructive in that readers apply strategies of analysis, synthesis, and judgment to decide "what to read, how much of it to read, at what pace, and in how much detail" (p. 24). They are able to synthesize information from varied sources and to balance their comprehension of the ideas read, their analysis of them, and their own ideas about them. They have the ability to construct knowledge at a high level of abstraction, creating their own "truths" from the "truths" of others, and understanding works of fiction at more than one level. Chall reported that it is debatable whether all individuals, even at the end of four years of college, reach this stage. This issue of the adult level of competence was also raised in Chapters 3 and 4 during discussions of the literate lexicon and syntax, respectively.

Whereas Chall's approach to development focused closely on reading itself, Odell (1973a, 1973b) took a more global approach and tried to relate reading development to more general advances in cognition. Odell related developments in reading to various cognitive developments that Piaget described. For example, Odell (1973b) emphasized the importance of *decentering* to the development of reading. Decentering involves "getting outside one's own frame of reference, understanding the thoughts, values, feelings of another person; . . . projecting oneself into unfamiliar circumstances, whether factual or hypothetical" (p. 455). Decentering, according to Piaget (1951, 1954, 1965), begins as early as the preoperational stage. In many ways, it continues throughout the life span as people move into unfamiliar tasks and environments.

Lunsford (1985) also took a more global approach and emphasized the importance of Vygotsky's (1962) work in organizing views of children's reading and writing development. Vygotsky agreed that children move through identifiable cognitive stages during the process of development, but he cautioned that even after the adolescent has learned to think in more elaborate ways, more elementary forms are not abandoned. Furthermore, Vygostky differentiated between *spontaneous concepts* that were formed as a result of ordinary, everyday experiences, and *scientific concepts* that were formed largely in conjunction with education.

Both Piaget's and Vygotsky's theories have appeal for attempting to understand the normal development of written language ability as well as the effects of education on development (e.g., for understanding how individuals develop abstract thinking abilities and the concept of audience). However, Lunsford (1985) reminded educators that no systematic research has been conducted to apply either Piaget's or Vygostsky's theories to the experiences of adolescents and young adults who are learning to write. Therefore, a related pedagogy has not yet been established.

Attempts to study the interactions of cognitive growth and writing in older children and adolescents have been problematic. One problem concerns the difficulties associated with identifying valid and reliable indices of writing maturity. In addition, some research has suggested that the kinds of developmental sequences that are implicit in school curricula are exactly the opposite from sequences of development that occur naturally in children (Brannon, 1985). For example, the tradition in the schools has been to emphasize the development of writing from stages of correctness, to clarity, and finally to fluency. However, it has been found that writing abilities develop naturally in the opposite direction—from fluency, to clarity, to correctness (Mayer, Lester, and Pradl, 1983). More recently, Brannon (1985) argued against the traditional view that writers grow by learning " 'the basics' in piecemeal fashion or by producing correct but perfunctory products" (p. 22), and suggested instead that writers grow by engaging repeatedly in the process of writing, including opportunities to write for different purposes. Consider, for example, the kind of personal writing that is illustrated in Figure 5-1. This note was written for a peer audience of one ("Nicky [only]"), and for social, not academic, purposes. The writing of this fourth-grade boy illustrates the dominance of fluency over correctness at this stage in spontaneous writing, especially when a teacher's red pencil is not expected. The importance of metalinguistic play with writing is also exemplified in the backwards writing, which is clearly labeled in case the reader has any difficulty with it, and the "sorry so sloppy" displays of this piece.

The lack of a significant number and variety of writing opportunities has also made it difficult for researchers to study developmental advances in written language. Britton, Burgess, Martin, McLeod, and Rosen (1975) began studying writing in London's schools with the intention of describing the development of writing abilities in youngsters of the ages of 11 to 18. However, they found that they could not describe those developmental stages fully because the youngsters were given so few opportunities to write outside

Nicky ~backward~
(s'tahw pu ro nWod?)

How's life, fine here - I guess.

I really sorry about calling you all those names the day before yesterday. I not glad that were not going together. Are you going or gonna go with Ryan. Because I wanna no if I can go back with you. please tell me yes or no. I'm writing this in math class. This palably a boring note but who cares. I don't. By the way tell out for recuss! gotta go by

sorry S/S/S/sloppy

Jarrod

Don't read

Write Bake soon

p.s. I still love ya a little but not a much as I did before. —

Figure 5-1. Spontaneous personal writing by a fourth-grade boy, illustrating the dominance of fluency over correctness at this stage of writing development, and the high focus on metalinguistic play.

of the restricted boundaries of school assignments (Brannon, 1985). Similarly, Applebee (1981) found restrictions in the kinds of writing opportunities offered in America's high schools.

Odell (1977) noted that it has not been possible to determine developmental stages in the use of intellectual processes in the writing of children and adolescents because of difficulty in identifying those processes. He proposed that six intellectual processes might be used as signs of growth in students' writing. These were *focus, contrast, classification, change, physical context,* and *sequence* (Pike, 1964a, 1964b). Odell also provided evidence that teaching students to be aware of the use of intellectual processes could increase the chances that the processes would be evinced in the students' work.

The kind of metacognitive strategies that were studied by Forrest-Pressley and Waller (1984) (see Chapter 2) have also been found to influence the ability to read, but to a lesser degree than the cognitive strategies have. Those authors found that both performance on each type of skill they studied (i.e., decoding, comprehension, strategies, language, attention, and memory), and the ability to verbalize about the skills, increased with grade level and with reading ability. However, performance scores tended to be better predictors of reading ability than verbalization scores. Other findings by Forrest-Pressley and Waller were that (1) there was a tendency for poor sixth-grade readers to mimic knowledge about decoding strategies but not to use them effectively in a performance task, (2) children began to use reading strategies at the third-grade level, but not until sixth grade did their comprehension increase under such conditions as making up a title, studying, and reading for fun, (3) the older and better readers were more able to use language skills and to talk about them, (4) the older and better readers were more able to read and to talk about memory skills, (5) although language skills had a strong link to reading ability at both third- and sixth-grade levels, developmental changes in attention and memory mainly affected students in the lower grade, (6) all in all, the third-grade readers were best characterized by their decoding performance scores, whereas sixth-grade readers were best characterized by their use of advanced strategies as indicated by efficiency. Forrest-Pressley and Waller also compared cognitive and metacognitive measures and determined that older and better readers were not only more proficient in using cognitive skills, they were also more proficient in verbalizing about those skills.

DISCOURSE STRATEGY DEVELOPMENTS

Schemata (i.e., internalized cognitive structures) are so important in determining whether individuals understand what they read that they can make a particular reader competent in one situation but less competent in another (Smith, Carey, and Harste, 1982). For example, a college student might find that he has no difficulty comprehending the information in a sports article, but that his economics textook might appear to be incomprehensible. Interestingly, the student's professor might experience the opposite set of reading-comprehension capabilities. The main difference between the two readers is in their schemata for the respective tasks. As Smith and colleagues (1982) commented, "Schemata form a mental concept important for finding meaning. Learning involves building up a repertoire of useful schemata for understanding new information. In short, what we comprehend depends in an important way on what we already know" (p. 24).

The familiar schema of narrative structures in stories is used almost universally to teach people to read because narrative structures are easy to perceive, their scripts are easy to follow, and they have been experienced in other modalities before children start to learn to read (Estes, 1982). However, at about the age of 9 (third or fourth grade), an important transition occurs in the literacy acquisition process, and children who have thus far been exposed primarily to texts with narrative structures must begin to comprehend the discourse that they read in their subject-matter textbooks, which is written as expository prose instead of as narrative stories. To compound the difficulty, it is known that the expository structure of textbooks is particularly difficult to perceive if the reader is unsophisticated about a given topic (Estes, 1982). Yet it is that same lack of sophistication that causes assignments to be made for students to read textbooks in the first place.

Children who begin encountering expository texts at the third- or fourth-grade level are the children who are moving gradually from Substage 3A to Substage 3B of Chall's (1983) progression. This is the time when they begin to read in order to acquire new knowledge and to read critically. If children are to be successful in making these transitions, they must acquire new strategies for recognizing the structures of different kinds of texts, not just narrative texts. Yet Tierney (1982) reported that recent studies have shown that many high school students lack skills for using hypotheses to develop interpretations of information represented by expository texts, or if they have those skills, they fail to use them. If students are to construct models that will assist them with their reading, Tierney indicated that they must be able to initiate and sustain simultaneously a variety of behavioral strategies that would include

> activating and refining predictions, maintaining and varying focus, interrelating ideas, self-questioning, attending to important information, dismissing irrelevant information, following topical development, recognizing relationships, evaluating understandings, considering the worth of ideas, deciding what is new information, sensing mood and

tone, sometimes visualizing, sometimes adding information, redefin-
ing, analogizing, editing, and reshuffling ideas. (p. 98).

It does not seem to be a lack of basic cognitive readiness that prevents
students from acquiring sophisticated text-analysis strategies. Tierney
reviewed a number of studies that demonstrated that students of a variety
of grade levels (as low as fifth grade) could learn strategies such as using
prior knowledge and textual cues to draw inferences if given specific instruction, modeling, and corrective feedback. Nevertheless, Tierney was concerned about the mismatch for most high-school students between their need
for self-regulatory abilities to cope with a variety of reading tasks and their
tendencies to restrict themselves typically to a single reading of a single textbook, for the single purpose of completing a class assignment, with the single
disposition to memorize.

Squire (1964) was concerned with the ability of adolescents (52 ninth
and tenth graders) to demonstrate global responses to literature. He studied seven categories of responses (literary judgment, interpretational, narrational, associational, self-involvement, prescriptive judgment, and
miscellaneous), using the unique strategy of having the adolescents comment, at predetermined divisions, on their responses while reading short
stories. Squire found that the most frequent responses from these young high-
school students were interpretational (more than 42 percent), narrational,
literary judgments, and self-involvement reactions. Less than 4 percent of
the responses were coded as associational, prescriptive judgment, or as
miscellaneous. Squire also identified six basic sources of difficulty that the
adolescents encountered in interpreting short stories: (1) failure to grasp the
meaning due to misunderstanding of key words, failure to grasp implications of details, or making incorrect inferences; (2) reliance on stock responses
(i.e., familiar and stereotyped patterns of thinking) for interpreting literature;
(3) "happiness binding" in the expectation of fairy-tale solutions, and unwill-
ingness to face the realities of unpleasant interpretation; (4) critical
predispositions to apply the same standards to all types of fiction (e.g.,
recognition of a "true-to-life" quality, or concern for "good description");
(5) irrelevant associations consisting of scattered, unrelated impressions; and
(6) the search for certainty, even when clues in the story were fragmentary
or minimal. Although Squire found general trends for all of the adolescents
he studied, individual differences, which he related to the "unique influence
of the abilities, predispositions, and experiential background of each reader"
(p. 50), were also noted. It is interesting that such difficulties as stereotyped
reactions, happiness bindings, and other misleading or distorted reactions
were found as often among the more intelligent readers as among those with
lower general intelligence scores. Also, the standardized reading instrument

Squire administered to his subjects did not prove to be a reliable index of the ability to interpret literary selections. All of Squire's subjects were of similar ages. However, he did compare his results with those from another study involving college freshmen and reported that the college students used a significantly higher percentage of interpretational responses than did the high-school students.

In 1979 and 1980, a national assessment of responses to reading and literature by a broad, representative sample of 9-, 13-, and 17-year-old students was conducted in the United States. It was entitled "National Assessment of Educational Progress" (NAEP) (1981). To interpret the results, the report was written with reference to a four-step model of the process through which comprehension might evolve: "(1) initial comprehension, leading to (2) preliminary interpretations, followed by (3) a reexamination of the text in light of these interpretations, leading to (4) extended and documented interpretation" (p. 2). The major findings of the study were that (1) almost all students recognized the value and utility of reading, (2) by the age of 17, most read a variety of materials appropriate for their ages, (3) older students displayed stronger comprehension skills, and by the age of 17 most students were able to answer multiple-choice questions requiring either literal or inferential comprehension and were able to summarize passages in writing, (4) by the age of 17, most students expressed their initial ideas and judgments about what they read, especially when personal reactions were involved, but only 5 to 10 percent of them seemed able to move beyond their initial interpretations, and (5) older students did provide more evidence to support their assertions than younger students.

Not only readers, but also writers, must learn to use a variety of organizational schemata and global analysis strategies when producing and evaluating written work. As in reading, it is difficult to measure a written schema structure with traditional quantitative techniques. For example, Brannon (1985) summarized the research on features of text in children's writing that demonstrate control of discourse strategies. She reported that "most of the technical and structural features of prose—facility with usage and the mechanics of written discourse as well as organizational facility—have been shown to be less reliable as developmental indicators than previously expected" (p. 20). This is partly because, as noted previously, when writers attempt greater intellectual complexity, the technical aspects of their work may falter.

In their attempts to study the development of writing abilities in youngsters of the ages of 11 to 18 in London schools, Britton and colleagues (1975) recognized that they needed to study the youngsters' ability to compose discourse of a variety of types. Four categories of discourse—*narration, description, exposition*, and *argument*—have traditionally been recognized in textbooks. However, Britton and colleagues found those categories inadequate to describe all of the kinds of writing in which older children and adolescents engaged. They also did not find it desirable "to attempt a developmental study that merely marked out stages of progress in terms of a descriptive catalogue of the end products" (p. 9). Rather, they found that they needed to consider both the students' sense of audience and the functions their written language served in order to consider adequately the contexts that determined the developmental sophistication of students' writing. For sense of audience, Britton and colleagues defined 10 subcategories that were subsumed under 5 major category headings for which children were primarily seen as writing: (1) self, (2) teacher, (3) a wider known audience, (4) an unknown audience, and (5) either a particular (named) audience or no discernible audience. Three main-function categories also were identified. In the *transactional* category, students took a participant role. At the opposite end of the continuum, was the *poetic* category, in which students took a spectator role. Prior to developing either of these two literary functions, students were found to function in an *expressive* mode. However, sense of audience and function of discourse interacted in complex ways to make it difficult to build developmental sequences. As noted previously, Britton and colleagues also found that it was difficult to clearly establish developmental stages in learning to write because students were given so few opportunities to write outside of the boundaries of restricted school assignments.

Britton and colleagues based their views of children's written language development on Vygotsky's (1962) theory that written language develops from inner language, and that expressive writing develops first because it has its foundations in talk. They also theorized that as writers mature, they become able to differentiate their own world views from those of others, and that their sense of audience develops as they become able to consider the needs of the reader. Children also learn to write for different functional purposes. Their writing moves outward in one direction along the continuum from expressive (writing inner thoughts) to transactional (expository or argumentative) writing, and in the other direction, from expressive to poetic (poems, short stories, novels, drama) writing. Consistent with their hypothesis that "development in writing is a process of dissociation, or progressive differentiation" (p. 190), Britton and colleagues (1975) found that informative (transactional) writing was largely developed in the school with the audience being sensed as "teacher-as-examiner." In contrast, they found that expressive and poetic writing developments were associated with teacher–learner dialogue, in which the child learned to write to the teacher as a trusted adult, or to an unknown audience. They also found that for 11- to 15-year-olds, writing for a public audience was virtually restricted to the poetic mode. Only at around the age of 16, did the students begin to produce transactional writing that demonstrated sensitivity to a public audience. The researchers hypothesized that early writing for unknown others was so much more likely to be poetic (or narrative) than expository in form because the students sensed that they had to be interesting to an unknown audience of strangers, with a "heightening of order imposed upon words and what they portray" (p. 193). When the students perceived themselves as functioning in a participant role (as in transactional writing), they apparently found less need to be interesting and organized, because they viewed themselves as writing for an audience of teacher-as-examiner.

Although the concept of *audience* has been a major focus of attention in recent discussions of rhetorical theory, Hillock (1986) reported that only a few studies have examined the development of audience sensitivity in written communication. He commented that "relatively little has been attempted in examining writers' knowledge of audience/product relations and their use of that knowledge" (p. 91). One study that did attempt to relate the ability of writers of different ages to modify their writing according to the needs of different audiences was conducted by Bracewell, Scardamalia, and Bereiter (1978). Those researchers asked students in the fourth, eighth, and twelfth grades and the junior year of college to describe two geometric shapes so they could be drawn by someone else: a student of the same age at a different school; a student in the same school; or a general audience. In a second experiment, students in fourth, eighth, and twelfth grades were told to write about the same shapes for one of three audiences: someone younger; a peer; or an adult. The researchers found that the writers' ability to use audience-orienting devices (four kinds of context-creating statements) was present as low as fourth grade, but that the use of such devices increased between fourth and twelfth grades. They also found that the ability to differentiate according to the needs of a specific audience was not clear until twelfth grade. Specifying audience age did result in differences in the numbers of context-creating statements in the twelfth grade, but not in the fourth or eighth grades.

Global text-organization strategies have also received little attention from researchers concerned with the writing abilities of older children and adolescents (Hillock, 1986). Studies thus far have tended to concentrate on oral story telling, or on younger writers. For example, one study conducted on written language samples produced by children in first and second grades (King and Rentel, 1981) showed steady increases in children's abilities to use lexical cohesion strategies, but another study (Sowers, 1981) showed that first grade children rarely (only 36 percent of a sample of 22 students) organized their stories into narratives (defined for her study as any piece of writing ordered chronologically). Rather, the children tended to use a strategy for writing that Bereiter and Scardamalia (1982) called the "what next" strategy, in which they jumped from one idea to another without any overall plan.

A more sophisticated rating scale for characterizing development in the ability to organize oral story telling was devised by Applebee (1978). He described six increasingly mature forms leading to the development of true narratives that were based on Vygotsky's (1962) views of developing cognitive organizational strategies. These forms were (1) *heaps*, which consist of a collection of statements related, perhaps, by free association, (2) *sequences*, which consist of a series of statements linked to adjacent statements, but with no overall cohesion, (3) *primitive narratives*, which consist of events surrounding a common nucleus, such as a character or a trip, but do not yield a linked story, (4) *unfocused chains*, which consist of a series of statements each linked concretely to the next, but in which the beginning has little relation to the ending, (5) *focused chains* which involve a central character or theme combined with a true sequence of events but with an ending that does not follow logically from the beginning, and (6) *true narratives*, which involve a central character or theme and a plot that is developed in logical sequence from beginning to ending, with a point often made at the end that relates to the beginning. Applebee's (1978) work showed that although oral narratives are attempted by children as young as the age of 2, the full narrative schema rarely appears until late elementary school.

The data on text organization (Nelson and Friedman, 1988) that were gathered as a part of the preparation for writing this chapter showed that youngsters continue to develop the ability to use narrative organizational strategies in their written language beyond elementary school and even beyond middle school. Nelson and Freidman used Applebee's (1978) six stages of development of the narrative schema for rating the stories of the fourth, seventh, and tenth graders, and college freshmen, with a score of one to six in the study that was mentioned previously. The results indicated that it was not until the freshman year of college that a mean story score representing use of full narrative structure (i.e., a mean score of 5.7) was reached in stories of personal experience written for unknown researchers who requested them to be made "interesting." This finding suggested that developmental events might be even more protracted than the earlier research by Britton and colleagues (1975) had indicated.

The mean story schema scores for the groups of fourth and seventh graders in the Nelson and Friedman (1988) study were 3.9 and 3.7, respectively. The narrative schema scores for the fourth and seventh graders did not differ significantly from each other, but they both differed significantly from narrative schema scores earned by tenth graders, whose mean score was 5.1. The mean score for the fourth graders was obtained by averaging the scores from three stories that rated 6 (true narratives), five stories that rated scores of 5 (focused chains), twelve stories that earned scores of 3 (primitive narratives), and two stories that earned scores of 2 (sequences).

As Applebee (1978) and Westby (1982) had reported, Nelson and Friedman found that unfocused chain stories (score = 4) were rare, indeed nonexistent. The narrative schema scores for seventh graders also showed considerable variance, with three scores of 6, three scores of 5, twelve scores of 3, and one score of 2. Eleven of the tenth graders earned true narrative scores of 6, thirteen of them earned scores of 5, and four earned scores of 3. No tenth graders earned narrative scores lower than 3.

Continued development in the ability to use true narrative structure for organizing written language during later adolescence is supported by the fact that the college freshmen earned narrative structure scores that were significantly better than those of the tenth graders. The mean score for the college freshmen was 5.7, and they also showed less variability in their scores. Fifteen of the college-freshman stories rated a score of 6 (full narrative) and five rated a score of 5 (focused chain). In the Nelson and Friedman study, it was clear that older students were better able to structure their writing as narratives than younger students (although no significant advances were made in this ability from fourth through seventh grade).

SEMANTIC STRATEGY DEVELOPMENTS

Reading and writing both involve the communication of meaning. Semantic processing strategies are an important aspect of written language development. Semantic strategies vary from those that deal with the comprehension or selection of individual words to strategies for processing meaning in the contexts of sentences and larger textual units.

The correlation between word knowledge and language comprehension is well established (Curtis, 1986). Loban (1963) found the correlation between vocabulary and intelligence test scores to be the highest in his longitudinal study of children's language from kindergarten through their first seven years of school. Loban also found that high vocabulary and intelligence test scores clustered with high language ability in all modalities—listening, speaking, reading, and writing.

Word knowledge and world knowledge are both important factors contributing to the development of literacy as it was discussed in Chapters 2 and 3. However, development of the ability to relate word knowledge to knowledge associated with larger context units has not been thoroughly investigated. Curtis (1986) wondered whether knowledge of word meanings facilitates comprehension or whether word knowledge is a product of comprehension. Her research suggested that the two hypothetical explanations addressed two different aspects of word knowledge. Curtis studied college students who were high scorers and low scorers on standardized multiple choice vocabulary tests. Previous research had shown that younger and less skilled students have difficulty using context to identify word meanings, and that older and more skilled students use context more effectively. This suggested that part of what it means to have a large vocabulary is to be able to use context efficiently to acquire new word meanings. However, Curtis' findings were not completely consistent with the results of earlier research. In her study, some of the skilled students were no more successful than the less skilled students in using context to acquire new word meanings. Curtis interpreted her results as suggesting that there are basic differences between the types word knowledge she called "knowing that. . ." (declarative knowledge) and "knowing how. . ." (procedural knowledge). She also suggested that differences of the two types of knowledge in students may represent differences in processing style more than differences in developmental level, at least during the college years.

The ability to read or write texts that use words with increased semantic maturity is also an important index of written language development. The fact that word frequency has been recognized for some time as an index of semantic difficulty is represented by the longstanding reputation of the Thorndike and Lorge (1944) *Teacher's Word Book of 30,000 Words.* Two other large scale word counts were provided by Kucera and Francis (1967) and by Carroll, Davies, and Richman (1971). Such counts are useful in determining how difficult material is for children to read.

Vocabulary measures can also be used to judge the maturity of children's compositions. However, the problem with using vocabulary counts is that it is difficult to establish standards for judging the maturity of particular word choices. Finn (1977) suggested that computers might provide an efficient way of identifying the semantic maturity of students' writing by comparing their word choices against words stored in a data base. He used themes written by fourth, eighth, and eleventh graders to illustrate his points. Although a data base for judging students' themes still has not become widely available more than a decade after Finn's paper was published, his suggestions for the kinds of word categories that such a data base should include are relevant today.

First of all, Finn suggested that some words have low-frequency scores (based on published vocabulary counts) for reasons other than that they represent mature choices. These words therefore should be eliminated from judgments of written language maturity. They include (1) words dictated by the topic (e.g., an assignment on "pollution" would presumably necessitate the use of that word several times in the theme), (2) proper nouns, (3) slang words, and (4) contractions, which would be avoided in formal textbook language written for children but be common in the language written by children. High-frequency words (e.g., function words) also do not distinguish among language written by children at different grade levels and should not be included. Finn presented a list of 240 words called "undistinguished word classes" (p. 80) that he placed in this category. The kinds of words that Finn thought should be identified as representing mature word choices on the part of the student author were (1) words that represent low-frequency word choices but that do not fall into any of the categories listed above, (2) abstract nouns (e.g., *alternatives, efforts, menace*), (3) verbs that indicate cognitive activity rather than physical activity (e.g., *blame, support, realize*), and (4) adjectives that reveal a judgment on the part of the author regarding an abstract state (e.g., *adequate, controversial, unnatural*).

One measure that has been suggested for quantifying the diversity of children's vocabulary is the type–token ratio (TTR). The TTR is the number of different words in a sample (types) divided by the total number of words (tokens) in the sample. Loban (1963) used the TTR in his longitudinal study of children through the elementary-school years. He indicated that, although the method has been criticized, "it can disclose important distinctions *when the size of the language sample is kept uniform*" [italics in original] (p. 22). The TTR decreases as sample length increases because of the relatively greater repetition of high-frequency function words in longer samples. No normative data are available for the TTR, but it has been suggested that they are appropriate for evaluating the written language samples of children (Isaacson, 1985).

In the Nelson and Friedman (1988) study, the analysis of variance (ANOVA) for TTR was significant for grade level, but differences in story length (shortest for the seventh graders) led the seventh graders to earn the highest TTR (mean = 0.59), followed by the tenth graders (mean = 0.54), and then the fourth graders (mean = 0.49) and the college freshmen (mean = 0.49), who had identical scores. Because of the known effect of length on TTR, an analysis of covariance (ANCOVA) was also conducted, with story length in words as the covariate. In this case, the results were also significant by grade level, but the adjusted means showed the expected developmental progression (fourth: 0.47; seventh: 0.52; tenth: 0.54; freshmen: 0.56).

Beyond individual word choices, readers and writers must develop strategies for processing words at the phrase and sentence levels. Indeed, as Curtis (1986) noted in the study reviewed previously, it is not always clear whether word-level knowledge leads to comprehension or vice versa. Goodman (1976) commented that "if the focus were on meaning rather than identification of words, there wouldn't be as many reading problems" (p. 64). To measure developmental advances in children's ability to demonstrate concern for meaning while reading, Goodman devised a formula that yielded a *comprehending percentage*. An individual's comprehending percentage is computed by "taking the percentage of miscues that are originally acceptable semantically and adding to that the percentage that aren't semantically acceptable but which are corrected" (p. 68). To study comprehending, Goodman had tenth graders of varied ability levels, and high-ability eighth graders, read stories of two levels of difficulty. He found that miscue percentages were affected by grade level, ability, and story difficulty. The high-ability eighth graders performed more like the high-ability tenth graders on the easy story, but not on the more difficult one. Percentages of both syntactically acceptable and semantically acceptable miscues increased with better ability and easier stories. Goodman summarized his findings as follows:

> First of all, more proficient readers make better miscues; they're better miscues not in the sense that we like them but in terms of their effect. They're less likely to produce unacceptable grammar. Furthermore, more proficient readers have an ability to recognize when their miscues need correction. When a reader is correcting a lot of miscues that don't change the meaning and not correcting a lot that do change the meaning, there is a pretty powerful insight that he's operating on a wrong model, that in effect he's not very efficient because he's wasting a lot of time trying to achieve accuracy that's unnecessary, while not being able to handle the situation where he loses the meaning. (p. 70)

Beyond the level of meaningful sentences, readers and writers must develop stategies for processing ideas in texts so that the texts can form a cohesive whole. The most influential recent work on text cohesion has been Halliday and Hasan's (1976) *Cohesion in English*. As Halliday and Hasan defined it, cohesion is a semantic (rather than syntactic) system of ties across sentence boundaries that bind a text together. Although they are basically semantic, cohesion strategies can also involve syntactic processes. Halliday and Hasan described five kinds of cohesion processes: *lexical* cohesion strategies, which involve semantic linkages among vocabulary items; *grammatical* cohesion strategies, which involve the three syntactic–semantic operations of *reference, substitution,* and *ellipsis*; and *conjunction* strategies, which relate ideas with a cohesion process that is largely grammatical but also lexical. The common feature among these strategies is that cohesion is established by writing so that linguistic items "point" to each other. Cohesion strategies can be used to point backwards to previously introduced lexical items (*anaphora*) or ahead to new information (*cataphora*). They can also provide immediate cohesion between two linguistic items; they can be chained in a sequence of immediate ties, or they can be remote in that they are separated by one or more sentences.

Developmental data on the use of cohesion strategies in written language are limited. Studies of higher-ability and lower-ability college freshmen that were reviewed by Strong (1985) all showed better writing to be associated with higher frequencies of cohesive ties, particularly cohesion using the lexical strategy of providing synonyms. Better writers also used many more referential ties than did poorer writers, including explicit signals of relations between ideas, such as *the same as*, *similar to*, and *different from*. Conjunctive ties were used more frequently by the better writers as well.

Nelson and Friedman's (1988) written language samples were not coded for all instances of cohesion. However, they were coded for instances in which cohesion failed, the writer made an illogical connection, or the reader felt the need for further information. These instances were totaled with other instances of semantic-reference difficulty that included word choices of the following types: (1) all-purpose words, indicating apparent lack of a more exact vocabulary item (e.g., a fourth grader wrote about going to *a motorbike place*); (2) word choices that were slightly inappropriate to the context (e.g., a tenth grader wrote that chores involved in painting a house were *literally killing people*; a college freshman wrote about large rocks that were *filled with messages* [instead of *covered*]; and (3) problems involving deictic choices for maintaining appropriate perspective regarding person (including pronoun errors), time (including verb-tense errors), or space.

The total of the pooled semantic errors for each subject in this study was then divided by the total number of words used by that subject and multiplied by 100 in order to obtain a frequency rate for word-choice errors per 100 words (i.e., a percentage error rate). The ANOVA performed on these rates for the four different grade levels showed significant differences. However, it was not the case that errors became consistently fewer as grade level increased. The fourth graders did show the highest error rate and the greatest variability (mean = 2.29; SD = 2.20), and they were found to be significantly different from all other grade levels. The seventh graders showed the next highest word-choice error rate (mean = 1.33; SD = 1.25). However, their semantic error rates were not significantly different from those of the tenth graders or the freshmen. In fact, although the error rate went down for the tenth graders to the lowest level (mean = 0.58; SD = 0.63), it went back up slightly for the college freshmen (mean = 1.18; SD = 0.85). Perhaps this occurred because the freshmen were willing to take more risks in their writing, particularly in their attempts to use abstract vocabulary.

Among the semantic errors that writers of all ages made, deictic word choices proved to be especially difficult. With deixis, a particular word must be chosen according to the perspective of the speaker or writer regarding person (e.g., *I* versus *you*), time (e.g., *now* versus *then*), and place (e.g., *here* versus *there*). Even college freshmen produced sentences like *I paid no attention to the time, even though I was due back ten minutes ago*, and *There was no doubt about it now*, indicating that it was difficult for them to maintain a consistent temporal perspective in their writing. Writers of all ages mixed references to themselves in the first person with references to themselves as the generic *you* (e.g., a college freshman wrote about his feelings concerning high-school graduation with the words, *This was the ending of the process that you had spent thirteen years of your life attempting to fulfill*). Such findings were consistent with the cautions mentioned previously that it is too simplistic to use error counts by themselves as signals of written language maturity. Nevertheless, it is important to know that the biggest jump in ability to avoid errors in semantic reference and the use of other cohesive devices came between fourth and seventh grade for these normally developing American youngsters.

SYNTACTIC STRATEGY DEVELOPMENTS

Syntactic complexity is a reliable indicator of advancing maturity in children's writing. It is also easier to measure than semantic complexity. Numerous studies (e.g., Hunt, 1965, 1970; Loban, 1963, 1976; O'Donnell, Griffin, and Norris, 1967) of written syntactic development were discussed in Chapter 4. Consistent with those earlier studies, the Nelson (1988) written language samples showed steady increases in the mean length of T-units across the four different grade levels. The means and standard deviations for each grade were as follows: fourth (8.75; 1.12); seventh (10.74; 2.09); tenth (12.06; 2.74); college freshmen (13.85; 1.65). In the Nelson study, mean length of T-unit was measured as the number of morphemes per T-unit because the SALT computer program has a convention of using slashes to indicate inflectional bound morphemes, and that convention was used when entering the written language samples. However, rather than entering sentences as the students had punctuated them, Hunt's (1965) system of T-unit division was used (as described in Chapter 4).

In the Nelson (1988) study, to investigate students' use of complex strategies to combine the sentences of simple T-units, several measures were available through the use of the SALT (Miller and Chapman, 1986) program. The program was designed to count both the number of conjunctions and the types of conjunctions. It also counted relative pronouns, and provided a way to code other features. For example, secondary verbs (sv) were coded whenever writers used participles or gerunds (not infinitives) to incorporate one T-unit into another, as when a college freshman produced this sentence: *After putting [sv] in my order, I let my eyes wander in order to pass the time.*

Several indirect measures of syntactic embedding and combination were significant in the Nelson (1988) study. For example, the ANOVA for incidence of secondary verbs per 100 words showed significant grade-level differences. Like T-unit length, the use of secondary verbs increased steadily with advancing grade level. However, in this case, the fourth graders (mean = 0.18) and the seventh graders (mean = 0.28) were not significantly different from each other; neither were the tenth graders (mean = 0.88) and the college freshmen (mean = 1.01). All other paired comparisons showed significant differences.

The findings regarding secondary verbs were interesting considering Hunt's (1965) earlier observation that older students are better at using such strategies to combine clauses. The data in the Nelson (1988) study suggested that older students were using secondary verbs to express ideas more efficiently, rather than using conjunctions to conjoin ideas into compound sentences. This was supported by the fact that the oldest students actually used the fewest types of conjunctions per 100 words. The ANOVA for types of conjunctions was significant, but the only significant difference between means was between those for the seventh graders, who used the most types (mean = 2.87), and the college freshmen, who used the fewest types (mean = 1.87). Both the fourth graders (mean = 2.25) and the tenth graders (mean = 2.49) used slightly fewer types of conjunctions than the seventh graders. However, incidence rates may have been affected by the fact that seventh graders wrote significantly shorter papers (even though they were given the same amount of time to write), and the results based on incidence percentages should be interpreted with caution. It is interesting that the relationships among the means according to grade level shifted somewhat when the measure of total conjunctions per 100 words was used (instead of type). In this case, the ANOVA was significant, but the fourth graders (mean = 7.86) used the most total conjunctions, followed by the tenth graders (mean = 7.75), and the seventh graders (mean = 6.07). In this study, neither the total, nor the type, of relative pronouns per 100 words was significantly different according to grade level. However, the fourth graders did use significantly more pronouns of all types per 100 words than did students at any of the other grade levels.

There is evidence that the ability to use more complex sentences in written language is susceptible to educational intervention. Since Hunt's original work was published in 1965, a number of educators have advocated the use of exercises to give students experience in combining deep-structure syntactic units to yield new surface structures. For example, Mellon (1969) and O'Hare (1973) both reported dramatic gains in "syntactic fluency" (also called "maturity") as a result of engaging students in systematic sentence-combining activities. Similarly, Daiker, Kerek, and Morenberg (1979) found that college students who practiced sentence combining for fifteen weeks improved in syntactic complexity more than students who were taught in more traditional ways. Bereiter and Scardamalia (1982) argued that the advances associated with such training efforts resulted from students gaining conscious access to their syntactic resources, perhaps through an executive procedure (metacognition) that would allow them to search systematically for alternative syntactic structures. Awareness of the syntactic synonymy of two sentences having different surface structures but similar deep structures is a metalinguistic skill that Hakes (1980) identified as emerging by the age of 6. The ability to see the similarity of meaning between two ways of saying or writing something is important because it enables children to write with greater fluidity and flexibility. It also enables children to perform complex reading comprehension tasks such as looking back into their textbooks to find material to answer questions at the end of chapters (Nelson, 1986).

Strong (1985) reported that not all researchers have agreed that increased syntactic complexity constitutes increased maturity in writing. Furthermore, as discussed in Chapter 4, syntactic complexity varies with the type of discourse. Hillock (1986) summarized research that has shown that "different modes of discourse entail different degrees of syntactic complexity, with argument and exposition or explanation generally involving greater complexity than narrative and expressive writing" (p. 70). Christensen (1968) and Moffett (1968) both warned against the use of artificial exercises for teaching writing. Christensen also argued against the use of the T-unit as a measure of syntactic complexity and emphasized that practice in sentence combining was likely to reinforce the kind of highly embedded, nominalized style that is characteristic of government documents. Moffett argued that students' language education was better served by having them "interact" in writing activities rather than having them "imitate." Hillock's (1986) review of studies that tried to relate length of T-units to quality of writing led him to conclude that "an underdeveloped theme may be a collection of lengthy but empty T-units, while a specific and effective piece of writing may be made up of relatively short T-units" (p. 76). However, Mellon's (1969) analysis of sentence-combining effects showed that students were not combining what they formerly would have written separately; they were elaborating more on what they were writing. He concluded that "the differences between mature and immature writing are a result more of elaboration than of condensation" (p. 58).

Strong (1985) stressed that any efforts to have students focus on their syntactic choices must be related to the larger issues of intuition about prose effectiveness. "The emphasis, always, is on shaping language to match intention" (p. 72). Educational processes, Strong argued, should employ activities to encourage students to integrate syntactic issues with semantic and pragmatic issues rather than to isolate them.

STRATEGIES FOR RELATING ORTHOGRAPHY, PRONUNCIATION, AND PUNCTUATION

Chall (1983) assigned the problems of dealing with the direct connections of reading and printed text to the earliest stages of reading when children are "glued" to the words on the page. In the later stages of learning to read and write, youngsters acquire more sophisticated strategies for relating printed letters to word and spelling patterns and for determining where to break utterances into sentences and sentences into paragraphs.

One area of controversy surrounding strategies for learning to read and write is the degree to which the English language orthography (spelling) system represents the way the English language sounds. Chomsky (1980) argued that the conventional orthography and the sound structure of the English language are much closer than they seem. She indicated that many spelling errors could be avoided if writers developed the habit of looking for regularities rather than simply memorizing the spellings of words as isolated examples. Applying this principle, Henderson (1981) suggested that students be provided with lists of words that illustrate derivations. For example, *divide*, *invade*, *explode*, and *include* are all transformed into nouns with the derivational morpheme *-sion*. In contrast, *ignite*, *incubate*, and *alternate* are all transformed into nouns with the derivational morpheme *-tion* (p. 122).

Smith (1973) expressed skepticism concerning the importance of certain "lower level" activities on the processes of learning to read and write:

> Briefly, I think that the connections between written language and speech matter far less than is often assumed, especially those between phonology and orthography. The sound-spelling relationship has practically nothing to do with immediate writing and immediate reading, except to the extent that the alphabetic characters make production easier and discrimination more difficult. The alphabetic principle has rather more relevance to some mediated writing and reading systems, but the relationship is complex and by no means always advantageous. The mere fact that sound-spelling correspondences exist does not necessarily entail that they are of critical importance in either writing or reading. (pp. 129-130)

Although top-down theorists such as Smith have dominated in recent years, earlier theoreticians and empirical researchers emphasized the importance of "subsystems" in controlling the perceptual aspects of the reading process. For example, Singer (1970) attempted to identify factors that affected the speed and power of reading from third through sixth grades. His findings supported the views of subsequent researchers that higher-level processes gradually come to override lower-level processes as children advance in age and grade level. For example, at the sixth-grade level, Singer found that fewer factors accounted for more of the variance in speed of reading than at the third-grade level. The important variables at the sixth-grade level were visual verbal meaning, auditory picture meaning, speed of word perception, and spelling recognition. However, at the third-grade level, such perceptual variables as recognition of affixes and roots, and dot figure-ground perception, assumed greater importance.

Other developments in the perceptual activities associated with later stages of learning to read were studied by Gibson and Levin (1975). They examined the degree to which reading and spelling might be truly reciprocal aspects of the same process, pointing out that the rules about how to pronounce a word were not necessarily reversible from the point of view of predictability. In summary comments, Gibson and Levin emphasized that

> Excellent readers are sometimes very bad spellers. The difference between reading and spelling is analogous to that between recognition and recall, acknowledged by psychologists to be different processes. Recognition is the easier process, in that it requires less information to distinguish and identify a display produced *for* one than to produce it for oneself. A word can be recognized correctly without full information about its sp-ll-ng [sic]. (p. 335)

The National Assessment of Educational Progress (NAEP) (1980) identified a number of errors that might occur in compositions written by 17-year-olds. This was a companion project to the NAEP (1981) project on reading and literature that was discussed previously in this chapter. Errors in written language included (1) run-on sentences (e.g., a sentence having two or more independent clauses with no punctuation or conjunction in between), (2) incomplete sentences (e.g., a sentence lacking an independent clause), (3) incorrect punctuation (involving commas, dashes, quotation marks, semicolons, apostrophes, and periods), (4) incorrect capitalization, and (5) incorrect spelling. These error types were examined in the Nelson (1988) study. Results showed that the frequency of run-on and incomplete sentences decreased as grade level increased. For the students in fourth, seventh, and tenth grades and college, the means for run-on and incomplete sentences (combined) per 100 T-units were 16.2, 10.1, 5.1, and 5.5, respectively. Differences between the fourth graders and tenth graders, and between the fourth graders and college freshmen were statistically significant. The frequency of punctuation and capitalization (combined) errors per 100 T-units also decreased as grade level increased, with mean percentage rates of 54, 52, 48, and 39 obtained by the four groups, respectively. However, no differences between subject groups were statistically significant for this error type. Finally, the results showed a steady decrease in the frequency of spelling errors as grade level increased. The mean number of spelling errors per 100 words was 6.34, 3.89, 1.76, and 1.13 for the four groups, respectively. For this variable, differences between all of the means were statistically significant except for those between the tenth graders and college freshmen, suggesting that improvement in spelling tapers off during high school.

CONCLUSIONS

Reading and writing are complex processes. They are integrally related to speaking and listening, but they differ in important ways. Part of becoming a literate person during the 9-through-19 age range involves the ability to capitalize on the similarities among basic language and cognitive skills no matter what the modality of processing. Part of it also seems to come from recognizing and emphasizing critical differences associated with processing in different modalities. Both perceptual and conceptual processes are involved in reading and writing, but the developmental data suggest that conceptual processes increasingly dominate perceptual processes as youngsters proceed through adolescence. The literate person possesses not only word knowledge and world knowledge, but also commands the tools for acquiring more knowledge in the most efficient way possible.

REFERENCES

Applebee, A.N. (1978). *The child's concept of story*. Chicago: University of Chicago Press.

Applebee, A.N. (1981). *Writing in the secondary school*. Urbana, IL: National Council of Teachers of English.

Bereiter, C., and Scardamalia, M. (1982). From conversation to composition: The role of instruction in a developmental process. In R. Glaser (Ed.), *Advances in instructional psychology* (Volume 2) (pp. 1-64). Hillsdale, NJ: Erlbaum.

Bracewell, R., Scardamalia, M., and Bereiter, C. (1978, March). *The development of the audience awareness in writing*. Paper presented at the annual meeting of the American Educational Research Association, Toronto, CAN (ERIC Document Reproduction Service No. ED 154 433).

Brannon, L. (1985). Toward a theory of composition. In B.W. McClelland and T.R. Donovan (Eds.), *Perspectives on research and scholarship in composition* (pp. 6-25). New York: The Modern Language Association of America.

Britton, J., Burgess, T., Martin, N., McLeod, A., and Rosen, H. (1975). *The development of writing abilities (11–18)*. London: Macmillan Education.

Carroll, J.B., Davies, P., and Richman, B. (1971). *Word frequency book*. Boston: Houghton Mifflin.

Chall, J.S. (1983). *Stages of reading development*. New York: McGraw-Hill.

Chomsky, C. (1980). Reading, writing, and phonology. In M. Wolf, M.K. McQuillan, and E. Radwin (Eds.), *Thought and language/Language and reading* (pp. 51-71). Reprint series No. 14. Cambridge, MA: Harvard Educational Review. Reprinted from *Harvard Educational Review*, 1970, *40*, 287-309.

Christensen, F. (1968). The problem of defining a mature style. *English Journal, 57*, 572-579.

Cooper, C.R. (1976). Tonawanda Middle School's new writing program. *English Journal, 65*, 56-61.

Crowhurst, M. (1980). Syntactic complexity and teachers' quality ratings of narrations and arguments. *Research in the Teaching of English, 14*, 223-232.

Curtis, M.E. (1986, October). *Vocabulary, literacy, and schooling*. Paper presented at the Boston University Conference on Language Development, Boston, MA.

Daiker, D., Kerek, A., and Morenberg, M. (1979). *The writer's options: College sentence combining.* New York: Harper and Row.

Estes, T.H. (1982). The nature and structure of text. In A. Berger and H.A. Robinson (Eds.), *Secondary school reading: What research reveals for classroom practice* (pp. 85–96). Urbana, IL: ERIC Clearinghouse on Reading and Communication Skills.

Finn, P.J. (1977). Computer-aided description of mature word choices in writing. In C.R. Cooper and L. Odell (Eds.), *Evaluating writing: Describing, measuring, judging* (pp. 69–90). Urbana, IL: National Council of Teachers of English.

Forrest-Pressley, D.L., and Waller, T.G. (1984). *Cognition, metacognition, and reading.* New York: Springer-Verlag.

Gibson, E.J., and Levin, H. (1975). *The psychology of reading.* Cambridge, MA: MIT Press.

Goodman, K.S. (1973). Psycholinguistic universals in the reading process. In F. Smith (Ed.), *Psycholinguistics and reading* (pp. 21–27). New York: Holt, Rinehart, and Winston.

Goodman, K.S. (1976). What we know about reading. In P.D. Allen and D.J. Watson (Eds.), *Findings of research in miscue analysis: Classroom implications* (pp. 57–70). Urbana, IL: National Council of Teachers of English.

Hakes, D. (1980). *The development of metalinguistic abilities.* New York: Springer-Verlag.

Halliday, M.A.K., and Hasan, R. (1976). *Cohesion in English.* London: Longman.

Henderson, E.H. (1981). *Learning to read and spell: The child's knowledge of words.* DeKalb, IL: Northern Illinois University Press.

Hillock, G., Jr. (1986). *Research on written composition.* Urbana, IL: ERIC Clearinghouse on Reading and Communication Skills.

Hunt, K.W. (1965). *Grammatical structures written at three grade levels.* Urbana, IL: National Council of Teachers of English.

Hunt, K.W. (1970). Syntactic maturity in school children and adults. *Society for Research in Child Development Monographs,* No. 134, *35,* No. 1. Chicago, IL: The University of Chicago Press.

Isaacson, S. (1985). Assessing written language skills. In C.S. Simon (Ed.), *Communication skills and classroom success: Assessment of language-learning disabled students* (pp. 403–424). San Diego, CA: College-Hill Press.

King, M.L., and Rentel, V.M. (1981). *How children learn to write: A longitudinal study.* Columbus, OH: The Ohio State University Research Foundation.

Kucer, S.B. (1987). The cognitive base of reading and writing. In J.R. Squire (Ed.), *The dynamics of language learning* (pp. 27–51). Urbana, IL: ERIC Clearinghouse on Reading and Communication Skills.

Kucera, H., and Francis, W.N. (1967). *Computational analysis of present-day English.* Providence, RI: Brown University Press.

Loban, W.D. (1963). *The language of elementary school children.* Urbana, IL: National Council of Teachers of English.

Loban, W.D. (1976). *Language development: Kindergarten through grade twelve.* Urbana, IL: National Council of Teachers of English.

Lunsford, A.A. (1985). Cognitive studies and teaching writing. In B.W. McClelland

and T.R. Donovan (Eds.), *Perspective on research and scholarship in composition* (pp. 145-161). New York: Modern Language Association of America.

Mayer, J., Lester, N., and Pradl, G. (1983). *Writing to learn: Learning to write.* Montclair, NJ: Boynton.

Mellon, J.C. (1969). *Transformational sentence-combining: A method for enhancing the development of syntactic fluency in English composition.* Urbana, IL: National Council of Teachers of English.

Miller, J., and Chapman, R. (1986). *Systematic Analysis of Language Transcripts* [Computer program; Ann Nockerts, Programmer]. Madison, WI: Language Analysis Laboratory, Waisman Center on Mental Retardation and Human Development.

Moffett, J. (1968). *Teaching the universe of discourse.* Boston: Houghton Mifflin.

National Assessment of Educational Progress. (1980). *Writing achievement, 1969-1979: Results from the Third National Writing Assessment.* Denver, CO: National Assessment of Educational Progress. (ERIC Document Reproduction Service Nos. ED 196 042, ED 196 043, ED 196 044)

National Assessment of Educational Progress. (1981). *Reading, thinking, and writing: Results from the 1979-80 National Assessment of Reading and Literature* (Report No. 11-L-01). Denver, CO: National Assessment of Educational Progress. (ERIC Document Reproduction Service No. 209 641)

Nelson, N.W. (1986). Individual processing in classroom settings. *Topics in Language Disorders, 6*(2), 13-27.

Nelson, N.W. (1988). *Written language abilities of older children and adolescents: Computer analysis techniques and results.* Manuscript submitted for publication.

Nelson, N.W., and Friedman, K.K. (1988). *The concept of story in narratives written by older children and adolescents.* Manuscript submitted for publication.

Odell, L. (1973a). Piaget, problem-solving, and freshman composition. *College composition and communication, 24,* 36-42.

Odell, L. (1973b). Teaching reading: An alternate approach. *English Journal, 22,* 450-463.

Odell, L. (1977). Measuring change in intellectual processes as one dimension of growth in writing. In C.R. Cooper and L. Odell (Eds.), *Evaluating writing: Describing, measuring, judging* (pp. 107-132). Urbana, IL: National Council of Teachers of English.

O'Donnell, R.C., Griffin, W.J., and Norris, R.C. (1967). *Syntax of kindergarten and elementary school children: A transformational analysis.* Urbana, IL: National Council of Teachers of English.

O'Hare, F. (1973). *Sentence combining: Improving student writing without formal grammar instruction.* Urbana, IL: National Council of Teachers of English.

Page, E. (1968). The use of the computer in analyzing student essays. *International Review of Education, 14,* 253-263.

Petrosky, A.R. (1982). Reading achievement. In A. Berger and H.A. Robinson (Eds.), *Secondary school reading: What research reveals for classroom practice* (pp. 7-19). Urbana, IL: ERIC Clearinghouse on Reading and Communication Skills.

Piaget, J. (1951). *The child's conception of the world.* New York: Humanities.

Piaget, J. (1954). *The construction of reality in the child.* New York: Basic Books.

Piaget, J. (1965). *Language and thought of a child* (translated by M. Bagain). New York: Free Press.

Pike, K.L. (1964a). A linguistic contribution to composition. *College Composition and Communication, 15*, 82-88.

Pike, K.L. (1964b). Beyond the sentence. *College Composition and Communication, 15*, 129-135.

Rubin, D.L. (1982). Adapting syntax in writing to varying audiences as a function of age and social cognitive ability. *Journal of Child Language, 9*, 497-510.

Rubin, D.L. (1984). The influence of communicative context on stylistic variation in writing. In A. Pellegrini and T. Yawkey (Eds.), *The development of oral and written language in social contexts* (pp. 213-231). Norwood, NJ: Ablex.

Singer, H. (1970). A developmental model for speed of reading in grades three through six. In H. Singer and R.B. Ruddell (Eds.), *Theoretical models and processes of reading* (pp. 198-218). Newark, DE: International Reading Association.

Smith, F. (1973). *Psycholinguistics and reading*. New York: Holt, Rinehart and Winston.

Smith, S.L., Carey, R.F., Harste, J.C. (1982). The contexts of reading. In A. Berger and H.A. Robinson (Eds.), *Secondary school reading: What research reveals for classroom practice* (pp. 21-37). Urbana, IL: ERIC Clearinghouse on Reading and Communication Skills.

Sowers, S. (1981). Young writers' preference for non-narrative modes of communication. In D.H. Graves (Ed.), *A case study observing the development of primary children's composing, spelling, and motor behaviors during the writing process* (pp. 189-206). Durham, NH: University of New Hampshire.

Squire, J.R. (1964). *The responses of adolescents while reading four short stories.* Urbana, IL: National Council of Teachers of English.

Squire, J.R. (1987). Introduction to Section I: Interrelating the processes of reading and writing, composing and comprehending. In J.R. Squire (Ed.), *The dynamics of language learning: Research in reading and English* (p. 7). Urbana, IL: ERIC Clearinghouse on Reading and Communication Skills.

Strong, W. (1985). Linguistics and writing. In B.W. McClelland and T.R. Donovan (Eds.), *Perspectives on research and scholarship in composition* (pp. 68-86). New York: Modern Language Association of America.

Thorndike, E.L., and Lorge, I. (1944). *The teacher's word book of 30,000 words.* New York: Bureau of Publications, Teachers College, Columbia University.

Tierney, R.J. (1982). Learning from text. In A. Berger and H.A. Robinson (Eds.), *Secondary school reading* (pp. 97-110). Urbana, IL: ERIC Clearinghouse on Reading and Communication Skills.

Vygotsky, L.S. (1962). *Language and thought.* Cambridge, MA: MIT Press. (Original work published 1934.)

Weaver, C. (1982). Welcoming errors as signs of growth. *Language Arts, 59*, 438-444.

Westby, C. (1982). Cognitive and linguistic aspects of children's narrative development. *Communication Disorders, 7*, 1-16.

Wittrock, M.C. (1987). Constructing useful theories of teaching English from recent research on the cognitive processes of language. In J.R. Squire (Ed.), *The dynamics of language learning* (pp. 371-380). Urbana, IL: ERIC Clearinghouse on Reading and Communication Skills.

CHAPTER 6

■

COGNITION

■

ALAN G. KAMHI AND
RENÉ FRIEMOTH LEE

S ignificant changes occur in cognition during the 9-through-19 age range. Two general approaches have been taken by developmental theorists to describe those changes—the Piagetian approach, and the information processing approach. The Piagetian approach provides the most comprehensive and far-reaching account of cognitive development. Before Piagetian psychology became widely known, cognitive development was regarded by most psychologists as a rather dull and unimportant process of simply accumulating knowledge. However, Piaget's portrayal of cognitive development as a series of stages, a sequential process of acquiring fundamental, broadly generalizable cognitive structures, made the topic seem far more interesting. The information processing approach to cognitive development provides the microscopic level of analysis that fills in the details that the Piagetian approach does not provide.

This chapter covers the Piagetian theory of cognitive development and three of the more comprehensive information-processing theories. These include Case's neo-Piagetian theory, Fischer's skill theory, and Sternberg's triarchic theory. As a group, these four theories show that cognitive development during the 9-through-19 age range is marked by both quantitative and qualitative changes. The chapter is divided into three general sections. In the first section, the four theories are presented. Here the focus is on how each theorist characterizes cognitive development in preadolescents and adolescents. The second section discusses each theorist's view of the mechanisms that underlie and motivate changes in cognitive development. The final section discusses the relationship between language and cognition, and some changes that might occur in that relationship as children get older.

THEORIES OF COGNITIVE DEVELOPMENT

Piagetian Theory

The notion of developmental stages is one of the central components of Piaget's theory. Piaget identified four basic stages of cognitive development: the sensorimotor stage (from birth to two years old); the preoperational stage (two to seven years old); the stage of concrete operations (7 to 11 years old); and the stage of formal operations (older than 11) (Ginsberg and Opper, 1979). According to Piaget, progression from one stage to the next is accomplished through interaction of the learner with the environment. Under appropriate conditions, these interactions lead to a restructuring of the way the individual interprets perceptions of the world. The discussion that follows emphasizes the stages of concrete and formal operations and the transition between these two stages. For more information about Piaget's overall theory of development, and a discussion of the early stages, several excellent references are available (e.g., Ginsburg and Opper, 1979; Gross, 1985, Pulaski, 1980).

Concrete Operations

The ability to manipulate thought is the hallmark of operational thinking (Gross, 1985; Inhelder and Piaget, 1958). Concrete operations are internalized, reversible actions or rules that might best be thought of as mathematical functions (e.g., combine [+], reverse [-], order [<], and substitute [=]). These operations allow children to reason about specific types of problems. During the stage of concrete operations, children are able to reason logically and organize thoughts into coherent structures involving hierarchical and sequential relationships. Children in this stage are able to use concrete operations to solve problems of classification, conservation, and seriation.

CLASSIFICATION. The ability to classify implies particular kinds of knowledge about classes and the properties that define them (Gross, 1985). Late preoperational children can sort objects into hierarchically defined sets using properties such as shape and color. However, an understanding of class inclusion defines the entry into concrete operations. Class inclusion is knowledge about how an item's membership in one group is related to groups that are both superordinate and subordinate to the one in which it is included (Inhelder and Piaget, 1958). For example, preoperational children might be able to group beads by composition (glass or wooden), size (large and small), and color (red and yellow). If a child is shown a handful of wooden beads where six are red and four are yellow, and is then asked if there are more red beads or more wooden beads, the preoperational child would answer that there are more red beads. In contrast, the concrete operational child would realize that the subordinate class (red beads) is also part of a higher class of objects (wooden beads) and that the subordinate class can never have more items in it than the superordinate class.

CONSERVATION. Perhaps the most familiar characteristic of concrete operational thought is the child's ability to conserve properties of objects. Conservation involves the realization that certain properties of objects remain invariant despite superficial alterations in an object's appearance. The ability to conserve, like other forms of reasoning, depends upon the availability of logical operations. Conservation occurs through the coordination of three logical operations: identity, negation, and reciprocity. Identity is the understanding that a property remains the same if nothing is added or taken away. Negation is the understanding that a change in one dimension can be reversed by an equal but opposite transformation. Reciprocity is the understanding that if something is taken away from one dimension, an equal amount has been added to another dimension.

Although Piaget believed that a common group of operations underlie children's performance on conservation tasks, he also acknowledged the influence of stimulus properties on performance (Piaget, 1954). Piaget suggested that properties of objects that were more easily dissociated from children's own actions would be conserved earliest. Gross (1985) listed the varieties of properties and the relative ages at which they are conserved by children. Number is one of the earliest properties conserved; children generally conserve number by the age of six or seven. In contrast, children do not conserve volume until the age of 10 or 11.

Several studies (e.g., Gelman and Gallistel, 1978) have provided evidence for early number conservation when the number of items in sets is not very large. Other studies (e.g., Bruner, 1964) have demonstrated that children are more likely to give conservation judgments if perceptually misleading cues are kept from view. For example, Bruner reported that 45 percent of 4-year-olds and 83 percent of 5-year-olds stated that the quantity of liquid poured from one jar to another of a different size remains the same when the jars were screened from view. Although all of the 4-year-olds said they had made a mistake when they were shown the jars, most of the 5-year-olds stuck to their original claim that the quantity of liquid did not change. In contrast, only 20 percent of the 5-year-olds tested in the traditional fashion showed the concept of conservation of liquid. Although the identity operator is clearly important in making conservation judgments, improved performance on conservation tasks also reflects the gradual extinction of reasoning based upon perceptually illusory cues.

SERIATION. Children's understanding of a series is typically assessed by presenting a set of rods of unequal lengths to be ordered in a stair-step fashion. The ability to order objects in a series implies the acquisition of the logical operator for seriation. By the age of six or seven, children are able to construct a series without effort. As with conservation, however, studies have shown that children can seriate much earlier than the age of six (e.g., Koslowski, 1980). Nevertheless, as Gross (1985) pointed out, the fact that a child correctly orders items does not necessarily imply that an operative understanding of seriation is present.

SUMMARY. During the concrete operational stage, children acquire a set of reversible operations (rules) that govern their thought. The action schemes that were overt during the preoperational period have become internalized mental schemes. During this stage, children develop more facility in using the most powerful symbolic code, language, to think about the world and to solve various kinds of experimental and real-life problems.

Formal Operations

Although the intellectual abilities of the concrete operational child are quite powerful, those abilities are limited to reasoning about tangible, concrete objects that exist in the real world. The problem-solving ability that characterizes the concrete stage of thought is often unsystematic and incomplete because the child does not have a complete set of logical operations. For example, concrete operational thinkers can make conservation judgments given superficial changes in appearance. However, when asked to reason about more abstract relationships (e.g., why some objects float and others sink), their responses are closely tied to the physical world. For example, they may explain that things float because they are light and others sink because they are heavy. Concrete operational children also have difficulty when confronted with contradictions in their arguments. They are unable to understand that alternative conclusions based on observations not present in their experience are also possible. Children in this stage do not consider all possible outcomes or alternatives in solving problems (cf. Flavell, 1982; Ginsburg and Opper, 1979; Gross, 1985).

The ability to reason sytematically and logically about abstract ideas that may have no basis in reality is the hallmark of formal operational thought (Inhelder and Piaget, 1958; Piaget, 1972). Piaget used the term "hypothetico-deductive thinking" to describe the mental operations of adolescents and adults. Hypothetico-deductive thinking refers to the ability to evaluate systematically all of the logical possibilities in a problem. Formal operational thought is also characterized as "reflective-abstractive." By this Piaget meant that the person in formal operations can think about thinking, and operate on ideas as well as on tangible objects and events.

Gross (1985) provided an excellent example of how formal operational thought differs from concrete operational thought. In his example, children were asked to determine if there was a relationship between the type of drug people were taking and whether or not they got better. Taking the drug can be represented by the symbol D, and not taking the drug by the symbol D'; getting better can be represented by B, and not getting better by B'. Some people who take the drug get better (BD), and some people who take the drug do not (B'D); some people who do not take the drug get better (BD'), and some people who do not take the drug do not get better (B'D'). A concrete operational child realizes these four possibile outcomes, but does not consider operating on the products of these operations. That is, all four conditions might occur (BD + B'D + BD' + B'D'), or three out of four might occur, and so forth. There are exactly 16 possible outcomes to the problem. An understanding of these 16 outcomes implies the existence of a complete combinatorial scheme.

One could substitute the logical symbols (p and q) for the values B and D and relate these values to logical connectors that symbolize logical propositions such as affirmation ($p * q$), disjunction ($p \lor q$), implication ($p \rightarrow q$), and so forth (see Gross, 1985). These symbols could then be used to symbolize the conditions represented by the 16 combinations of B and D. This example should illustrate how reasoning in the formal operational stage takes on the form of propositional logic rather than the mathematical quality that characterized operations during the concrete operational period. The individual whose thought is propositionally based is freed from the concrete and contextual aspects of problems. Propositional thought does not rely on experiential evidence. Rather, the accuracy of a particular proposition is determined logically from truth values of other propositions to which it bears a formal, logical relationship (Neimark, 1975).

In the discussion that follows, various concepts requiring formal operational thinking are addressed. These concepts include conservation of volume, combinatorial operations and isolation of variables, hypothetical thought, and proportion, probability, and correlation.

CONSERVATION OF VOLUME. The ability to conserve does not develop all at once. Concrete operational children can conserve liquid, number, and substance, but the ability to conserve volume and area do not emerge until the formal operational stage. The asymmetry in the development of conservation is thought to be partly a function of the individual's ability to dissociate the object from its attributes (Pinard and Chasse, 1977). Because volume is an intrinsic part of any object, it is less dissociable and, therefore, conserved much later in development.

Conservation of volume typically is assessed by placing two balls of plasticene in two identical beakers, each filled with equal quantities of liquid. The subject sees that the balls displace an equal volume of liquid in both beakers. One ball is then changed into the shape of a sausage. The question is whether the subject recognizes that both the ball and the sausage continue to displace equal volumes of water. Elkind (1962) found that in a sample of college students, 74 percent of the boys and 58 percent of the girls conserved exterior volume (i.e., how much water an object displaces when it is submerged). Conservation of interior volume (how much a container holds) was achieved a year or two earlier. However, Pinard and Chasse (1977) found that only 36 percent of their adult subjects conserved volume. Thus, it appears that even older adolescents and adults have difficulty realizing volume changes as a function of alterations in the surface structure of an object.

COMBINATORIAL OPERATIONS AND ISOLATION OF VARIABLES. A variety of tasks have been used to examine adolescents' ability to deduce sets of possible orderings, derive complete combinatorial schemes, and use deductive reasoning to solve problems.

The "pendulum problem" is one of Piaget's best known tasks of formal operational thinking. Subjects are given a number of weights that can be tied to a long string to make a pendulum. They are allowed to vary the length of the string, the amount of weight attached to it, and the height of release. The task is to determine which of these factors, alone or in combination, affects the speed of the pendulum. Two factors can be isolated: the length of the string and the weight of the pendulum. There are four possible combinations of length and weight that will produce one of two outcomes: the pendulum will either swing faster or slower. The set of possible combinations can be delineated in a truth table that considers all of the possible outcomes and the truth value of the proposition. Experiments can then be devised to determine the solution to the problem. Formal operational thinkers, who are capable of this planned and systematic reasoning, soon discover that the critical factor is the length of the string: the shorter the string, the faster the pendulum swings.

The "colorless liquid problem" is another popular task for assessing formal operational thinking. In this task, the subject is presented with four similar flasks, numbered 1, 2, 3, and 4. Each flask contains a clear liquid. The subject is then given another flask, also containing a clear liquid, and a dropper. The subject is told that the liquid in the fifth flask is an indicator and, when mixed with one or more of the other liquids, will produce a yellow color. The problem is to produce the yellow color.

Performance on this task is evaluated on two criteria: whether or not the yellow color is produced, and how the subject goes about doing it (Inhelder and Piaget, 1958). Three stages of performance have been identified. Preoperational children simply mix two elements at a time in a relatively random fashion and render an illogical explanation for the results. Concrete operational children approach the task systematically to the point of combining each liquid with the indicator, but do not consider combinations of two flasks with the indicator. Formal operational youngsters, in this case age 13 or older, do not begin to pour immediately. Instead, they pause, consider the alternatives, and then map out a problem-solving plan. They consider all possible alternatives, and often label the purposes of each liquid; for example, "This is the substance that keeps it from coloring," or "This must be water because it didn't do anything." Also, they often ask for a pencil to keep track of what they are doing. Thus, formal operational youngsters are not influenced by the perceptual aspects of this task. They also are not satisfied with an accidental demonstration that produces the desired color. Because they reason deductively, they are interested in all possible procedures for the problem.

The last task to be discussed here is called "the possibilities of life on other planets problem." Subjects are asked to list all of the possible combinations of animal life that might be found on a newly discovered planet if all life forms could be categorized as either vertebrates or invertebrates and terrestrial or aquatic. Elkind, Barocas, and Rosenthal (1968) found that about half (52 percent) of the 14-year-olds generated 15 of these combinations, usually omitting the zero combination of no life forms. Martorano (1977) reported that by tenth grade (the age of 15), 70 percent of her adolescent subjects succeeded in this task.

By the age of 13 to 15, adolescents are fairly adept at generating combinatorial schemes and using that set of possibilities to isolate variables to solve problems. Gross (1985) suggested, however, that their reasoning at this age may be limited to an intuitive understanding of the principles of combination. When adolescents are asked to evaluate propositions and reason about specific logical relationships, they perform more poorly. Although they may understand the basic principles necessary to solve a problem, they often have difficulty recognizing the similarities in propositional statements that are based on the same principles.

HYPOTHETICAL REASONING. The stage of formal operations is marked by the adololescent's ability to reason hypothetically and to think creatively. This is evidenced with the "third-eye problem." Shaffer (1985) presented the following hypothetical situation to 9- and 11-year-olds:

Suppose you were given a third eye and you could choose to place this eye anywhere on your body. Draw a picture to show where you would place your "extra" eye, and then tell me why you would put it there.

Shaffer found that all of the 9-year-olds placed the third eye on the forehead between their two natural eyes. These children all used their concrete experiences to complete the assignment: eyes are found somewhere around the middle of the face in all people. In contrast, the older, formal operational children gave a wide variety of responses that were not dependent on what they had seen previously. These youngsters also provided imaginative rationales for placing the extra eye in unique locations. For example, one child put the eye in the palm of his hand so he could see around corners and see what kind of cookie he would get out of the cookie jar. Another child drew the eye in his mouth so he could see what he was eating. Another difference between the concrete and formal operational children was in their appreciation of the task. The younger children found it silly and uninteresting, or as one child remarked, "This is stupid. Nobody has three eyes." The older children, however, enjoyed the task to the extent of pestering their teacher during the remainder of the school year for more "fun art assignments" like the eye problem.

PROPORTION, PROBABILITY, AND CORRELATION. Several formal operational problems involve setting up ratios and appreciating proportional relationships. For example, to predict the direction that a balance beam will tilt, it is necessary to derive the ratio between units of weight and units of distance relative to the fulcrum. Concrete operational children are physically able to restore the balance beam to a state of equilibrium, but they are not able to predict how the beam will operate. The formal operational child, in contrast, is able to construct a ratio between weight and distance. For example, this child can reason that two units of weight are equal to one unit of distance. By about age 15, most adolescents can solve problems concerned with ratios and proportionality (Lunzer and Pumfrey, 1966; Pumfrey, 1968; Wavering, 1984). Martorano (1977) found that these kinds of problems were among the more difficult formal operational problems.

Another type of knowledge that develops late in the formal operational period is probability and chance. Piaget and Inhelder (1975) studied children's knowledge of chance by having them predict the outcome of purely random events, such as the position of a set of black and white marbles after they had been shaken up and come to rest in a box. On this task, someone who truly understands chance would conclude that no predictions can be made about where the marbles will end up. Green (1978) found that formal operational judgments about chance and probability occur in most adolescents by the age of 16.

Knowledge of correlated events has been evaluated by asking children to interpret the significance of the frequencies with which two properties covary with one another. In one problem (e.g., Gross, 1985), children are told that of 100 people, 47 have blond hair (+A) and blue eyes (+B), 38 have dark hair (−A) and brown eyes (−B), 15 have dark hair (−A) and blue eyes (+B), and none have blond hair (+A) and brown (−B) eyes. A matrix of possible events is constructed, and by summing the diagonals, the strength of the relationships are deduced. Martorano (1977) found that correlations were one of the easier formal operational problems to solve: 70 percent of the 10-year-olds and 95 percent of the 12-year-olds solved these problems correctly.

OPPOSING EVIDENCE. Questions have been raised about some of the fundamental aspects of Piaget's theory, including the validity of the proposed stages, his clinical method used to collect data, and the existence of general cognitive structures (e.g., Broughton, 1984). The following discussion will be limited to possible shortcomings of Piaget's theory in relation to formal operations.

Commons, Richards, and Armon (1984) noted that Piaget's model of adolescent thought has been subject to two principle types of criticism. First, it has been argued (e.g., Brainerd, 1978) that the model lacks parsimony in that it proposes a logical competency that is too extensive and complex. Indeed, the logical competency proposed in adolescents is often not found. Consequently, a less elaborate model would be sufficient to explain adolescent thought. The second frequent criticism is that the model of formal operations is too limited to capture the richness of adolescent and adult thought. Types of thinking exist, such as dialectical thought (i.e., reasoning that juxtaposes contradictory ideas and attempts to resolve their conflict), that do not have the logical structure of formal operations or of lower stages (Broughton, 1984). Several additional questions have been raised concerning Piaget's description of formal operational thought.

Can concrete operational children solve formal operational problems? There is evidence suggesting that concrete operational children are capable of formal operational thought. For example, instructing children to list all possible combinations in the colorless liquid problem or the possibilities of life on other planets problem leads to improved performance on these tasks (Gross, 1985). Also, Siegler (1984) reported that 10- and 11-year-old concrete operational children could learn to solve formal operational problems if certain scientific concepts were defined and the children were encouraged to think logically and systematically about the problems. In light of these findings, Gardner (1978) suggested that concrete operational children simply may need assistance, rather than a total reorientation in thinking, to solve formal operational problems.

Does everyone reach the stage of formal operations? Several investigators have found that adolescents are much slower to acquire formal operations than Piaget had believed. Indeed, some studies (Grinder, 1975; Neimark, 1975, 1979) found that only 30 to 40 percent of adolescents and adults exhibit formal operations. Formal operations are also virtually absent in nonliterate cultures (Berry and Dasen, 1974; Neimark, 1975). Some people might not attain formal operational thought because they simply do not have the intellectual capacity to move from concrete to formal operations. For example, individuals who score below average on standardized intelligence tests rarely reason at the formal level (Inhelder, 1966; Jackson, 1965). It should also be noted that Piagetian problems are biased in favor of students who have taken formal science and mathemetics courses: many of the problems are taken from chemistry, physics, and mathematics. Therefore, students who have taken these kinds of courses have an advantage over those who have not in solving formal operational problems.

One possibility raised by Shaffer (1985) is that nearly all adults are capable of formal operations but will exhibit these operations only on problems of interest to them. Flavell (1977) gave the example of a competent auto mechanic who reasons hypothetically when troubleshooting an engine problem but reverts to a more concrete level when reasoning about other problems. The success of teaching individuals to reason formally (see Siegler, 1984) suggests that one should not underestimate the cognitive capabilities of adolescents and adults who do not seem to reason at the formal level.

Are there higher stages of intellectual development? Some researchers have suggested that formal operational thinking is not the most mature form of reasoning (Commons et al., 1984). Arlin (1975), for example, called formal operations a "problem solving" stage that describes the way bright adolescents and adults think about problems that someone else presents to them. She suggested, however, that truly creative and insightful thinkers, such as Einstein, Aristotle, and Piaget himself, operate on a higher plane that enables them to rethink and reorganize existing knowledge and then ask important questions or define totally new problems. Arlin referred to this higher intellectual ability as a "problem finding stage."

Commons, Richards, and Kuhn (1982) suggested that there may be two levels of intellectual functioning beyond Piaget's formal operations. The first level, "systematic reasoning," refers to the ability to combine sets of formal operations into higher-order structures or systems. The next level, "metasystematic reasoning," is the ability to operate on and organize general systems into supersystems. Commons and colleagues (1982) asked undergraduate and graduate students to indicate how four story problems were similar or dissimilar to one another. Although the vast majority of students could solve Piagetian problems of formal operations, fewer than 20 percent of the undergraduates organized the stories into abstract systems or supersystems. In contrast, nearly 70 percent of the graduate students showed some evidence of systematic and metasystematic reasoning. It is possible, however, as Shaffer (1985) pointed out, that these cognitive abilities may represent very complex formal operations rather than distinct higher stages of intellect that are qualitatively different from formal reasoning.

SUMMARY. The stage of formal operational thought is characterized by the ability to reason systematically and logically about abstract ideas that are far-removed from the physical world. Although questions have been raised about the universal characteristics of formal operational thought and the age at which youngsters reach this stage, most developmental psychologists would agree that adolescents reason differently than preadolescents.

Information Processing Theories

As Gross (1985) noted, "information-processing theory is concerned with how information is taken into the organism, interpreted, represented, transformed, and acted upon" (p. 19). In the discussion that follows, three of the more fully developed information-processing approaches to cognitive development and problem solving are reviewed. These include Case's neo-Piagetian theory, Fischer's skill theory, and Sternberg's triarchic theory.

Neo-Piagetian Theory

In response to some of the criticisms of Piaget's theory, several neo-Piagetian positions have emerged. Each of these positions postulates an executive system that governs the way individuals use information; each position also specifies age-related restrictions on processing capacity (Case, 1984, 1985; Pascual-Leone, 1980). For Case (1985), the major developmental change is that the child becomes able to assemble executive control structures for solving different classes of problems. An executive control structure is defined as a mental blueprint or plan for solving a class of problems. Executive control structures have at least three components: (1) a representation of the problem situation; (2) a representation of the problem objectives; and (3) a representation of the problem strategy. In this way, control structures for solving dissimilar problems are similar in their underlying form.

DEVELOPMENTAL STAGES. Like Piaget, Case (1985) proposed four major stages of cognitive development. Case's stages correspond to the following age ranges: birth to 18 months; 18 months to 5 years; 5 to 11 years; and 11 to 18 years. The period of middle childhood (the third stage) is marked by the use of dimensional thought. Dimensional thought is characterized by the ability to focus on dimensions such as weight and distance to solve problems such as the balance-beam task. Between five and seven years of age, children can focus on a variety of dimensions, but they can only focus on one dimension at a time. However, at around the age of seven, they begin to focus on a second dimension. On the balance beam task, this is seen when an equal number of weights is placed on each side of the fulcrum. Instead of predicting that the beam will balance, they compute the distance of each weight from the fulcrum. Then they predict that the weight that is further away from the fulcrum will go down. The ability to focus on two dimensions, however, does not always lead to success, because weight and distance are never directly related to one another. When given a problem in which there is a difference in both weight and distance, children usually choose weight as the basis for prediction. However, between 9 and 11 years of age, children realize this problem and no longer base their decisions entirely on weight (Siegler, 1976). Case (1985) suggested that children use an addition or subtraction strategy to solve the problems. With the addition strategy, children simply add the number of weight and distance units on each side, and pick the one with the greater total value as the one that will go down. Such a strategy marks the pinnacle of dimensional thought.

Adolescence is characterized by the emergence of vectorial operations and abstract systems of thought. The major operations that adolescents demonstrate include bi-dimensional classification, seriation, compensation, and combination, as well as ratio, analogy, and trait abstraction. A vectorial operation is a second-order dimensional operation. Youngsters who compare the magnitude of one quantitative dimension with that of a second are said to be executing a second-order or abstract dimensional operation.

Beginning at around the age of nine, children are no longer limited to focusing separately on concrete dimensions, such as distance and weight in the balance-beam problem. Instead, they are now able to focus on a more abstract dimension: the vector that results from the opposition of the two concrete dimensions. In the balance-beam problem, the vectorial operation is ratio. In order to balance the beam, the individual must focus on the second-order dimension (ratio) that remains constant, while two lower-order dimensions (weight and distance) change. In the same vein, to understand an analogy, the individual must recognize a higher-order vector along which two lower-order dimensions may be compared ($A : B :: C : D$). (See Chapter 7.)

Case (1985) proposed four substages of cognitive development during the preadolescent and adolescent years. Substage 0, ages 9 to 11, marks the end of the dimensional period of thought and the beginning of vectorial operations. An example of a problem that youngsters can solve with isolated vectorial operations is as follows: "For two dollars you get eight francs. How many francs will you get for one dollar?" However, by the ages of 11 to 13, youngsters can begin to coordinate vectorial operations. For example, faced with a problem where two weights on the left of the balance beam are opposed by one weight on the right, while two distance pegs on the left are opposed by four distance pegs on the right, they no longer simply count pegs. Instead, they note that there are twice as many weights on the left (two for one) and that there are twice as many distance pegs on the right (two for one). Therefore, they conclude that the two sides will balance.

Youngsters of the ages of 11 to 13 can use the notion of ratio only when the operation has a single and very simple focus, as was the case in the previous example. By the ages of 13 to 15, however, adolescents are capable of taking a second division operation into account. One of the problems they can solve at this stage is what will happen when the distances on the two sides of the balance beam are five and two, and the weights are two and one. These adolescents compare the unit ratio of the weights (2 : 1) with the unit ratio of the distances ($2\frac{1}{2}$: 1), and pick the larger ratio as the more potent one.

In the final substage, the ages of 15 to 18, the particular set of operations that were used to adjust one of the dimensions can now be executed for the second dimension as well. Adolescents now can deal with problems in which neither quantity is stated in unit form. For a problem involving seven weights and three weights, at distances of two and five units, they may reason that two distance pegs and five distance pegs are the same as one for two and one-half, while three weights and seven weights are the same as one for two and one-third. Thus, the weight factor should predominate. This type of thinking has truly abstract quality, because neither of the entities being compared has any direct visual counterpart in the physical world (Case, 1985).

SUMMARY. According to Case's (1985) neo-Piagetian theory, the major change that occurs in development is in the child's ability to assemble executive control structures for solving different types of problems. Preadolescence is marked by the use of increasingly complex dimensional operations, while adolescence is marked by the use of increasingly complex and abstract operations.

Skill Theory

Fischer and his colleagues have been the major proponents of skill theory (Fischer, 1980; Fischer and Corrigan, 1981; Fischer and Pipp, 1984). Skill theory postulates a series of 10 developmental levels that occur in 3 cycles or tiers. The tiers are sensorimotor, representational, and abstract. Sensorimotor actions eventually produce representations, which in turn produce abstractions. Sensorimotor actions involve specific actions performed on objects or directed toward people. Representations designate concrete characteristics of particular objects, people, or events, whereas abstractions designate general, intangible characteristics of broad categories of objects, people, or events. A representation for subtraction, for example, is a specific arithmetic problem. In contrast, an abstraction for subtraction would involve a general definition of the operation that could be applied to all of the specific arithmetic problems. Sensorimotor actions occur from birth to the age of four or five. Representations occur from the age of 4 or 5 to the age of 10 or 12. Abstract mappings occur after the age of 14 to 16, abstract systems after 18 to 20, and systems of abstract systems after about age 24.

Within each tier there are four successive developmental levels, each involving a new type of skill organization. At the first level, the individual can control variations in only one set. Sets can involve actions, representations, or abstractions, depending on the tier of development. At the second level, the individual can combine several sets to produce a new structure. Termed a "mapping," this structure defines a simple relation between two or more sets. The third level involves the integration of several mappings to produce a system. Finally, the individual combines several systems at the fourth level to produce a system of systems. Structures formed at the fourth level represent a new building block and become a new set at the first level of the next tier. Thus, the fourth level of one tier is the first level of the next tier, and the cycle starts over again.

Consider some differences between the representation and abstraction tiers. A child in the third level of representations (the ages of six to eight) might make two dolls simultaneously carry out two intersecting social roles. One doll might be both the doctor and father to the other doll, who is both his patient and daughter. Fischer and Pipp (1984) gave the example of a 7-year-old saying to her grandmother, "I get it! You're my grandmother, and you're mommy's mother too!" By the age of 10, children are able to coordinate two or more systems to produce a system of systems, which is a single abstraction. Fischer and Pipp gave the example of a 12-year-old who coordinated her system for understanding her mother's and father's parental and spouse roles (mother/wife and father/husband) with her system for understanding the parental and spouse roles of her best friend's mother and father. The result was an abstraction for the family as a system of parental and spouse roles. A more detailed discussion of the abstract tier follows.

THE DEVELOPMENT OF ABSTRACTIONS. At around the age of 10 or 11, preadolescents begin to demonstrate Level 7 single abstractions, such as the arithmetic concepts of addition or subtraction or the interactional concepts of intention or responsibility (Fischer, Hand, and Russell, 1984). For example, the concrete actions and intentions of two individuals are not merely compared but are integrated under a single abstraction, such as "taking responsibility means a person shows she really cares about the effects her actions have on other people" (p. 49).

Single abstractions are the most primitive form of abstraction. With single abstractions, preadolescents have difficulty differentiating two similar abstract concepts, such as liberal and radical in politics, or addition and multiplication in mathematics. Fischer and colleagues (1984) gave the example of preadolescents (the ages of 10 to 11) saying that "addition and multiplication are the same thing; both combine numbers to make a bigger number" (p. 51).

According to Fischer and colleagues (1984), it is not until about the age of 14 or 15 that adolescents can coordinate two or more abstractions in a single skill. This is referred to as a Level 8 abstract mapping. By this age, adolescents can compare addition and multiplication. One student exlained the difference in the following way: "Addition and multiplication are similar operations. Both combine numbers to produce a larger number, but in different ways: by single units in addition and by groups of numbers in multiplication" (p. 50). Regarding intention and responsibility, adolescents are now able to relate the two concepts to explain what it is about taking responsibility that absolves one person from having shown a negative intention toward another person. Fischer and colleagues (1984) acknowledged that there has been relatively little research focusing on this developmental change. As discussed previously in relation to Piaget's and Case's work, however, several studies have shown that changes in performance on cognitive tasks do occur during this period (Case, 1985; Martorano, 1977; Neimark, 1975).

At about age 18 or 19, adolescents start to coordinate several aspects of two or more abstractions. This ability is referred to as Level 9 abstract systems. Adolescents are now able to understand the subtleties and complexities of relations between abstractions. They are also able to understand the relations between dissimilar arithmetic operations, such as division and addition. Similarly, older adolescents are able to consider several types of intention and responsibility. For example, in the context of harm inflicted on another person, they are able to consider two types of intention (deceit and unintentional harm) and two types of responsibility (dealing with the flaw in a harmful person's character and being concerned for the person harmed). The two types of intention require that one take different types of responsibility (Fischer et al., 1984).

One final level of development is postulated by skill theory. According to Fischer and colleagues (1984), individuals can begin to integrate abstract systems to form Level 10 general principles at around the age of 25. General principles are involved in many general ideologies (Broughton, 1978) and scientific theories. With the attainment of Level 10 general principles, individuals are able to construct a fully mature organization of identity, morality, or political ideology.

DEVELOPMENTAL ASYNCHRONIES. The levels posited by Fischer's skill theory are different than the stages proposed by Piaget or Case. Stage theorists tend to assume that when a particular stage is reached, most of the skills exist at that level. In contrast, skill theory assumes that the optimal level merely sets the upper limit on skills. Below that limit, behavior can vary widely across levels. The most spontaneous behavior often involves skills below a person's optimal level, especially for older children and adults (Fischer et al., 1984).

Another major difference between skill theory and stage theory concerns the way optimal-level capacity is extended to different content domains. For example, with stage theory, once concrete operations emerge, they are automatically applied to any content. Although the child might not always exhibit concrete operational thought, this reflects a performance problem rather than a competence or structural deficit. In contrast, with skill theory, when the person develops a new optimal level, the capacity to perform at the new level is present; however, competencies at that level are not present until particular skills are built; the person must work to develop skills in specific content domains.

Skill theory attempts to describe as well as to explain individual differences in cognitive abilities. Whereas most stage theorists assume that individuals pass through the same stages of development, skill theory postulates that when specific skills are considered, different people follow different developmental paths. In other words, the steps an individual takes to master a domain vary from one person to another. These differences are attributed to variations in the environment and in the cognitive abilities individuals bring to a particular task. For example, people differ widely in their verbal, spatial, and mathematical skills. The similarities across children of the same cognitive levels are seen when skills are analyzed globally.

There is a growing body of evidence indicating that experiences during adolescence lead to more unevenness in development than occurs at younger ages (Flavell, 1970; Neimark, 1975). During the elementary-school years, youngsters are more likely to be exposed to the same kinds of subject matter. At the secondary level, however, there is much more diversity in the courses that students can take. For example, students can select courses in physics, chemistry, geometry, calculus, foreign languages, and psychology. A student with experience in literature might show advanced performance in criticism and text analysis, but show average performance in physics or algebra. Variations in prior experience, personal preferences, and task difficulty all contribute to the unevenness of adolescent development.

Skill theory also postulates about individual differences in intelligence (Fischer and Pipp, 1984). According to skill theory, variations in intelligence stem from differences in optimal level and skill acquisition. High intelligence is associated with the ability to build more complex, flexible, and generalizable skills at each optimal level. An exceptionally bright child will initially reach each optimal level at approximately the same age as an average child. Once the new level has emerged, however, the bright child will quickly construct a wide range of skills at that level, whereas an average child will take much longer to extend that new capacity to other content domains. Skill theory also postulates that large individual differences are best seen under formal testing conditions. When individuals are tested under optimal performance conditions, the discrepancies in optimal levels virtually disappear.

PERFORMING AT OPTIMAL LEVELS. Fischer and colleagues (1984) found that when people have difficulty performing a task, they often resort to a "fallback" strategy in which they use a low-level skill to perform the task. Fallback strategies are very common in adolescent and adult behavior, especially in spontaneous settings. The frequent use of fallback strategies means that adolescents and adults do not do their best in many situations. Siegal (1975) suggested that the use of fallback strategies might be caused by the lack of a strong incentive to do the hard work necessary to achieve a high level of abstraction. Fischer and colleagues (1984) speculated that as adolescents move up the abstract tier, they become less and less likely to demonstrate optimal-level performance in their spontaneous behavior.

SUMMARY. The notion that cognitive development is best viewed as the acquisition of particular skills has behavioristic undertones. As conceptualized by Fischer and colleagues (1984), however, skill theory attempts to account for broadly based qualitative changes in cognitive development as well quantitative differences in particular skills that exist within a particular development level. Skill theory differs from Piagetian and neo-Piagetian stage theories in its formal recognition of the different paths children follow in acquiring specific skills.

Triarchic Theory

The last theory of cognitive development to be discussed was developed by Sternberg over the last 10 years or so. Triarchic theory attempts to account for intellectual development in terms of changes in the availability, accessibility, and ease of execution of different kinds of information-processing components. Unlike the theories discussed so far, triarchic theory does not specify precise developmental levels or stages. The attractiveness of the theory lies in its description of what develops and the mechanisms that underlie developmental changes.

Sternberg (1985) described intelligence as "mental activity directed toward purposive adaptation to, and selection and shaping of, real-world environments relevant to one's life" (p. 44). His triarchic theory designated the information-processing component as the basic unit of analysis. In fact, for several years, the theory was referred to as a componential theory of intelligence (e.g., Sternberg, 1984). A component was defined as an elementary information process that operates on internal representations of objects or symbols (Sternberg, 1985). Each component has three important properties: duration, difficulty (the probability of being excecuted incorrectly), and probability of execution.

There are three kinds of components, each serving different functions: metacomponents, performance components, and knowledge-acquisition components. Metacomponents are higher-order executive processes used in planning, monitoring, and decision making; performance components are processes used in performing a task; and knowledge-acquisition components are processes used in learning new information.

METACOMPONENTS. Sternberg (1985) identified seven metacomponents:

1. Recognizing what the problem is which needs to be solved
2. Selecting the components that actually execute the task
3. Selecting the mental representations or organization on which the components or strategy can operate
4. Selecting a strategy for combining lower-order components into a working algorithm for problem solving
5. Deciding how to allocate attentional resources
6. Monitoring what one has done, what one is doing, and what one still needs to do in problem solving
7. Being sensitive to external feedback

PERFORMANCE COMPONENTS. Although the number of possible performance components is quite large, these components tend to organize themselves into stages of task solution that are fairly general across different tasks. These stages include encoding of stimuli, combination of, or comparison between, stimuli, and response. Encoding components are concerned with initial perception and storage of new information. Quantitative and qualitative changes in encoding are a major source of intellectual development. With increasing age, encoding tends to be more exhaustive (Brown and DeLoache, 1978), is executed more slowly, and operates on different representations of information (Sternberg and Rifkin, 1979).

Combination and comparison components are involved in putting together or comparing information. The importance of these components is much more variable than encoding components. For example, solving analogies (see Chapter 7) would involve these components, but other problems might not. The response component is dependent upon the

metacomponents. Sternberg (1985) contended that metacomponential processes are more fundamental sources of individual differences than performance components.

KNOWLEDGE-ACQUISITION COMPONENTS. Knowledge-acquisition components are processes used in gaining new knowledge. Sternberg proposed
that three components are involved in the acquisition of declarative and
procedural knowledge across virtually all domains of knowledge: (1) selective
encoding; (2) selective combination; and (3) selective comparison. Selective encoding involves differentiating between relevant and irrelevant information. Selective combination involves combining information that is
selectively encoded to form an integrated whole. Selective comparison involves
relating newly acquired or retrieved information to previously acquired information or knowledge.

LEVEL OF GENERALITY. Sternberg classified components into three levels
of generality: general, class, and specific. General components, such as
encoding, are required to perform all tasks. Class components are required
to perform a representative subset of tasks within a particular task domain.
Inference is an example of a class component in that it is required for the
solution of certain kinds of induction problems, but is not required for all
problems. Specific components are required to perform single tasks within
a task domain. Tasks necessarily differ in the number and type of components
they require for completion.

SUMMARY. Sternberg's triarchic theory of cognitive development
describes the factors or components that are involved in intelligent thinking. Metacomponents, knowledge-acquisition components, and performance
components are the three essential elements of intelligence. Sternberg's theory
is unique in the role it gives to metacomponents as crucial mechanisms in
cognitive development.

MECHANISMS OF CHANGE IN COGNITIVE DEVELOPMENT

In the first section of this chapter, four different but overlapping views
of cognitive development for the 9-through-19 age range were presented:
Piaget's theory, Case's neo-Piagetian theory, Fischer's skill theory, and Sternberg's triarchic theory. In this second section, the discussion focuses on how
each of the four developmental theorists conceptualize the mechanisms
underlying cognitive development. This discussion is particularly relevant
to professionals who might be attempting to improve youngsters' cognitive
performance. The ability to translate proposed mechanisms of change into

practical educational and clinical programs is the best empirical test of the viability of the mechanism. In general, structural-based, stage theories, such as Piaget's, must invoke very powerful mechanisms of change to account for the far-reaching changes that occur at certain points in development. In contrast, theories that conceptualize development in terms of specific skill acquisitions need invoke less powerful mechanisms to account for developmental change. The following discussion considers how Piaget, Case, Fischer, and Sternberg explain developmental change.

Piagetian Approach to Mechanisms of Change

Piaget (1970) believed that change in intellectual structures occurs as a consequence of two complementary processes: adaptation and organization. The process of adaptation refers to the interaction between the organism and the environment. He contended that biological maturation of the brain and nervous system interacted with the child's experiences to promote cognitive development.

Adaptation is the interplay between the two processes of assimilation and accommodation, and adaptation occurs when there is an equilibrium between assimilatory and accommodative processes. Equilibrium is viewed as a necessary condition toward which the organism constantly strives. According to Piaget (1970), the tendency to seek equilibrium is what produces or motivates development. The process of alternating states of stability (equilibrium) followed by instability (disequilibrium) produces a spiral of ever higher levels of cognitive development.

One problem with Piaget's theory is that it does not clearly indicate how children progress from one stage of cognitive development to another. Presumably, children are always assimilating new experiences, accommodating those experiences, and reorganizing their cognitive schemata into increasingly complex mental structures (Shaffer, 1985). It is unclear what maturational changes must occur or what kinds of experiences a child must have in order to move from one stage to the next. Another problem with Piaget's theory is that concepts of conservation have been found to be teachable when there was no apparent cognitive disequilibrium (see Case, 1985).

There are other problems with the notion of equilibration as the mechanism of change. Brainerd (1978), for example, pointed out that equilibration would predict that development should be characterized by rapid and abrupt changes in skill levels, followed by periods of consolidation or no change. There is evidence, however, (e.g., Flavell, 1982) that individual development is better characterized as a continuous and gradual acquisition of concepts and skills.

Finally, Case and other neo-Piagetians (e.g., Pascual-Leone, 1970) found a paradox in Piaget's conceptualization of equilibration. They questioned how new intellectual structures could develop from what are described as basically rigid, permanent, and habitual schemes. In other words, how does the child come to conceptualize some higher level of thought while operating at some lower level?

Neo-Piagetian Approach to Mechanisms of Change

According to Case (1985), the process of stage transition involves two components. The first is the hierarchical integration of two existing structures that previously served a different purpose. The second is the hierarchical subordination of one of these structures to the other. Recall that Case proposed four major stage boundaries. Those boundaries occur at 4 months, 20 months, 5 years, and 11 years of age. At each of those points in time, children are thought to integrate (hierarchically) a variety of their existing control structures into new structures that are qualitatively different from each of their component parts. The operation or strategy of one structure often serves as the means towards the attainment of an end that is specified by the other higher-level structure. For example, ratio computation becomes a means for resolving dimensional conflicts in children around the age of 11.

Case proposed that children come equipped with four general regulatory processes that make them predisposed to and capable of hierarchical integration and subordination. These processes are problem solving, exploration, imitation, and mutual (social) regulation. Although these processes appear to be quite different on the surface, they all involve a sequence of basic subprocesses that entail five basic components: (1) goal setting; (2) experimenting with novel scheme sequences; (3) evaluating the consequences of those sequences; (4) restructuring valuable sequences so that they can be used in the future; and (5) practicing these new sequences or structures until they become consolidated. Case provided some limited evidence suggesting that engaging a child in one of these four regulatory processes could facilitate cognitive development.

To address the variability in performance that exists in children, Case proposed a set of general factors that are not invariant in development. These variable functions set a limit on the effectiveness of the four regulatory processes that are invariant. A particularly important variable function is the size of a child's short-term storage space. It is well established that human organisms have limited attentional resources (e.g., Norman, 1976). These resources must be divided between two functions: executing current operations, and storing or retrieving the products of operations previously executed. Case (1985) referred to these two functions as operating space (OS) and short-term storage space (STSS). Case's research suggested that the growth of STSS plays an important regulating role in stage transition. The growth of STSS can result from a developmental change in the capacity of the individual's total processing space (i.e., OS + STSS), or by a decrease in the proportion of total processing space devoted to operating.

In a series of studies, Case found support for the second explanation. Subjects of different ages were administered two tests: a test of STSS (e.g., counting span) and a test of the efficiency with which they could execute the STSS task (for counting, counting speed was measured). Next, a group of adults were taught a new operation, such as counting in a foreign language, which temporarily reduced their operational efficiency and increased the amount of OS required. The STSS of the adults was determined under the new conditions and compared with young children who had the same degree of operational efficiency. The results from several studies (e.g., Case, 1985; Case, Kurland, and Goldberg, 1982) indicated that the STSS of young children and adults was not different for new operations. Thus, the total processing space of adults and children is the same, and the measured increases in STSS with development are a function of decreases in the proportion of this space that is devoted to executing basic operations.

A second variable function is practice. The most obvious reason for a developmental increase in operational efficiency is operational practice. In school, children receive intensive practice in basic operations, such as enumeration, size estimation, and word decoding. Practice might also contribute to increases in representational precision that occur across stage boundaries. Case (1984), however, provided evidence that factors other than practice influence operational efficiency. He reported a study in which 40 children between the ages of 6 and 10 were exposed to intensive practice in counting over a three month period. Children in the experimental group received 5,000 trials in counting, but did not appear to be more accelerated in their counting efficiency. Case concluded that practice will improve an individual's operational efficiency but only within the limits set by other factors, factors in which either biological maturation or general experience play the determining role.

The neo-Piagetian view of how children move from stage to stage is clearly more explicit than the one proposed by Piaget. Although still acknowledging the existence of general stages of cognitive development, the neo-Piagetian view specifies the regulatory processes involved in stage transitions, the potential influence of practice and instruction on development, and the changes that occur in the allocation of attentional resources with changes in development.

Skill Theory: Mechanisms of Change

Skill theory proposes two types of processes to account for structural changes in development: optimal-level processes and skill-acquisition processes. Processes based on optimal level account for most of the major changes in development (macrodevelopment). As indicated earlier, the optimal level reflects the upper limit on the complexity of a skill that an individual can control. Optimal levels increase over a "relatively long age span," producing changes in the kinds of skills a person can exhibit (Fischer and Pipp, 1984). These changes are characterized in terms of the ten developmental levels discussed earlier.

The important question regarding developmental change concerns the factors that lead to changes in optimal level. Skill theory, like Piagetian and neo-Piagetian theories, acknowledges that both organismic and environmental factors underlie developmental changes. Fischer and Pipp suggested that there are three important environmental influences: practice, instruction, and environmental support (indicating the kinds of performance expected). They conducted a study that examined the influence of these three environmental factors. Subjects ranging from 9 through 20 years old were given problems that required explanation of one of four relations between similar arithmetic operations; for example, how does addition relate to subtraction, multiplication to addition, and so forth. In the spontaneous condition (no practice or support), performance showed a slow, gradual improvement between the ages of 15 and 20, but never even reached the level of 50 percent accuracy. In the practice-and-support condition, performance spurted sharply between the ages of 15 and 16, from near 0 percent to over 80 percent accuracy. Optimal level was thus achieved under conditions predicted to promote optimal performance.

Organismic factors also contribute to changes in optimal level. Although initially skeptical about the generality of biological correlates of cognitive development, Fischer and Pipp reported that spurts in head circumference and brain waves appeared at the appropriate ages for each level tested (all but Level 10). Fischer and Pipp emphasized, however, that these data only suggested a possible relationship between biological changes and cognitive development. They further cautioned against thinking of biological changes as prerequisites in any simple sense for changes in cognitive level.

As indicated earlier, changes in optimal level do not lead directly to changes in all of an individual's skills. Changes in particular skills require processes of skill acquisition in which the person combines and differentiates more elementary skills to produce more advanced skills (Fischer et al., 1984). The processes of skill acquisition are described by a set of transformation rules that specify how simpler skills can be combined to form more complex skills. Skills in different domains might share the same microdevelopmental transformational rule.

To illustrate, Fischer and colleagues (1984) offered the example of an 11-year-old girl who had just begun to use Level 7 single abstractions. Her new optimal level allowed her to coordinate two specific, concrete arithmetic problems, such as $9 - 7 = 2$ and $15 - 5 = 10$, to form an abstract skill for subtraction. The transformation rules "Shift of Focus" and "Compounding" describe two kinds of possible extensions of this rule. With Shift of Focus, the girl can shift from coordinating the original two problems to coordinating one of the original problems and a new one. With this transformation, she has extended her concept to one additional problem, but still cannot coordinate the three problems at the same time. However, the transformation rule Compounding allows her to coordinate all three problems. Now all three specific problems are treated as instances of the same concept of subtraction. In this way, a generalized, differentiated concept of subtraction is gradually constructed.

Skill theory is highly explicit in describing how microdevelopmental transformations lead to a specific developmental sequence in a particular content domain. However, Fischer and colleagues (1984) would be the first to admit that the theory is less explicit in describing the macrodevelopmental processes that characterize shifts in optimal level. More information is needed concerning the way in which environmental and organismic factors lead to changes in optimal-level performance.

Triarchic Theory: Mechanisms of Change

Sternberg's (1985) theory of intelligence provides several sources of developmental change in cognition. First, the component of knowledge acquisition provides the mechanisms for a steadily developing knowledge base. As the knowledge base increases, more sophisticated forms of knowledge-acquisition are possible, which lead, in turn, to greater facility in executing performance components. Sternberg viewed development as an unending feedback loop where the components lead to increased knowledge. This increased knowledge, in turn, leads to more effective use of the components and to further increases in the knowledge base, and so on.

A second source of developmental variation is the child's ability to self-monitor the metacomponents. In young children, the allocation of metacomponential resources may be less than optimal. As children get older, they become better at self-monitoring. This leads to improved allocations of metacomponential resources, in particular self-monitoring of the metacomponents. As was the case with knowledge-acquisition components, there is an unending feedback loop that is specific to the metacomponents themselves.

It is the metacomponents that form the major basis for the development of intelligence in Sternberg's triachric theory. All activation and feedback are filtered through these components. If they do not perform their function well, it will not matter much what the other kinds of components do (Sternberg, 1984). Cognitive development, however, arises not only from improved performance within each of the componential systems, but also from the automatization of the functioning of each subsystem. The functioning of a particular subsystem proceeds from controlled to automatic. As seen with Case's (1985) neo-Piagetian theory, the automatization of particular tasks or processes frees up memory and attentional resources.

Sternberg's triarchic theory seems to add the final piece to the puzzle of what mechanisms underlie changes in cognitive development. That final piece is the metacomponential aspect of the theory; that is, the ability to monitor the function of the metacomponents. The ability to monitor and evaluate the effectiveness of the problem-solving strategies is a crucial aspect of adolescent thought.

LANGUAGE AND COGNITION

The relationship between language and cognition has been explored most extensively in infants and young children. A variety of positions have been proposed to characterize this relationship (see Rice and Kemper, 1984). At one extreme is the position that language is a necessary prerequisite for thought. This position, often referred to as *linguistic determinism*, gained great popularity through the writings of Sapir and Whorf (cf. Slobin, 1979). However, this position was largely discredited through the work of Bruner (e.g., Bruner, Goodnow, and Austin, 1956) and Brown (1958).

At the other extreme is the Piagetian or strong cognitive view that language is a product of intelligence. According to Piaget (1980), language emerges at the end of the sensorimotor period as part of the more general symbolic function. The symbolic function is defined as the ability to represent mentally an external event or object in its absence. Language is not the only symbolic ability that emerges at this time; others include symbolic play, deferred imitation, representational drawing, dreams, and mental imagery. The Piagetian view postulates that developments in these non-linguistic symbolic abilities should parallel developments in language. In relation to older children and adolescents, Piaget (1926) contended that formal operational thinking was a necessary prerequisite for the comprehension of abstract forms of language such as proverbs (e.g., "Every cloud has a silver lining"). Many investigators (e.g., Arlin, 1978; Billow, 1975; Cometa and Eson, 1978; Holden, 1978; Siltanen, 1981; Smith, 1976) subsequently tried to prove Piaget's theory in relation to proverbs and other types of figurative language, such as metaphors, but none were successful (see Chapter 8). Van Kleeck (1984) suggested that certain metalinguistic tasks (e.g., judgments of synonymy and grammatical acceptability) require concrete operational thinking and that others (e.g., dealing with figurative language) require formal operational thinking. However, she also suggested that factors other than Piagetian cognitive level, such as a youngster's creativity, vocabulary development, and cognitive style (i.e., reflective versus impulsive), may affect performance on metalinguistic tasks.

Between these two extremes are various correlational (e.g., Bates, 1979) and interactionist (e.g., Schlesinger, 1977) views. Both of these views acknowledge the bidirectional influences of language and cognition. Proponents of the interactionist view argue that language experiences influence children's cognitive development. The interactionist view emphasizes the role that the child's social interactions have on language development, as well as how specific language experiences influence the child's thinking. Case, Fischer, and Sternberg would all be considered interactionists.

The correlational (homologue) view, as espoused by Bates (1979), contends that language and cognition derive from a common, deeper underlying system of cognitive operations and structures. This view accounts for the finding that certain cognitive structures and linguistic knowledge appear at the same time but are not always positively correlated. Studies of figurative language comprehension have tended to support the correlational view of the relation between language and cognition (e.g., Billow, 1975; Holden, 1978; Nippold, Martin, and Erskine, 1988).

There is also the view that there are specific language acquisition structures or strategies available to young children learning language. These structures are necessarily independent from the more general cognitive system. This view is consistent with Chomsky's (1965) theory of language acquisition. (For further discussion of these views, see Rice and Kemper, 1984).

The different views on the relationship between language and cognition all allow for some independence of language and cognition. There are many mental experiences that are nonlinguistic, including imagistic, sensory, musical, and motoric experiences. Many creative thinkers, for example, describe the phenomenon of resolving a problem but then having tremendous difficulty expressing the solution in some form (e.g., using oral or written language). Artists and composers often do not think out their works in words. Slobin (1979) described the familiar experience of groping for a word or struggling to find the best way to say something. In addressing this phenomenon, William James (cited in Slobin, 1979, p. 146) posed the question of what kind of a mental fact is the "intention of saying something"?

The independence of verbal language proficiency and cognition is readily apparent in many of the tasks used to evaluate adolescent thought.

Although developmentalists agree that language plays a more central role in thinking as children get older, many of the problems used to evaluate adolescent thought do not require sophisticated verbal skills. In the pendulum problem, for example, one need merely indicate that the key variable is the length of the string. In the balance-beam problem, a simple "Yes" (the beam will be balanced) or "No" will suffice. Clearly, it is not necessary to be a great orator or a proficient debater to attain the levels of adolescent thought described in this chapter. However, as discussed in Chapter 7, other types of cognitive problems presented to adolescents do require a fair amount of linguistic sophistication. For example, solving verbal analogies often depends on an understanding of subtle differences in word meanings (e.g., "*heterogeneity* is to *divergence* as *homogeneity* is to ?").

Nevertheless, the fact that language and cognition are not isomorphic makes it possible for the thinking that characterizes preadolescents and adolescents to be manifested not only in the verbal or written expression of ideas but also in the ability to solve problems in mathematics, physics, chemistry, and so forth. Fischer (1980) suggested that individuals often do not acquire similar proficiencies across different content or knowledge domains. The independence of language and thought suggests that language proficiency (both expressive and receptive) might be considered a separate knowledge domain in the same way that mathematics, physics, and chemistry are considered distinctive. However, the fact that language and thought exist and often function independently of one another does not mean that they have no influence on one another.

Most developmentalists recognize the bidirectional influences of language and cognition. During the first 18 months of life, the relationship clearly favors cognition because the child is prelinguistic. However, as the child's language competencies improve during the preschool years, language begins to play an increasingly more important role in thinking. The influence of language on cognition has received considerable attention. There is a rich tradition of research in behavioral psychology that has examined the ways in which language mediates thought. For example, verbal descriptions of response alternatives and verbal coding strategies have been shown to be effective mediators in performance (e.g., Spiker, 1963). Verbal mediators can guide performance in psychological experiments and also in real-life situations.

In a similar vein, language has been shown to function as an executive or regulator of thinking. Luria (1982) and Vygotsky (1962) are generally credited with first recognizing the regulatory role of language. Behavior is first regulated by others' language and gradually becomes directed by the child's own verbalizations. As children get older, language plays an increasingly more important role in thinking (Vygotsky, 1962). Thus, although verbal proficiency is not necessarily required to demonstrate abstract thought, language can play an important role in regulating the problem-solving strategies older children use. Indeed, the use of language to regulate and monitor behavior has been employed effectively to modify impulsive behavior (Meichenbaum, 1977) as well as to improve problem solving and academic performance (e.g., Segel, Chipman, and Glaser, 1985). Future research should examine the changes that take place in the relationship between language and cognition during the 9-through-19 age range.

CONCLUSIONS

In this chapter, four different views of cognitive development were presented for the 9-through-19 age range: Piaget's theory, Case's neo-Piagetian theory, Fischer's skill theory, and Sternberg's triarchic theory. Despite the differences in these views, the major proponent of each would agree that preadolescent and adolescent cognition is characterized by growth in the following areas: (1) hypothetical reasoning that involves inductive and deductive processes; (2) the coordination of abstract ideas, rules, and systems; and (3) the use of various abstract symbol systems, such as those that characterize mathematics, physics, formal logic, and language.

Two of the theorists, Case and Fischer, provided evidence of changes occurring about every two years throughout the preadolescent and adolescent periods. The theories of Case and Fischer were the most integrative in terms of describing how quantitative changes in knowledge and skill interrelate and cause qualitative changes in cognitive structures. With the exception of Piaget, each of the theorists acknowledged that adults are capable of higher levels of thinking than adolescents. Fischer, for example, noted that around the age of 25, individuals begin to integrate abstract systems to form Level 10 general principles. Other kinds of higher-level thinking were also discussed, including Arlin's (1975) problem-finding stage, and the systematic and metasystematic reasoning levels proposed by Commons and colleagues (1982).

The four theorists proposed quite different mechanisms of developmental change, though all agreed that both organismic and environmental factors influence development. Case, Fischer, and Sternberg provided very explicit descriptions of the mechanisms that underlie and motivate developmental change. Case, for example, described how changes in the allocation of attentional and memory resources were associated with developmental spurts. Fischer described how instruction, practice, and environmental support lead to optimal-level performance. For Sternberg, children's improving ability to allocate and monitor metacomponential resources provided the major basis for developmental change.

The relationship between language and cognition was discussed in the final section of the chapter. Four views of this relationship were considered, including the Piagetian strong cognitive view, the interactionist view, the correlational (homologue) view, and the language-specific view. Case, Fischer, and Sternberg would all be considered interactionists. The independence of language and cognition was discussed, as was the bidirectional influences of language and cognition. It is generally agreed that language plays a more important role in thinking as children get older. However, future research should address how the relationship between language and cognition changes during preadolescence and adolescence. In the next chapter, verbal reasoning is discussed, a construct where language and cognition are closely related.

REFERENCES

Arlin, P. (1975). Cognitive development in adulthood: A fifth stage? *Developmental Psychology, 11,* 602-606.

Arlin, P. (1978, February). *Piagetian operations in the comprehension, preference, and production of metaphors.* Paper presented at the Annual International Interdisciplinary Conference on Piagetian Theory and the Helping Professions, Los Angeles, CA.

Bates, E. (1979). *The emergence of symbols: Cognition and communication in infancy.* New York: Academic Press.

Berry, J., and Dasen, P. (Eds.). (1974). *Culture and cognition: Readings in cross-cultural psychology.* London: Methuen.

Billow, R.M. (1975). A cognitive developmental study of metaphor comprehension. *Developmental Psychology, 11,* 415-423.

Brainerd, C. (1978). The stage question in cognitive-developmental theory. *Behavioral and Brain Sciences, 2,* 173-213.

Broughton, J. (1978). The development of concepts of self, mind, reality, and knowledge. In W. Damon (Ed.), *New directions for child development, Number 1, Social cognition.* San Francisco: Jossey-Bass.

Broughton, J. (1984). Not beyond formal operations but beyond Piaget. In M. Commons, F. Richards, and C. Armon (Eds.), *Beyond formal operations* (pp. 395-411). New York: Praeger Scientific.

Brown, R. (1958). *Words and things.* New York: The Free Press.

Brown, A., and DeLoache, J. (1978). Skills, plans, and self-regulation. In R. Siegler (Ed.), *Children's thinking: What develops?* Hillsdale, NJ: Erlbaum.

Bruner, J. (1964). On the course of cognitive growth. *American Psychologist, 19,* 1-15.

Bruner, J., Goodnow, J., and Austin, G. (1956). *A study of thinking.* New York: Wiley.

Case, R. (1984). The process of stage transition: A neo-Piagetian view. In R. Sternberg (Ed.) *Mechanisms of cognitive development* (pp. 19-44). New York: Freeman.

Case, R. (1985). *Intellectual development: Birth to adulthood.* Orlando, FL: Academic Press.

Case, R., Kurland, D., and Goldberg, J. (1982). Operational efficiency and the growth of short-term memory span. *Journal of Experimental Child Psychology, 33,* 386–404.

Chomsky, N. (1965). *Aspects of the theory of syntax.* Cambridge, MA: MIT Press.

Cometa, M.S., and Eson, M.E. (1978). Logical operations and metaphor interpretation: A Piagetian model. *Child Development, 49,* 649–659.

Commons, M., Richards, F., and Armon, C. (Eds.). (1984). *Beyond formal operations.* New York: Praeger Scientific.

Commons, M., Richards, F., and Kuhn, D. (1982). Systematic and metasystematic reasoning: A case for levels of reasoning beyond Piaget's stage of formal operations. *Child Development, 53,* 1058–1069.

Elkind, D. (1962). Quantity conceptions in college students. *Journal of Social Psychology, 57,* 459–465.

Elkind, D., Barocas, R., and Rosenthal, B. (1968). Combinatorial thinking in adolescents from graded and ungraded classrooms. *Perceptual and Motor Skills, 27,* 1015–1018.

Fischer, K. (1980). Learning as the development of organized behavior. *Journal of Structural Learning, 3,* 253–267.

Fischer, K., and Corrigan, R. (1981). A skill approach to language development. In R. Stark (Ed.), *Language behavior in infancy and early childhood.* New York: Elsevier/North Holland.

Fischer, K., Hand, H., and Russell, S. (1984). The development of abstractions in adolescence and adulthood. In M. Commons, F. Richards, and C. Armon (Eds.), *Beyond formal operations* (pp. 43–73). New York: Praeger Scientific.

Fischer, K., and Pipp, S. (1984). Processes of cognitive development: Optimal level and skill acquisition. In R. Sternberg (Ed.), *Mechanisms of cognitive development* (pp. 45–81). New York: Freeman.

Flavell, J. (1970). Cognitive changes in adulthood. In L. Goulet and P. Baltes (Eds.), *Life-span developmental psychology: Research and theory* (pp. 53–82). New York: Academic Press.

Flavell, J. (1982). On cognitive development. *Child Development, 53,* 1–10.

Gardner, H. (1978). *Developmental psychology: An introduction.* Boston: Little, Brown and Company.

Gelman, R., and Gallistel, C. (1978). *The young child's understanding of number: A window on early cognitive development.* Cambridge, MA: Harvard University Press.

Ginsburg, H., and Opper, S. (1979). *Piaget's theory of intellectual development* (Second edition). Englewood Cliffs, NJ: Prentice-Hall.

Green, M. (1978). Structure and sequence in children's concepts of change and probability: A replication of Piaget and Inhelder. *Child Development, 49,* 1045–1053.

Grinder, R. (Ed.). (1975). *Studies in adolescence* (Third edition). New York: Macmillan.

Gross, T. (1985). *Cognitive development.* Monterey, CA: Brooks/Cole.

Holden, M.H. (1978, February). *Proverbs, proportions, and Piaget.* Paper presented at the Annual International Interdisciplinary Conference on Piagetian Theory and the Helping Professions, Los Angeles, CA.

Inhelder, B. (1966). Cognitive development and its contribution to the diagnosis of some phenomena of mental deficiency. *Merrill-Palmer Quarterly, 12*, 299-319.

Inhelder, B., and Piaget, J. (1958). The early growth of logical thinking. New York: Basic Books.

Jackson, S. (1965). The growth of logical thinking in normal and subnormal children. *British Journal of Educational Psychology, 35*, 255-258.

Koslowski, B. (1980). Quantitative and qualitative changes in the development of seriation. *Merrill-Palmer Quarterly, 26*, 391-405.

Lunzer, E., and Pumfrey, P. (1966). Understanding proportionality. *Mathematics Teaching, 34*, 7-13.

Luria, A. (1982). *Language and cognition.* New York: Wiley.

Martorano, S. (1977). A developmental analysis of performance on Piaget's formal operational tasks. *Developmental Psychology, 13*, 666-672.

Meichenbaum, D. (1977). *Cognitive-behavior modification: An integrative approach.* New York: Plenum Press.

Neimark, E. (1975). Longitudinal development of formal operations thought. *Genetic Psychology Monographs, 91*, 171-225.

Neimark, E. (1979). Current status of formal operations research. *Human Development, 22*, 60-67.

Nippold, M.A., Martin, S.A., and Erskine, B.J. (1988). Proverb comprehension in context: A developmental study with children and adolescents. *Journal of Speech and Hearing Research, 31*, 19-28.

Norman, D. (1976). *Memory and attention: An introduction to human information processing* (Second edition). New York: Wiley.

Pascual-Leone, J. (1970). A mathematical model for the transition rule in Piaget's development stages. *Acta Psychologica, 32*, 301-345.

Pascual-Leone, J. (1980). Constructive problems for constructive theories: The current relevance of Piaget's work and a critique of information processing simulation psychology. In H. Speda and P. Kluwe (Eds.), *Psychological models of thinking* (pp. 176-203). New York: Academic Press.

Piaget, J. (1926). *The language and thought of the child.* New York: Harcourt, Brace.

Piaget, J. (1954). *The construction of reality in the child.* New York: Basic Books.

Piaget, J. (1970). *Science of education and the psychology of the child.* New York: Orion Press.

Piaget, J. (1972). Intellectual evolution from adolescence to adulthood. *Human Development, 15*, 1-12.

Piaget, J. (1980). Language within cognition. In M. Piatelli-Palmarini (Ed.), *Language and learning: The debate between Jean Piaget and Noam Chomsky* (pp. 163-184). Cambridge, MA: Harvard University Press.

Piaget, J., and Inhelder, B. (1975). *The origin of the idea of chance in children.* New York: Norton.

Pinard, A., and Chasse, G. (1977). Pseudoconservation of the volume and surface area of a solid object. *Child Development, 48*, 1559-1566.

Pulaski, M. (1980). *Understanding Piaget.* New York: Harper and Row.

Pumfrey, P. (1968). The growth of the schema of proportionality. *British Journal of Educational Psychology, 38*, 202-204.

Rice, M., and Kemper, S. (1984). *Child language and cognition.* Austin, TX: Pro-Ed.

Schlesinger, I. (1977). The role of cognitive development and linguistic input in language acquisition. *Journal of Child Language, 4,* 153-169.

Segal, J., Chipman, S., and Glaser, R. (Eds.). (1985). *Thinking and learning skills: Volume 1. Relating instruction to research.* Hillsdale, NJ: Erlbaum.

Shaffer, D. (1985). *Developmental psychology.* Monterey, CA: Brooks/Cole.

Siegal, M. (1975). Spontaneous development of moral concepts. *Human Development, 18,* 370-383.

Siegler, R. (1976). The effects of simple necessity and sufficiency on children's causal inferences. *Child Development, 47,* 1058-1063.

Siegler, R. (1984). Mechanisms of cognitive growth: Variation and selection. In R. Sternberg (Ed.), *Mechanisms of cognitive development* (pp. 141-163). New York: Freeman.

Siltanen, S.A. (1981). Apple noses and popsicle toeses: A developmental investigation of metaphorical comprehension. Unpublished doctoral dissertation, Ohio State University.

Slobin, D. (1979). *Psycholinguistics* (Second Edition). Glenview, IL: Scott Foresman and Company.

Smith, J.W.A. (1976). Children's emphasis of metaphor: A Piagetian interpretation. *Language and Speech, 19,* 236-243.

Spiker, C. (1963). Verbal factors in the discrimination learning of children. *Monographs of the Society for Research in Child Development, 28,* 53-68.

Sternberg, R. (Ed.). (1984). *Mechanisms of cognitive development.* New York: Freeman.

Sternberg, R. (1985). *Beyond IQ: A triarchic theory of human intelligence.* New York: Cambridge University Press.

Sternberg R., and Rifkin, B. (1979). The development of analogical reasoning processes. *Journal of Experimental Child Psychology, 27,* 195-232.

van Kleeck, A. (1984). Metalinguistic skills: Cutting across spoken and written language and problem-solving abilities. In G.P. Wallach and K.G. Butler (Eds.), *Language learning disabilities in school-age children* (pp. 128-153). Baltimore, MD: Williams and Wilkins.

Vygotsky, L. (1962). *Thought and language.* Cambridge, MA: MIT Press.

Wavering, M. (1984). Interrelationships among Piaget's formal operational schemata: Proportion, probability, and correlation. *Journal of Psychology, 118,* 57-64.

CHAPTER 7

■

VERBAL REASONING

■

MARILYN A. NIPPOLD

Verbal reasoning is a mental construct where language and cognition converge. This is evidenced in the following problem for eighth-grade math students:

> To make spaghetti sauce, add one can of tomato paste and two cans of water to one package of mix. Add a spoonful of salad oil. How many cans of water would you use with three packages of mix? How many cans of tomato paste would you use with eight cans of water? (*Growth in Mathematics*, Level 8, 1978, p. 132)

To solve this problem, students must call on both linguistic and nonlinguistic abilities as they read and comprehend the sentences, set up the proportions, and perform the operations of multiplication and division. An important topic, youngsters' competence in verbal reasoning reflects their intelligence and language development, and is predictive of their academic success (Achenbach, 1979, 1970; Lorge and Thorndike, 1957; Sternberg, 1982).

Problems in verbal reasoning are either inductive or deductive. Inductive problems include solving analogies (e.g., "*Bear* is to *cub* as *cow* is to _____?_____"), proportions (e.g., "One package is to two cans as three packages is to *n* cans"), series completions (e.g., "June, August, October, _____?_____"),

---

Parts of this chapter were published by Marilyn A. Nippold in the article Verbal analogical reasoning in children and adolescents. *Topics in Language Disorders*, 6(4), 51-63, 1986. Reprinted with permission of Aspen Publishers, Inc.

and classifications (e.g., "Which of the following words does not go with the others?: aunt, cousin, sister, friend"), and interpreting metaphors (e.g., "The house was a box with no lid"), and proverbs (e.g., "The fat pig gets all the pears"). Deductive problems include solving syllogisms (e.g., "All blocks are green. This is a block. Therefore, _____?_____"), probability problems (e.g., "You toss a coin. It can land heads or tails. Toss it 100 times. How many times can you expect it to land heads?"), and combinations (e.g., "Here are three different shapes—a triangle, circle, and square. Show me all the different ways you can combine them").

Inductive and deductive reasoning problems differ in the extent to which the preceding information in a problem is logically (although not necessarily psychologically) sufficient evidence for the conclusion (Sternberg, 1982). With inductive reasoning, the preceding information supports the conclusion but is not sufficient evidence for it. For example, to solve the "bear–cub" analogy just presented, one must draw on outside information concerning the relationship between *bear* and *cub* in order to generate an item that goes with *cow* in the same way that *cub* goes with *bear*. With deductive reasoning, however, the preceding information is logically sufficient evidence for the conclusion. For example, the conclusion to the "This block is green" syllogism just presented is based entirely on the two preceding statements.

Youngsters are called on to reason both inductively and deductively during the elementary-, middle-, and high-school years. Therefore, it is important to examine the findings from developmental studies in these two areas. Space limitations in the present chapter prevent a review of all types of inductive and deductive reasoning. Therefore, analogies will be the focus for examining inductive reasoning, and syllogisms for examining deductive reasoning, two types of problems that have been studied extensively for the 9-through-19 age range. The developmental literature concerning metaphors and proverbs for this age range is reviewed in Chapter 8.

ANALOGIES: INDUCTIVE REASONING

Youngsters' ability to solve analogy problems has been examined through tasks where incomplete analogies of the form "A is to B as C is to ?" (A : B :: C : D) are presented, and the appropriate D item must be generated by the subject or selected from several alternatives. Studies have demonstrated that performance on such tasks steadily improves during the 9-through-19 age range; growth is characterized by increased speed and accuracy, greater use of systematic strategies, and enhanced comprehension of semantically complex problems (Achenbach, 1969, 1970; Feuerstein, 1979; Gallagher and Wright, 1979; Goldman, Pellegrino, Parseghian, and Sallis, 1982; Goldstein, 1962; Levinson and Carpenter, 1974; Sternberg and

Downing, 1982; Sternberg and Nigro, 1980). Growth also occurs metalinguistically in that children become more adept at explaining their answers to analogy solutions (Goldman, Pellegrino, Parseghian, and Sallis, 1982; Levinson and Carpenter, 1974). A variety of internal and external factors related to performance will now be discussed.

Internal Factors

A youngster's age, intelligence, level of academic achievement, and problem-solving style are factors related to performance on tasks of verbal analogical reasoning. Several investigators have examined age-related improvements in analogical reasoning. For example, Feuerstein (1979) examined groups of youngsters of the ages of 8 through 14 ($n = 253$). A written multiple-choice task involving 20 problems was presented. Each problem consisted of a 2×2 matrix in which each of the two boxes at the top contained printed words (e.g., *house* and *door*). Together, these words implied a certain relationship (e.g., "One enters a house through a door"). For the lower half of the matrix, the box on the left also contained a printed word (e.g., *garden*), and the box on the right was empty. The subject's task was to select a word from a set of six choices (*gate, plot, fence, apartment, flowers*) that best completed the matrix (i.e., *gate*). All analogies were composed of high-frequency words selected from children's books. Mean scores obtained by the 8-, 9-, 10-, 11-, 12-, 13-, and 14-year-olds, respectively, were 23, 60, 72, 75, 87, 89 and 91 percent, indicating that accuracy improved as subjects got older. By the age of 12, however, performance appeared to reach a plateau, perhaps because the analogies were composed of simple vocabulary. Had more complex vocabulary been used (e.g., "Stethoscope is to physician as pestle is to: sculptor, pharmacist, teacher, author"), the task might have challenged the older subjects to a greater extent.

Achenbach (1970) also examined age-related improvements in analogical reasoning. He developed the *Children's Associative Responding Test* (CART), a measure designed specifically to distinguish children who solve analogies through word association from those who use analogical reasoning skills. This is a written multiple-choice test consisting of 68 analogies of the form A : B :: C : D. Of these, the first three terms, called the stem of the analogy, are presented, and the fourth is left to be inferred. Each stem is followed by five single-word answer choices. For half of the test items, the correct choice is a distant associate of the C term, but one of the other choices, a plausible foil, is a close semantic associate of C. For example, for the item "*Bear* is to *cave* as *boy* is to ____?____" the correct answer, *house*, is pitted against the foil *girl*. For the other half of the test items, none of the choices is a particularly close associate of C (e.g., "*Piano* is to *fingers* as *whistle* is to *lips, throat, loud, face, song*"). Associative responding on the test is measured by subtracting the number of nonfoil errors from the number of foil errors to obtain a difference (D) score. Thus, the higher the D score, the greater the tendency to respond associatively.

Achenbach administered the CART to youngsters 11, 12, 13, and 14 years old ($n = 1085$). Mean accuracy scores of 71, 81, 85, and 89 percent were obtained by the four age groups, respectively, indicating that the CART was sensitive to age-related improvements in analogical reasoning. Achenbach also examined the relationships between performance on the CART and the subjects' IQ scores, grade point averages, and scores on standardized tests of academic achievement, and found that for all four age groups the low D scorers (i.e., $D \leq 1$) surpassed the high D scorers (i.e., $D \geq 4$) on all three variables. Interestingly, although the high D scorers made more errors on the test items for which associative responding was possible, the two groups performed equally well on the items for which this was not possible, indicating that the associative responders had the capacity to solve the problems through analogical reasoning, but did not consistently do so.

A difference in problem-solving style between associative and nonassociative responders also was explored by Achenbach (1969) using the *Matching Familiar Figures Test* (MFFT) (Kagan, Rosman, Day, Albert, and Phillips, 1964). This is a timed test requiring careful and systematic analysis. In it, a pictured object (e.g., a teddy bear) is displayed, and a child must pick out the identical object from a set of six choices, five of which represent subtle variations of the target picture (e.g., the shape of the mouth or feet, or the angle of the head or bow tie vary). Children with an impulsive problem-solving style tend to perform the task quickly and inaccurately, while those with a reflective style perform more slowly and accurately. In Achenbach's study, a short version of the CART was administered to 191 11-year-olds. The 20 with the highest D scores (associative responders) and the 20 with the lowest D scores (nonassociative responders) were then given the MFFT. As predicted, the high D scorers showed an impulsive problem-solving style on the MFFT, while the low D scorers were more reflective on this test.

Research has indicated that the associative response strategy diminishes during preadolescence and that by early adolescence, analogies of the form A : B :: C : D (second-order analogies) are usually solved through appropriate reasoning processes (Gallagher and Wright, 1979; Goldman et al., 1982; Sternberg and Nigro, 1980). This change in strategy represents a qualitative improvement in analogical reasoning. However, Sternberg and Downing (1982) hypothesized that young adolescents would revert to the old associative response strategy when confronted with more complex third-order analogies of the form [(A : B :: C : D) :: (A : B :: C : D)]. As with second-order analogies, these "analogies between analogies" can vary in their "goodness" depending on the relationships expressed by the terms. For example, for each of the component analogies, the C and D terms must be related to one another in the same way as the A and B terms (Criterion 1); in addition, the component analogies must be related to one another analogously (Criterion 2). The following third order analogy meets these two criteria:

[(sand : beach :: star : galaxy) :: (water : ocean :: air : sky)]

In contrast, the next example satisfies the first criterion but fails to satisfy the second because the two component analogies are associatively related to one another:

[(bench : judge :: pulpit : minister) :: (chair : courtroom :: pew : church)]

To test the "associative reversion" hypothesis, Sternberg and Downing constructed a task consisting of 60 third-order analogies. All of the problems satisfied the first criterion for goodness but varied in the extent to which the second criterion was satisfied, with many of the component analogies associatively related. Adolescents of the ages of 13, 16, and 18 ($n = 60$) were asked to judge the relatedness of the component analogies in each problem using a scale of 1 ("extremely poorly related") to 9 ("extremely well related"). According to the investigators, high scores assigned to the associatively related problems constituted an associative response strategy in dealing with third-order analogies. Results indicated that ratings of the associative problems were highest among the youngest adolescents and declined with each successive age group. This lead the investigators to conclude that the associative response strategy observed among preadolescents in relation to second-order analogies resurfaces among adolescents in relation to third-order analogies, but shows the same diminishing pattern as a function of age.

External Factors

Semantic and structural factors also influence youngsters' performance on tasks of verbal analogical reasoning. To study the role of semantics, Goldstein (1962) constructed a task to determine whether analogies expressing different types of meanings would present variations in difficulty. He developed a written multiple-choice test similar to Achenbach's (1970) CART, which consisted of 120 analogies of the form A : B :: C : D, with the D term omitted. Each stem was accompanied by five answer choices. The task consisted of 15 analogies of eight different types shown in Table 7-1.

In contrast to Achenbach (1969, 1970), Goldstein (1962) attempted to exclude problems that could be solved by simple word association and therefore did not require analogical reasoning. For example, an analogy such as "*glove* is to *hand* as *shoe* is to *foot*" would not be included because the correct answer, *foot*, is a close associate of the third term, *shoe*. However, an item such as "*garden* is to *gate* as *room* is to *door*" was acceptable because *door* is not a particularly close associate of *room*. The degree of association between words had been determined through prior screening procedures. Goldstein's task was administered to youngsters of the ages of 8 through 13

Table 7-1. *Types of analogies used by Goldstein.*

1. *Antonymous* (e.g., *clear* is to *cloudy* as *shallow* is to: narrow, pool, muddy, swift, *deep*)
2. *Synonymous* (e.g., *weep* is to *cry* as *smile* is to: joke, *grin*, play, sorry, mouth)
3. *Characteristic Property* (e.g., *wheel* is to *round* as *arrow* is to: bow, strong, wood, shoot, *straight*)
4. *Part–Whole* (e.g., *leg* is to *knee* as *arm* is to: hand, wrist, *elbow*, sleeve, head)
5. *Superordinate–Subordinate* (e.g., *shirt* is to *clothing* as *hammer* is to: nails, hit, claw, *tools*, screwdriver)
6. *Functional* (e.g., *time* is to *clock* as *weight* is to: pound, size, hour, watch, *scale*)
7. *Sequential* (e.g., *Tuesday* is to *Sunday* as *Friday* is to: Monday, *Wednesday*, Sunday, Thursday, week)
8. *Causal* (e.g., *fire* is to *smoke* as *water* is to: liquid, wet, ice, *steam*, drink)

Adapted from Goldstein, 1962.

($n = 120$). To ensure that the subjects' performance was not hampered by reading difficulties, the vocabulary of the analogies did not exceed a third-grade level. Results indicated that the synonymous, antonymous, and characteristic property analogies were easiest to solve, followed by superordinate and part-whole analogies. Causal, functional, and sequential analogies were the most difficult. Task performance was found to improve with age, and mean scores of 40, 39, 44, 56, 59, and 64 percent were obtained by the six age groups, respectively. With the exception of the 8-year-olds, these percentages are markedly lower than those obtained by Feuerstein (1979). Reasons for this discrepancy are unknown, as both investigators carefully controlled the vocabulary level of their analogies, presented similar types of analogies (e.g., synonymous, functional, part-whole, etc.), used a written multiple-choice task, and took steps to ensure that the children understood the task prior to testing.

Sternberg and Nigro (1980) also examined the influence of semantic factors in a developmental study of verbal analogical reasoning but used subjects of a wider age range: 9-, 12-, 15-, and 18-year-olds ($n = 80$). Sixty analogies of the form used by Goldstein (1962) were presented in a written multiple-choice task, with 12 items representing each of five semantic types: synonymous, antonymous, functional, linear ordering (i.e., sequential), and category membership (i.e., superordinate–subordinate). Unlike the Goldstein study, Sternberg and Nigro (1980) did not attempt to exclude (or include) items that could be solved by word association. As with Goldstein's study, the vocabulary of the analogies did not exceed a third-grade level.

Results indicated that both functional and antonymous relationships were considerably easier than synonymous, linear ordering, and category membership. These findings were only partially consistent with Goldstein (1962) who found that functional analogies were quite difficult and that synonymous analogies were quite easy to solve. This discrepancy suggests that it is important to consider variations in difficulty within any particular type of analogy. For example, it is possible that the component meanings of Goldstein's functional analogies (e.g., *compass* is to *direction* as *tape measure* is to *distance*) were conceptually more difficult than those used by Sternberg and Nigro (1980) (e.g., *horn* is to *play* as *horse* is to *ride*). Nevertheless, the results of the Sternberg and Nigro study were consistent with Goldstein's results in that overall performance steadily improved as a function of subject age. However, accuracy for the 9-, 12-, 15-, and 18-year-olds, respectively, was 72, 78, 83, and 92 percent—means that were much higher than those obtained by Goldstein for the two overlapping age groups, the 9- and 12-year-olds. This inconsistency may be due in part to the presence of analogies in Sternberg and Nigro's study that could be solved by word association. In fact, Sternberg and Nigro noted that the two youngest age groups did show greater accuracy on the analogies of this type compared with those that actually required analogical reasoning, a discrepancy that was not seen in the older subjects. This suggested to Sternberg and Nigro that younger children use different strategies in solving verbal analogies than older children, who are more likely to rely on their reasoning skills.

Gallagher and Wright (1979) also considered the possibility that different types of meanings would affect the difficulty level of analogies. However, these investigators focused on a different aspect of meaning than Goldstein (1962) and Sternberg and Nigro (1980). In Gallagher and Wright's study, a written multiple-choice task consisting of 20 analogies was designed. Ten of the test items were "concrete" analogies in which the relationship shared by the two pairs of terms was easily observable (e.g., *picture* is to *frame* as *yard* is to *fence*); the other 10 analogies were "abstract" in that the common relationship was less observable (e.g., *engine* is to *car* as *man* is to *bicycle*). The response choices always included at least one plausible foil, which was a term that was related to the analogy but not in the appropriate manner (e.g., *tree* was a foil in the "picture" analogy). Following each response, children were asked to explain their answers in writing.

Children of the ages of 9, 10, 11, and 12 ($n = 260$) participated in the study. Results indicated that the abstract analogies were more difficult to solve than the concrete. Performance on the multiple-choice task steadily improved with age, with the younger children more easily swayed by plausible foils, thus showing a greater tendency to respond associatively. Developmental changes in the written explanations of answers were characterized by an improved ability to capture the shared relationship between the two pairs of terms. For example, the 9-year-olds tended to think of the pairs as independent units (e.g., "A car needs an engine, a bicycle needs a person"), while the 12-year-olds were better able to integrate the two (e.g., "Because engine and man power the car and the bicycle").

The studies discussed so far have focused on the semantic issue by comparing the difficulty of analogies expressing different types of meanings or levels of abstractness. However, it should be mentioned that the difficulty of analogies can also be increased simply by raising the vocabulary level (Sternberg, 1982). For example, the following analogies both express antonymous meanings that are easily observed, but the second example is more complex because of the particular words employed:

    1.   "top : bottom :: front : back"
    2.   "apex : base :: anterior : posterior"

A group of 19-year-olds obviously will understand the second analogy better than a group of 9-year-olds. This raises an important issue concerning the differential contribution of logical thinking versus semantic knowledge to the development of verbal analogical reasoning. When studies control the vocabulary level of their analogies, age-related improvements do occur (Feuerstein, 1979; Goldstein, 1962; Sternberg and Nigro, 1980) and therefore seem attributable to growth in logical thinking. However, the common practice of choosing words from elementary reading lists does not fully consider the child's understanding of those words, which may be incomplete. Thus, the degree to which logical thinking versus semantic knowledge affects performance on analogy tasks remains in question. Although semantic knowledge is always necessary in solving analogy problems, it may play a greater role on some tasks than on others. For example, it appears to be quite important on the Woodcock-Johnson Psycho-Educational Battery (Woodcock and Johnson, 1977), which contains the analogy "*purr* is to *cat* as *bark* is to _____?_____ (*dog*)" for 9-year-olds and "*accumulate* is to *dissipate* as *collect* is to _____?_____ (*disperse*)" for 19-year-olds. Thus, it would be interesting to conduct a developmental study where youngsters of the ages of 9 through 19 are administered all of the Woodcock-Johnson analogies and subsequently questioned about the items they miss so that vocabulary complexity versus logical factors could be isolated.

Several investigators have examined structural factors affecting verbal analogical reasoning. For example, Goldman and colleagues (1982) examined 8- and 10-year-olds ($n = 47$) under two different conditions—a generation task and a multiple-choice task. In the generation task, 50 analogy stems were presented (e.g., *cat* is to *tiger* as *dog* is to _____?_____), and the child was asked to supply the missing term (i.e., *wolf*). Two weeks later, each child received a multiple-choice task in which the same 50 stems were presented but each was followed by five alternative answers, some of which were close associates of the third term of the analogy. After the child selected an answer, he or she was asked to explain that choice to the examiner.

Results indicated that the generation task was more difficult than the multiple-choice task, and that the 10-year-olds as a group outperformed the 8-year-olds on both tasks. In agreement with the findings of Gallagher and Wright (1979) and Sternberg and Nigro (1980), the younger children in this study showed a greater tendency to respond associatively on the multiple-choice task. However, much variability within age groups was found, with some 8-year-olds outperforming the less skilled 10-year-olds. Goldman and colleagues also found that less skilled children in both age groups had greater difficulty justifying their correct responses on the multiple-choice task, tending to provide irrelevant (e.g., "Dogs and wolves bark") or personalized (e.g., "I like wolves") explanations compared with those of skilled children, whose answers more often reflected proportional thinking (e.g., "Cats and tigers are in the same family and dogs and wolves are too").

Levinson and Carpenter (1974) also addressed the issue of structural factors in analogical reasoning. These investigators used a generation task in which youngsters of the ages of 9, 12, and 15 ($n = 42$) were asked to solve a set of 16 analogies written in two different forms—quasi and true. A true analogy is written in the form of a proportion (e.g., *bird* is to *air* as *fish* is to *water*), whereas a quasi analogy is written in sentence form and contains verbs that specify the relationship between the terms (e.g., a *bird* flies in the *air*; a *fish* swims in the *water*). In this study, each age group received a different set of analogies (with missing fourth terms) so that the vocabulary level could be controlled for each group. In addition, care was taken to ensure that none of the correct answers to the analogies was a close associate of the third term. Half of the subjects in each group received the analogies in the true form first, followed one week later by the quasi analogies; the other half in each group received the two forms in the reverse order. Four subjects, randomly selected from each group, were also asked to explain their solutions orally for both the true and quasi analogies so that proportional thinking could be examined.

The results of the study revealed that quasi analogies were significantly easier than true analogies for the 9-year-olds, with mean scores of 64 versus 50 percent, respectively, for this age group. However, the quasi analogies offered no advantage to the 12- or 15-year-olds, who outperformed the younger subjects on both types of analogies. In the oral explanations of solutions, the extent to which proportional thinking was evinced for the true analogies steadily increased as a function of subject age, a result that supplements the research of Gallagher and Wright (1979) and Goldman and colleagues (1982), who found that children who were better at solving analogies were also better at explaining them. However, the explanations for the quasi analogies showed no age-related improvements. Perhaps this lack of change was due to the fact that the key relationship was already provided for the children in the verbs of the quasi analogies, thus reducing the advantage of the older children, who could identify the relationships themselves.

Summary

During the 9-through-19 age range, youngsters show an increasing ability to solve semantically complex analogies and to provide logical explanations of those solutions. Improvement also occurs in the strategies used to solve analogy problems. For example, by early adolescence, the associative response strategy observed during preadolescence in relation to second-order analogies has been replaced by analogical reasoning. Although the associative strategy resurfaces during early adolescence in relation to third-order analogies, it later diminishes as it did during preadolescence.

Aside from these age-related findings, research has demonstrated that youngsters within any particular age group show a wide range of competence in solving analogy problems, with the more competent youngsters also showing higher intelligence, better academic achievement, and a more reflective problem-solving style. Because these youngsters also provide better explanations of analogy solutions, their verbal skills in general may be above average.

Youngsters' ability to solve analogies is affected by semantic factors. For example, concrete analogies are easier than abstract, and analogies expressing antonymous relationships are easier than those expressing sequential or causal relationships. Structural factors also affect performance, with quasi analogies easier than true analogies for younger children and multiple choice response modes easier than generational modes. Another structural factor concerns the juxtaposition of second-order analogies to create third order analogies. The greater difficulty of these "analogies between analogies" is evinced by the fact that adolescents who respond analogically to second-order analogies nevertheless respond associatively when first confronted with third-order analogies.

SYLLOGISMS: DEDUCTIVE REASONING

Consistent with improvement in analogical reasoning, performance on syllogism tasks steadily improves during the preadolescent and adolescent years (e.g., Keating and Caramazza, 1975; Roberge and Flexer, 1980; Roberge and Paulus, 1971; Sternberg, 1979, 1980; Taplin, Staudenmayer, and Taddonio, 1974), and is related to internal factors such as age, intelligence, and language ability (e.g., Keating and Caramazza, 1975; Sternberg, 1979). Performance is also related to external factors such as type of syllogism (e.g., class versus conditional), content dimensions (e.g., common objects versus abstract symbols), and presentation mode (e.g., written versus naturalistic) (e.g., Kuhn, 1977; Roberge and Flexer, 1979; Roberge and Paulus, 1971; Sternberg, 1979; Taplin et al., 1974). These findings will now be discussed.

Internal Factors

In a developmental study that examined factors of age, intelligence, and language ability, Keating and Caramazza (1975) presented 64 *if–then* conditional syllogisms in a written multiple-choice format (e.g., "If Bill is better than Joe, and Joe is better than Tom, then who is best — Bill, Tom, or Joe?") to groups of 11- and 13-year-old boys ($n = 109$). Each age group was composed of a "bright" subgroup and an "average" subgroup. All bright subjects had scored at the 98th or 99th percentile on the composite arithmetic scale of the *Iowa Tests of Basic Skills* (Lindquist and Hieronymous, 1956), whereas all average subjects had scored between the 45th and 55th percentiles on this measure. Results indicated that the 13-year-olds performed the syllogisms task significantly better than the 11-year-olds, with mean accuracy scores of 81 and 76 percent obtained by the two age groups, respectively. In both age groups, it was also found that the bright subgroup performed the task significantly better than the average subgroup. To examine the relationships between syllogistic reasoning and other abilities, all subjects in both age groups were also administered a vocabulary test and a nonverbal reasoning test, the *Standard Progressive Matrices* (Raven, 1960). Low but significant correlation coefficients were obtained between syllogistic reasoning and both of those measures, suggesting that competence with syllogisms involves both linguistic and nonlinguistic processes. Sternberg (1979) also reported that language was an important component of syllogistic reasoning in a study discussed later in this chapter.

In another study, Sternberg (1980) examined improvements in speed and accuracy in syllogistic reasoning during the preadolescent and adolescents years. Youngsters of the ages of 8, 10, 13, 15, and 16 ($n = 124$) were tested using a written multiple-choice task that contained 32 linear syllogisms (e.g., "John is taller than Mary. Mary is taller than Pete. Who is tallest — John, Mary, or Pete?"). The individual responses of each subject were timed automatically using a tachistoscopic device with an attached centisecond clock. The subject read each problem silently and pushed a button to indicate an answer choice. Results showed that accuracy improved significantly as subjects got older, with mean scores of 60, 75, 77, 82, and 84 percent obtained by the five age groups, respectively. Response latency steadily declined with each successive age group, a finding that was consistent with research in analogical reasoning (Sternberg and Nigro, 1980).

Roberge and Flexer (1980) also demonstrated age-related improvements in syllogistic reasoning in a study with youngsters 12 and 14 years old ($n = 80$). The task consisted of 16 syllogisms of various types such as biconditional (e.g., "A bug is big if and only if it is red. This bug is red. Therefore, ___?___") and *if–then* conditional (e.g., "If a bug is big, then it is red. This bug is not big. Therefore, ___?___"). Subjects were asked to select a conclusion that followed logically from the two premises. Results showed that the 14-year-olds performed the task significantly better than the 12-year-olds, with mean accuracy scores of 70 and 64 percent obtained by the two age groups, respectively. Subjects were also administered the Word Knowledge subtest of the Metropolitan Achievement Tests because the investigators had predicted that syllogistic reasoning was related to vocabulary development. However, the correlation coefficient between the two tasks was not significant, a result that was inconsistent with other studies supporting a relationship between language development and syllogistic reasoning (Keating and Caramazza, 1975; Sternberg, 1979). Perhaps this was due to the fact that the vocabulary level of Roberge and Flexer's syllogisms was quite simple.

External Factors

In addition to examining developmental improvements in syllogistic reasoning, a number of investigators have examined the effects of external factors on youngsters' facility with syllogisms. For example, Roberge and Paulus (1971) examined syllogistic reasoning in youngsters of the ages of 9, 11, 13, and 15 ($n = 200$) by comparing two types of syllogisms: class (i.e., "All *A*s are *B*s. *X* is an *A*. Therefore, *X* is a *B*.") and *if–then* conditional (i.e., "If *A* then *B*. *A*. Therefore, *B*."). Another purpose of their study was to determine if content dimensions affected the difficulty of the syllogisms. Content dimensions included "concrete-familiar," where common objects were used in the problems in unimaginative ways, "suggestive," where common objects were used in imaginative ways, and "abstract," where letters, symbols, or nonsense words were used. Examples of class and conditional syllogisms expressing the three different content dimensions are contained in Table 7-2. For both class and conditional syllogisms, 12 problems were presented for each of the three content dimensions, and subjects were asked to provide a "Yes," "No," or 'Maybe" response to the last statement in each problem.

Results showed that class syllogisms were significantly easier to solve than conditional for the subjects as a whole. Significant differences also were obtained as a function of content dimension: when grade levels and types of syllogisms were combined, concrete-familiar problems were easiest, followed by suggestive and abstract problems. Consistent with other developmental studies, accuracy in responding to both the class and conditional syllogisms improved significantly with age: combining the three content dimensions, mean accuracy scores for class syllogisms were 43, 45, 54,

Table 7-2. *Types of syllogisms used by Roberge and Paulus.*

Concrete–Familiar:
    Class
        All of the green coats in the closet belong to Sarah.
        The coat in the closet is green.
        Therefore, the coat in the closet does not belong to Sarah.
    Conditional:
        If the hat on the table is blue, then it belongs to Sally.
        The hat on the table is blue.
        Therefore, the hat on the table does not belong to Sally.

Suggestive:
    Class:
        All ants that can fly are bigger than zebras.
        This ant can fly.
        Therefore, this ant is bigger than a zebra.
    Conditional:
        If mice can fly, then they are bigger than horses.
        Mice can fly.
        Therefore, mice are bigger than horses.

Abstract:
    Class:
        All pittles are cloots.
        This is not a cloot.
        Therefore, this is a pittle.
    Conditional:
        If there is a nupittle, then there is a coolt.
        There is not a coolt.
        Therefore, there is a nupittle.

Adapted from Roberge and Paulus, 1971.

and 63 percent for the 9-, 11-, 13-, and 15-year-olds, respectively; for conditional syllogisms, those scores were 42, 41, 56, and 59 percent, respectively.

    Other investigators have also documented the greater difficulty of conditional syllogisms in comparison to other types. For example, Roberge and Flexer (1979) administered a syllogistic reasoning task to groups of 13-year-olds and adults ($n = 144$). The task consisted of 16 syllogisms, with four representing each of the four different types shown in Table 7-3: biconditional, conditional, exclusive disjunctive, and inclusive disjunctive. For each problem, subjects were asked to write a conclusion that followed logically from the two premises. Results showed that exclusive disjunctive problems were easiest to solve, that conditional were most difficult, and that inclusive disjunctive and biconditional problems were intermediate in difficulty. Mean

Table 7-3. *Types of syllogisms used by Roberge and Flexer.*

Biconditional:
    There is an *A* if and only if there is a *B*.
    There is an *A*.
    Therefore, _____.

Conditional:
    If there is an *A*, then there is a *B*.
    There is not an *A*.
    Therefore, _____.

Exclusive Disjunctive:
    Either there is an *A* or there is a *B* (but not both).
    There is not a *B*.
    Therefore, _____.

Inclusive Disjunctive:
    Either there is an *A* or there is a *B* (or both).
    There is a *B*.
    Therefore, _____.

Adapted from Roberge and Flexer, 1979.

accuracy scores for those four types, respectively, were 85, 63, 71, and 70 percent.

Similar results were obtained by Sternberg (1979) who conducted a larger developmental study of syllogistic reasoning. Subjects in his study were 7, 9, 11, 13, 17, and 19 years old ($n = 224$). The task involved a cardboard box, a towel to cover the box, and two objects such as a cardboard circle and a square. A game was played where the examiner secretly placed one, both, or neither of the two objects into the box. The subject's goal was to figure out what the examiner had done. To assist the subject, the examiner always gave two "hints" which were actually the first two premises of a syllogism. The subject was then asked to respond "True," "False," or "Maybe" to the conclusion of the syllogism. The premises and conclusion were always presented both orally and in written form. The task consisted of 80 syllogisms, with 16 representing each of five different types — conjunctive, disjunctive (both inclusive and exclusive), *if–then* conditional, *only if* conditional, and biconditional. Examples of each type are contained in Table 7-4. Sternberg called this the "combination task" because the subject had to mentally combine the first two premises in order to evaluate the validity of the conclusion. To accomplish this, the subject had to comprehend each of the three sentences ("linguistic encoding") and then reason deductively ("logical combination").

Table 7-4. *Types of syllogisms used by Sternberg.*

Conjunctive:
  There is a circle in the box *and* there is a square in the box.
  There is a circle in the box.
  There is a square in the box.

Disjunctive:
  Inclusive (*A* or *B* or both):
    There is a circle in the box *or* there is a square in the box.
    There is a circle in the box.
    There is a square in the box.
  Exclusive (*A* or *B* but not both):
    There is a circle in the box *or* there is a square in the box.
    There is a square in the box.
    There is not a circle in the box.

If-then Conditional:
  If there is a circle in the box *then* there is a square in the box.
  There is a square in the box.
  There is a circle in the box.

Only-if Conditional:
  There is a circle in the box *only if* there is a square in the box.
  There is not a circle in the box.
  There is not a square in the box.

Biconditional:
  There is a circle in the box *if and only if* there is a square in the box.
  There is not a square in the box.
  There is not a circle in the box.

Adapted from Sternberg, 1979.

Mean accuracy scores for the subjects as a whole indicated that the conjunctive syllogisms (69 percent) were easiest, followed by the exclusive disjunctive syllogisms (35 percent); the *only if* conditional (21 percent) and the biconditional (20 percent) were intermediate in difficulty, and the inclusive disjunctive (6 percent) and the *if–then* conditional (6 percent) were the most difficult. Results also showed that performance improved significantly with age: mean accuracy scores obtained by the groups of 7-, 9-, 11-, 13-, 17-, and 19-year-olds, respectively, were 8, 17, 24, 31, 44, and 57 percent.

Another purpose of Sternberg's study was to compare the contribution of linguistic versus logical competence to the development of syllogistic reasoning. To accomplish this, another task, called "encoding," was presented to the same groups of subjects. The encoding task employed the same problems and procedures as in the combination task, except that the second premise of each problem was omitted (e.g., "There is a circle in the box *and* there is a square in the box. There is not a circle in the box—True, False, Maybe"). Note that by omitting the second premise, the need for deductive reasoning dissolves and the task simply assesses the subject's linguistic comprehension of the sentences. By comparing the difficulty of the encoding and combination tasks, one can infer the contribution of linguistic versus logical factors to performance on the combination task. In the present study, that comparison showed that the two tasks were approximately equal in difficulty for each of the six age groups. Sternberg therefore concluded that linguistic competence is more important than logical competence in the development of syllogistic reasoning.

Taplin, Staudenmayer, and Taddonio (1974) also compared the difficulty of different types of syllogisms but focused specifically on variations of *if–then* conditional problems. Subjects in their study were 9, 11, 13, 15, and 17 years old ($n = 296$). The task consisted of 96 conditional problems, with 12 representing each of the eight types shown in Table 7-5. Each problem consisted of two premises that were always true and a conclusion that varied in its truthfulness. Capital letters were used in all problems, as shown in the following example, which affirmed the antecedent and had an affirmative conclusion.

Table 7-5. *Types of conditional syllogisms used by Taplin, Staudenmayer, and Taddonio.*

Type of Syllogism	Conclusion	1st Premise	2nd Premise	Conclusion to Evaluate
1. Affirming the antecedent	affirmative	if p then q	$+p$	$+q$
2. Affirming the antecedent	negative	if p then q	$+p$	$-q$
3. Denying the antecedent	affirmative	if p then q	$-p$	$+q$
4. Denying the antecedent	negative	if p then q	$-p$	$-q$
5. Affirming the consequent	affirmative	if p then q	$+q$	$+p$
6. Affirming the consequent	negative	if p then q	$+q$	$-p$
7. Denying the consequent	affirmative	if p then q	$-q$	$+p$
8. Denying the consequent	negative	if p then q	$-q$	$-p$

Adapted from Taplin, Staudenmayer, and Taddonio, 1974.

A. If there is a Z, then there is an H.
B. There is a Z.
C. There is an H.

In responding to an argument, subjects were asked to evaluate the truthfulness of the conclusion (C) by circling the appropriate choice — "always correct," "sometimes correct," or "never correct." For all subjects combined, the most difficult types of syllogisms were both forms of denying the antecedent and both forms of affirming the consequent. In contrast, the syllogisms for both forms of affirming the antecedent (Table 7-5, items 1 and 2) and denying the consequent (items 7 and 8) were much easier. As expected, performance on the task improved significantly as a function of subject age: combining the various types of syllogisms, mean accuracy scores for the 9-, 11-, 13-, 15-, and 17-year-olds, respectively, were 39, 44, 45, 54, and 63 percent.

The syllogistic reasoning tasks employed in the studies discussed so far have been quite formal. However, Kuhn (1977) suggested that formal written tasks of syllogistic reasoning might underestimate children's competence in this area. She therefore developed a more naturalistic task where pictures were presented and a child was asked questions that called on class or conditional syllogistic reasoning. In one task, the child was shown a large color photograph of a "far-away city" called Tundor and additional pictures of people who lived there. The examiner made various statements about the pictures (e.g., "All of the people in Tundor are happy. Here is a picture of Jean. Jean lives in Tundor") and then asked questions requiring a "Yes," "No," or "Maybe" response (e.g., Is Jean happy?). Although 6- through 9-year-olds participated in the study, only the performance of the 9-year-olds ($n = 15$) is relevant to the present chapter. Results indicated that the 9-year-olds achieved mean accuracy scores of 77 and 67 percent for the questions requiring class and conditional reasoning, respectively, results that were markedly higher than those obtained by the 9-year-olds in the Roberge and Paulus (1971) study (43 and 42 percent for class and conditional items, respectively), or by the 9-year-olds in the Taplin and colleagues (1974) study (39 percent) who were presented with conditional items only. These comparisons across studies suggest that problems in class and conditional syllogistic reasoning are easier to solve when more naturalistic assessment methods are employed.

Summary

Youngsters' speed and accuracy on tasks of syllogistic reasoning steadily improves during the 9-through-19 age range. Growth in this area continues even into adulthood, as college students remain challenged by certain types of syllogisms. Although studies have shown that competence with syllogisms is related to intelligence and language development, the differential contribution of each of these factors is unknown. However, Sternberg (1979) argued that growth in linguistic knowledge rather than in logical competence is largely responsible for the improved performance that occurs as a function of age.

Studies have also shown that syllogisms expressing conjunction, exclusive disjunction, and class relationships are generally easier than those expressing inclusive disjunction and the *if–then* conditional. Biconditional and *only if* conditional syllogisms appear to be intermediate in difficulty. Factors responsible for these differences among types are unknown, although frequency of occurrence in conversation may be important. For example, speakers use the exclusive *or* (e.g., "I'll take strawberry or chocolate") more often that the inclusive variety (e.g., "I'll take strawberry or chocolate or both") (Sternberg, 1979). It is also noteworthy that syllogisms within a particular type can vary in difficulty according to content factors. For example, *if–then* conditionals that deny the antecedent or affirm the consequent are more difficult to understand than those that affirm the antecedent or deny the consequent, and syllogisms containing abstract terms (capital letters) are more difficult than those with concrete terms (e.g., names of common objects). Mode of presentation also has been found to affect performance. For example, formal written syllogisms are more difficult to solve than syllogisms occurring in naturalistic tasks.

CONCLUSIONS

The development of inductive and deductive verbal reasoning during the 9-through-19 age range has been discussed in relation to analogies and syllogisms. During this period, growth in solving both types of problems steadily improves in terms of speed and accuracy and in the ability to handle semantic and structural complexities. Age, intelligence, and language ability are important factors related to performance on tasks of analogical and syllogistic reasoning. However, the debate concerning the relative contribution of logical versus linguistic factors to performance in these two areas has not been resolved.

REFERENCES

Achenbach, T.M. (1969). Cue learning, associative responding, and school performance in children. *Developmental Psychology, 1,* 717–725.

Achenbach, T.M. (1970). Standardization of a research instrument for identifying associative responding in children. *Developmental Psychology, 2,* 283–291.

Feuerstein, R. (1979). *The dynamic assessment of retarded performers: The learning potential assessment device, theory, instruments, and techniques.* Baltimore, MD: University Park Press.

Gallagher, J.M., and Wright, R.J. (1979). Piaget and the study of analogy: Structural analysis of items. In M.K. Poulsen & G.I. Lubin (Eds.), *Piagetian theory and the helping professions: Proceedings from the eighth interdisciplinary conference* (Volume 2) (pp. 100-104). Los Angeles: University of Southern California.

Goldman, S.R., Pellegrino, J.W., Parseghian, P., and Sallis, R. (1982). Developmental and individual differences in verbal analogical reasoning. *Child Development, 53,* 550-559.

Goldstein, G. (1962). *Developmental studies in analogical reasoning.* Unpublished doctoral dissertation, University of Kansas, Lawrence, KS.

Growth in mathematics (Level 8). (1978). New York: Harcourt Brace Jovanovich.

Kagan, J., Rosman, B.L., Day, D., Albert, J., and Phillips, W. (1964). Information processing in the child: Significance of analytic and reflective attitudes. *Psychological Monographs, 78* (Whole No. 578).

Keating, D.P., and Caramazza, A. (1975). Effects of age and ability on syllogistic reasoning in early adolescence. *Developmental Psychology, 11,* 837-842.

Kuhn, D. (1977). Conditional reasoning in children. *Developmental Psychology, 13,* 342-353.

Levinson, P.J., and Carpenter, R.L. (1974). An analysis of analogical reasoning in children. *Child Development, 45,* 857-861.

Lindquist, E.F., and Hieronymous, A.N. (1956). *Iowa Tests of Basic Skills.* Boston: Houghton Mifflin.

Lorge, I., and Thorndike, R.L. (1957). *Lorge-Thorndike Intelligence Tests.* Boston: Houghton Mifflin.

Nippold, M.A. (1986). Verbal analogical reasoning in children and adolescents. *Topics in Language Disorders, 6*(4), 51-63.

Raven, J.C. (1960). *Guide to the Standard Progressive Matrices.* London: Lewis.

Roberge, J.J., and Flexer, B.B. (1979). Further examination of formal operational reasoning abilities. *Child Development, 50,* 478-484.

Roberge, J.J., and Flexer, B.B. (1980). Control of variables and propositional reasoning in early adolescence. *The Journal of General Psychology, 103,* 3-12.

Roberge, J.J., and Paulus, D.H. (1971). Developmental patterns for children's class and conditional reasoning abilities. *Developmental Psychology, 4,* 191-200.

Sternberg, R.J. (1979). Developmental patterns in the encoding and combination of logical connectives. *Journal of Experimental Child Psychology, 28,* 469-498.

Sternberg, R.J. (1980). The development of linear syllogistic reasoning. *Journal of Experimental Child Psychology, 29,* 340-356.

Sternberg, R.J. (1982). Reasoning, problem solving, and intelligence. In R.J. Sternberg (Ed.), *Handbook of human intelligence* (pp. 225-307). Cambridge, England: Cambridge University Press.

Sternberg, R.J. and Downing, C.J. (1982). The development of higher-order reasoning in adolescents. *Child Development, 53,* 209-221.

Sternberg, R.J., and Nigro, G. (1980). Developmental patterns in the solution of verbal analogies. *Child Development, 51,* 27-38.

Taplin, J.E., Staudenmayer, H., and Taddonio, J.L. (1974). Developmental changes in conditional reasoning: Linguistic or logical? *Journal of Experimental Child Psychology, 17,* 360-373.

Woodcock, R.W., and Johnson, M.B. (1977). *Woodcock-Johnson Psycho-Educational Battery.* Hingham, MA: Teaching Resources.

CHAPTER 8

■

FIGURATIVE LANGUAGE

■

MARILYN A. NIPPOLD

Two butterflies are on a daisy in a polo field with poloists bearing down upon a ball at rest beneath them. The caption, a speech of one of the butterflies, connects the language of teenagers incongruously with the situation of pastoral: 'The first one to fly off is chicken.' (Redfern, 1984, p. 23)

Figurative language often occurs in spoken form during conversations, lectures, and news reports, and in written form in newspapers, poems, novels, and textbooks. Major types of figurative language include metaphors, similes, idioms, and proverbs. When used effectively, such language captures an individual's attention, stimulates the imagination, and helps to educate, entertain, and encourage. It also may enhance peer acceptance as when adolescents exchange figurative expressions unique to their social groups (Donahue and Bryan, 1984). Gaining competence with figurative language during the 9-through-19 age range is an important part of becoming a literate person.

Youngsters' development of figurative language has been studied for over 60 years. Much of the interest in this topic stems from the belief that figurative competence reflects an individual's cognitive level (e.g., Arlin, 1978; Billow, 1975; Cometa and Eson, 1978; Smith, 1976), creativity (e.g., Gardner, Kircher, Winner, and Perkins, 1975; Paivio, 1979; Schaefer,

Parts of this chapter were published by Marilyn A. Nippold in the article Comprehension of figurative language in youth. *Topics in Language Disorders, 5*(3), 1-20, 1985. Reprinted with permission of Aspen Publishers, Inc.

179

1975), and abstract reasoning ability (e.g., Brown, 1965; Hoffman and Honeck, 1980; Kogan, Connor, Gross, and Fava, 1980; Ortony, 1979). Although figurative language is first understood during the preschool years (e.g., Boynton and Kossan, 1981; Dent, 1984; Gardner, 1974; Gentner, 1977; Vosniadou and Ortony, 1983), comprehension steadily improves throughout childhood, adolescence, and into the adult years (e.g., Boswell, 1979; Gorham, 1956; Lodge and Leach, 1975; Richardson and Church, 1959; Watts, 1944). Less is known about the development of figurative language in terms of production. However, it has been suggested that growth in production follows a U-shaped curve such that novel, imaginative expressions are frequently produced by preschoolers, decrease during the elementary school years, but increase during adolescence (Gardner et al., 1975; Gardner, Winner, Bechhofer, and Wolf, 1978). Further research is necessary to confirm this developmental pattern.

This chapter discusses the development of figurative language for youngsters in the 9-through-19 age range. Comprehension of metaphors, similes, idioms, and proverbs is emphasized. Aspects of production are also discussed where information is available. Although younger children participated in many of the studies to be reviewed, their performance is generally not reported because of this book's emphasis on preadolescents and adolescents.

METAPHORS AND SIMILES

A metaphor contains a term, called the topic, which is likened to another term, called the vehicle, on the basis of one or more shared features, called the ground (Gardner et al., 1978). For example, in the metaphor "The giraffe was a flagpole living at the zoo," *giraffe* is the topic, *flagpole* the vehicle, and *tallness* the ground. Two major types of metaphors are the predicative (also known as similarity) and the proportional (Billow, 1977; Miller, 1979). In a predicative metaphor, such as the "giraffe–flagpole" example, there is one topic and one vehicle (Ortony, 1979; Winner, Engel, and Gardner, 1980a). Proportional metaphors contain two topics and two vehicles that express an analogical relationship at an underlying level; at the surface level, however, one topic is unstated (Gardner et al., 1978; Miller, 1979; Ortony, 1979). For example, the proportional metaphor "Johnny's knee was a tomato that squirted juice" contains the analogy "*Tomato* is to *juice* as *knee* is to _____," leaving the topic *blood* to be inferred.

A simile is a variation of a predicative metaphor that makes the comparison between the topic and vehicle more explicit by inserting the word *like* (e.g., "The giraffe was like a flagpole living at the zoo") or the phrase *as (adjective) as* (e.g., "The giraffe was as tall as a flagpole living at the zoo"). Note that in the latter type of simile, the comparison is so explicit that the ground is actually stated.

Metaphor and Simile Comprehension

Internal Factors

Chronological age, verbal ability, and cognition are factors that have been studied in relation to metaphor and simile comprehension. For example, Siltanen (1981) studied metaphor comprehension by grouping youngsters of the ages of 9 through 18 ($n = 126$) into Piagetian cognitive stages: concrete-operational (ages 9 through 11), late concrete–early formal operational (ages 12 through 14), and formal operational (ages 15 through 18). The experimental task consisted of 16 metaphors which had been classified as "easy" (e.g., "Butterflies are rainbows"), "moderate" (e.g., "Jealousy is a green-eyed monster"), or "difficult" (e.g., "Genius is perseverence in action"). Each metaphor was presented within a contextually supportive paragraph. Subjects read the paragraphs and wrote down the meanings of the metaphors.

Explanations of the metaphors were analyzed in terms of accuracy and completeness. As expected, the formal operational group outperformed the transitional group, which outperformed the concrete-operational group. However, even the formal operational group had not completely mastered the task, and found the set of "difficult" metaphors especially challenging. Verbal-ability scores from certain subtests of the *Iowa Tests of Basic Skills* (Lindquist and Hieronymus, 1956) were available for some of the subjects, and significant correlation coefficients were obtained between metaphor comprehension and "Language Use," "Language Total," "Reading Comprehension," and "Total Listening."

Billow (1975) also examined metaphor comprehension in relation to Piagetian cognitive level. Youngsters 9, 11, and 13 years old ($n = 30$) were asked to explain the meanings of 12 similarity metaphors (e.g., "Hair is spaghetti") and 12 proportional metaphors (e.g., "My head is an apple without any core"). Billow hypothesized that concrete-operational thinking was required before a child could comprehend similarity metaphors, and that formal operational thinking was required before the more difficult proportional metaphors could be understood. Each subject was also administered a class-inclusion task as a measure of concrete operations, and a combinatorial reasoning task as a measure of formal operations.

Results showed that for both types of metaphors, explanations steadily improved as subject age increased. For the similarity metaphors, mean accuracy scores obtained by the 9-, 11-, and 13-year-olds, respectively, were 60, 85, and 90 percent. For the proportional metaphors, those means were 47, 65, and 75 percent, respectively. In addition, significant correlations were obtained between class inclusion and similarity metaphor comprehension, and between combinatorial reasoning and proportional metaphor comprehension. However, the cognitive-prerequisite hypothesis was not supported for either type of metaphor: youngsters who performed poorly on the class-inclusion task sometimes understood the similarity metaphors, and those who performed poorly on the combinatorial task sometimes understood the proportional metaphors.

Other investigators such as Arlin (1978), Cometa and Eson (1978), and Smith (1976) also tried to show that certain Piagetian cognitive stages are prerequisites to metaphor comprehension, but none were successful. A recent discussion of this issue was published by Vosniadou (1987), who delineated the major methodological weaknesses characterizing the research in this area.

The relationship between cognition and metaphor comprehension has also been examined from a non-Piagetian perspective, but the results have been inconsistent. For example, Kogan and colleagues (1980) examined the relationship between performance on a metaphoric-triads task (MTT) and performance on various standardized tests such as the *Otis-Lennon Mental Ability Test* (Otis and Lennon, 1967) and the *Iowa Tests of Basic Skills* (Lindquist and Hieronymous, 1956). The MTT is a measure of metaphor comprehension where three pictures are displayed in a row in front of the subject. Two pictures express a metaphoric relationship (e.g., a coiled snake and a winding river) whereas the third picture (e.g., a fish) is related to the other two in a literal manner. The subject's task is to select and explain all possible pairs. A response is credited if the metaphoric relationship is appropriately identified. Kogan and colleagues found that the MTT was sensitive to age-related improvements in metaphor comprehension: mean accuracy scores for groups of 9-, 10-, 12-, 18-, and 19-year-olds ($n = 448$) were 29, 28, 41, 61, and 60 percent, respectively. Scores on the *Iowa* and *Otis-Lennon* tests were available for some of the 9-year-olds and for all of the 12-year-olds, but no correlations between these measures and the MTT reached significance. However, some of the 9-year-olds were also administered the *Children's Associative Responding Test* (CART; Achenbach, 1969), a measure of analogical reasoning (see Chapter 7), and it was found that better performance on the MTT was associated with better performance on the CART.

Malgady (1977) also employed a non-Piagetian approach to the study of metaphoric language. In his investigation, 11 different similes (e.g., "The hair is like spaghetti," "The clouds are like ice cream," etc.) were presented in written form and youngsters were asked to write down the meanings of each. Results showed that a group of 11- and 12-year-olds ($n = 20$) produced a greater percentage of valid interpretations than a group of 8- and 9-year-olds ($n = 20$), with means of 83 and 71 percent obtained by the two groups, respectively. For the older group, it was also found that performance on the simile task was significantly correlated to verbal intelligence as measured by the *Lorge-Thorndike Intelligence Test* (Lorge and Thorndike, 1957), to reading comprehension as measured by the *Metropolitan Achievement Tests*

(Durost, 1959), and to academic performance as measured by teacher ratings. However, the correlations for the younger group were not significant with respect to any of the standardized tests.

SUMMARY. Studies focusing on internal factors have shown that metaphor and simile comprehension steadily improve during the 9-through-19 age range. Some studies have reported that better figurative comprehension is associated with higher performance on tasks of cognitive, verbal, or academic ability; however, no studies have identified any specific prerequisites for the comprehension of metaphors or similes. In fact, the *cognitive prerequisite theory* is no longer well accepted, as it has been shown that even preschool children can comprehend metaphors when age-appropriate materials and testing procedures are employed (Vosniadou, 1987). In contrast, a more plausible theory is the *language experience view*, which states that metaphor comprehension is largely dependent upon the amount of exposure a youngster has had to such language (Ortony, Turner, and Larson-Shapiro, 1985).

External Factors

Research has shown that a variety of linguistic, metalinguistic, and non-linguistic factors affect youngsters' metaphor comprehension. These include syntactic form, conceptual domain, response condition, novelty, and the element of movement.

For example, Nippold, Leonard, and Kail (1984) examined the influence of syntactic form and conceptual domain on children's metaphor comprehension. A group of 9-year-olds ($n = 30$) were included in their study. A multiple-choice listening task was presented which contained nine instances of four different types of metaphoric sentences: (1) perceptual-predicative (e.g., "The bird was a rainbow flying in the sky"); (2) psychological-predicative (e.g., "Tom was a vaccuum cleaner listening to the story"); (3) perceptual-proportional (e.g., "The bird's nest was a piggybank that had no coins"); and (4) psychological-proportional (e.g., "The artist was an apple tree that had no fruit"). Perceptual metaphors expressed a visual resemblance between different items, whereas psychological metaphors expressed an emotion, mental state, or personality characteristic.

In constructing the task, Nippold and colleagues ensured that the sentences were approximately the same length, that the vocabulary was simple, and that the metaphors were novel so that children would actively think about their meanings. In presenting the task, the examiner read each sentence aloud, asked the child to repeat it, and read two alternative interpretations for the child to choose from. One alternative always represented an appropriate figurative interpretation, whereas the foil expressed an inappropriate nonliteral interpretation. For example, in presenting the alternatives for the "bird–rainbow" metaphor, the examiner said, "That means the bird: (1) was very colorful; (2) was making a nest." Results showed that the children had more difficulty with proportional metaphors than with predicative, but that psychological metaphors did not differ from perceptual in ease of understanding.

Although Nippold and colleagues did not find that psychological metaphors were more difficult to comprehend that perceptual, other investigators have reported differences in metaphor comprehension related to the conceptual domain. For example, Winner, Rosenstiel, and Gardner (1976) compared children's understanding of "psychological-physical" metaphors to "cross-sensory" metaphors. Psychological-physical metaphors were said to express "a psychological experience by appealing to an event in the physical domain" (p. 290) (e.g., "After many years of working at the jail, the prison guard had become a hard rock that could not be moved" [p. 293]), and cross-sensory were said to express "an experience in one sensory modality by referring synesthetically to another sensory modality" (p. 290) (e.g., "The smell of my mother's perfume was bright sunshine" [p. 293]).

Youngsters of the ages of 10, 12, and 14 ($n = 90$) were included in their study. The examiner read 16 metaphoric sentences to each subject: eight psychological-physical and eight cross-sensory. Comprehension of each sentence was assessed under two different conditions; explanation, and multiple choice. To accomplish this, the examiner asked half the subjects in each age group to explain the meanings of the sentences, and the other half to select from four alternative interpretations the examiner read to them. For each sentence, the four choices always included one appropriate metaphoric interpretation and three foils that expressed various literal interpretations.

The results for both response conditions showed that comprehension steadily improved through the age of 14, and that the cross-sensory metaphors were easier to understand than the psychological-physical, particularly for the 10-year-olds. The results also showed that for both conditions literal interpretations decreased and figurative interpretations increased as subjects got older. The multiple choice condition revealed a higher level of performance than the explanation condition. However, this was not surprising, given the greater metalinguistic demands of an explanation task in requiring a child to talk about language as an entity itself.

Gardner (1974) also found that an explanation condition was more difficult than a receptive condition in assessing metaphor comprehension. His study included subjects 11 and 19 years old ($n = 50$). Each subject was asked to match familiar polar adjectives, such as *happy–sad* and *loud–quiet*, to stimuli in various sensory modalities, such as colors, facial expressions, and auditory tones. Materials had been collected to represent the literal and metaphoric interpretations of the adjective pairs in various modalities. For example, the literal interpretation of the pair *happy–sad* was represented by pictures of happy and sad faces, and the metaphoric interpretations by yellow-orange and violet-blue color swatches, and by musical tones played in a major key and in a minor key. Gardner had ensured that the metaphoric matches were legitimate by presenting them to adult judges in a prior experiment.

Each subject was first presented with materials representing the literal interpretations of an adjective pair, such as a happy face and a sad face, and was told to decide, for example, which was happy and which was sad. Then the examiner presented pairs of stimuli representing metaphoric interpretations from the various modalities (e.g., two colors or two tones) and the subject was told to decide which was happy and which was sad. After deciding, the subject was asked to explain each match. Accuracy in assigning the metaphoric interpretations to the sensory stimuli was equally high for the 11- and 19-year-olds, with means of 89 and 91 percent obtained by the two groups, respectively. The groups differed, however, in terms of their explanations: Although the 11-year-olds explained their matches adequately, the 19-year-olds gave an even greater variety of appropriate explanations, evinced less concreteness, and showed greater awareness of the multiple meanings of words.

Returning now to the issue of syntactic form and metaphor comprehension, Winner and colleagues (1980a) constructed a task that included 15 predicative metaphors (e.g., "The skywriting was a scar marking the sky"). For each metaphor, four syntactically different but semantically equivalent versions were also included, which were in the form of topicless metaphors (e.g., "The scar marked the sky"), similes (e.g., "The skywriting was like a scar marking the sky"), quasi analogies (e.g., "A scar marks someone's skin and something marks the sky"), and riddles (e.g., "What is like a scar but marks the sky?").

The subjects included a group of 9-year-olds ($n = 40$). The examiner read the 15 metaphors to each child, presenting three for each of the five different forms. As in the earlier study (Winner et al., 1976), half the children responded through a multiple-choice condition, and half were asked to explain the meanings of the metaphors. In the multiple-choice condition, the examiner read four alternative answers and asked to child to choose the best one. Consistent with the earlier study (Winner and colleagues, 1976), the multiple-choice condition yielded greater accuracy than the explanation condition for all five versions of the metaphors. For both response modes, topicless metaphors were easier to understand than predicative, and riddles were easier to understand than topicless metaphors, but similes and predicative metaphor were equal in difficulty. Whereas quasi analogies were easier to understand than topicless metaphors for children in the multiple choice condition, they were equal in difficulty for children in the explanation condition.

Although Winner and colleagues (1980a) had predicted that similes would be easier to comprehend than predicative metaphors, suggesting that the additional word *like* might help a child realize that the metaphorical statement was not intended literally, their results did not support that prediction. Reynolds and Ortony (1980) had made that same prediction, but tested it using a more naturalistic task involving contextual support. Children 9, 10, and 11 years old ($n = 112$) read short stories and selected the most appropriate continuation sentence for each from among four alternatives. The continuation sentences were expressed either as predicative metaphors or as semantically matched similes. For example, one story was about a boy who wanted to hide his new baseball mitt from his friends. Expressed as a metaphor, the appropriate continuation sentence was "Johnny was a dog burying a bone in the backyard," and as a simile it was "Johnny was like a dog burying a bone in the backyard." However, the results of the study showed that metaphors and similes were equal in difficulty for these three age groups. It was also shown that for the metaphors and similes combined, accuracy in selecting the appropriate continuation sentence steadily improved as subject age increased: mean scores of 67, 72, and 80 percent were obtained by the 9-, 10-, and 11-year-olds, respectively.

A developmental study conducted by Pollio and Pollio (1979) indicated that the novelty of a metaphoric expression affects its understandability. These investigators presented a comprehension task involving 17 frozen and 17 novel metaphors to youngsters in the fourth through the eighth grades (9 through 14 years old; $n = 149$). A frozen metaphor was defined as one that frequently occurred in the language, whereas a novel metaphor rarely occurred. Each metaphor in the study had been classified as frozen or novel by a panel of adult judges. To assess comprehension, each metaphor was presented within the context of a short paragraph or sentence that was followed by four randomly ordered answer choices. One choice expressed the correct nonliteral meaning of the metaphor and the others were foils, as shown in the two examples below (Pollio and Pollio, 1979):

Frozen:
> I went into the kitchen and *ate up a storm*.
> a. I ate a lot.
> b. I like to eat when it's raining.
> c. I ate so much it rained.
> d. I drank some white lightning from the refrigerator.

Novel:
> I saw a coffin and was scared. I walked slowly toward it. I was amazed *my feet were brave enough to take me there*.

    a. I did not think I would have the courage to do it.
    b. Somehow I was pulled to the coffin against my will.
    c. My feet have a mind of their own.
    d. My new sneakers made me feel I could do anything. (p. 114)

Children read the test items and circled the best answer choice for each. As predicted, the frozen metaphors were easier to comprehend than the novel for all five grade levels. The results also showed a pattern of steady improvement as grade level increased: in fourth grade, accuracy in comprehending the novel and frozen metaphors was 45 and 58 percent, respectively, but increased to 60 and 80 percent, respectively, by eighth grade.

Pollio and Pickens (1980) later presented that same comprehension task to additional groups of subjects representing a broader age range. Youngsters of the ages of 8 through 17, from third, fifth, sixth, seventh, ninth, and eleventh grades ($n = 180$), participated in the second study. Consistent with the first study (Pollio and Pollio, 1974), frozen metaphors were easier to comprehend than novel, and comprehension of both types of metaphors steadily improved as subjects got older. Although the two oldest subject groups approached a ceiling on the task, accuracy in comprehending the novel and frozen metaphors was 88 and 95 percent, respectively, by eleventh grade.

Dent (1984) examined the nonlinguistic factor of movement in relation to metaphor comprehension in the visual modality. Ten-year-olds and adults ($n = 32$) were included in her study. Each subject was shown triads of filmed scenes (e.g., a ballerina leaping, a ballerina spinning, a top spinning) and was told to pick the two that went together. In each triad, there were three possible pairings: (1) literal, in which the same type of object was shown in two different ways (e.g., ballerina leaping, ballerina spinning); (2) metaphoric, in which one particular property characterized two different types of objects (e.g., ballerina spinning, top spinning); and (3) control, in which there was little similarity between two scenes (e.g., top spinning, ballerina leaping).

Ten triads were presented to each subject, half consisting of moving or *event* scenes, such as the ballerina and top, and half consisting of stationary or *object* scenes, such as a wrinkled face, a smooth face, and a wrinkled apple. After a metaphoric pairing was made, the subject was asked to think about the two scenes at the same time and to describe what came to mind. The purpose of this description task was to determine the extent to which the subject could explain the overlapping properties (i.e., the ground) between the topic and the vehicle of a visual metaphor when specifically probed for such information.

As predicted, both the 10-year-olds and the adults had greater success in detecting the event metaphors than the object metaphors, a finding which Dent attributed to the greater "attention-capturing" properties of the former.

The results also showed that the adults made more metaphoric pairings than the 10-year-olds, that control pairings occurred infrequently, but that literal pairings were frequent at both ages. Interestingly, the two age groups performed equally well in explaining the metaphoric pairings, a finding that contrasted with many other studies that showed metaphoric explanations steadily improving during the preadolescent and adolescent years (Billow, 1975; Gardner, 1974; Kogan et al., 1980; Malgady, 1977; Pollio and Pickens, 1980; Siltanen, 1981; Silberstein, Gardner, Phelps, and Winner, 1982; Winner et al., 1976).

SUMMARY. Developmental studies focusing on external factors have shown that metaphor comprehension steadily improves during the 9-through-19 age range, and that it is influenced by a number of factors. One important factor is syntactic form. For example, predicative metaphors are easier to understand than proportional, whereas riddles, quasi analogies, and topicless metaphors are easier to understand than predicative metaphors. Similes and predicative metaphors are equal in understandability for this age range, although similes may be easier than predicative metaphors for children younger than nine years of age (Reynolds and Ortony, 1980). Conceptual domain also affects metaphor comprehension such that cross-sensory metaphors are easier to understand than psychological-physical. Novelty is also an important factor in that frozen metaphors are easier to understand than novel. It was also shown that tasks involving matching or multiple-choice response conditions are considerably easier than explanation tasks, which place additional metalinguistic demands on the interpreter, but that metaphoric explanations steadily improve during the 9-through-19 age range. Finally, a nonlinguistic factor affecting metaphor comprehension is the element of movement. For example, if metaphoric relationships are presented within a visual modality, those involving action seem to be easier to detect than static presentations.

Metaphoric Productions

A number of questions might be asked concerning metaphoric productions during the 9-through-19 age range. For example, what is the frequency of metaphoric productions, and under what conditions do they occur? Does the frequency of productions increase or decrease as youngsters get older? What types of metaphors are produced during this age range, and to what extent are they novel versus frozen? Investigators have started to address these questions, but much remains to be learned.

Formal Tasks

Most of the research focusing on metaphoric productions in older children and adolescents has been conducted using formal elicitation tasks. For example, Pollio and Pollio (1974) studied the development of metaphoric productions in third-, fourth-, and fifth-grade children, of the ages of 8 through 11 (n = 174). In a compositions task, students wrote stories about imaginative topics (e.g., a talking goldfish, adventures in space), and the frequency of novel and frozen metaphors occurring in their stories was analyzed. The results showed that the production of both types of metaphors steadily decreased as grade level increased, and that all three grade levels produced a greater proportion of frozen than novel metaphors. Pollio and Pollio suggested that during formal writing assignments, elementary-school students are increasingly concerned about achieving good grades so are less likely to "rock the boat" by using words in unconventional or nonliteral ways.

However, when Pollio and Pollio presented a different task to the same students in that study, the results suggested that the capacity for figurative production actually increased during the 8-through-11 age range. The second task required the students to make comparisons between different items. Pairs of unrelated words (e.g., boy–clock) were presented, and the students were asked to describe how the two items were similar. As before, the students' responses were analyzed for the frequency of frozen and novel metaphors. In contrast to the composition task, the comparison task showed that for all three grade levels, a greater proportion of novel than frozen metaphors occurred in the responses. The results also showed that the production of both types of metaphors steadily increased as grade level increased.

To study the development of metaphoric productions over a wider age range, Pollio and Pickens (1980) administered a compositions task similar to the one used by Pollio and Pollio (1974) to groups of students 8 through 17 years old who were enrolled in the third, fifth, sixth, seventh, ninth, and eleventh grades (n = 180). Consistent with the previous study (Pollio and Pollio, 1974), a greater proportion of frozen than novel metaphors were produced by each grade level, and both types of metaphors steadily decreased in frequency from third through sixth grades, thus reflecting the "don't rock the boat" strategy seen earlier with the composition task. Whereas novel metaphors continued to decrease through eleventh grade, interestingly, the frequency of frozen metaphors sharply increased from seventh to eleventh grades. Pollio and Pickens (1980) suggested that these results were consistent with the view that formal writing tasks tend to discourage unusual usages of words, and that adolescents are even more sensitive to this issue than younger students. The fact that frozen metaphors actually increased during adolescence was simply interpreted to mean that as students got older, they no longer considered the frozen metaphors unusual.

Gardner and colleagues (1975) employed a sentence-completion task to study metaphoric productions developmentally. Youngsters 11, 14, and 19 years old (approximately 60 subjects) were included in this study. Each subject was presented with a set of short stories and asked to complete the last sentence in each, which was actually a simile. Gardner and colleagues provided the following example:

Things don't have to be huge in size to look that way. Look at that boy standing over there. He looks as gigantic as. . . . (p. 128)

Youngsters' productions were subsequently scored as literal, conventional (i.e., frozen), appropriate (i.e., novel), or inappropriate. Results indicated that frozen metaphoric productions were the most frequent response at all age levels but did not show any developmental changes. Literal, inappropriate, and novel metaphoric productions were low at all age levels, but novel productions did show a slight increase in frequency as subject age increased.

Gardner and colleagues' finding that frozen metaphors were produced more frequently than novel metaphors during a sentence-completion task was consistent with the findings of Pollio and Pollio (1974) and Pollio and Pickens (1980), where youngsters wrote compositions. However, Gardner and colleagues' (1975) findings were inconsistent with those two studies in terms of the developmental patterns for the two types of metaphors. Thus, it is difficult to draw firm conclusions concerning the development of metaphoric productions during the 9-through-19 age range. More research should be conducted in this area, particularly in natural settings where youngsters are interacting with peers, parents, and teachers during daily activities.

Spontaneous metaphors spoken by preschool children in natural settings were recorded and analyzed in several investigations (e.g., Billow, 1981; Chukovsky, 1968; Winner, 1979; Winner, McCarthy, and Gardner, 1980b; Winner, McCarthy, Kleinman, and Gardner, 1979), and a relatively high incidence of such language was reported. No known investigator has conducted that type of systematic study of youngsters in the 9-through-19 age range. However, several investigators have informally examined older children's spontaneous production of metaphors in the form of sounding and slang expressions.

Informal Tasks

SOUNDING. Ortony and colleagues (1985) questioned black youngsters from fourth, fifth, and sixth grades ($n = 319$) living in Harlem, New York, about their participation in "sounding," a verbally aggressive street game where insults are exchanged that often contain metaphors and other types of figurative language. Ortony and colleagues provided the following example of sounding:

Larry: "Man, you so poor your roaches and rats eat lunch out!"
Reggie: "Well, you so poor the rats and roaches take you out to lunch!" (p. 26)

Many of the youngsters in the study reported that they often engaged in sounding, which, when executed skillfully, is a mark of status among preadolescent and adolescent blacks. The investigators also were interested in the relationship between sounding and the comprehension of figurative language. Therefore, all subjects were also administered the Reynolds and Ortony (1980) metaphor-simile comprehension task previously described, and it was found that those who engaged more frequently in sounding also understood figurative language better than those who engaged in it less often. Consistent with Reynolds and Ortony (1980), performance on the figurative comprehension task steadily improved as subjects got older, but the frequency of sounding for the different grade levels was not reported. Thus, it is unknown to what extent developmental changes may occur in black youngsters' sounding behavior.

SLANG. Slang is another type of figurative language that has been studied informally in older children. The use of slang expressions unique to the peer group is reportedly an important aspect of language development, particularly during adolescence (Donahue and Bryan, 1984; Hyde, 1982; Leona, 1978; Lewis, 1963; Nelsen and Rosenbaum, 1972; Schwartz and Merten, 1967). Slang expressions used by adolescents often occur in the form of metaphors. For example, Leona (1978) studied adolescents at a high school near Boston, Massachusetts, and reported that the general student population had special names for members of various cliques. These cliques included "jocks," who were actively involved in sports, "motorheads," who spent most of their time driving or repairing their cars, and "fleabags," who used drugs and had a countercultural lifestyle. In addition, each of these cliques had its own metaphoric expressions that served to distinguish it from outsiders. For examples, jocks had special names for other athletes (e.g., *The Jumping Machine, Speedy, East to West*), motorheads had names for particular cars (e.g., *Bondo, Six-Pack, Goat*), and fleabags had names for drugs (e.g., *joints, bones, j's*).

Little is known about developmental changes that may occur in the spontaneous production of slang expressions in older children and adolescents. However, Nelsen and Rosenbaum (1972) indirectly examined this issue in a study where boys and girls ($n = 1916$) from seventh through twelfth grades (12 through 18 years old) were compared in their ability to generate lists of slang words used by their peers when talking about various topics. Nine different topics were presented, one at a time, which included money, cigarettes and smoking, autos and motorbikes, alcohol and drinking, clothing and appearance, boys, girls, popular people, and unpopular people. Students worked in groups of four individuals of the same gender from the same grade level. Each group was allowed five minutes per topic to generate as many slang words as possible.

Results showed that boys generated more slang words than girls for the topics of money, and autos and motorbikes, but that girls outperformed boys on the topics of clothing and appearance, boys, popular people, and unpopular people. The results also showed that the mean number of slang words steadily increased as a function of grade level, and that larger increases were seen for some topics than for others. For example, seventh-grade boys generated a mean of 10.4 words for the topic of girls, whereas twelfth-grade boys generated a mean of 24.4 words for this topic. Other topics showing large increases for boys included cars and motorbikes, and alcohol and drinking. Topics showing large increases for girls included unpopular people, alcohol and drinking, and girls.

Although the Nelsen and Rosenbaum study showed that older adolescents knew more slang words than younger ones, this did not prove that the older adolescents actually used more slang words. Thus, it would be interesting to examine systematically the frequency with which slang words are actually used by adolescents of different ages. To accomplish this, instead of asking adolescents to generate lists of slang words, an indirect approach might be employed where adolescents in small groups are asked to discuss among themselves various topics of interest (e.g., "What do clothes tell you about another person?," "What makes a boy or girl popular? Unpopular? Why?"). As the youngsters are talking, tape recordings could be made so that the spontaneous usage of slang words could later be analyzed. Adolescents of different ages (e.g., 13, 15, 17, and 19 years old) should be studied in this manner so that developmental differences could be observed. It would also be important to study adolescents' use of slang words in a variety of different settings and with co-conversationalists of different ages, sexes, and levels of status.

Another interesting aspect of slang expressions is that they can have multiple *nonliteral* meanings, often signaled by subtle variations in vocal stress, pitch, and intonation, and by nonlinguistic contextual factors. For example, the popular expression *awesome* can serve as a sincere comment about the excellence of a particular person or entity (e.g., "We have an *awesome* basketball team!" spoken after winning the state championship). However, it can also be used sarcastically to deflate another's ego (e.g., "Jim's an *awesome* athlete," in reference to the weakest player on a team). Little is known about the ability of older children and adolescents to use and understand the multiple nonliteral meanings of slang expressions, a topic for future research.

Summary

Research suggests that the capacity for metaphoric productions during the 9-through-19 age range increases, but that the actual usage of such language is greatly affected by situational factors. For example, formal writing assignments tend to discourage spontaneous metaphoric productions, whereas divergent production tasks (e.g., comparing dissimilar objects, generating lists of slang words) tend to encourage its use, and show increases in frequency as youngsters get older. Informal encounters with peers tend to encourage spontaneous metaphoric productions in the form of sounding and slang expressions, but developmental changes in these behaviors are unknown. The extent to which youngsters actually create novel metaphors during social encounters is also unknown. In addition to these issues, it would be interesting to examine systematically the extent to which youngsters' capacity for metaphoric productions is related to social factors such as leadership and dominance, and to nonsocial factors such as intelligence and general language ability.

IDIOMS

Idioms are expressions, such as *hot potato, on the rocks,* and *upper crust,* that can have both a literal and a figurative meaning depending on the linguistic context. For example, the literal meaning of *upper crust* comes to mind upon reading "The baker rolled out the upper crust," but the figurative meaning of that expression is sparked by the sentence "Only children from the upper crust can attend Worthly Academy" (Nippold and Martin, in press).

Figurative meanings of idioms have become fixed in the language through repeated use (Ackerman, 1982). Sometimes the figurative meaning of an idiom is known mainly by a specific subgroup of the population, as when idioms occur in the form of slang expressions produced by adolescents. For example, Leona (1978) reported that the jocks in a Boston high school told other athletes "Your socks are on fire" to indicate smelly feet, and that the motorheads talked about "riding the gun," which meant sitting in the passenger seat of a car. It is often assumed that there is little relationship between the literal and figurative meanings of idioms and, therefore, that knowing the literal meaning of an idiom is not very helpful in learning its figurative meaning (Ortony, Schallert, Reynolds, and Antos, 1978). This view has led several investigators to hypothesize that people learn idioms as giant lexical units rather than by analyzing their constituents (e.g., Ackerman, 1982; Hoffman and Honeck, 1980; Strand and Fraser, 1979). However, Gibbs (1987) recently distinguished two types of idioms: *metaphorically opaque* and *metaphorically transparent.* With the opaque type (e.g., *beat around the bush, at the drop of the hat, spill the beans*), there is little relationship between the literal and figurative meanings. However, with the transparent type (e.g., *hold your tongues, skating on thin ice, right under our noses*), the figurative meaning is actually a metaphorical extension of the literal meaning. For example, *skating on thin ice* implies a precarious situation both literally and figuratively. Gibbs therefore hypothesized that metaphorically transparent idioms would be easier for children to figure out than metaphorically opaque.

Idioms as giant lexical units are an important part of vocabulary development. Although they often occur in textbooks for school children (Arter, 1976; Hollingshed, 1958), research has shown that youngsters' reading comprehension is sometimes hindered by the presence of idioms in written passages (May, 1979). An understanding of idioms is therefore necessary for the child's attainment of literacy. A small number of studies have formally examined the development of idiom comprehension during the 9-through-19 age range. However, youngsters' production of idioms during this period has only been studied informally (e.g., Leona, 1978).

Lodge and Leach (1975) conducted an idiom comprehension study that included 9-, 12-, and 21-year-olds ($n = 60$). The task consisted of 10 idiomatic sentences (e.g., *He kicked the bucket, He spilled the beans*), each accompanied by four pictures. Two of the pictures were accurate illustrations — one of the literal meaning and one of the figurative — and two were foils. After each sentence was read aloud by the examiner, the subject was asked to point to the pictures that best expressed its two meanings. All groups clearly understood the literal meanings, but the figurative meanings were considerably more difficult, particularly for younger subjects. Mean accuracy scores for the figurative meanings obtained by the 9-, 12-, and 21-year-olds, respectively, were 20, 50, and 80 percent. Thus, it appeared that the figurative meanings of idioms were not well understood until after age 12.

However, Lodge and Leach's findings were questioned by Strand and Fraser (1979), who suggested that the simultaneous presentation of literal and figurative pictures in that investigation may have been confusing. Therefore, Strand and Fraser designed a task in which comprehension of the literal meanings of idiomatic sentences was assessed separately from comprehension of the figurative meanings. Strand and Fraser's study included 9- and 11-year-olds ($n = 20$). Each child listened to 20 idiomatic sentences, each of which was accompanied by two sets of four pictures — one set for the literal meanings and one for the figurative meanings. Each set contained one correct illustration and three foils. The literal and figurative comprehension tasks were both administered during one session, with the literal task always following the figurative. For both tasks, the examiner read a sentence and asked the child to choose the one picture that best expressed its meaning. For the figurative task, the child was also asked to explain the meaning of the sentence.

In agreement with Lodge and Leach (1975), Strand and Fraser (1979) found that both groups comprehended the literal meanings of the idioms better than the figurative. For the figurative meanings, however, comprehension was higher in the Strand and Fraser study, where mean accuracy scores of 62 and 79 percent were obtained by the 9- and 11-year-olds, respectively. However, it should be mentioned that factors other than presentation style may have contributed to the discrepancy between the findings of these two studies. For example, different sets of idioms were presented in the two studies, and Strand and Fraser's task contained twice as many idioms. Although there was some overlap in the idioms presented, it is possible that Strand and Fraser's set was simply easier. Although a comparable item analysis was not conducted by Lodge and Leach (1975), Strand and Fraser (1979) reported that 11 out of 20 idioms in their task were understood at a figurative level by all of the 11-year-olds. Interestingly, only one of those "easy" idioms (*He hit the sack*) had also been used by Lodge and Leach (1975).

The remaining idioms in the Strand and Fraser study ranged in accuracy from 20 to 90 percent for the 11-year-olds. To explain this range, the investigators informally compared the syntactic structure of the "difficult" and "easy" idioms but found no consistent differences. Therefore, they suggested that ease of understanding may be a function of the extent to which children are exposed to various idioms and find them relevant to their own experiences.

As with comprehension of metaphors, research has demonstrated that comprehension of idioms is influenced by the manner in which it is assessed. For example, Prinz (1983) compared the difficulty of idiom comprehension under two conditions—multiple choice versus explanation. Youngsters of the ages of 9, 12, and 15, and a group of adults ($n = 48$), were included in the study. The same procedures and idiomatic sentences that had been used by Lodge and Leach (1975) served as the multiple-choice task in this investigation, and for the explanation task, each subject was simply asked to explain the meanings of the idiomatic sentences. Performance on both tasks steadily improved as subject age increased, but multiple choice was easier than explanation: for multiple choice, mean accuracy scores for the 9-, 12-, 15-year-olds, and adults, respectively, were 50, 80, 90, and 100 percent; for explanation, those means were 20, 35, 50, and 95 percent, respectively. Thus, the active interpretation of idioms lagged behind their passive understanding for all subject groups except the adults, for whom the tasks were equally easy. It should be noted that on the multiple-choice task, the 9- and 12-year-olds in the Prinz study performed at a higher level than those two age groups did in the Lodge and Leach (1975) study. This suggests that individuals of a particular age group may show a wide range of competence in idiom comprehension.

Many questions remain unanswered concerning youngsters' comprehension of idioms. For example, in the three studies just described (Lodge and Leach, 1975; Prinz, 1983; Strand and Fraser, 1979), idioms were presented within a pictorial context. However, it is unknown to what extent pictures may facilitate youngsters' comprehension of figurative meanings. It is also possible that youngsters respond differently to idioms that occur in contrived testing situations compared to natural settings.

Douglas and Peel (1979) developed a more naturalistic procedure for examining idiom comprehension. In their study, 120 children from first, third, fifth, and seventh grades listened to six different idioms, each presented in a spoken story context (e.g., "Billy was racing his model car. Waiting at the starting line, he was so excited that he *jumped the gun*."). The subject was then asked to explain the idiom (e.g., "What does the phrase *jumped the gun* mean?"). Responses were evaluated for the degree to which literal interpretations (e.g., "Billy stepped over the gun") versus figurative interpretations (e.g., "Billy started too soon") were provided. Consistent with other studies (e.g., Lodge and Leach, 1975; Prinz, 1983; Strand and Fraser, 1979), Douglas and Peel (1979) found that idiom comprehension steadily improved as subject age increased. Although a full understanding of the idioms was not attained until seventh grade, even the first graders often provided figurative interpretations.

Ackerman (1982) also examined idiom comprehension in context. Children 8 and 10 years old and a control group of adults ($n = 72$) were included in his study. Each subject listened to a series of simple short stories, each of which ended in an idiomatic sentence (e.g., "Karen said, I'll *fix his wagon*"). The stories were biased towards different interpretations of the final sentence—idiomatic, literal, or neutral—and the question of interest was the extent to which subjects could interpret the figurative meaning of the final sentence in the presence of varying contexts. Results showed that the 8-year-olds could interpret the sentences mainly in the presence of idiomatic contexts, whereas the 10-year-olds and the adults could interpret them not only in the presence of idiomatic contexts but also in the presence of literal and neutral contexts. These findings suggested to Ackerman that younger children rely on idiomatically biasing contexts to a greater extent than older children when interpreting idioms, and that for older children and adults "idiom interpretations are relatively fixed and not strongly dependent on contextual support" (p. 450). However, it is important to point out that the idioms presented in Ackerman's study were considered to be "common"; it is possible that if less common idioms had been presented, the older subjects might have relied on context to a greater extent than they did in that study.

Nippold and Martin (in press) examined idiom interpretation in adolescents. They had predicted that idioms in context would be easier for adolescents to interpret than idioms in isolation. Their subjects were 14, 15, 16, and 17 years old ($n = 475$). The task consisted of a modified version of the idioms subtest from the *Fullerton Language Test for Adolescents* (Thorum, 1980). Normally, the idioms subtest is administered individually and a student is asked to explain to the examiner the meanings of 20 different idioms which are presented out of context (e.g., *take a back seat, talk shop, chip on one's shoulder*, etc.). However, in the Nippold and Martin study, the 20 idioms were presented in written form and the subjects were asked to write down their interpretations of each. The task was modified in this way so that a large number of subjects could be tested quickly. The task was also modified so that half the idioms were presented in isolation (e.g., "What does it mean to *take a back seat?*") and half were presented within two-sentence story contexts where the idiom was the last phrase in the second sentence (e.g., "Billy often gets into fights with other kids at school. His mother says he has a chip on his shoulder. What does it mean to have a *chip on one's shoulder?*"). Care was taken to ensure that the idioms assigned to the two conditions, in isolation and in context, were balanced for difficulty. In writing the stories, familiar situations were depicted and simple vocabulary and syntax were used so that idiom comprehension would not be hampered by reading complexities.

Results showed that idioms in context were significantly easier for adolescents to interpret than idioms in isolation. For all subjects combined, the mean accuracy score was 60 percent for idioms in isolation and 69 percent for idioms in context. Although the contextual advantage was small, a greater advantage might have accrued had the idioms been presented within larger contextual units (e.g., paragraphs). The study also showed that performance under both presentation modes improved as subject age increased. Mean accuracy scores obtained by the 14-, 15-, 16-, and 17-year-olds, respectively, were 54, 57, 63, and 67 percent for idioms in isolation, and 65, 68, 72, and 72 percent for idioms in context. Although accuracy of idiom interpretation slowly improved as subject age increased, even the oldest subjects had not completely mastered the task in either presentation mode. These results were consistent with Prinz (1983) in showing quantitative improvement but nonmastery of idiom interpretation during adolescence; however, they were inconsistent with Douglas and Peel (1979) who reported complete mastery by the age of 13. This discrepancy may be due, in part, to the fact that different sets of idioms were employed in the various studies. Qualitative analyses of subjects' explanations in the Nippold and Martin study indicated that no response, literal (e.g., *throw light on something*: "Turn on the light"), and unrelated (e.g., *throw light on something*: "Leave something alone") error types occurred most often among the 14-year-olds but decreased as subject age increased.

In the Nippold and Martin (in press) study, recent results of the *National Educational Development Tests* (NEDT; 1984) were available for 97 of the 16-year-olds. This is a group-administered, standardized test of academic achievement that contains three subtests which measure literacy: English Usage, Natural Sciences Reading, and Social Studies Reading. Significant correlations were obtained between the idiom-interpretation task and each of these subtests.

Gibbs (1987) recently examined the effects of context on children's interpretation of idioms while comparing the difficulty of metaphorically opaque (e.g., *shoot the breeze*) versus metaphorically transparent (e.g., *slap in the face*) idioms. He also compared the difficulty of two response modes: explanation versus forced choice. Subjects included a group of 9-year-olds ($n = 20$). Ten opaque and 10 transparent idioms were presented. Half of the children received the idioms in context while the other half received them in isolation. In the context condition, each idiom served as the final sentence of an idiomatically biasing story. The examiner read each story aloud and then asked to child to explain the final sentence. Following the explanation, the child was asked to choose the best interpretation of the idiom from two alternatives. Examples of opaque and transparent test items, respectively, are as follows (Gibbs, 1987):

1. When Betty got home from school early for disrupting the class, she knew that her mother would be angry. When her mother asked her why she was home so early, Betty started to ask her mother what was for dinner that night. Finally her mother said, "Stop beating around the bush."

   Explanation Question:
   What did Betty's mother mean when she said "Stop beating around the bush"?
   Forced-Choice Questions:
   A. Did she want Betty to stop avoiding the question?
   B. Did she want Betty to stop hurting the plants?

2. Jim and Tina got into a big argument out on the playground over whose turn it was to get on the swing. When the teacher came over to see what the problem was, Jim and Tina shouted their complaints at her at the same time. The teacher said, "Hold your tongues."

   Explanation Question:
   What did the teacher mean when she said "Hold your tongues"?
   Forced-Choice Questions:
   A. Did she want them to grab their tongues?
   B. Did she want them to be quiet?

In the isolation condition, the child was asked to explain the meaning of each idiomatic sentence without hearing the story and then to choose the best interpretation of the sentence from two alternatives.

Results showed that idioms in context were easier to interpret than idioms in isolation, that transparent idioms were easier than opaque in the explanation mode, and that the forced-choice was easier than the explanation mode. For the explanation mode, mean accuracy scores for idioms in context were 92 and 78 percent for transparent and opaque idioms, respectively; for idioms in isolation, however, those scores were only 32 and 18 percent, respectively. For the forced-choice mode, mean accuracy scores for idioms in context were 96 percent for both transparent and opaque idioms; for idioms in isolation, however, those scores were 58 and 67 percent for transparent and opaque idioms, respectively. Therefore, idiom interpretation was easiest in the forced-choice–contextual condition and most difficult in the explanation–isolation condition. These results are consistent with other studies of figurative language (e.g., Nippold, Martin, and Erskine, 1988; Prinz, 1983; Winner et al., 1976; 1980a) in showing that receptive tasks, are easier than explanation tasks and that contextually supportive information facilitates children's understanding of figurative expressions. In addition, the finding that transparent idioms were easier to explain than opaque adds an exciting dimension to the literature concerning children's idiom interpretation: prior to Gibbs' (1987) study, the common assumption that there is little relationship between the literal and figurative meanings of idioms had not been questioned.

Summary

Developmental studies have shown that idioms are well understood at a literal level at the age of nine, but that a figurative understanding is acquired more gradually and remains incomplete even at the age of 19. However, individual idioms vary greatly in their ease of understanding, and certain idioms are well understood at a figurative level by the age of nine, particularly if they occur frequently in the child's linguistic environment and are metaphorically transparent. The relevance of a particular idiom to a child's own experiences may also affect its understandability. As with comprehension of metaphors, idiom comprehension in older children and adolescents is influenced by certain task factors. For example, idioms presented in isolation are more difficult than idioms presented in biasing contexts, and tasks requiring youngsters to explain the figurative meanings of idioms are more difficult than multiple-choice tasks where youngsters can choose an appropriate interpretation or simply point to a picture that best illustrates the meaning. Explanation tasks therefore tend to underestimate a youngster's passive understanding of idioms. However, they do provide insight into qualitative changes that occur as children get older, and indicate, for example, that literal interpretations of idioms decline as figurative interpretations increase. It has also been shown that youngsters having higher levels of literacy provide better explanations of idioms than their less literate peers.

Much remains to be learned concerning youngsters' competence with idioms. For example, it is unknown to what extent idiom comprehension occurring in natural settings (e.g., listening to Grandfather talk about sports or politics) differs from that which occurs in contrived testing situations.

In addition, little is known about the development of youngsters' ability to produce spontaneously appropriate idioms in natural settings. Another topic for future research suggested by Gibbs (1987) is the comprehension of "ambiguous idioms," expressions such as *give a hand* which have two distinct figurative meanings (i.e., to applaud or to assist another person). It would be interesting to compare youngsters' comprehension of ambiguous idioms with other types of linguistic ambiguities such as sentences, jokes, and riddles (see Chapter 9).

PROVERBS

Proverbs are statements that can offer encouragement (e.g., "Every cloud has a silver lining") or advice (e.g., "Don't count your chickens before they're hatched"), warn a person of danger (e.g., "When a wolf shows his teeth, he isn't laughing"), or comment upon events (e.g., "When the cat's away, the mice will play"). At a literal level, proverbs can be true or false, but at a figurative level, they express opinions that cannot be clearly denied or affirmed (Honeck, Voegtle, Dorfmueller, and Hoffman, 1980).

Compared to metaphors, similes, and idioms, proverbs are generally more difficult for children to comprehend (Billow, 1975; Douglas and Peel, 1979). In fact, many investigators have reported that children have little or no comprehension of proverbs before adolescence (Billow, 1975; Douglas and Peel, 1979; Gorham, 1956; Holden, 1978; Lutzer, 1988; Piaget, 1926; Richardson and Church, 1959; Watts, 1944). Proverb comprehension typically has been assessed by presenting children with lists of proverbs out of context and asking them to explain their meanings.

For example, Richardson and Church (1959) read seven different proverbs to children of the ages of 9 through 12 ($n = 47$) and wrote down their explanations. They also tested adolescents and adults ($n = 30$) in this manner for purposes of comparison. Examples of proverbs used in their study were "You can't teach an old dog new tricks," "Every cloud has a silver lining," and "All that glitters is not gold." The results showed that explanations of the 9-year-olds were primarily literal and situationally specific. For example, one 9-year-old explained the "dog" proverb by saying, "It's hard for the dog. . .cuz he's so slow and old," and another 9-year-old explained the "cloud" proverb by saying, "Maybe it's a man that has a silver lining in his coat." Although explanations gradually became more figurative as subject age increased (e.g., "It means it's futile to try to change old habits" for the "dog" proverb), the 12-year-olds still had difficulty with many of the proverbs, and even the adolescents and adults sometimes offered immature explanations.

Similar findings were reported by Watts (1944), who examined proverb comprehension in children of the ages 11 through 14. Watts, however, constructed a multiple-choice task in which children read a list of proverbs (e.g., "Empty vessels make the most sound") followed by four alternative interpretations. The choices always included one correct figurative interpretation (e.g., "The people who talk most are often the most ignorant") and three foils. Although accuracy improved as subject age increased, not even the oldest children approached mastery of the task.

Gorham (1956) also developed a multiple-choice task very similar to Watts' (1944) which included 40 proverbs, each followed by four alternative interpretations. The task was then administered to students at every level from fifth grade through the senior year of college ($n = 651$). The results showed a low level of comprehension for the youngest students but steady improvement with increasing grade level: mean accuracy scores ranged from 33 percent for the fifth graders to 81 percent for the college seniors. Holden (1978) later administered Gorham's task to students in fifth, seventh, and ninth grades (ages 10 through 15; $n = 79$) and obtained similar results for those three grade levels: 28, 47, and 55 percent accuracy, respectively.

Some investigators, however, have questioned the view that preadolescents have limited comprehension of proverbs. For example, Honeck, Sowry, and Voegtle (1978) questioned the validity of assessing youngsters' proverb comprehension through explanation tasks. Noting that children often display discrepancies between their comprehension and production of language, these investigators designed a task where children could point to pictures to indicate their comprehension of proverbs. Honeck and colleagues were also concerned with confounding factors related to the proverbs themselves, such as syntactic and semantic complexity. Therefore, they developed a list of 10 proverbs that had relatively simple syntactic structure and familiar content words. An example of such a proverb was "Bees give honey from their mouths and stings from their tails," which could be translated as "A thing can be both good and bad at the same time."

For each proverb, two pictures were provided, one illustrating the correct figurative meaning and the other illustrating an incorrect interpretation (foil). Neither picture contained items that represented the literal meanings of the words in the proverbs. For example, the "bee" proverb was correctly illustrated by a girl roasting a hot dog over a camp fire while the fire was burning her slacks. The foil showed another girl opening a present as a ball was about to strike her. In presenting the task, the examiner first displayed the two pictures and told the child to study them carefully. Ten seconds later, the examiner read the corresponding proverb and asked the child to point to the picture that meant the same thing. Practice trials were given prior to the test items to ensure that the child understood the procedures.

A group of 9-year-olds ($n = 20$) who participated in the Honeck and colleagues' study obtained a mean accuracy score of 68 percent. Although performance of this group was well above the level of chance, they did not approach mastery, even though task demands were carefully controlled. This is an important finding because it suggests that the gradual improvement in proverb comprehension during adolescence observed in other studies (Billow, 1975; Douglas and Peel, 1979; Gorham, 1956; Holden, 1978; Piaget, 1926; Richardson and Church, 1959; Watts, 1944) may not be due entirely to an increasing ability to deal with confounding factors.

Resnick (1982) also documented proverb comprehension in preadolescents. In his investigation, students in the third through seventh grades (of the ages of 8 through 13; $n = 438$) were presented with 10 different proverbs that contained simple vocabulary and depicted familiar situations (e.g., "If you cut down the forest, you will catch the wolf," "Don't plant thorns if you walk barefoot"). Comprehension of each proverb was assessed using three different multiple-choice tasks, "Story Matching," "Proverb Matching," and "Paraphrase." For Story Matching, a short story followed by four different proverbs was presented; the child was asked to choose the proverb that best completed the story. For Proverb Matching, the child chose a proverb that had the same meaning as the target proverb. For Paraphrase, each proverb was followed by four different interpretations to choose from. Each child was also administered an analogies task as a measure of general intelligence. This task consisted of 10 analogy problems from the *Cognitive Abilities Test* (Thorndike and Hagen, 1971).

Results showed that Story Matching was the easiest comprehension task, that Paraphrase was the most difficult, and that Proverb Matching was intermediate in difficulty. Resnick (1982) suggested that Story Matching was easiest because the stories provided contextual support for the proverbs. It was also shown that even the youngest children performed above the level of chance and that proverb comprehension steadily improved with increasing grade level. Combining the three different proverbs tasks, mean accuracy scores were 45, 58, 65, 74, and 89 percent for the third, fourth, fifth, sixth, and seventh graders, respectively. Correlation coefficents were calculated between the analogies task and each of the three proverbs tasks for the subjects as a whole. All were significant and indicated moderately strong relationships. Resnick concluded that intelligence plays an important role in proverb comprehension. However, he also argued that grade level was an even more important factor.

Other developmental studies have compared the difficulty of proverbs with other types of figurative language. For example, in the Douglas and Peel (1979) study of idiom comprehension previously described, the same youngsters from the third, fifth, and seventh grades were also asked to explain six different proverbs presented within story contexts (e.g., "The teacher said, 'You can go to recess after the test, because *sweet is pleasure after pain*' "). Although proverb explanations steadily improved with increasing grade level, they were consistently more literal than idiom explanations at all three grades.

As another example, Billow (1975) compared children's comprehension of proverbs and metaphors. In his investigation, 9-, 11-, and 13-year-olds were asked to explain the meanings of 12 proverbs (e.g., "There is many a slip between cup and lip") and 24 metaphors (e.g., "Hair is spaghetti"). The results showed that proverbs were considerably more difficult to explain than metaphors for all three age groups. Although proverb explanations improved as subject age increased, they remained quite literal before adolescence, a finding that was consistent with other proverb studies that employed explanation tasks (e.g., Douglas and Peel, 1979; Lutzer, 1988; Piaget, 1926; Richardson and Church, 1959).

Piaget (1926) believed that proverb comprehension requires advanced cognitive processes that are acquired during the stage of formal operational thinking. Research, however, has not supported this cognitive prerequisite hypothesis in relation to proverb comprehension (Billow, 1975; Holden, 1978). Nevertheless, research has shown that that proverb comprehension in adolescents is at least correlated to performance on various Piagetian tasks of formal operational thinking involving syllogistic reasoning and mathematical probability (Holden, 1978).

Although the sources of proverb difficulty remain to be identified with certainty, the syntactic and semantic complexity (e.g., "To teach a fool is as easy as to cure a corpse," "A bad compromise is better than a good battle") of proverbs undoubtedly contributes. In addition, proverbs often express meanings that require world experience to be fully appreciated (e.g., "The bread of strangers can be very hard"). It is also possible that proverbs require greater analytical effort from the interpreter. For example, many proverbs are similar to metaphors in that they involve a comparison of entities that are normally viewed as distinct. The comparison provided in proverbs is more elusive than that provided in metaphors, however, because proverbs usually contain more than one vehicle and never state the topics. In fact, the topics of a proverb are variable and can only be found in the context in which the figurative statement occurred. These points are illustrated by the situation in which a fourth-grade teacher leaves her normally obedient classroom for five minutes only to return to chaos, and remarks, "When the cat's away, the mice will play!" Here, the two topics "teacher" and "students" are being likened to the vehicles "cat" and "mice," respectively, but are not contained in the proverb itself. The same proverb with different topics might be just as appropriate if uttered by a track coach who assigns his runners an unsupervised 10-mile workout but shortly finds them frolicking at the beach.

The reported difficulty of proverbs may also be a function of the methods used to examine comprehension. Although context is necessary for the full appreciation of a proverb, few investigators have considered its importance. In most studies, proverb comprehension has been examined by presenting youngsters with lists of proverbs out of context and asking them to come up with their own explanations of the proverbs or to choose the best explanation of each from a set of answer choices also lacking contextual information (e.g., Billow, 1975; Gorham, 1956; Holden, 1978; Piaget, 1926; Richardson and Church, 1959; Watts, 1944). Presenting proverbs in isolation, however, ignores the fact that proverbs typically occur in conversations, lectures, or stories where linguistic and nonlinguistic contextual information may faciliatate comprehension. Therefore, tasks that present proverbs out of context may underestimate a child's comprehension of proverbs in natural settings (Nippold et al., 1988). Explanation tasks may also underestimate proverb comprehension: research has shown that when receptive tasks are used to assess comprehension of other types of figurative language such as idioms and metaphors, youngsters demonstrate an understanding of those expressions several years before they can adequately explain their meanings (Ackerman, 1982; Dent, 1984; Gardner, 1974; Winner et al., 1976, 1980a).

Nippold and colleagues (1988) suggested that a task involving contextual information and a nonspoken response mode would be a better method of assessing proverb comprehension than a task where proverbs are presented out of context and the youngster must explain their meanings. These investigators designed a proverbs task incorporating those features and presented it to students from fourth, sixth, eighth, and tenth grades (of the ages of 9 through 16; $n = 240$). To determine if performance on a non-Piagetian reasoning task was related to performance on the proverbs task, they also administered a perceptual analogies task to all subjects.

The proverbs task consisted of 30 items presented in a written multiple-choice format. The individual proverbs were borrowed from various sources (Chambers, 1979; Gorham, 1956; Hoffman and Honeck, 1980; Honeck et al., 1978; Piaget, 1926; Reston, 1985; Watts, 1944), and represented different levels of familiarity and semantic and syntactic complexity. For each test item, a proverb was used by a named individual and was followed by four different contextual descriptions. An example follows:

The teacher said, "The new broom sweeps clean."
a. The new principal likes to coach the basketball team.
b. The new principal likes to eat lunch with the students.
c. The new principal fired all of the old teachers.
d. The new principal likes to have spelling contests every week.

The subject's job was to select the context in which it was most appropriate for the proverb to be used. In writing the response alternatives for each test item, care was taken to ensure that none could be literally true and therefore misleading. An attempt also was made to write about situations thought to be meaningful to students in the fourth through the tenth grades, and to use relatively simple vocabulary and sentence structure so that proverb comprehension would not be hampered by reading difficulties. The proverbs task was written at about the fourth-grade level (Fry, 1972). As a further safeguard against possible reading and vocabulary confounds, subjects were told before the testing began that during the testing they should ask the examiner about any words they could not read or did not understand. The Figure Analogies subtest from the nonverbal battery of the *Lorge-Thorndike Intelligence Tests* (Lorge and Thorndike, 1957) served as the perceptual reasoning task. This task contains 30 perceptual analogies expressing the relationship "*A* is to *B* as *C* is to *D*"; three designs (*A*, *B*, and *C*) are presented in a row and a fourth (*D*) is left to be inferred. Each test item is followed by five answer choices, only one of which best completes the analogy.

Results showed that the perceptual reasoning task was more difficult than the proverbs task, but that performance on both tasks steadily improved with increasing grade level. For the proverbs task, mean accuracy scores of 67, 77, 83, and 85 percent were obtained by the subjects in the fourth, sixth, eighth, and tenth grades, respectively, while on the reasoning task, scores of 61, 70, 76, and 81 percent were obtained by those four groups. With chance performance equal to 25 percent on the proverbs task and 20 percent on the reasoning task, even the youngest subjects, the fourth graders, performed well above the level of chance on both experimental tasks. Proverb comprehension among preadolescents was markedly better than in other studies where explanation tasks were employed or proverbs were presented out of context (e.g., Billow, 1975; Gorham, 1956; Richardson and Church, 1959; Watts, 1944). Results also showed that correlation coefficients between proverb comprehension and perceptual analogical reasoning were significant for each of the four grade levels.

Summary

This discussion of proverb comprehension has highlighted the contrast between two points of view, one negative and one positive, regarding youngsters' competence with this type of figurative language. Whereas the negativists (Billow, 1975; Gorham, 1956; Holden, 1978; Piaget, 1926; Richardson and Church, 1959; Watts, 1944) contended that proverb comprehension was largely an adolescent attainment, the positivists (Honeck et al., 1978; Nippold et al., 1988; Resnick, 1982) contended that it was possible well before the adolescent years. Whereas the negativists presented proverbs in isolation and required explanations of their meanings, the positivists showed that when task demands were simplified, preadolescents comprehended proverbs reasonably well, a finding that was consistent with research in metaphors and idioms. Also consistent with metaphors and idioms, it appears that the active explanation of proverbs lags behind their passive understanding. Although the Piagetian cognitive prerequisite hypothesis has been examined in relation to proverbs, the results have not been supportive. Nevertheless, it has been shown that proverb comprehension is related to general cognitive ability as measured by tasks of inductive (e.g., analogical) and deductive (e.g., syllogistic) reasoning (see Chapter 7).

CONCLUSIONS

This chapter has discussed the development of figurative language during the 9-through-19 age range. Figurative understanding was emphasized more than production, a reflection of the available research on this topic. Common developmental patterns were seen with metaphors and similes, idioms, and proverbs. For example, 9-year-olds have a basic understanding of each of these types of figurative expressions, but major improvements will occur as these youngsters progress through adolescence. For example, growth will occur in lexical knowledge, syntactic complexity, world knowledge, and analytical reasoning. These linguistic and cognitive advances will allow for gradual improvements in the understanding and explanation of figurative expressions and in the ability to infer meaning from context. Also during adolescence, it is likely that youngsters will find these expressions increasingly relevant to their own life experiences, a factor which may stimulate further interest in learning new figurative expressions. Youngsters attending high schools where language and literature are highly regarded may acquire figurative competence more rapidly than those whose institutions place less of an emphasis on literacy, a position which is consistent with the language experience view (Ortony et al., 1985) of figurative development. However, it does not appear that figurative language is ever completely mastered, even by the age of 19, because new expressions can always be created or encountered in spoken and written contexts.

REFERENCES

Achenbach, T.M. (1969). Cue learning, associative responding, and school performance in children. *Developmental Psychology, 1*, 717-725.

Ackerman, B.P. (1982). On comprehending idioms: Do children get the picture? *Journal of Experimental Child Psychology, 33*, 439-454.

Arlin, P.K. (1978, February). *Piagetian operations in the comprehension, preference, and production of metaphors.* Paper presented at the Annual International

Interdisciplinary Conference on Piagetian Theory and the Helping Professions, Los Angeles, CA.

Arter, J.L. (1976). *The effects of metaphor on reading comprehension.* Unpublished doctoral dissertation. University of Illinois at Urbana-Champaign.

Billow, R.M. (1975). A cognitive developmental study of metaphor comprehension. *Developmental Psychology, 11,* 415-423.

Billow, R.M. (1977). Metaphor: A review of the psychological literature. *Psychological Bulletin, 84,* 81-92.

Billow, R.M. (1981). Observing spontaneous metaphor in children. *Journal of Experimental Child Psychology, 31,* 430-445.

Boswell, D.A. (1979). Metaphoric processing in the mature years. *Human Development, 22,* 373-384.

Boynton, M., and Kossan, N.E. (1981, October). *Children's metaphors: Making meaning.* Paper presented at the Sixth Annual Boston University Conference on Language Development, Boston, MA.

Brown, S.J. (1965). *The world of imagery: Metaphor and kindred imagery* (pp. 226-240). New York: Haskell House.

Chambers, J.W. (1979, March). *Proverb comprehension with pictorial and verbal scenarios.* Paper presented at the Biennial Meeting of the Society for Research in Child Development, San Francisco, CA.

Chukovsky, K. (1968). *From two to five.* Berkeley, CA: University of California Press.

Cometa, M.S., and Eson, M.E. (1978). Logical operations and metaphor interpretation: A Piagetian model. *Child Development, 49,* 649-659.

Dent, C.H. (1984). The developmental importance of motion information in perceiving and describing metaphoric similarity. *Child Development, 55,* 1607-1613.

Donahue, M., and Bryan, T. (1984). Communicative skills and peer relations of learning disabled adolescents. *Topics in Language Disorders, 4*(2), 10-21.

Douglas, J.D., and Peel, B. (1979). The development of metaphor and proverb translation in children grades one through seven. *Journal of Educational Research, 73,* 116-119.

Durost, W.N. (1959). *Metropolitan Achievement Tests.* New York: Harcourt, Brace, and World.

Fry, E. (1972). *Reading instruction for classroom and clinic.* New York: McGraw-Hill.

Gardner, H. (1974). Metaphors and modalities: How children project polar adjectives onto diverse domains. *Child Development, 45,* 84-91.

Gardner, H., Kircher, M., Winner, E., and Perkins, D. (1975). Children's metaphoric productions and preferences. *Journal of Child Language, 2,* 125-141.

Gardner, H., Winner, E., Bechhofer, R., and Wolf, D. (1978). The development of figurative language. In K. Nelson (Ed.), *Children's language* (Volume 1) (pp. 1-38). New York: Gardner Press.

Gentner, D. (1977). Children's performance on a spatial analogies task. *Child Development, 48,* 1034-1039.

Gibbs, R.W. (1987). Linguistic factors in children's understanding of idioms. *Journal of Child Language, 14,* 569-586.

Gorham, D.R. (1956). A proverbs test for clinical and experimental use. *Psychological Reports, 2,* 1-12.

Hoffman, R.R., arfd Honeck, R.P. (1980). A peacock looks at its legs: Cognitive science and figurative language. In R.P. Honeck and R.R. Hoffman (Eds.), *Cognition and figurative language* (pp. 3-24). Hillsdale, NJ: Erlbaum.

Holden, M.H. (1978, February). *Proverbs, proportions, and Piaget.* Paper presented at the Annual International Interdisciplinary Conference on Piagetian Theory and the Helping Professions, Los Angeles, CA.

Hollingshed, J.C. (1958). *A study of figures of speech in intermediate grade reading.* Unpublished doctoral dissertation. Colorado State College, Fort Collins, CO.

Honeck, R.P., Sowry, B.M., and Voegtle, K. (1978). Proverbial understanding in a pictorial context. *Child Development, 49,* 327-331.

Honeck, R.P., Voegtle, K., Dorfmueller, M.A., and Hoffman, R.R. (1980). Proverbs, meaning, and group structure. In R.P. Honeck and R.R. Hoffman (Eds.), *Cognition and figurative language* (pp. 127-161). Hillsdale, NJ: Erlbaum.

Hyde, J.P. (1982). Rat talk: The special vocabulary of some teenagers. *English Journal, 71,* 98-101.

Kogan, N., Connor, K., Gross, A., and Fava, D. (1980). Understanding visual metaphor: Developmental and individual differences. *Monographs of the Society for Research in Child Development, 45*(Serial No. 183). Chicago: University of Chicago Press.

Leona, M.H. (1978). An examination of adolescent clique language in a suburban secondary school. *Adolescence, 13,* 495-502.

Lewis, M.M. (1963). *Language, thought, and personality in infancy and childhood* (pp. 163-228). London: Harrap.

Lindquist, E.F., and Hieronymus, A.N. (1956). *Iowa tests of basic skills.* Boston: Houghton Mifflin.

Lodge, D.N., and Leach, E.A. (1975). Children's acquisition of idioms in the English language. *Journal of Speech and Hearing Research, 18,* 521 5 29.

Lorge, I., and Thorndike, R.L. (1957). *Lorge-Thorndike intelligence tests.* Boston: Houghton Mifflin.

Lutzer, V.D. (1988). Comprehension of proverbs by average children and children with learning disorders. *Journal of Learning Disabilities, 21,* 104-108.

Malgady, R.G. (1977). Children's interpretation and appreciation of similes. *Child Development, 48,* 1734-1738.

May, A.B. (1979). All the angles of idiom instruction. *The Reading Teacher, 32,* 680-682.

Miller, G.A. (1979). Images and models, similes and metaphors. In A. Ortony (Ed.), *Metaphor and thought* (pp. 202-250). Cambridge, England: Cambridge University Press.

National educational development tests (1984). Chicago: Science Research Associates.

Nelsen, E.A., and Rosenbaum, E. (1972). Language patterns within the youth subculture: Development of slang vocabularies. *Merrill-Palmer Quarterly, 18,* 273-285.

Nippold, M.A. (1985). Comprehension of figurative language in youth. *Topics in Language Disorders, 5*(3), 1-20.

Nippold, M.A., Leonard, L.B., and Kail, R. (1984). Syntactic and conceptual factors in children's understanding of metaphors. *Journal of Speech and Hearing Research, 27,* 197-205.

Nippold, M.A., and Martin, S.T. (in press). Idiom interpretation in isolation versus context: A developmental study with adolescents. *Journal of Speech and Hearing Research*.

Nippold, M.A., Martin, S.A., and Erskine, B.J. (1988). Proverb comprehension in context: A developmental study with children and adolescents. *Journal of Speech and Hearing Research, 31*, 19-28.

Ortony, A. (1979). The role of similarity in similes and metaphors. In A. Ortony (Ed.), *Metaphor and thought* (pp. 186-201). Cambridge, England: Cambridge University Press.

Ortony, A., Schallert, D.L., Reynolds, R.E., and Antos, S.J. (1978). Interpreting metaphors and idioms: Some effects of context on comprehension. *Journal of Verbal Learning and Verbal Behavior, 17*, 465 4 77.

Ortony, A., Turner, T.J., and Larson-Shapiro, N. (1985). Cultural and instructional influences on figurative language comprehension by inner city children. *Research in the Teaching of English, 19*, 25-36.

Otis, A.S., and Lennon, R.T. (1967). *Otis-Lennon mental ability test*. New York: Harcourt, Brace, and World.

Paivio, A. (1979). Psychological processes in the comprehension of metaphor. In A. Ortony (Ed.), *Metaphor and thought* (pp. 150-171). Cambridge, England: Cambridge University Press.

Piaget, J. (1926). *The language and thought of the child*. New York: Harcourt, Brace.

Pollio, M.R., and Pickens, J.D. (1980). The developmental structure of figurative competence. In R.P. Honeck and R.R. Hoffman (Eds.), *Cognition and figurative language* (pp. 311-340). Hillsdale, NJ: Erlbaum.

Pollio, M.R., and Pollio, H.R. (1974). The development of figurative language in school children. *Journal of Psycholinguistic Research, 3*, 185-201.

Pollio, M.R., and Pollio, H.R. (1979). A test of metaphoric comprehension and some preliminary data. *Journal of Child Language, 6*, 111-120.

Prinz, P.M. (1983). The development of idiomatic meaning in children. *Language and Speech, 26*, 263-272.

Redfern, W. (1984). *Puns*. New York: Blackwell.

Resnick, D.A. (1982). A developmental study of proverb comprehension. *Journal of Psycholinguistic Research, 11*, 521-538.

Reston, J. (1985, February 19). A useful book of Russian proverbs. *The Eugene Register-Guard*, p. 15A.

Reynolds, R.E., and Ortony, A. (1980). Some issues in the measurement of children's comprehension of metaphorical language. *Child Development, 51*, 1110-1119.

Richardson, C., and Church, J. (1959). A developmental analysis of proverb interpretations. *Journal of Genetic Psychology, 94*, 169-179.

Schaefer, C.E. (1975). The importance of measuring metaphorical thinking in children. *Gifted Child Quarterly, 19*, 140-148.

Schwartz, G., and Merten, D. (1967). The language of adolescence: An anthropological approach to the youth culture. *The American Journal of Sociology, 72*, 453-468.

Silberstein, L., Gardner, H., Phelps, E., and Winner, E. (1982). Autumn leaves and old photographs: The development of metaphor preferences. *Journal of Experimental Child Psychology, 34*, 135-150.

Siltanen, S.A. (1981). *Apple noses and popsicle toeses: A developmental investigation of metaphorical comprehension.* Unpublished doctoral dissertation, Ohio State University, Columbus, OH.

Smith, J.W.A. (1976). Children's emphasis of metaphor: A Piagetian interpretation. *Language and Speech, 19,* 236–243.

Strand, K.E., and Fraser, B. (1979). *The comprehension of verbal idioms by young children.* Unpublished paper, Boston University, School of Education.

Thorndike, R., and Hagen, E. (1971). *Cognitive abilities test.* Boston: Houghton Mifflin.

Thorum, A.R. (1980). *The Fullerton language test for adolescents: Experimental edition.* Palo Alto, CA: Consulting Psychologists Press.

Vosniadou, S. (1987). Children and metaphors. *Child Development, 58,* 870–885.

Vosniadou, S., and Ortony, A. (1983). The emergence of the literal-metaphorical-anomalous distinction in young children. *Child Development, 54,* 154–161.

Watts, A.F. (1944). *The language and mental development of children* (pp. 195–217). London: Harrap.

Winner, E. (1979). New names for old things: The emergence of metaphoric language. *Journal of Child Language, 6,* 469–491.

Winner, E., Engel, M., and Gardner, H. (1980a). Misunderstanding metaphor: What's the problem? *Journal of Experimental Child Psychology, 30,* 22–32.

Winner, E., McCarthy, M., and Gardner, H. (1980b). The ontogenesis of metaphor. In R.P. Honeck and R.R. Hoffman (Eds.), *Cognition and figurative language* (pp. 341–361). Hillsdale, NJ: Erlbaum.

Winner, E., McCarthy, M., Kleinman, S., and Gardner, H. (1979). First metaphors. In D. Wolf (Ed.), *Early symbolization: New directions for child development* (pp. 29–41). San Francisco, CA: Jossey-Bass.

Winner, E., Rosenstiel, A., and Gardner, H. (1976). The development of metaphoric understanding. *Developmental Psychology, 12,* 289–297.

CHAPTER 9

■

LINGUISTIC AMBIGUITY

■

MARILYN A. NIPPOLD

Metalinguistic awareness, the ability to consciously reflect on the nature of language (van Kleeck, 1984), is called on when words are used in unique or unexpected ways. This occurs, for example, when an individual encounters linguistic ambiguity. The humor in riddles, jokes, and comic strips often stems from linguistic ambiguity (e.g., Q: "What did the short tree say to the tall tree?" A: "I'm stumped"), a phenomenon that can also serve as an attention-capturing device in newspaper headlines (e.g., "Bike sales ride on all-terrain cycles"), bumper stickers (e.g., "You can't hug your kids with nuclear arms"), and advertisements (e.g., ad for Ford Tempo cars: "Designed to move you").

To understand these types of ambiguous messages, an individual must know the double meanings of words and appreciate the linguistic contexts in which they occur. Nonlinguistic information may also be required. For example, a full understanding of the newspaper headline "Night owls flock back to Hoots" requires knowledge that Hoots is a 24-hour restaurant in Eugene, Oregon where students can study all night.

Developmental studies have examined youngsters' understanding of linguistic ambiguity in three different domains: (1) isolated sentences (e.g., "It's too hot too eat"); (2) humor (e.g., Q: "Why did the hungry man go into the lamp store?" A: "Because he wanted a light snack"); and (3) advertisements (e.g., "Grounds for owning a Subaru") (Brodzinsky, Feuer, and Owens, 1977; Keil, 1980; Kessel, 1970; Muus and Hoag, 1980; Nippold, Cuyler, and Braunbeck-Price, in press; Shultz, 1974; Shultz and Horibe, 1974; Shultz and Pilon, 1973; Wiig, Gilbert, and Christian, 1978). Major findings from those studies are discussed in this chapter. Although younger children participated in many of the studies, their performance is not reported because of this book's focus on the 9-through-19 age range.

SENTENCES

Four different types of sentential ambiguity have been examined in terms of their relative difficulty: phonological (e.g., "I have enough for eight tea/eighty cups"), lexical (e.g., "The lady wiped the glasses"), surface structure (e.g., "He fed her // *dog* biscuits" versus "He fed her dog // *biscuits*"), and deep structure (e.g., "The duck is ready to eat"). The double meaning of a phonological ambiguity results from varying the pronunciation of one or more words in the sentence. For a lexical ambiguity, however, the double meaning results from a word or phrase having two different meanings. A surface-structure ambiguity is a sentence in which double meanings result from variations in stress and juncture. A deep-structure ambiguity contains a noun that serves as an agent in one meaning but as an object in the other meaning (Nippold, Cuyler, and Braunbeck-Price, in press).

Research with adults (MacKay and Bever, 1967) showed that when subjects were asked to interpret different types of ambiguous sentences, the two meanings of lexical ambiguities were detected faster than those of surface-structure ambiguities, which were detected faster than those of deep-structure ambiguities. Phonological ambiguities were not presented. On the assumption that response latency reflects processing complexity, these findings led many investigators (Brodzinsky, Feuer, and Owens, 1977; Keil, 1980; Kessel, 1970; Shultz and Pilon, 1973; Wiig, Gilbert, and Christian, 1978) to predict that children's understanding of sentential ambiguity would mirror this pattern developmentally such that lexical ambiguities would be understood earlier than surface-structure ambiguities, which in turn would be understood earlier than deep structure ambiguities. However, the experimental evidence has only partially supported that prediction.

For example, Kessel (1970) examined understanding of sentential ambiguity in a study that included 9- and 12-year-olds ($n = 20$). The task consisted of 12 sentences, with four representing each of the following three types: lexical, surface structure, and deep structure. For each sentence, the child was shown four pictures, two illustrating the correct interpretations and two illustrating foils. For example, pictures accompanying the sentence "The eating of the chicken was sloppy" were (1) a chicken eating grain sloppily, (2) a chicken eating grain neatly, (3) a boy and girl eating chicken sloppily, and (4) a boy and girl eating chicken neatly. The examiner read each sentence aloud two times and asked the child to choose the pictures that went with it. The child was then asked to explain those choices. The purpose of the questioning was to assess the child's depth of understanding and to control for random guessing. Because each of the four surface-structure ambiguities could be spoken with two different suprasegmental patterns corresponding to different interpretations, the examiner used a different pattern for the two readings of each of these sentences; for example, "He fed her dog // *biscuits*" versus "He fed her // *dog* biscuits." To receive full credit for a sentence, the child had to select the correct pictures and provide acceptable explanations of each.

Results showed that the 12-year-olds outperformed the 9-year-olds, with mean scores of 91 and 58 percent obtained by the two age groups, respectively. As predicted, the lexical ambiguities were easier to understand than the other two types. However, the surface- and deep-structure ambiguities were about equal in difficulty, which was inconsistent with Kessel's prediction. Qualitative differences between the groups were evident from their explanations, with the 12-year-olds able to target the ambiguous elements in a sentence more readily than the 9-year-olds.

Using different procedures from Kessel's, Shultz and Pilon (1973) examined understanding of ambiguous sentences in a study that included 9-, 12-, and 15-year-olds ($n = 84$). The task contained phonological, lexical, surface-structure, and deep-structure ambiguities, with six sentences per type. For each sentence, understanding was assessed first with a paraphrase measure and then with a picture measure. For the paraphrase measure, the child listened to a sentence and then explained what it meant. If only one meaning was explained, the examiner prompted the child by asking if the sentence meant anything else. For the picture measure, two pictures illustrating the correct meanings of the sentence were presented and the examiner asked the child to point to the picture or pictures that illustrated the sentence. As an example, one picture for the sentence "He saw a man eating fish" showed a ferocious shark and another showed a man at a table eating fish. If only one picture was chosen, the examiner prompted the child by asking if the sentence meant anything else. The child was then asked to explain the picture choices. For both the paraphrase and picture measures, a sentence was credited only if the child could explain both meanings adequately.

Results showed that the picture measure elicited more correct responses than the paraphrase measure. On both measures, understanding of the four ambiguity types steadily improved as subject age increased, with phonological ambiguities easier than lexical, and lexical easier than surface- and deep-structure, which were equally difficult to understand. Although the phonological and lexical ambiguities were nearly mastered by the age of 15, the surface- and deep-structure ambiguities were infrequently understood before the age of 12, and continued to challenge even the 15-year-olds. Despite procedural variations, Shultz and Pilon's results were consistent with Kessel's (1970) in showing that lexical ambiguities were easier to understand than the two syntactic types, that the surface- and deep-structure ambiguities were equal in difficulty, and that 12-year-olds outperformed 9-year-olds.

Using the same task as Shultz and Pilon, Brodzinsky, Feuer, and Owens (1977) examined children's understanding of linguistic ambiguity in relation to their problem-solving styles. Children 10 and 13 years old ($n = 96$) participated in the study. The *Matching Familiar Figures Test* (MFFT) (Kagan, Rosman, Day, Albert, and Phillips, 1964) was administered to establish each child's problem-solving style. This is a task that measures speed and accuracy in matching identical pictures, and yields four different response patterns: slow-accurate ("reflective"), fast-inaccurate ("impulsive"), slow-inaccurate, and fast-accurate. In the present study, it was predicted that impulsive children, known to perform quick and cursory analyses of stimuli, would be less successful in understanding both meanings of ambiguous sentences than reflective children, known to be more systematic in their analyses. However, it was also predicted that the prompting procedures employed in the Shultz and Pilon (1973) task ("Does it mean anything else?") would eliminate any differences between the reflective and impulsive children by encouraging a closer analysis of the sentences.

Results showed that on both the paraphrase and picture measures, the reflective children spontaneously understood a greater number of double meanings than the impulsive or slow-inaccurate children. Fast-accurate children performed between these two extremes. However, the impulsive and slow-inaccurate youngsters performed as well as the reflective youngsters after prompting had occurred. This pattern was particularly strong for the 10-year-olds in relation to the surface- and deep-structure ambiguities. Consistent with Shultz and Pilon, it was also shown that phonological ambiguities were easier to understand than lexical, that lexical were easier to understand than deep- and surface-structure, and that the two syntactic types were equally difficult. Not surprisingly, the 13-year-olds were more successful than the 10-year-olds at spontaneously explaining the double meanings of the sentences and pictures. Combining the problem-solving styles and ambiguity types, mean accuracy scores on the spontaneous paraphrase measure (before prompting) were 40 and 23 percent for the 13- and 10-year-olds, respectively. On the picture measure, those scores were 73 and 54 percent, respectively. It was also reported that understanding of linguistic ambiguity was positively correlated to intelligence test scores for the subjects in this study.

Wiig, Gilbert, and Christian (1978) examined speed and accuracy in relation to youngsters' understanding of ambiguous sentences. Subjects included 10-, 12-, and 18-year-olds ($n = 30$) who were administered a picture-pointing task that contained eight lexical, five surface-structure, and three deep-structure ambiguities. Unlike previous studies, some of the lexical ambiguities in this task had both a literal and an idiomatic interpretation rather than two literal interpretations only. These included "She did not press the suit," "This restaurant even serves crabs," and "The man kept the watch." In addition, some of the lexical ambiguities were also deep-structure ambiguities (e.g., "This restaurant even serves crabs"). Each ambiguous sentence was accompanied by four picture choices, two illustrating the correct meanings and two representing foils. For example, the pictures for the lexical ambiguity "He is drawing a gun" were (1) a man drawing a picture of a gun, (2) a cowboy drawing a gun from his holster, (3) a man throwing a gun, and (4) a man holding a smoking gun. The examiner read each sentence aloud and the subject pointed to the picture(s) expressing the appropriate meaning(s). Each pointing response was timed with a stopwatch. Subjects were not required to explain their picture choices.

Consistent with previous studies, the number of correct responses increased as a function of age, with mean scores of 46, 58, and 59 percent obtained by the 10-, 12-, and 18-year-olds, respectively. However, not even the oldest subjects had mastered the task, and no developmental changes occurred in response times. It was also found, in contrast to previous studies, that no ambiguity type was significantly easier than another for any age group. This may be due to the fact that several of the lexical ambiguities had idiomatic interpretations, and thus were not typical examples of this sentence type.

In an examination of the psychological bases of ambiguity, Keil (1980) predicted that children's competence with linguistic ambiguity would be related to their competence with nonlinguistic ambiguity. Pictures that could be interpreted in two different ways served as the nonlinguistic stimuli. For example, a sketch of a ladder could also be viewed as a railroad track, and a sketch of a horse's head could also be viewed as a seal if the ears were thought of as flippers and the nostrils as eyes. The ambiguous sentences in this study consisted of 24 lexical and 24 syntactic (12 surface and 12 deep structure). All sentences were presented on audiotape. Because lexical ambiguities tend to be easier to understand than syntactic, it was also predicted that lexical ambiguities would be more closely related to easier "symbolic" pictorial ambiguities (e.g., the ladder–railroad track picture), and that syntactic ambiguities would be more closely related to more difficult "structural" pictorial ambiguities (e.g., the horse–seal picture). Twelve symbolic and 12 structural pictorial ambiguities were presented. Subjects included 10- and 13-year-olds ($n = 36$), who were told that all sentences and pictures would have two meanings which they should explain. To receive credit for a test item, both meanings of a sentence or picture had to be expressed.

Despite Keil's predictions, no picture–sentence correlations reached significance for either age group. Thus, it was concluded that sentential and pictorial ambiguities have different psychological bases. Consistent with previous studies, however, the syntactic sentences were more difficult than the lexical, and the deep- and surface-structure ambiguities were equally difficult to understand. Although the 13-year-olds understood the sentences and pictures better than the 10-year-olds, even the oldest subjects remained challenged by the two tasks.

Summary

Developmental studies have shown that the ability to identify and explain sentential ambiguity steadily improves during the preadolescent and adolescent years. In general, phonological ambiguities are easier than lexical, and lexical are easier than surface- or deep-structure ambiguities, which are about equal in difficulty. However, it appears that ambiguous sentences of any particular type can vary widely in their difficulty. For example, certain lexical ambiguities having both a literal and an idiomatic interpretation (e.g., "She did not press the suit") are more difficult than certain deep-structure ambiguities having two literal interpretations only (e.g., "The duck is ready to eat"). Studies have also shown that youngsters' competence with ambiguous sentences is enhanced by picture cues, and that competence is related to intelligence and to problem-solving style. It is noteworthy that similar findings regarding intelligence and problem-solving style occurred with respect to verbal analogical reasoning (see Chapter 7).

However, it should be emphasized that the studies just reviewed presented youngsters with sentences out of context—sentences that would not be ambiguous during ongoing discourse because of linguistic and non-linguistic information provided by natural settings (van Kleeck, 1984). For example, if people were discussing the menu at a new seafood restaurant, the comment "This restaurant even serves crabs" would not be ambiguous. Therefore, studies of sentential ambiguity provide little information about youngsters' understanding of language that is truly ambiguous in naturalistic contexts. Jokes and riddles, however, are humorous forms of language occurring in social situations where an understanding of the double meanings of words and phrases is often required (Shultz, 1974; Shultz and Horibe, 1974). Youngsters' performance in these types of settings provides insight into their competence with "real world" language experiences.

HUMOR

An understanding of humor is interwoven with linguistic and cognitive development, abstract reasoning ability, and factual knowledge (Masten, 1986; McGhee, 1979; Prentice and Fathman, 1975; Zigler, Levine, and Gould, 1966). It also is positively associated with academic achievement (Masten, 1986) and a reflective problem-solving style (Brodzinsky, 1977). Spontaneous humor expressed by older children and adolescents promotes peer accep-

tance, self-esteem, and personal adjustment, and provides a socially acceptable way of releasing tension associated with dating, sexuality, and bodily
changes (Damico and Purkey, 1978; Masten, 1986; Ransohoff, 1975). Humor
is therefore a topic that must be taken seriously.

Youngsters' understanding of humor based on linguistic ambiguity has
been investigated by a small number of researchers. The first known study
in this area was conducted by Shultz and Horibe (1974), who examined
youngsters' understanding of jokes that were based upon the four major types
of ambiguity: phonological, lexical, surface structure, and deep structure.
Jokes of each type are contained in Table 9-1. The humor in each joke resulted
from the incongruity between two sentences and its subsequent resolution.
For example, in the lexical ambiguity, "Order! Order in the court!" "Ham
and cheese on rye, please, Your Honor," *order* first implies a request for quiet
but then implies a request for food. Resolution of this incongruity requires
knowledge of two distinct meanings of *order*, and the ability to consider both
meanings simultaneously. In Shultz and Horibe's study, the task contained
six jokes of each of the four types. Each joke was presented audibly in the
form of a tape-recorded dialogue, and visually in written form. Subjects
included 10- and 12-year-olds ($n = 60$) who were asked to explain what was
funny about the jokes. Results showed that the 12-year-olds outperformed
the 10-year-olds in targeting the critical ambiguous elements. Jokes based
on phonological ambiguity were generally easiest, followed successively by
surface-structure, lexical, and deep-structure ambiguities, results that were
inconsistent with studies of sentential ambiguity.

Table 9-1. *Types of jokes used by Shultz and Horibe.*

Phonological:
    SPEAKER A: "Waiter, what's this?"
    SPEAKER B: "That's bean soup, ma'am."
    SPEAKER B: "I'm not interested in what it's been. I'm asking what it is now."

Lexical:
    SPEAKER A: "Order! Order in the court!"
    SPEAKER B: "Ham and cheese on rye, please, Your Honor."

Surface Structure:
    SPEAKER A: "I saw a man eating shark in the aquarium."
    SPEAKER B: "That's nothing. I saw a man eating herring in the restaurant."

Deep-Structure:
    SPEAKER A: "Call me a cab."
    SPEAKER B: "You're a cab."

Adapted from Shultz and Horibe, 1974.

Muus and Hoag (1980) conducted the only study known to examine adolescents' understanding of jokes based on lexical and syntactic ambiguity. In their investigation, a group of 14- and 15-year-olds ($n = 38$) were asked to explain the humor involved in jokes similar to those employed by Shultz and Horibe (1974). Ten lexical and 10 syntactic ambiguities were presented in written form, and explanations were scored in terms of the number of legitimate meanings expressed. The subjects obtained an overall accuracy score of 83 percent, with lexical and syntactic ambiguities equally easy to explain. Thus, it appears that by middle adolescence, youngsters are quite adept at understanding jokes involving linguistic ambiguity. Muus and Hoag also reported that adolescents in their study who had performed better on a Piagetian task of formal operational thinking also performed better on the ambiguity task, compared to age-matched subjects with lower cognitive performance. This finding supported the view that cognition plays a role in youngsters' understanding of humor.

Youngsters' understanding of riddles has also been examined in terms of the four major types of ambiguity. Like jokes, riddles express incongruity that is resolvable through an understanding of ambiguous elements. Riddles differ from jokes, however, by employing a question and answer format (e.g., Q: "Where does a walnut stay the night?" A: "In the Nutcracker Suite"). Shultz (1974) examined the understanding of riddles in a study that included 10- and 12-year-olds ($n = 60$). The task consisted of six riddles of each of the four types, as shown in Table 9-2. Each riddle was presented audibly and in written form, and youngsters were asked to explain the humor in each. In contrast to the Shultz and Horibe (1974) study on jokes, the

Table 9-2. *Types of riddles used by Shultz.*

Phonological:
QUESTION: "Why did the cookie cry?"
ANSWER: "Because its mother had been a wafer so long."

Lexical:
QUESTION: "Why did the farmer name his hog Ink?"
ANSWER: "Because he kept running out of the pen."

Surface-Structure:
QUESTION: "Tell me how long cows should be milked."
ANSWER: "They should be milked the same as short ones, of course."

Deep-Structure:
QUESTION: "What animal can jump as high as a tree?"
ANSWER: "All animals. Trees cannot jump."

Adapted from Shultz, 1974.

10-year-olds in the study on riddles understood them as well as the 12-year-olds. It was also found that the lexical riddles were easiest to understand, and that the phonological, surface-structure, and deep-structure riddles were about equal in difficulty. This finding is inconsistent with studies of sentential ambiguity, which showed that phonological ambiguities were easiest to understand (Brodzinsky et al., 1977; Shultz and Pilon, 1973). However, this finding is consistent with the view that ambiguities of any particular type can vary widely in their difficulty.

No known studies have examined the understanding of riddles in adolescents, and thus it is unknown to what extent performance in this area improves beyond the age of 12. However, in view of the studies on sentential ambiguity, improvements might be expected to occur during adolescence, especially in relation to riddles involving more advanced vocabulary (e.g., Q: "How did Shakespeare find out everything?" A: "A little bard told him"), world knowledge (e.g., Q: "What did the cyclops say to Ulysses?" A: "Watch your step. I've got my eye on you"), or idiomatic meanings (e.g., Q: "What should you do if you have insomnia?" A: "Don't lose any sleep over it").

Summary

Studies of humor development have not made any consistent findings with regard to the four different types of linguistic ambiguity, a pattern which contrasts with the studies on isolated sentences. Nevertheless, the two domains are consistent in reporting that understanding improves as subject age increases. Less is known about humor development during adolescence, but it appears that growth occurs in this area at least through the age of 15. However, McGhee (1979) reported that adolescence is a time when humor based on ambiguity is no longer considered funny because of its simplistic nature. Adolescents are often bored by memorized jokes and riddles and prefer more sophisticated forms of humor where abstract themes (e.g., irony) are involved and greater cognitive challenges are presented. Humor expressed in the form of witty remarks and spontaneous anecdotes is also enjoyed by adolescents, especially when social or sexual conflicts are highlighted (Ransohoff, 1975; Wolfenstein, 1978). However, adolescence is also a time when preferences for humor become quite individualistic (Laing, 1939), a phenomenon which is consistent with the increasing individualism that occurs in other aspects of linguistic and cognitive development (see Chapter 1).

ADVERTISEMENTS

As with jokes and riddles, advertisements that play on the double meanings of words and phrases require an understanding of linguistic ambiguity in naturalistic settings. Youngsters' understanding of ambiguous ads reflects their metalinguistic development and their competence with "real world" language experiences. It is therefore an important topic for research.

Nippold, Cuyler, and Braunbeck-Price (in press) examined youngsters' explanations of ambiguous advertisements. Subjects 9, 12, 15, and 18 years old ($n = 40$) were individually administered the "Ambiguous Ads Task." This task required the subject to explain the meanings of 18 different advertisements. The ads had been taken from magazines, newspapers, and brochures, and each represented a common product or service. Examples of the ads are provided in Table 9-3. Each ad displayed a picture of the product and a main caption. Fourteen ads had two different meanings, and four were foils having only one meaning each. The ambiguous ads were all considered to be lexical ambiguities, and each contained a word or phrase having a physical and a psychological meaning. The physical meaning pertained to a concrete object or activity, whereas the psychological meaning pertained to a concept, mental state, or other abstract entity. For example, an ad for Subaru cars displayed a station wagon driving on various types of rugged terrain and a caption that read "*Grounds* for owning a Subaru." To present each test item, the examiner displayed the ad, read the main caption aloud, and asked the subject to explain what it meant. If only one meaning was explained, the examiner asked the subject if it meant anything else. Responses to the four foils were not scored.

Results of the study showed steady improvement with increasing age:

Table 9-3. *Examples of ambiguous advertisements used by Nippold, Cuyler, and Braunbeck-Price.*

1. Here's an ad for Ford Tempo cars. It says, "Designed to move you."
   (picture shows Ford Tempo car driving down highway)
   Acceptable answers:
   (1) transportation move
   (2) emotion move
2. Here's an ad for Diaparene Corn Starch Baby Powder. It says, "The absorbing facts about cornstarch."
   (picture shows container of Diaparene)
   Acceptable answers:
   (1) absorbs moisture
   (2) interesting, engrossing
3. Here's an ad for some new dinners from Stouffer's foods. It says, "Introducing the Upper Crusts. Two sensational new entrees from Stouffer's."
   (picture shows top-crusted meat dishes served on elegant table setting)
   Acceptable answers:
   (1) pie crusts
   (2) wealthy social class

Adapted from Nipold, Cuyler, and Braunbeck-Price, in press.

mean accuracy scores for the 9-, 12-, 15-, and 18-year-olds, respectively, were 33, 64, 71, and 84 percent. The most improvement occurred between the ages of 9 and 12, perhaps reflecting the transition into formal operational thinking, the stage of cognitive development when abstract reasoning comes into fruition (see Chapter 6). Performance improved beyond the age of 12, but at a slower pace. Qualitative analyses indicated that the explanations of the youngest subjects often were incomplete or overly general. For example, for the Diaparene ad (Table 9-3, item 2), one 9-year-old simply responded, "It's for powdering babies." As subjects got older, however, their explanations became more complete and specific. For example, one 18-year-old explained the Diaparene ad as follows:

> By absorbing, they mean the interesting or appealing facts about corn-starch. The facts that perhaps you didn't know before. But at the same time, they mean absorbing, as in naturally absorbing. . .the cornstarch keeps your baby dry.

However, even the 18-year-olds had not completely mastered the task and sometimes struggled to express themselves. For example, another 18-year-old responded to that same ad as follows:

> . . .absorbing. . .I don't know how to explain it. It kind of has a dou-ble meaning. . . . Well, something. . . . It's kind of like the facts about cornstarch, like here's what it's going to do, if that makes any sense. I can't really describe it.

The results also showed that accuracy was greater in response to the physical meanings of the ads than to the psychological, particularly for the 9-year-olds. Perhaps this was due to the fact that the pictures provided clearer visual clues for the physical meanings. For example, for the Stouffer's ad (Table 9-3, item 3), the picture showed top-crusted dinners being served. In contrast, the visual clues for the psychological meanings of the ads were much more subtle (e.g., an elegant table setting for the Stouffer's ad). The fact that some of the psychological meanings were idiomatic (e.g., *in his eyes, the upper crusts, swing of things, looks like a million*) may also have contributed to the greater difficulty of the psychological meanings, because idiomatic meanings are more difficult to understand than literal (see Chapter 8). This discrepancy between the physical and psychological meanings of the ads was also consistent with Asch and Nerlove (1960), who found that the physical meanings of double-function terms are understood several years before their psychological meanings. Double-function terms are words such as *bright, sweet,* and *warm* that have a related physical and psychological meaning. Interestingly, in the present study, six of the ads contained ambiguous words that were actually double-function terms (i.e., *move, delivers, absorbing, appetite, support,* and *deliver*). Further details of the study are available elsewhere (Nippold et al., in press).

Summary

Youngsters' performance on the Ambiguous Ads Task (Nippold et al., in press) was consistent with developmental studies of linguistic ambiguity involving isolated sentences, jokes, and riddles in showing steady improvement during the preadolescent and adolescent years. However, all of the ambiguous ads in the Nippold study were lexically based. Therefore, no statement can be made concerning the extent to which ads containing phonological or syntactic ambiguities might challenge youngsters of this age range. It should also be emphasized that not even the 18-year-olds had completely mastered the Ambiguous Ads Task. This suggests that growth in understanding of ambiguous ads may continue to improve into adulthood, as it does in relation to other types of multiple-meaning stimuli such as proverbs, metaphors, and idioms (see Chapter 8).

CONCLUSIONS

Youngsters' understanding and explanation of linguistic ambiguity steadily improves during the 9-through-19 age range. However, certain tasks remain challenging throughout this period, especially when idiomatic or unfamiliar word meanings are involved. Greater skill with linguistic ambiguity is associated with high intelligence, above-average academic achievement, and a reflective problem-solving style.

Studies where ambiguity occurs in naturalistic contexts (e.g., jokes, riddles, and advertisements) yield important information concerning the development of communicative competence in specific discourse settings during the preadolescent and adolescent years. Youngsters' understanding of ambiguity that occurs in other naturalistic contexts such as newspaper headlines, comic strips, and bumper stickers could also be examined as well as their spontaneous production of linguistic ambiguity, particularly during peer interactions. Another topic for research concerns the spontaneous production of ambiguity in situations where humorous stories or anecdotes are exchanged. Cognitive and linguistic factors closely associated with spontaneous production could also be examined in youngsters during the 9-through-19 age range.

REFERENCES

Asch, S.E., and Nerlove, H. (1960). The development of double function terms in children. In B. Kaplan and S. Wapner (Eds.), *Perspectives in psychological theory: Essays in honor of Heinz Werner* (pp. 47-60). New York: International Universities Press.

Brodzinsky, D.M. (1977). The role of conceptual tempo and stimulus characteristics in children's humor development. *Developmental Psychology, 11*, 843-850.

Brodzinsky, D.M., Feuer, V., and Owens, J. (1977). Detection of linguistic ambiguity by reflective, impulsive, fast/accurate, and slow/inaccurate children. *Journal of Educational Psychology, 69,* 237-243.

Damico, S.B., and Purkey, W.W. (1978). Class clowns: A study of middle school students. *American Educational Research Journal, 15,* 391-398.

Kagan, J., Rosman, B.L., Day, D., Albert, J., and Phillips, W. (1964). Information processing in the child: Significance of analytic and reflective attitudes. *Psychological Monographs, 78* (Whole No. 578).

Keil, F. (1980). Development of the ability to perceive ambiguities: Evidence for the task specificity of a linguistic skill. *Journal of Psycholinguistic Research, 9,* 219-229.

Kessel, F.S. (1970). The role of syntax in children's comprehension from ages six to twelve. *Monographs of the Society for Research in Child Development, 35*(6), Serial No. 139.

Laing, A. (1939). The sense of humour in childhood and adolescence. *British Journal of Educational Psychology, 9,* 201.

MacKay, D.G., and Bever, T.G. (1967). In search of ambiguity. *Perception and Psychophysics, 2,* 193-201.

Masten, A.S. (1986). Humor and competence in school-aged children. *Child Development, 57,* 461-473.

McGhee, P.E. (1979). *Humor: Its origin and development* (pp. 125-167). San Francisco: Freeman.

Muus, L.A., and Hoag, L.A. (1980, November). *Cognition and the detection of linguistic ambiguity by adolescents.* Paper presented at the Annual Convention of the American Speech-Language-Hearing Association, Detroit, MI.

Nippold, M.A., Cuyler, J.S., and Braunbeck-Price, R. (in press). Explanation of ambiguous advertisements: A developmental study with children and adolescents. *Journal of Speech and Hearing Research.*

Prentice, N.M., and Fathman, R.E. (1975). Joking riddles: A developmental index of children's humor. *Developmental Psychology, 11,* 210-216.

Ransohoff, R. (1975). Some observations on humor and laughter in young adolescent girls. *Journal of Youth and Adolescence, 4,* 155-170.

Shultz, T.R. (1974). Development of the appreciation of riddles. *Child Development, 45,* 100-105.

Shultz, T.R., and Horibe, F. (1974). Development of the appreciation of verbal jokes. *Developmental Psychology, 10,* 13-20.

Shultz, T.R., and Pilon, R. (1973). Development of the ability to detect linguistic ambiguity. *Child Development, 44,* 728-733.

van Kleeck, A. (1984). Metalinguistic skills: Cutting across spoken and written language and problem-solving abilities. In G.P. Wallach and K.G. Butler (Eds.), *Language learning disabilities in school-age children* (pp. 128-153). Baltimore, MD: Williams & Wilkins.

Wiig, E.H., Gilbert, M.F., and Christian, S.H. (1978). Developmental sequences in perception and interpretation of ambiguous sentences. *Perceptual and Motor Skills, 46,* 959-969.

Wolfenstein, M. (1978). *Children's humor: A psychological analysis.* Bloomington, IN: Indiana University Press.

Zigler, E., Levine, J., and Gould, L. (1966). Cognitive processes in the development of children's appreciation of humor. *Child Development, 37,* 507-518.

CHAPTER 10

■

LANGUAGE AND SOCIALIZATION

■

DOUGLAS C. COOPER
AND LYNNE ANDERSON-INMAN

Socialization is usually viewed as the process of growing up in a particular society. The term is used to describe the acquisition of the cultural knowledge required to operate successfully and appropriately in the everyday world. It is usually thought that parents and other adults are the teachers or transmitters of this culture and that children or other new members of the society are the learners. This view of socialization is not erroneous, but it is somewhat incomplete. Socialization is actually an interactive process. For example, as parents teach their children how to be children, children teach their parents how to be parents. Socialization occurs as a function of this cultural teaching and learning. Through the process of socialization, people assume a variety of different roles in life (e.g., child, parent, friend, student, teacher) and learn how to act appropriately in those roles. Acting appropriately is essential to feelings of social membership and solidarity.

An important but often overlooked dimension of the socialization process is language. Language is most commonly perceived as a "conduit" into which speakers pour their thoughts (Reddy, 1979). At the other end of the conduit is the listener, receiving the meaning of the words spoken. This conduit view makes clear distinctions between language, thought, and experience. Language, however, has a far more intimate connection to thought and behavior than this view indicates. Indeed, language is not only the bearer of thoughts but also the shaper of thoughts. From this perspective, the study of language and socialization is an attempt to understand processes that in everyday experience are inseparable. To be socialized is to learn the language of the surrounding society.

This chapter is divided into three main sections. The first section describes the interactionist view of socialization in detail. The next section examines the role that language plays in the socialization process. The final section presents examples of linguistic socialization in relation to five different issues affecting youngsters in the 9-through-19 age range.

SOCIALIZATION AS INTERACTION

In their now classic treatise, *The Social Construction of Reality*, Berger and Luckmann (1966) explained that socialization is a complex process of interaction, mediated by language, through which a person's social reality is constructed. This notion of the social construction of reality contrasts with the idea that reality is simply out there to be discovered through exploratory activity. An interactionist view of socialization holds that what people think of as reality is the result of their interaction with worldly or social structures, and the relations that ensue from that experience. These social structures (e.g., nuclear family, suburban neighborhood, school) are the frameworks which the person uses to understand and make sense out of day-to-day existence.

Language is one of the structures that confronts a child during socialization. During the interactive process of socialization, children learn how to use the structure of language to express and understand subjective meanings. In other words, children learn "how to mean" within the context of their culture (Halliday, 1975, 1978). Cultural meaning is not passively absorbed by the child but is acquired through active participation in social life. This notion of active participation is fundamental to the interactionist view of socialization. Berger (1967) explained it as follows:

> The individual is not molded as a passive, inert thing. Rather, he is formed in the course of a protracted conversation (a dialectic in the literal sense of the word) in which he is a participant. That is, the social world (with its appropriate institutions, roles, and identities) is not passively absorbed by the individual, but actively appropriated by him. (p. 18)

Another way to describe the interactive nature of socialization is the concept of *embeddedness*. Children are not just observers of social life but are embedded in it. What they understand of their culture "is something that is attained in and structured by the process of social interaction" (Durkin,

1986, p. 207). Embeddedness means that socialization and the use of language are the very means by which a person *realizes* a cultural role. Yet socialization also *regulates* the developmental process. This realization-regulation relationship is an important characteristic of social life.

The concept of socialization as a product of social interaction implies a relationship between the individual and a larger social group. Conversation is one of the principal means by which a person communicates with and is influenced by this larger group. Conversation is also the principal means by which an individual tries to resolve the tension that inevitably surfaces between individuality and group identity. Tannen (1986) explained this as the contradiction between involvement and independence. She cited the analogy of porcupines. In the winter cold they huddle together for warmth but prick each other with their sharp quills, so they pull away. The very nature of their being is a source of both comfort and pain. An analogous process takes place during socialization and the maintenance of mature relationships. For most people there is no possibility and probably no desire to achieve either absolute independence or absolute involvement. As Tannen explained it, "We are individual and social creatures. We need other people to survive, but we want to survive as individuals" (p. 17).

The social use of language and other communication strategies can be viewed as an attempt to construct a dynamic balance between independence and involvement. This suggests that socialization is not a neat undisturbed process, but rather a process that is subject to discontinuities. Because people can reflect on their experience, they can sometimes opt for involvement, while at other times choose independence. This tacking back and forth between involvement and independence it is not done haphazardly. In general, the experience is guided by certain principles, one of which is *typification*. Typification is the process of recognizing a given instance of something as representative of a larger category. Just as a child will recognize an unfamiliar species of dog as part of the canine family, certain behaviors are recognized as representative of social roles or social identities. These social roles serve as categories for assessing and interpreting social situations. They act as yardsticks for evaluating the behavior of others, and as guides in determining appropriate responses to that behavior.

These categories are learned during the socialization process and provide a framework for action. As children mature, they construct a range of familiar categories for themselves and for those with whom they interact. Behavior or action within these familiar categories is taken for granted. For example, a person does not have to deliberate about the role of child or parent for each interactional instance in the family. Through the process of typification, the structure of these recurring communicative interactions becomes "typical." In this sense, they are constraining because people usually follow the established patterns without examination or question. This "taken-for-grantedness," however, is essential for the conduct of everyday life. People simply do not have the capacity or intellectual energy to deliberate about every instance of social behavior. To do so would be disruptive to the flow of social interaction.

A familiar theme of the interactionist model of socialization is that social practices are both the medium through which the process occurs and the outcome of the process (Giddens, 1979). The social practices of significant others in a child's life (e.g., parents, teachers, friends, siblings) structure the child's perceptions of the social world, defining and modifying "reality" as they introduce the child to it. In other words, children's perceptions of the social world are mediated by the social practices of those with whom they interact. In the process of interacting with others, however, social practices can change. They are modified by experience and become more complex and varied over time.

This discussion brings up the issue of the idiosyncratic nature of socialization. Significant others select certain features of the world according to their particular location in the social structure, and also in accordance with their biographically rooted indiosyncrasies. For example, parents in one family may emphasize formal politeness and require children to refer to adult neighbors as "Mr. Smith," "Miss Jones," or "Mrs. Brown." In another family, polite familiarity may be the strategy that is taught to young children, resulting in elder friends and acquaintances being called by first names or even nicknames.

LINGUISTIC SOCIALIZATION

The idea that social practices are both the medium and the outcome of the socialization process also pertains to language use. The child has no choice as to native language. The linguistic structures of the native language, and the world view those structures reflect, are imposed on the child. Language acquisition requires the internalization of these constraints on cognition and language activity. Yet, as Giddens (1984) pointed out, "The learning of a language greatly expands the cognitive and practical capacities of the individual" (p. 170).

Although the constraining nature of language is unavoidable, it becomes so taken-for-granted that people lose sight of its powerful impact on consciousness and behavior. Berger and Luckmann (1966) suggested that "an understanding of language is. . .essential for any understanding of the reality of everyday life" (p. 37). This is true because of language's influential nature. "I encounter language as a facticity external to myself and it is coercive in its effect on me. Language forces me into its patterns" (p. 38). It should be kept in mind that this obligatory nature of language is not deterministic but merely constraining. A zone of meaningfulness is linguistically circumscribed for and by the speaker. "In this manner language marks the coordinates of my life in society and fills that life with meaningful objects" (p. 22).

Halliday (1978) wrote about language and the social structure it reflects as a system of meaningful relations. For him, language was one of the "systems that constitutes a culture; one that is distinctive in that it also serves as the encoding system for many (though not all) of the others" (p. 2). The point here is that language is much more than a labeling process. The meaning of a sentence consists of more than the aggregate of the lexical items syntactically strung together. The sentence's meaning also depends on the context in which it is uttered. When someone at a party is invited by the host to sit in "the old dog chair," the meaning might not be clear to the guest unless it is understood that the chair was the one in which the host's deceased dog slept. Although the chair has been cleaned and made acceptable for human occupation, the sentence has immense significance to the speaker. It signifies a range of complex relationships which are not apparent unless the listener shares the same social knowledge base as the speaker.

Meaning is not always made explicit. The socialized use of language relies on a body of shared knowledge. For a simplistic illustration, think of a couple leaving a movie theater. One of them may remark, "That was a very powerful film." The other person might respond, "Yes, I agree." Virtually no explicit discussion takes place, and none is necessary to establish communicative understanding. But suppose on their way home this couple stops to visit another couple. The above claim about the powerfulness of the movie is met with a series of inquiries for more details about the content of the movie. The couple who just saw the movie must explicate the content in order to make their interpretation understood. In order for understanding to occur between these two couples, they must first establish shared knowledge. Much of everyday talk in familiar settings like families proceeds in a manner similar to that of the couple who shared the film. A taken-for-granted world built on shared experience provides the basis for understanding and getting on with everyday life.

Even when there is shared knowledge, language is not simply a process for labeling reality, but rather a process for defining or interpreting it. Blumer (1969) explained as follows:

> Human beings interpret or "define" each other's actions. Their "response" is not made directly to the actions of another but is instead based on the meaning which they attach to such actions. Thus, human interaction is mediated by the use of symbols, by interpretation, or by ascertaining the meaning of one another's action. (p. 79)

Language is the principal means of expressing social values to a developing child. It is also the means by which the child reinterprets those values and internalizes them in biographically unique ways.

Just as members of the same culture simultaneously exhibit uniqueness and commonality, speakers of the same language accomplish communicative tasks with a high degree of variability. Prucha (1983) offered an explanation for the increasing variability in language use during the developmental path from childhood to adulthood:

The real existence of language (its use by an individual as well as its functioning in society as a whole) is substantially bound up with social needs. All linguistic reality (system, process, product) serves social needs (objectively existing purposes), and these needs are the causes of an immense variety of language use and great diversity of linguistic messages. (p. 287)

Prucha called this a sociofunctional explanation of language use. Language functions to satisfy social needs, and those needs develop in particular social contexts. For example, a girl at school may say to her teacher, "I wasn't doing anything and Carl splashed paint all over me!" This "tattling" is a communicative strategy that satisfies the girl's need to inform the teacher about some other child's misdeeds, but also to avoid implicating herself in the matter.

One of the principal achievements of the person undergoing socialization is the integration of the self into the complex structure of everyday life. Socialization is, in part, the process whereby a person learns to refer to self and others. This referencing activity builds up a grid which provides the individual with a stable order of meaningful social relationships. Children not only learn and use increasingly complex and sophisticated grammatical forms, but "more significantly. . .their usage comes to reflect the complexities of social relationships" (Hewitt, 1984, p.98). The more the child masters grammatical and relationship terms, "the better able he or she is to represent these relationships internally, thus incorporating the social world into itself" (Hewitt, 1984, p. 98). As the child matures, the semantic range of linguistic elements and relationships increases along with the growth of interactive experience. Hewitt (1984) explained as follows:

An essential part of linguistic socialization goes far beyond the learning of words, their definitions, and their possible grammatical relationships. It involves learning the relationship between words and deeds, between the system of labels for objects. . .and the range of social acts that are possible in the world in which the child lives. In short, the child learns how to represent its own conduct and that of others linguistically, and also how to link the two together. (p. 100)

Language is the critical factor that links the life styles of children undergoing socialization and the significant others with whom they interact.

"Our use of language represents a crucial link between the collective, cultural, and cognitive individual domains in our everyday lives" (Forgas, 1985, p. 253). The view that language is a living communication system for social interaction is crystallized in Halliday's (1978) question, "How else can one look at language except in a social context?" (p. 10). Or as Wurm (1976) reported, "It is now commonly accepted that communication systems such as language have a real existence only in the social and cultural settings in which they appear" (cited by Forgas, 1985, p. 254).

Developing Communicative Competence

Linguistic socialization is much more than learning linguistic rules. Competent use of language also requires knowing situational rules. Understanding how language and socialization are related means understanding context, because all linguistic experience is situated in a meaningful context. Meaning is not derived from any absolute linguistic reality but from the interdependence of language use and the situations in which language is uttered. In this sense, the study of language and the study of socialization are not two distinct phenomena but a single process. To be socialized is to learn the language.

Chomsky (1965) described competence as the language user's tacit knowledge of the finite set of underlying grammatical rules out of which the speaker can produce or the listener can understand an infinite number of grammatical sentences. Chomsky's formulation provides a framework for understanding language acquisition, but it has less explanatory power for understanding the development of expertise in everyday talk. In discussing the development of competent performance in everyday talk, Hymes (1972) proposed the construct *communicative competence*. Communicative competence is the use of speech forms that are appropriate for particular social settings:

> We have to account for the fact that the normal child acquires knowledge of sentences, not only as grammatical but also as appropriate. He or she acquires competence as to when to speak, when not, and as what to talk about with whom, when, where, and in what manner. (p. 108)

The development of communicative competence is at issue throughout a person's life. This has not always been recognized. Harris and Coltheart (1986) suggested there are good reasons why language development is now understood as occurring over a longer period of time. They explained that

> Our concept of what a child has to acquire in order to become a fully competent adult language user has broadened beyond mere lexical and syntactic competence, to include such skills as the ability to understand

and produce coherent discourse. . .and to produce language which is appropriate for a particular listener and a particular situation. (p. 80)

Saville-Troike (1982), cited by Romaine (1984), listed linguistic knowledge, interactional skills, and cultural knowledge as three domains of expertise that must be accounted for in a theory of communicative competence. Speakers must perceive and choose salient features in each of these three categories in order to communicate effectively. They must make choices among the range of possible utterances (e.g., "How are you?," "Hi," "What's happening?"), be sensitive to the norms governing a particular interaction (e.g., the question "How are you?" is a greeting, not a parting comment), and display an awareness of the prevailing cultural values and attitudes (e.g., the greeting "How are you?" is not a serious inquiry about a person's well-being). These three types of skills and knowledge, internalized during early periods of socialization, are employed at a tacit level of awareness during communication, and are refined throughout life.

Language and Social Power

The linguistic forms and interactional strategies employed by speakers do not necessarily conform to standard or preferred patterns. Understanding communicative competence requires a sensitivity to particular social contexts. For example, children who are judged linguistically deficient in the school environment sometimes display sophisticated and competent communication skills in the home, neighborhood, or peer group situation. Vernacular forms of speech, or ways of talking that are appropriate for the speaker's social group, may not reflect the standards of the preferred speech norms but can be judged competent because of their appropriateness for some of the situations in which they are used. It must be noted, however, that not all situationally competent communicative performances have the same influence in terms of social power, nor are they equally acceptable across a range of social contexts.

The concept of *sociolinguistic code* can help explain how different forms of talk are invested with different weights of social power. Bernstein (1974) used the notion of sociolinguistic code to describe how different ways of talking enable access or limit access to the language of power in a given situation. For example, to the extent that the language children bring to school does not conform to the standards of school language, the ability of these children to express, comprehend, and otherwise employ the sociolinguistic code of the school is limited. The initial site for the development of a sociolinguisitc code is the family. Family talk or discourse is particular in two ways: the uniqueness of the family itself, and the family's location in the social structure. World views that are particular to the family's social location are intergenerationally transmitted through the unconscious development and sharing of a family's sociolingusitic code (Bernstein, 1981). As adolescence approaches and children move out of the tight circle of family socialization, family influence wanes. Peer groups become more important and their sociolinguistic codes become more influential.

Atkinson (1985) used the example of clothing as a code. When people get dressed, they are involved in selection and combination. Certain principles are at work; for example, from top to bottom (head to toe) and from inside out (underwear to outerwear). Each garment slot can be filled from a diverse (or perhaps sparse) collection resulting (hopefully) in an integrated clothing system. For the foot slot, a person may select from a variety of footwear. For the torso slot, the person may choose from among a variety of shirts, blouses, or sweaters. "The code will regulate the selection and combination of cultural elements, and will articulate that array with social occasions and contexts of use" (p. 85). In an analogous manner, particular linguistic and communicative features are made available to children as they mature. The available choices enable children to act out particular social roles that are, in turn, constrained by those very choices. For example, when children want to join a particular peer group, they choose specific words and speaking styles that will gain entry into the desired group. In order to maintain membership, they are constrained to use the group's code.

The internalization of a sociolinguistic code creates zones of relevant meanings. The quality of children's interactions in both verbal and nonverbal terms orients them to particular orders of meaning. Heath (1983) showed how differences in language use in three southeastern United States communities influenced the children's relationship to school language codes. For example, in one home environment talk about books used language forms similar to those used in school. In another environment, talk about books was almost nonexistent. In the latter case, books had little relevance in the child's life, while in the former they were seen as important. The different zones of relevance internalized by these children as a result of the language used (or not used) at home have a tremendous impact on the children's socialization in other environments, in this case in school.

When learning to talk, children do not just learn a native language, they learn particular versions of the language. The learned language contains social knowledge as well as linguistic structures. This social knowledge is internalized through experience and language use. During social interactions, speakers retrieve the particular sociolinguistic code they have learned. This code is a tacit principle that regulates the selection and combination of meaningful features of the social world. Through socialization, the child integrates these features into a coherent world view. As children mature, they develop an understanding of the contextual constraints and determinants of appropriate ways of speaking. The use of varying linguistic forms by children in face-to-face interaction not only increases their control over linguistic resources, but also their control over the social world which the language system reflects. Understanding how the language system works means understanding how the world works.

EXAMPLES OF LINGUISTIC SOCIALIZATION

This final section of the chapter provides examples of linguistic socialization in relation to five different issues that affect preadolescents and adolescents: identity; gender; cross-sex communication; the peer group; and friendship.

Identity

One of the most consistent themes running through the literature on adolescence is that of the identity crisis. Although the adolescent identity crisis may appear as an abrupt developmental disjuncture, it is actually related to a number of changes that have been taking place for a long period of time. It is the failure to anticipate these changes in the sociophysiological environment of children that contributes to the perception that adolescence prompts the onset of an abrupt identity crisis. Coleman (1980) pointed out that adolescence is usually thought of as a time of both change and consolidation. There are a number of reasons for this. First, many physical changes that occur prior to and during adolescence are accompanied by changes in body image and sense of self. Second, adolescent intellectual growth "makes possible a more complex and sophisticated self concept involving a greater number of dimensions" (p. 13). Children in this age range are increasingly able to consider another person's perspective. Third, increasing emotional independence, and an increasing concern with fundamental social decisions involving occupation, sexual behavior, and friendship, intensify the development of the self-concept. Finally, the transitional nature of adolescence seems to be associated with additional changes in self-concept.

As children approach adolescence, their language reflects this search for a secure identity. The use of slang by preadolescents and adolescents sets them apart from younger children, but more pointedly from their parents and other adults (see Chapter 8 for a discussion of slang development). Slang and other stylistic variations distinguish the adolescent culture from the adult world and help to maintain group identity. Language has been the principal means of socialization, and this is tacitly recognized by children's efforts to display lexical uniqueness through slang and communicative strategies like "Gimme five!" Le Page (1978) posited a sociolinguistic theory of speech acts that views every utterance a person makes as an act of identity. Speakers can employ various linguistic resources to establish and maintain a sense of self- and peer-group identity. The theory of socialization presented in the first section of this chapter identified language as the principal factor mediating the construction of reality, which includes a person's identity. Identity is a dynamic concept, particularly during childhood and adolescence. Certain stylistic variations and words gain symbolic function as the person emerges from childhood. Subsequently, those same language variations lose symbolizing power as the adolescent approaches adulthood.

Despite the striving for autonomy, communication with parents remains a significant factor in the life of preadolescents and adolescents (Walker and Greene, 1986). But peer relationships have increasing importance for the adolescent who is developing a sense of personal identity. It may appear that children are rejecting one sphere of influence—parental—for another— the peer group. It is more likely, however, that the world for adolescents is becoming more complex. They are able to take more into account when dealing with their identity and the issues surrounding it. Prestige forms of talk, that is, forms that most closely conform to formal patterns, may be used to show respect, manipulate parental behavior, or to express maturity. Sometimes youthful slang will be used in adult–child interaction to build camaraderie.

It is not uncommon to hear middle and late adolescents say "I can...." These statements of confidence often refer to adult activities that are becoming possible. Examples include, "I can drive a car," or, "I can take care of myself." The bravado that often accompanies this "can do" attitude is an effort to communicate confidence and strength during a period of life characterized by intense transition. From preadolescence to young adulthood, people pass through a period which, as Lyell (1973) argued, is devalued. This is so because the adolescent "does not work. American culture primarily values competition, productivity, and achievement" (p. 85). Furthermore, adolescents seem to be taken seriously only by their peers "because the activities of adolescents are culturally not valued" (p. 85) by others. Lyell's view may be an oversimplification, but it does suggest some explanation for the context in which preadolescents and adolescents grow up. Communicative strategies are employed to balance the demands that come from home, school, friendships, and peer groups.

Gender

An important dimension of socialization and the socialized use of language for adolescents is gender identity. A fundamental dimension of self and social identity is gender. The way that parents and significant others address children from birth in terms of gender has a pervasive impact on the child's identity structure. The manner in which parents and other caregivers handle, play with, and speak to children communicates clear messages about appropriate gender labels and gender behavior. So quite early in life, children are both perceptually and productively sensitive to gender categories. They can recognize gender-differentiated behavior, including speech, and they can act in ways that reflect that difference. As children participate in communicative interactions, they acquire tacit knowledge that is displayed in gender-appropriate behavior (or sometimes in a conscious violation of gender-appropriate behavior). The social meaning of linguistic structures is demonstrably appreciated by maturing children when they speak and act in ways that are appropriate to their gender role.

Gender issues are intense during adolescence. The task of adolescence is to fashion a coherent sense of identity, verifying that identity through numerous and varied social interactions. To some degree, this coherence is achieved through reenactment of peer-group rituals and behavior norms. The member-marking function of certain linguistic forms provides an organizational drift that binds members of peer groups together. As Romaine (1984) expressed it, "Socialization in sex-specific peer groups exerts pressure towards conformity in linguistic and other behavior" (p. 12). Conformity to sex-specific peer group linguistic and behavioral norms produces sameness and difference. Gender specificity also means gender differentiation.

Numerous studies (Biondi, 1975; Cheshire, 1982; Labov, 1972; Lakoff, 1975; Romaine, 1984) have pointed to the existence of marked differences in male and female speech patterns. According to Macaulay (1977), these differentiated speech patterns are regularized by middle adolescence. The research of Macaulay (1977), Romaine (1978, 1984), and Cheshire (1982) indicated that women "produce forms that are nearer the prestige norm more frequently than men" (Romaine, 1984, pp. 112–113). Similarly, Cheshire noted that for the verbs *do, was, see, came,* and *ain't,* the boys she studied produced more nonstandard forms than girls. For example, boys were more likely to say "she do" or "we does" than girls. In the case of utterances such as "You ain't no boss," or "You ain't been around here," girls used *ain't* significantly less often than boys.

Explanations have been offered for gender-differentiated linguistic and communicative strategies (Fishman, 1978; Hirschman, 1973; West and Zimmerman, 1977). The social-power argument put forth by these writers and others says that the way women and men communicate reflects the prevailing masculine dominance in society. For example, in cross-sex conversations, men make more interruptions, are more disputatious, exert greater topic control, and make more factual declarations. Thus, as Lakoff (1975) claimed, the task of becoming both an adult and a woman may seem almost impossible for adolescent girls. The difficulty arises from the effort to acquire adult confidence and strength while using communicative strategies that deny women interactional control.

Maltz and Borker (1982) complemented the social-power argument by claiming that boys and girls grow up in different subcultures and learn to use words for different purposes. They concluded that

> Basically girls learn to do three things with words: (1) to create and maintain relationships of closeness and equality; (2) to criticize others in acceptable ways; and (3) to interpret accurately the speech of other girls. (p. 205)

In task-oriented activities, Goodwin (1980) found that girls predominantly used inclusive forms such as *let's, we gonna, we could*, and *we gotta*. These inclusive forms of speech indicate an orientation toward language as an adhesive that binds relationships. Adolescent girls spend much time "talking, reflecting, and sharing intimate thought. Loyalty is of central concern to the 12- to 14-year-old girl, presumably because, if innermost secrets are shared, friends may have 'dangerous knowledge' at their disposal" (Brooks-Gunner and Matthews, 1979, p. 280). So, as Lever (1976) commented about best friends, "sharing secrets binds the union together, and 'telling' the secrets to outsiders is symbolic of the 'break-up' " (cited by Maltz and Borker, 1982, p. 206).

Group relationships among boys are more hierarchically based. Status is the principal variable manipulated by interactional strategies. Maltz and Borker (1982) explained as follows:

> The world of boys is one of posturing and counter-posturing. In this world speech is used in three ways: (1) to assert one's position of dominance; (2) to attract and maintain an audience; and (3) to assert oneself when other speakers have the floor. (p. 207)

If it is true that "the use of speech for the expression of dominance is the most straightforward and probably the best-documented sociolinguistic pattern in boys' peer groups" (p. 207), then communicative strategies that reflect this purpose will be noticeably different from those of girls, whose social purposes are more cooperative and relationship oriented.

Social success becomes increasingly important for boys and girls when they enter school and takes on more complex dimensions as adolescence is approached. Talking is the principal means by which adolescents present themselves to their peers and to the rest of the world. Inadequate communication skills are much more difficult to compensate for than, say, poor clothing. In order to feel competent as a social being, boys and girls need to have the linguistic resources and be able to make appropriate communicative choices in terms of both situation and timing. The fact that these choices may be limited by gender-specific linguistic patterns may play a significant role in the future of an individual.

Cross-Sex Communication

Boys and girls are frequently in close proximity, yet the evidence presented so far suggests that they live in somewhat different worlds. Same-sex peer groups are the common pattern from early childhood through adolescence. Dweck (1981) argued that "from a very early age, boys and girls form their own quite different cultures" (p. 325). This divergence is evidenced by the development of "different interests, values, and goals that relate to activities they will engage in and persons with whom they will associate" (p. 325). Once this separation is established, girls and boys structure their worlds in ways that reflect different spheres of relevance. According to Maltz and Borker (1982), women's speech reflects a concern with support. For example, women exhibit a greater tendency to use inclusive pronouns such as *we* and *you*. Men's speech, however, reflects an interest in challenging others and is characterized by various forms of verbal aggression such as practical jokes, put-downs, and insults.

If these differences are so pronounced, even at an early age, what communicative strategies are used by girls and boys to talk with each other? After studying the development of interactional norms among early adolescent girls, Eden and Sanford (1982) reported that by the sixth grade, girls were beginning to interact with boys on a regular basis. By the seventh and eighth grades, boyfriends were not uncommon. Eden and Sanford pointed out that "the addition of more frequent interactions with boys added another level of complexity to girls' interpersonal relations and required new interactional norms" (p. 11). However, male–female relationships are viewed by adolescents as difficult to talk about. For example, Varenne (1983) found that his teenage informants in a suburban high school repressed any talk of a sexually related nature. The students talked easily about "the jocks," "the freaks," or social events, but were usually unwilling to discuss male–female relationships. To do so seemed to require special communicative strategies.

One strategy employed by the girls in Eden and Sanford's (1982) study was the use of an intermediary to communicate with a boy. Girlfriends would agree to talk with a boy for a friend, but this talk was strictly constrained by rules that governed its intimacy. The girlfriend acting as the intermediary must not be too friendly or intimate with the boy. One of Eden and Sanford's examples is illustrative. Carol had been talking with Betty's boyfriend for her but Betty thought that Carol had been too friendly:

> Mary [another member of the girls' group] said it wasn't Carol's fault, but Betty said, "Yes, it was. You flirt. You flirt. Carol you're mean. I don't like you anymore." Carol asked Betty if she still wanted to talk with him for her. She said, "Yes" and immediately got happier and began singing about peanut butter cookies. (p. 11)

What is apparent in this example is that Carol's intermediary role is of paramount importance. The need for their friendship quickly supersedes Betty's suspicion of Carol's intimacy with Betty's boyfriend. These girls exhibit the effort to balance considerations for maintaining their own relationship with the more competitive features of cross-sex communication.

An area where content of the messages communicated is very important is learning about birth control. Where do young people learn about this sensitive area of social knowledge? A study by De Pietro and Allen (1984) identified four interactional styles for learning about birth control: "(1) home-oriented style; (2) peer-oriented style; (3) professionally-oriented style; and (4) multi-source user" (p. 828). Multi-source users gained information from a variety of sources such as home, peers, professionals, and public media. On birth control knowledge tests, girls scored significantly higher for peer-group style than for home style, and multi-source users scored highest of all. Boys scored significantly higher for home style than peer style, and scores were just slightly lower for multi-user style. According to these data, girls gained a significant amount of birth control knowledge from their peers. They talked with their friends about birth control in an informative manner much more than boys did. One possible explanation for this is that females have borne the cultural expectation that birth control is a female responsibility. This study also confirmed that women talked more frequently about intimate problems with their friends than boys did.

Little research has been conducted on the nature of cross-sex interaction during the preadolescent and adolescent years. As Eden and Sanford (1982) pointed out, "We still know little about either the content of adolescent norms or the processes by which these norms are developed and maintained" (p. 1). Given the intense interest in and importance of gender socialization, further study of the way children acquire adult communicative strategies for cross-sex interaction is warranted.

The Peer Group

Children move into new contexts both subjectively and objectively with the onset of puberty. New zones of relevance are noticed and mutually constructed through peer group interaction. The systematic variations that mark gender-specific and peer-group "forms of life" play a significant role in incorporating the child into a desired group. Gaining control over marked linguistic features shows a growing competence in the use of communicative strategies that both realize and regulate behavior and speech patterns appropriate to gender and peer group membership.

Hewitt's study (1987) of the use of Creole, or London Jamaican, by white adolescents demonstrates one way that speakers use linguistic resources to associate with and to distinguish themselves from certain groups. White adolescents learned Creole from their association with West Indian blacks living in London. One 16-year-old black boy gave his reasons for enjoying the use of Creole:

> Yes. Cos I feel. . .sounds funny. . . I feel black and I'm proud of it to speak like that. That's why, when I talk it. I feel better than when I'm talking like now [to the interviewer]. (p. 89)

Hewitt observed that "for many black adolescents Creole is a source of identity and its use an assertion of cultural difference" (p. 87). Yet the use of Creole does not go unchallenged in the black community. Many black parents have reservations about its use due to its low prestige in the wider community. Thus, the linguistic growth of Creole is somewhat independent of parental speech, and it grows despite parental reservations. This demonstrates Labov's claim (1972) that "children do not speak like their parents. . . [they] follow the pattern of their peers" (p. 304). In the midst of conflicting claims for appropriate speech, "many black adolescents have made their own 'provision' for improving their prestige and that of their dialect within the contexts that are most meaningful and in relation to the power structures in which they see themselves embedded" (Hewitt, 1987, p. 91).

This is the social context in which the white adolescents who are motivated to adopt Creole patterns of speech immerse themselves. Hewitt (1987) noticed that a common pattern among white Creole users begins with its use in play. Jocular use of Creole is an attempt to establish in-group relations between speakers of different ethnic backgrounds and speaker styles. As young white speakers interact with black youth and are motivated to mediate cultural differences, Creole utterances become more spontaneous:

> WHITE BOY: "Oh, Rayston, ya goin football on Saturday?"
> BLACK BOY: "Mi na go football! Wha for?"
> WHITE BOY: "Check some gyal later."
> BLACK BOY: "Na. Mi na wan check gyal now."
> WHITE BOY: "Rasschalt! Fink ya bent." (p. 94)

When both boys were using strong Jamaican pronunciation, the white boy was almost indistinguishable from the black boy. Through the acquisition and use of Creole, the white boy has identified with the speech values of black youth culture. Thus, through the adoption of a set of linguistic resources, peer in-group identity is accomplished.

Association with peers is an important feature of striving for autonomy during the 9-through-19 age range. While withdrawal from dependence on parents is significant, the acquisition of peer interactional norms in terms of verbal and nonverbal elements is of paramount concern. Children are attracted to certain ongoing peer groups in which they must integrate themselves. Eden and Sanford (1982) pointed out that because interactional norms among early adolescents "are constantly changing, it is important for children of all ages to have frequent contact with peers in order to be aware of relevant norms" (p. 21). The way in which the norms are communicated is also constantly changing. For example, Eden and Sanford reported that "openly making fun of others became increasingly less common between sixth and eighth grades as students became more aware of the feelings of others" (p. 21). Thus, the communicative strategies used to talk about other people undergo modification in response to sensitivity development. At the age of 9 or 10, the overweight child may often be the object of open ridicule or teasing. However, a few years later (at the age of 12 or 14) it is less common that this type of talk is expressed in the presence of the object person.

Varenne (1983) reported that in the suburban high school he investigated, it was generally admitted that cliques existed, yet there was "no example of a student seriously acknowledging membership in a clique" (p. 256). Students in this school recognized friendship as "a good thing" and cliquishness as a "bad thing" (p. 256). The students were reluctant to call their close and frequent associates a clique. Instead, those associates were called friends. Friends and peer group membership were not exclusive categories. But linguistic discriminations were made by these students. Why is this so? Varenne pointed out that as students attempt to sort out the *I, we,* and *they* relationships, "the external social situation of a participant does not determine his symbolic expression of this situation" (p. 270). Thus, a student who was a top athlete and spent most of his waking hours with other top athletes was organizationally a jock, a member of a readily distinguishable clique. Yet this student was not obligated to talk about the jocks as *we* against the *they* of other groups. In fact, this student differentiated himself from the jocks by referring to them as *they.* In this case, language does not reflect the objective status of experience but displays an effort to understand the increasingly complex social conditions that confront the growing adolescent.

The transition from childhood to adolescence is accompanied by an intensity of peer interaction. This in part is a process of separating from parents. According to a study conducted by Brendt (1979), conformity to peers peaks during middle adolescence. This isolation of parents from peers is accomplished at least in part by the children not discussing peers with their parents. Adolescents who share too much of the peer world with parents may feel like they are compromising adolescent autonomy. If there are two worlds, the adolescent and the parent–adult (as is often claimed by both sets of participants), that separation is established and maintained in part by differentiated linguistic worlds. While this may be true, it should be emphasized that positive parent–child communication at any age enhances the relationship for both.

Friendship

Friendship is a social relation most people are involved in throughout their lives. Changes in social knowledge concerning friendship follow a developmental curve. In their research, Stein and Goldman (1981) noticed that 12-year-olds were more aware than 9-year-olds of the fact that "shared interests facilitate the establishment of friendship and that the interests of others may differ from those of self" (p. 313). The 12-year-olds in their research were also more aware that potential friends may have goals of their own and other activities in which they might be engaged. This indicates that along with the cognitive ability to assess another person's perspective comes the communicative ability to express that knowledge appropriately. For example, a 9-year-old boy might say to a new friend, "Let's go the park and play football," whereas a 12-year-old boy might ask a new friend, "Would you like to play football?" These two utterances reflect different abilities to assess the social situation, with the 12-year-old showing greater awareness of the "need to match or establish common interests" (p. 313). In addition, the older boy shows greater usage of his linguistic resources to gain insight into the friend's perspective, thereby obtaining information that can be helpful in future interactions with the friend.

Youniss and Smollar (1985) reported some interesting conclusions from their study of adolescent relations with parents and friends:

> Adolescents talk to their close friends about school, sex and dating, opposite-sex friends, friendships, family, and the future. More females than males, however, reported discussions of these topics with their close friends, and regardless of the topic, more females than males selected the close friend as the preferred or most likely discussion partner. (p. 99)

Communication between close male friends seemed to be more restricted than that between close female friends. For example, 69 percent of girls in one study chose a close friend as the most likely partner with whom to discuss problems about an opposite-sex friend. In contrast, only 50 percent of the boys made a similar choice. In general, discussion of intimate problems and feelings was more prevalent among close female friends than among males.

Youniss and Smollar also examined the quality of communication between adolescent friends. If it was reported that close friends both explained their reasons for ideas and sincerely tried to understand the other friend's ideas, the discussion was characterized as *symmetrical*. If only one of these functions was performed, it was labeled *asymmetrical*. Female communication was significantly more symmetrical than male communication. There were also differences in younger and older adolescents' perceptions of friendship. Both boys and girls judged friendship to be more meaningful and important as they grew older. The girls in Youniss and Smollar's research expressed a feeling about friendship that is consistent with the research findings referred to in the discussion on gender. They were almost unanimous in depicting the primary function of female friendship as intimate sharing. For example, one girl said, "The relationship is deeper, less superficial. When you're younger you look for good times. Now you want someone you can share the bad times as well as the good" (p. 105). While this feature of intimacy and closeness was not entirely absent from the boys' communicative life, it was engaged in much less often.

As this discussion of friendship implies, comments about interaction among adolescent friends are often differentiated along gender lines. This is partly due to the fact that researchers have methodically researched the problem this way, and to the consistent pattern of same-sex friendship selection (Toman, 1976). There is a need for more research on adolescent cross-sex friendship communication. It is known that boys and girls learn to talk like men and women (see Edelsky, 1977). But little is known about how those communication styles constructed among adolescent friends and peer groups.

CONCLUSIONS

Language use and socialization are a unified process, a view that is captured by Berger and Luckmann's (1966) notion that social life is a protracted conversation. As children carry on this conversation, they acquire a range of communicative skills that enable them to gain control over a greater range of linguistic resources. These resources are used by individuals to situate themselves in the social world. Whether children talk with their friends, initiate a romantic conversation, or make a delicate request of their parents, competent use of language skills is required. This chapter has illustrated how linguistic socialization is a complex process that exceeds the usual understanding of what it means to talk. To talk is to interact with the world. Through this interactive process, children make connections with the world and also with themselves.

REFERENCES

Atkinson, P. (1985). *Language, structure and reproduction: An introduction to the sociology of Basil Bernstein.* London: Methuen.

Berger, P. (1967). *The sacred canopy.* Garden City, NY: Doubleday.

Berger, P., and Luckmann, T. (1966). *The social construction of reality.* Garden City, NY: Doubleday.

Bernstein, B. (1974). *Class, codes and control: Theoretical studies towards a sociology of language.* New York: Schoken.

Bernstein, B. (1981). Codes, modalities and the process of reproduction. *Language in Society, 10,* 327-363.

Biondi, L. (1975). *The Italian-American child: His sociolinguistic enculturation.* Washington, DC: Georgetown University Press.

Blumer, H. (1969). *Symbolic interactionism.* Berkeley, CA: University of California Press.

Brendt, T. (1979). Developmental changes in conformity to peers and parents. *Developmental Psychology, 15,* 608-616.

Brooks-Gunner, J., and Matthews, W. (1979). *He and she: How children develop sex role identity.* Englewood Cliffs, NJ: Prentice-Hall.

Chesire, J. (1982). *Variation in English dialect.* Cambridge: Cambridge University Press.

Chomsky, N. (1965). *Aspects of a theory of syntax.* Cambridge, MA: MIT Press.

Coleman, J. (1980). *The nature of adolescence.* London: Methuen.

Di Pietro, R., and Allen, R. (1984). Adolescents' communication and learning styles about birth control. *Adolescence, 19,* 827-837.

Durkin, K. (1986). Language and cognition during the school years. In K. Durkin (Ed.), *Language development in the school years* (pp. 203-233). London: Croom Helm.

Dweck, C. (1981). Social-cognitive processes in children's friendships. In S. Asher, and J. Gottman (Eds.), *The development of children's friendships* (pp. 322-333). Cambridge, England: Cambridge University Press.

Edelsky, A. (1977). Acquisition of an aspect of communicative competence: Learning what it means to talk like a lady. In S. Ervin-Tripp, and S. Mitchell-Kernan (Eds.), *Child Discourse* (pp. 225-243). New York: Academic Press.

Eden, D., and Sanford, S. (1982, August). *The development and maintenance of interactional norms among early adolescents.* Paper presented at the International Sociological Association Meeting, Mexico City.

Fishman, P. (1978). Interaction: The work women do. *Social Problems, 25,* 397-406.

Forgas, J. (1985). *Language and social situations.* New York: Springer-Verlag.

Giddens, A. (1979). *Central problems in social theory.* New York: Basic Books.

Giddens, A. (1984). *The constitution of society.* Berkeley, CA: University of California Press.

Goodwin, M. (1980). Directive-response speech sequences in girl's and boy's task activities. In S. McConnell-Ginet, R. Borker, and N. Furman (Eds.), *Women and language in liberation and society* (pp. 157-173). New York: Praeger.

Halliday, M. (1975). *Learning how to mean.* New York: Elsevier.

Halliday, M. (1978). *Language as a social semiotic.* Baltimore, MD: University Park Press.

Harris, M., and Coltheart, M. (1986). *Language processing in children and adults.* London: Routledge, Paul and Kegan.

Heath, S. (1983). *Ways with words.* Cambridge, England: Cambridge University Press.

Hewitt, J. (1984). *Self and society.* Boston: Allyn and Bacon.

Hewitt, R. (1987). White adolescent Creole users and the politics of friendship. In B. Mayor, and A. Pugh (Eds.), *Language, communication and education* (pp. 85-106). London: Croom Helm.

Hirschman, L. (1973). *Female–male differences in conversation interaction.* Paper presented at the Linguistics Society of America, San Diego, CA.

Hymes, D. (1972). On communicative competence. In J. Pride, and J. Holmes (Eds.), *Sociolinguistics* (pp. 269-293). Harmondsworth, England: Penguin.

Labov, W. (1972). *Sociolinguistic patterns*. Philadelphia: University of Pennsylvania Press.

Lakoff, R. (1975). *Language and women's place*. New York: Harper and Row.

Le Page, R. (1978). *Projection; focusing; diffusion: Steps towards a socio-linguistic theory of language*. Caribbean Linguistics Society Occasional Paper No. 9.

Lever, J. (1976). Sex differences in games people play. *Social Problems, 23*, 478-483.

Lyell, R. (1973). Adolescent and adult self-esteem as related to cultural values. *Adolescence, 7*, 85-92.

Macaulay, R. (1977). *Language, social class and education: A Glasgow study*. Edinburgh: University of Edinburgh Press.

Maltz, D., and Borker, R. (1982). A cultural approach to male-female miscommunication. In J. Gumperz (Ed.), *Language and social identity* (pp. 196-216). Cambridge, England: Cambridge University Press.

Prucha, J. (1983). Using language: A sociofunctional approach. In B. Bain (Ed.), *The sociogenesis of language and human conduct* (pp. 287-295). New York: Plenum Press.

Reddy, M. (1979). The conduit metaphor—A case of frame conflict in our language about language. In A. Ortony (Ed.), *Metaphor and thought* (pp. 284-324). Cambridge, England: Cambridge University Press.

Romaine, S. (1978). Post-vocalic /r/ in Scottish English: Sound change in school children. In P. Trudgill (Ed.), *Sociolinguistic patterns in British English* (pp. 144-158). London: Edward Arnold.

Romaine, S. (1984). *The language of children and adolescents: The acquisition of communicative competence*. Oxford: Basil Blackwell.

Saville-Troike, M. (1982). *The ethnography of communication*. Baltimore, MD: University Park Press.

Stein, N. and Goldman, S. (1981). Children's knowledge about social situations: From causes to consequences. In S. Asher, and A. Pugh (Eds.), *The development of children's friendships* (pp. 297-321). Cambridge, England: Cambridge University Press.

Tannen, D. (1986). *That's not what I meant! How conversational style makes or breaks relationships*. New York: Ballentine Books.

Toman, W. (1976). On the extent of sibling influence. In K. Reigel, and J. Meacham (Eds.), *The developing individual in a changing world* (pp. 707-736). Chicago: Aldine.

Varenne, H. (1983). *American school language*. New York: Irvington Publishers.

Walker, L., and Greene, J. (1986). The social context of adolescent self-esteem. *Journal of Youth and Adolescence, 15*, 315-322.

West, C., and Zimmerman, D. (1977). Women's place in everyday talk: Reflections on parent-child interaction. *Social Problems, 24*, 521-529.

Wurm, S. (1976). Summary of discussion. In W. McCormack and S. Wurm (Eds.), *Language and man*. The Hague, Netherlands: Mouton.

Youniss, J., and Smollar, S. (1985). *Adolescent relations with mothers, fathers, and friends*. Chicago: University of Chicago Press.

CHAPTER 11

∎

PRAGMATICS

∎

M. IRENE STEPHENS

The phone rings at a residence. The circumstances, caller, and query are the same for all three points in time:

Caller: May I please speak with your mother?

JB at age 4: Mommy's going potty. (hangs up)

JB at age 12: Mom can't come to the phone right now. Can you call back later? (waits for acknowledgment)

JB at age 17: Mother can talk with you in a minute but first tell me about your trip. How did you enjoy England? (continues the conversation, offering some comments on his impressions of London when he visited there at the age of 14, until his mother appears)*

The ability to handle the same situation with increasing pragmatic competence is apparent from these three responses. At the age of 4, the child offers a factual report and terminates the conversation. At the age of 12, he shows more social awareness both in his appropriately vague statement regarding his mother's inability to come to the phone and in waiting for some form of acknowledgement. However, he does not indicate any interest in continuing the conversation. At the age of 17, he estimates correctly that his mother will be available shortly and now views the caller as a longtime family friend with whom he has topics in common. He becomes a full-fledged conversational partner, continuing the conversation until his mother is ready

---

*From the author's files.

to take her turn. Pragmatic development, illustrated by this vignette, epitomizes the interaction between language and socialization.

The literature on pragmatic development takes a number of forms. In some studies, anecdotal evidence involving a single child is offered in support of a pattern of development, just as in the example above. In other studies, observations are made in naturalistic settings (e.g., mother–child interactions) and the exchanges are recorded and analyzed to display the child's abilities in a particular facet of conversational partnership (e.g., requesting). These studies, longitudinal or cross-sectional in design, trace children's progress in a selected domain. Other studies are more structured and probe the child's ability to respond to predetermined linguistic stimuli (e.g., indirect requests) or to predetermined verbal tasks (e.g., referential communication studies). The number of children observed can include one or more, and the resulting data might be reported in terms of patterns noted, percentages of responses within a category of behaviors, or more formal statistical analyses.

However, studies of pragmatic development for the 9-through-19 age range are limited in number. Phillipps (1985) lamented that a major problem for anyone "who is searching for guidelines on children's spoken language development after they have passed the age of 9 is the fact that almost none exists" (p. 60). McTear (1985) agreed, stating that, "In contrast to the extensive literature on the development of conversation in preschool children, . . . little has been written as yet on development into school age and beyond" (p. 201). He offered several explanations for this. One reason is that older children are more aware of being observed and may fall shy and silent, or may offer a stilted performance they believe is somehow expected. Another reason is that older children's sites of interaction become widely extended. For example, they visit a friend, talk on the phone, roam around in groups, shop, play team sports, and engage in other social activities which make unobtrusive observation nearly impossible. Also, "A further problem which besets research into later conversational development is that there is no model of the skilled adult conversationalist which might inform such work" (p. 201). However, it would be difficult to construct such a model because communicative competence develops throughout the life span and is largely defined by the social context (see Chapter 10). Consequently, "most reported studies of older children have involved either experimental settings or classroom interaction, where the situation is more formal and controlled" (p. 201).

This is indeed the case. What is known about pragmatic development in the 9-through-19 age range falls into four subtopics: classroom discourse, peer instruction, narrative ability, and special settings. Each of these subtopics is discussed in this chapter.

CLASSROOM DISCOURSE

Cazden (1986) explained that two research approaches have traditionally been employed in the study of classroom discourse: a *process-product* approach and a *sociolinguistic* approach. She contrasted the approaches as follows:

> A fundamental difference between process-product and sociolinguistic research is evident just from a glance at their research reports. Because process-product researchers code classroom talk on the spot into preestablished categories, their reports contain tables of frequencies, but include samples of classroom language only as examples of code categories, and even then not necessarily from the classroom under study. Sociolinguistic researchers, by contrast, work from transcriptions of audio or video recordings of classroom life or, less often, from detailed observational notes. Their reports may also include frequency counts, but an important place is given to qualitative analyses of excerpts of actual classroom talk. (p. 433)

Both of these approaches are represented in studies of classroom discourse in older school-age children, conducted in either the United States or the United Kingdom.

A common type of classroom exchange occurs when the teacher elicits a response from a student and then evaluates the response before moving to another student. The following example (McTear, 1985) is typical of this exchange type:

Teacher: What is the opposite of *polite?*
Student: *Impolite.*
Teacher: That's right.
(pp. 209–210)

This exchange type has often been described as an IRE (Initiation-Response-Evaluation) or an IRF (Initiation-Response-Followup) cycle. The average 9-year-old has had years of experience in classroom discourse and has encountered many instances of the IRE or IRF teacher–student interaction. This youngster has learned the accompanying classroom communicative rules of giving a brief, specific answer, and only when called upon. If the teacher's second turn in the sequence is another question, upper-grade students recognize this as a request for clarification, expansion, or a different answer; that is, the teacher need not directly say "that's wrong." There is little growth during adolescence in students' responses given in this direct instructional format because, apparently, they have already mastered the form.

A less formal context for examining classroom discourse skills is small group discussions. Barnes and Todd (1978) observed 13-year-olds in small groups discussing topics chosen by their teachers. One of the topics was a set of problems associated with providing national parks for outdoor pursuits and tourism while at the same time preserving the natural landscape and protecting farming. The authors described the salient characteristics of these discussions. They noted that at the age of 13, the youngsters were not simply reproducing previously digested knowledge but were actually shaping and reorganizing their knowledge as they talked. The hesitant nature of the talk was seen as a positive feature (called *exploratory talk*) in which youngsters, collaboratively and without pressure of being assessed, worked toward an expression of their shared meanings. Meanings were not predetermined but actually developed during the course of the discussion. Various speech acts were produced, which rarely occur in open classroom discussions. These included initiating discussion of a new topic, qualifying another's contribution, providing examples, and using evidence to challenge an assertion.

Phillipps (1985) found similar and additional characteristics when he studied small groups of students in the school setting. He observed 10- through 12-year-olds during peer group conversations, again associated with school tasks, and noted that the students were likely to adopt one of five discourse modes after signalling their individual preferences in mode-marked language. The modes were:

1. Hypothetical: Speculation is marked by utterances such as *how about, what if, say that, could, might*.

2. Experiential: Personal preface or anecdote is marked by utterances such as *once, I remember, It reminds me of when. . . .*

3. Argumentational: Utterances contain phrases such as *yes but, on the other hand, because if. . .then*, and assertive tags such as *is it?, will he?, don't they?*

4. Operational: Consists of commentaries on ongoing activities with frequent use of deictics such as *that, these, it, them*, and occasional directives such as *push it down, now take that off, hang on a minute*.

5. Expositional: This is similar to the IRF exchange that occurs when a teacher is present. Children appear reluctant to use this mode and do so only for brief stretches of time in answer to WH-questions; for example, Q: *Where was that wall?* A: *Along our street.* Q: *What street?* A: *Wingate Road*.

The children in Phillipps' study also demonstrated a readiness to make responses compatible with previous utterances. As a result of this collaborative behavior, the children often produced conversation which had a distinctive and cohesive style. Because of what seemed to be a highly developed ability to communicate indirectly their preference for a particular way of conversing, 10- through 12-year-olds working in peer groups were able to organize their conversation cohesively without it ever becoming necessary for any individual to take charge, either by dictating an agenda or by prescribing the language and the discourse strategies to be used.

These two studies (Barnes and Todd, 1978; Phillips, 1985) are in the sociolinguistic tradition. Detailed, naturalistic observations were made of youngsters 10 through 13 years old interacting in small groups, and patterns in their discourse skills were described.

Brown, Anderson, Shillcock, and Yule (1984), on the other hand, had a different purpose for their process-product study of 14- through 17-year-olds in Scottish secondary schools. They were concerned with how a spoken-language curriculum could be developed such that students' ability to use more advanced discourse skills could be measured and improved. First, the authors made a distinction between *chat* and *information-related talk*. Chat is a social type of exchange, while information-related talk, frequently occurring in school settings, is used to transfer information on a particular topic for a specific purpose.

As part of the research project, Brown and colleagues interviewed more than 500 students in a range of Scottish secondary schools. They found very few students who could not chat competently, but found many who had considerable difficulty with more demanding forms of information-related talk. In an attempt to delineate communicative factors associated with information-related talk, these researchers devised three types of tasks in ascending order of difficulty: a Static Task, a Dynamic Task, and an Abstract Task. An example of a Static Task is the Diagram Task, in which a speaker is given a folder containing a simple diagram. The listener, who sits opposite the speaker and behind a low screen, is given a blank sheet of paper and colored pens. The speaker is to tell the listener how to draw the diagram so that eventually the diagrams will look exactly alike. An example of a Dynamic Task is the Car Crash Scene, in which a speaker is asked to provide an eyewitness account of a car crash for a listener who was not present when the car crash occurred. The most demanding is the Abstract Task, in which the student is to give an opinion on a controversial topic such as whether or not additional nuclear plants should be built. This task is similar to a debate format.

Brown and colleagues showed that the students who were first presented with an easy task performed better than those who were first presented with a more difficult task. They also found that, in both the Static Task and the Car Crash Task, speakers who had first served as listeners scored better than those who had not. That is, speakers with experience in the listener's role had greater referential success. This suggested that serving as the listener enhanced the students' perspective taking ability and sensitivity to the communicative needs of another. Additional information on social perspective-taking, and its relationship to language development, is contained in Chapter 10.

PEER INSTRUCTION

Another useful context for examining pragmatic development is peer instruction. Here upper-grade students assume a teaching role and display those pragmatic skills they have observed to accompany that role. Two studies involving preadolescents showed that they lack a number of pragmatic skills associated with mature teaching.

In the first study (Ellis and Rogoff, 1986), 8- and 9-year-olds were compared with adults as they taught 6- and 7-year-olds individually. The child dyads were of the same sex, but were unacquainted. The task, which took place in a single session, involved learning to sort items found in grocery stores and school cafeterias, such as sorting snacks, fruits, sandwich spreads, and condiments. Each "teacher" was encouraged to examine the items in a sorted array until familiar with the category system. A cue sheet was available for the teacher but not for the "student." As anticipated, the children differed significantly from adults in their teaching styles. In general, the children neglected to help their students understand the category system underlying the sorting task; instead, they focused more on the physical manipulation of the items ("Put that in this pile"). More specifically, three important teaching processes were used less often by the children than by the adults: orienting, explaining, and preparing the student for the memory test.

The second study (Cook-Gumperz, 1977) involved 10-year-olds and employed a task similar to the Static-Diagram task of Brown and colleagues (1984). Forty pairs of fifth-grade children were asked to make a model using a kit of color-coded straight and circular pieces of wood. One child was the "builder" and the other was the "instructor." The builder was blindfolded so that the instructor had to rely on verbal cues to guide the building process. The instructor was told, "You can say anything you want to tell your friend how to make the model but don't touch the pieces." As in the Ellis and Rogoff (1986) study, Cook-Gumperz observed that the 10-year-old instructors provided little orientation for the builders. For example, they did not begin by telling the builders what they were going to build (a car), nor did they explain the general sequence of actions. Instead, a typical introduction consisted of the builder picking up a piece and the instructor responding with either "Yes, keep that one you have in your hand" or "Put that one down." Again, these findings were similar to those of Ellis and Rogoff (1986) whose 8- and 9-year-old teachers did not help their students understand the underlying category system in the sorting task. In addition, the 10-year-old instructors in Cook-Gumperz' study focused on the physical manipulation of the items (e.g., "Take that . . . yes, that one") just as the 8- and 9-year-old teachers had done in the Ellis and Rogoff study.

In a similar experiment with 5- and 6-year-olds as students, Cook-Gumperz (1977) reported that 10-year-old instructors displayed a second style for correcting instructions that failed: with peers, they used pronominal imperatives (e.g., "Put it right there") but with younger children, they used lexicalized specifications (e.g., "Put the round one in your hand straight down"). In this way, the 10-year-olds displayed a pragmatic strategy which they had in their "teacherese" repertoire, but only used it with the younger children.

The weaknesses in the children's teaching strategies uncovered in these two studies (Cook-Gumperz, 1977; Ellis and Rogoff, 1986) indicate that preadolescents have a number of important pragmatic skills to acquire before reaching an adult level. In view of the findings of Brown and colleagues (1984), it would be interesting to determine if preadolescents can improve their teaching strategies if they first serve as students or builders before serving as teachers or instructors.

NARRATIVE ABILITY

During the last 10 years, there has been a renewed interest in the development of children's narrative ability. The broad base of this interest is reflected in the variety of participating researchers' disciplines. Contributions have come from anthropologists (e.g., Heath, 1983), linguists (e.g., Labov, 1972a, 1972b), cognitive theorists (e.g., Bruner, 1985), child language specialists (e.g., Kernan, 1977), speech–language pathologists (e.g., Johnston, 1982), and educators (e.g., Stein and Glenn, 1979, 1982; Westby, Van Dongen, and Maggart, in press).

Why has this topic attracted the interest of such a wide range of investigators? Why is the acquisition of narrative ability so important? Speaking philosophically, life can be viewed as a series of sequenced events in time, and it can be said that cultures reveal their particular knowledge of the world through stories. Representing events through narration permits people to make sense of these events, and "story" is one invention of the human mind that helps to organize and interpret experiences. More particularly, developing adequate narrative skills at the expected age levels greatly affects communicative competence in both social and academic domains, especially during the 9-through-19 age range. The ability to relate personal anecdotes in a coherent and relevant manner as part of a conversational exchange, and to understand the anecdotes of others, affects peer interaction. Narrative ability also affects academic performance, particularly in language-arts classes at the upper elementary level, and in literature, government, and history classes at the high school and college levels.

Just exactly what is learned when a child gradually acquires the concept of story? Investigators such as Stein and Glenn (1979) have suggested that the child induces an underlying story grammar, which is akin to the rules the child induces for syntax. A simple story grammar proposed by Stein and Glenn (1982) contains the following elements: the setting; the problem; the characters' internal responses, goals, or plans; the solution; and the ending.

Some of these elements are included in young children's stories but, as Westby (1984) pointed out, the "characters' internal plans to deal with problems set up in the initiating events are not frequent in stories told by children under 9 years of age" (p. 118). Apparently, the ability to plan and the awareness of others' planning is slow to develop, and is a matter of life-long learning. Because a character's internal reponses (including plans for problem solving) are often not explicitly stated within the story line, young children do not easily discern this element within story grammars.

Stein and Glenn (1982) discussed the relationship between story grammars and story schemata, and explained that a basic assumption underlying story grammars

> is that some type of schematic knowledge is used to guide the encoding and retrieval of story information. This knowledge may be acquired in two ways: by listening to or reading stories, and by participating in and developing an understanding of everyday social interaction. As comprehenders become more exposed to the variations in story structure and to different social situations, their schematic knowledge is gradually thought to correspond to the structural descriptions given in the story grammar. (p. 256)

In this fashion, children gradually learn that an "episodic motive-resolution" schema defines the basic core of most stories. Stein and Glenn examined the gradual learning of this schema in kindergarteners and in third and sixth graders ($n = 162$). These researchers constructed three story stems which contained the setting element of a story grammar; for example, "Once there was a girl named Alice who lived in a house near the ocean" (p. 270). The children were tested individually and were "told that they would be given the very beginning of a story. Their task was to take the beginning and construct a full-blown story that would have everything in it that a good story should" (p. 270). Results showed that "at the kindergarten level, 50 percent of the children told at least two out of three stories with a basic episodic structure; at third grade, 72 percent of the children's stories met this criterion; and at sixth grade, 78 percent of all stories were episodically organized" (p. 270).

Stein and Glenn reported that the nonepisodic stories could be classified into three major types. Listed from least mature to most mature approximation to the episodic motive-resolution status, they were:

1. Descriptive Sequence Story: The traits and actions of a protagonist are included but there are no temporal indicators on the sequence of events; thus, the sequences are more like elaborated setting statements than episodic sequences.
2. Action Sequence Story: The protagonist's actions are temporally arranged in order of occurrence but with no direct causal connection between events; thus, the story lacks a discernible motive-resolution sequence with a logical beginning and ending.
3. Reactive Sequence Story: The story contains a beginning and an ending with events causally related to each other; however, the protagonist never develops a goal or plan so that his or her well-being

is totally dependent on environmental circumstances or the actions
of other people. The core of the story is therefore omitted. (p. 271)

Here again, it appears that the major character's internal responses are
developmentally the last element of the story grammar or the story schema
to be included. Duffer and Stephens (1987) reported a similar finding in
their study of story solution abilities in children of the ages of 9 through
12 ($n = 30$). In their research, however, the story to be completed was more
detailed than the stems offered by Stein and Glenn (1982). The children
were provided with information about the setting, initiating event, problem, and even several internal responses of the protagonist, as well as the
ending, so that the children knew that the protagonist's goal was reached.
The subject's task was to retell the story and to give precise details of *how*
the goal was reached.

Duffer and Stephens (1987) devised a scoring system which involved two
domains, Scope of Information and Quality of Solution, with two categories within each domain. Each category was worth three points for a total
possible score of 12 points. Results showed that the scores ranged from 0
to 12; however, 24 of the 30 children scored six or better. The scoring category most relevant to the present discussion is the "active versus passive solution." Results showed that most of the high-scoring children generated an
active solution. A passive solution occurred when the protagonist reached
his goal through external circumstances such as good luck or the kind efforts
of others. This result parallels Stein and Glenn's (1982) third and most mature
nonepisodic story type, the Reactive Sequence Story.

Waggoner, Messe, and Palermo (1985) conducted an interesting developmental study with second, fourth, and sixth grade students ($n = 96$) that
examined the interrelationships among story grammar elements and the
understanding of metaphoric and literal language. These researchers
embedded metaphors or their literal counterparts in stories at either the
Reaction or Outcome positions of a story grammar. For example, in a story
entitled "Jill at the Zoo," at the Reaction position, the metaphoric version
contained the sentence "Jill was a kitten in a room filled with balls of yarn,"
while the literal version contained the sentence "Jill was really excited about
all the different animals" (p. 1165). Results showed that accurate recall of
both metaphoric and literal propositions improved as a function of increasing grade level, and that both types of propositions were recalled better in
the Outcome position than in the Reaction position. When children were
asked to explain the meanings of the metaphoric propositions, the frequency
of correct explanations also improved with increasing grade level. The
researchers concluded that "the use of a grammar for constructing the stories
used in this research provided a structure that the children could use not
only to aid recall but also to allow them to succeed in the more difficult

task of verbalizing the meaning of the metaphors" (p. 1163). Chapter 8 contains further information on the development of metaphoric language and the extent to which contextual information facilitates children's understanding of metaphors.

Other studies of narrative ability in older children have been conducted. For example, Kernan (1977) examined 18 stories told by black American girls to black female interviewers familiar to the girls. There were six stories of personal experiences from each of three groups: second and third graders; fifth and sixth graders; and eighth and ninth graders. In general, Kernan found a large difference between the narratives of the second and third graders and the fifth and sixth graders, and a negligible difference between the narratives of the fifth and sixth graders and the eighth and ninth graders. For example, the youngest group used an abstract introducer (e.g., "Once upon a time. . . .") only once to begin their narratives, the middle group used it five times, and the oldest group, four times. Orientation-information clauses (e.g., time, place) were found in 11 percent of the youngest group's narratives, 27 percent of the middle group's narratives, and 22 percent of the oldest group's narratives. Background information was 27, 69, and 71 percent for the three groups, respectively. A protagonist's status or characteristics were mentioned twice as often by the two older groups than by the youngest group. Attitudes or feelings of the narrator toward ongoing events (e.g., "I was so scared") were displayed by 19 percent of the youngest group, 26 percent of the middle group, and by 31 percent of the oldest group. However, there was one form used *only* by the oldest group; namely, paraphrase for the sake of exaggeration, dramatic effect, or emphasis.

In his observations of the verbal facility of teenage gangs in New York City, Labov (1972a and 1972b) described the complex rules associated with exchanges such as sounding (see Chapter 8) and ritual insults. One form used by these black working-class adolescents was "story-telling as threat." This occurred when a violent incident (real or imagined) that happened to a rival gang member was related within hearing distance of a rival gang peer with the purpose of posing a threat (e.g., "Last dude stand in my way come home to his momma wif no teef"). Labov's studies of black adolescents showed that they possessed sophisticated narrative abilities.

One of the later-acquired story comprehension abilities is that of drawing inferences. Often a narrative will not contain explicit information about an occurrence or a character's thoughts. In these instances, the listener must infer that a certain action took place or that a character must have made a particular decision. In other words, the listener must fill in some important piece of information in order to fully understand the story. In a study of accurate inferencing (Crais and Chapman, 1987), 9- and 10-year-olds outperformed 6- and 7-year-olds in drawing correct inferences as well as answering factual questions about a set of stories. It was also found that for both age groups, "inference questions were significantly more difficult than premise questions" (p. 50).

A crucial aspect of advanced narrative development is the ability to provide a summary. Johnson (1983) identified six competencies associated with successful summarizing:

> (1) comprehending the individual propositions of a story; (2) establishing connections between propositions; (3) identifying the constituent structure of the story; (4) remembering the information in the story; (5) selecting the information to be represented in the summary; and (6) formulating a concise but coherent representation of that information. (p. 346)

There is evidence that the first four competencies are well developed by school entry, but that the last two are gradually refined during the upper elementary grades.

In Johnson's (1983) study of summarization skills, children in first, third, and fifth grades ($n = 55$) and college students ($n = 20$) were asked to recall and summarize two stories, a "Pig" story and a "Rabbit" story. The stimuli and procedures were chosen to maximize the probability that even the youngest children would achieve at least partial success. A practice task was included which stressed the difference between telling the *whole* story and just telling *about* the story. All subjects were told they would hear stories played on a tape recorder and they should try to remember them. After a practice story ("Goldilocks and the Three Bears") was presented, subjects were asked to pretend that they were on the way home from school with a friend who had never heard that story before. The friend would like to hear it and the subject had plenty of time to tell the whole story. After retelling the practice story, the subject was given instructions which described a different situation. Now, however, there was not enough time to tell the *whole* story so the subject should just tell *about* the story. After the subject's attempt, the experimenter offered a sample summary. The subject then heard the experimental stories and performed the recall and summary tasks. The data were analyzed to determine if subjects produced summaries for both stories that were shorter than their recall versions. This criterion was met by 78 percent of the first graders, 90 percent of the third graders, 95 percent of the fifth graders, and by all of the college students.

As discussed in Chapter 5, Applebee (1978) examined the concept of story as it developed in British youngsters 2 through 17 years old. One aspect of his research examined children's ability to summarize stories. Subjects of the ages of 6, 9, 13, and 17 were required to discuss a story of their choice. The 6- and 9-year-olds were asked "What is your favorite story? Tell me about it," whereas the older subjects received a questionnaire which directed them to "Pick any story or poem you know well and write about it." For the group of 6-year-olds, 27 percent gave no scoreable response, 50 percent retold the story, 17 percent offered a synopsis–summary,* and only 4 percent made evaluative comments. For the group of 9-year-olds, none gave no scoreable response, 9 percent retold the story, 72 percent offered a synopsis–summary, and 18 percent made evaluative comments. From these data, a clear developmental progression in the ability to summarize emerges, with the largest advance occurring between 6 and 9 years. Most of the 13- and 17-year-olds offered both a synopsis-summary and complex evaluative comments. It is interesting to compare the evaluative comments of the different age groups. A typical 6-year-old was likely to say "It was a good story" or "I liked it," and a 9-year-old was likely to say "It was exciting" or "I like lots of action." In contrast, the 13- and 17-year-olds utilized four different categories of evaluative comments. For example, it was the 13-year-olds "who first showed a substantial tendency to make use of analysis" (p. 112) by looking at factors in the story which made them identify with the major character, by considering cause and effect relationships, and by posing aesthetic criteria by which the story should be judged. Sixty-three percent of the 13-year-olds attempted some form of analysis in their evaluations (although it did not appear at all in the responses of the younger children), and at the age of 17, 95 percent of the evaluative comments contained analytic remarks. In describing the last stage to emerge when adolescents were asked why they like or dislike stories, Applebee explained as follows:

> [it] involves a generalization about the meaning or theme of a work, rather than an analysis of its parts. Though both analysis and generalization seem to require the resources of formal operational thought, analysis emerges sooner and more fully in these samples . . . we find that analysis occurs alone but generalization rarely does . . . . (pp. 112–113)

Thus, the ability to offer a sophisticated judgment or evaluation of a narrative develops gradually during adolescence.

Additional narrative abilities that develop during the preadolescent and adolescent years include detecting deceit in a character's words or actions, recognizing flashbacks in the story line, realizing the symbolism intended, and comprehending allegories (Westby, Van Dongen, and Maggart, in press).

---

*(Applebee's 6 year old group would be equivalent to Johnson's first graders. The discrepancy in the percentages of children providing a summary can be explained by the difference in both directions and analyses. Johnson told her subjects to summarize and gave them some practice and simply required them to produce summaries shorter than their recalls while Applebee gave only very general instructions and required that the summaries contain set characteristics.)

SPECIAL SETTINGS

This section of the chapter discusses youngsters' pragmatic behaviors in special settings, which include role-playing activities, analyzing gender-related talk, and participating in a holiday ritual.

In the first study to be reviewed, Mitchell-Kernan and Kernan (1977) assumed that a "competent member of a speech community has internalized the norms for the appropriate use of directive types, and possesses not only an intuitive knowledge of which forms to use in which speech situations, but also the ability to interpret forms as directives which, on the surface, would seem to be serving some other speech function" (p. 189). These investigators studied the use of directives in a group of black American children of the ages of 7 through 12. The data consisted primarily of directives used during a role-playing activity involving hand puppets on an improvised stage with the children hidden from view. These data were augmented with examples drawn from more naturally occurring speaking situations. The research team had observed the children almost daily for a period of about seven months.

Ervin-Tripp's (1976, 1977) classification scheme of six directive types was used in the analysis:

1. Need Statements (e.g., "I want a green milkshake")
2. Imperatives (e.g., "Be back here at three o'clock")
3. Imbedded Imperatives (e.g., "John, would you please tell that lady to quit")
4. Permission Directives (e.g., "Can I speak to her?")
5. Question Directives (e.g., "Hey, you got a quarter, Mac?")
6. Hints (e.g., "Last person talk to me like that is in his grave")

A total of 261 directives were analyzed for social distribution of directive types, and for the relationship between particular directives and broader interactional goals. All six types were used by the children, but imperatives were the most common type with 200 instances. Of these 200 imperatives, 71 percent that occurred in a personal or family situation were used where the speaker and listener were of perceived equal status. In Transactional Situations, 70 of the imperatives were used in perceived situations where the speaker was of a higher status addressing one of a lower status. Mitchell-Kernan and Kernan (1977) summarized their results as follows:

> On the basis of the directives exhibited in the role-play data, and in their spontaneous speech, we can say that the children in our sample have acquired all of the conventional forms that directives may take in American English as described by Ervin-Tripp. Although the children

ranged in age from 7-12 years, there was no apparent difference by age in their ability or willingness to use the various types (pp. 206-207).

Consequently, there is little perceived growth in the use of directives in the age span of interest here.

In Edelsky's study (1977) of awareness of gender-related talk, 122 adults and 122 first, third, and sixth graders served as subjects. The subjects were presented with a list of 24 printed sentences and asked to choose who would most likely say each sentence — men, women, or both with equal likelihood. For example, it was assumed from past research that men would be likely to say "Damn, I lost my keys," that women would say "That's adorable," and that either men or women might say "I was very tired." After making the choices, the subjects were interviewed. The sixth graders performed similarly to the adults in defining the variables and in explaining gender-related linguistic forms. The sixth graders also possessed the adult knowledge that weakness and elaboration of expression are assumed to be gender-related female traits, and that some adverbs, because they weaken the relation between the speaker's convictions and the topic following the adverb, are a linguistic means for conveying such traits (e.g., "I was just furious"). However, only the adults occasionally assigned profanity to females, and only adults were aware of tag questions being used to elicit agreement rather than information.

Berko Gleason and Weintraub (1976) studied the pragmatic skills of children 2 years to 11+ years during the *Trick or treat* Halloween ritual. They reported that "The children's behavior was very consistent. The youngest children — two and three year olds — typically said nothing at all. Four and five year olds tended to say nothing but *Trick or treat*. . . . Somewhat older children say *Trick or treat* and *Thank you*; and children over ten produce the whole routine — *Trick or treat*, *Thank you* and *Goodbye*" (p. 132-133).

The authors observed that although adults gave a great deal of explicit teaching or coaching either before the children set out on their rounds or while accompanying them, there was no attempt to embed the routine in an explanation of its significance. Consequently, parents tend to take for granted that children understand the purpose of this October ritual. Only when children's questions or comments reveal that they do not understand is an explanation provided. J.B., the child discussed at the beginning of this chapter, revealed his misconceptions about the *Trick or treat* ritual when he asked on the night before Halloween, "What will be my trick?" After a little more conversation, it became clear to his mother that he believed the trick-or-treater first performed a magic trick of some kind and was then rewarded with a treat. Many years later he confided that he was 13-years-old when he fully comprehended the history behind the current *Trick or treat* ritual.

CONCLUSIONS

Pragmatic development has been reviewed in terms of four main sub-topics: classroom discourse, peer instruction, narrative ability, and special settings. During the 9-through-19 age range, as growth occurs in social perspective taking, youngsters are increasingly able to adjust the content and style of their speech when addressing peers, younger children, and adults. For example, they learn to give more precise instructions to others, and they learn what to do and say during holiday rituals. They also show greater awareness of the speaking styles of others as evinced by their growing ability to make appropriate judgments about gender-related talk. Growth in social perspective taking is also manifested during story retelling tasks, as youngsters show greater ability to infer the thoughts and feelings of characters, and enhanced sensitivity to characters' internal responses and goals. Youngsters' organizational skills also improve during the 9-through-19 age range as they display advances in their ability to summarize and evaluate stories, an important academic skill related to the acquisition of literacy. Researchers should continue the investigation of pragmatic development in older children and adolescents, particularly in naturalistic contexts wherever possible.

REFERENCES

Applebee, A.N. (1978). *The child's concept of story.* Chicago: University of Chicago Press.

Barnes, D., and Todd, F. (1978). *Communication and learning in small groups.* London: Routledge and Kegan Paul.

Berko Gleason, J.B., and Weintraub, M. (1976). The acquisition of routines in child language. *Language in Society, 5,* 129-136.

Brown, G., Anderson, A., Shillcock, R., and Yule, G. (1984). *Teaching talk.* Cambridge, England: Cambridge University Press.

Bruner, J. (1985). Narrative and paradigmatic modes of thought. In E. Eisner (Ed.), *Learning and teaching the ways of knowing* (pp. 97-115). Chicago: University of Chicago Press.

Cazden, C.B. (1986). Classroom discourse. In M.C. Wittrock (Ed.), *Handbook of research on teaching* (Third edition) (pp. 432-463). New York: Macmillan.

Cook-Gumperz, J. (1977). Situated instructions: Language socialization of school age children. In S. Ervin-Tripp and C. Mitchell-Kernan (Eds.), *Child discourse* (pp. 103-121). New York: Academic Press.

Crais, E.R., and Chapman, R.S. (1987). Story recall and inferencing skills in language/learning-disabled and nondisabled children. *Journal of Speech and Hearing Disorders, 52,* 50-55.

Duffer, T.A., and Stephens, M.I. (1987, November). *Story solution abilities in normal/ language impaired children ages 9–12.* Paper presented at the Annual Convention of the American Speech-Language-Hearing Association, New Orleans, LA.

Edelsky, A. (1977). Acquisition of an aspect of communicative competence: Learning what it means to talk like a lady. In S. Ervin-Tripp, and S. Mitchell-Kernan (Eds.), *Child Discourse* (pp. 225-243). New York: Academic Press.

Ellis, S., and Rogoff, B. (1986). Problem solving in children's management of instruction. In E.C. Mueller, and C.R. Cooper (Eds.), *Process and outcome in peer relationships* (pp. 301-325). Orlando, FL: Academic Press.

Ervin-Tripp, S. (1976). Is Sybil there? The structure of some American English directives.. *Language in Society, 5*, 25-66.

Ervin-Tripp, S. (1977). Wait for me, roller skate! In S. Ervin-Tripp & C. Mitchell-Kernan (Eds.), *Child Discourse* (pp. 165-188). New York: American Press.

Heath, S.B. (1983). *Way with words: Language, life and work in communities and classrooms.* Cambridge, England: Cambridge University Press.

Johnson, N.S. (1983). What do you do when you can't tell the whole story? The development of summarization skills. In K.E. Nelson (Ed.), *Children's language* (Volume 4) (pp. 315-383). Hillsdale, NJ: Erlbaum.

Johnston, J. (1982). Narratives: A new look at communication problems in older language-disordered children. *Language, Speech, and Hearing Services in Schools, 13*, 144-155.

Kernan, K.T. (1977). Semantic and expressive elaboration in children's narratives. In S. Ervin-Tripp, and C. Mitchell-Kernan (Eds.), *Child discourse* (pp. 91-102). New York: Academic Press.

Labov, W. (1972a). Rules for ritual insults. In W. Labov (Ed.), *Languages in the Inner City* (pp. 297-353). Philadelphia: The Univ. of Penn. Press, Inc.

Labov, W. (1972b). *Sociolinguistic patterns.* Philadelphia: University of Pennsylvania Press.

McTear, M. (1985). *Children's conversation.* New York: Basil Blackwell.

Mitchell-Kernan, C., and Kernan, K. (1977). Pragmatics of directive choice among children. In S. Ervin-Tripp, and C. Mitchell-Kernan (Eds.), *Child discourse* (pp. 189-208). New York: Academic Press.

Phillips, T. (1985). Beyond lip-service: Discourse development after the age of nine. In G. Wells, and J. Nicholls (Eds.), *Language and learning: An interactional perspective* (pp. 59-82). Philadelphia: The Falmer Press.

Stein, N.L., and Glenn, C.G. (1979). An analysis of story comprehension in elementary school children. In R.O. Freedle (Ed.), *New directions in discourse processing* (Volume 2) (pp. 53-120). Norwood, NJ: Ablex.

Stein, N.L., and Glenn, C.G. (1982). Children's concept of time: The development of a story schema. In W.J. Friedman (Ed.), *The developmental psychology of time* (pp. 255-282). New York: Academic Press.

Waggoner, J.E., Messe, M.J., and Palermo, D.S. (1985). Grasping the meaning of metaphor: Story recall and comprehension. *Child Development, 56*, 1156-1166.

Westby, C.E. (1984). Development of narrative language abilities. In G.P. Wallach and K.G. Butler (Eds.), *Language learning disabilities in school-age children* (pp. 103-127). Baltimore, MD: Williams and Wilkins.

Westby, C.E., Van Dongen, R., and Maggart, Z. (in press). Assessing narrative competence. *Seminars in Speech and Language.*

SUBJECT INDEX

Abstract language, learning, 4–5
Abstract nouns, 114
Abstract task, 251
Abstractions, development of, 140–141
Action Sequence Story, 254
Adjectives, 114
Adolescent Language Screening Test, 8
Adult model of syntactic structure, 52–53
Adverbial clauses, 70–72
Adverbial conjuncts, 74–76
Adverbs, comprehension of, 34–35
Advertisements, understanding, 219–221
  ambiguous, 220–221
  Ambiguous Ads Task, 220, 222
  summary on, 222
Agent-focused (AF) discourse, 77
Ambiguous Ads Task, 220, 222
Analogy problems, ability to solve with inductive reasoning, 160–168
Analysis of covariance (ANCOVA) for TTR, 114

Analysis of variance (ANOVA) for TTR, 114, 116, 117, 118–119
Anaphora, 115
ANCOVA. *See* Analysis of covariance
ANOVA. *See* Analysis of variance
Argument as category of discourse, 108
Argumentational mode of language, 250
Asymmetrical discussion, 242
The Atlantic Monthly, 53
Audience, concept of in spoken and written communication, 18, 22, 110

Car Crash Task, 251
CART. *See Children's Associative Responding Test*
Cataphora, 115
Chat versus information-related talk, 251
Children's Associative Responding Test (CART), 161–162, 163, 182

Key: (*t*) indicates table.

Classroom discourse, study of, 249-251

Clause length as quantitative measure of syntactic development, 57-58

Clause level, structures at, 68-69. *See also* Subordinate clauses

Cognition
  conclusions on, 151-154
  development, mechanisms of change in, 145-151
    neo-Piagetian approach to, 147-148
    Piagetian approach to, 146-147
    skill theory, 149-150
    triarchic theory, 150-151
  language and, 151-154
  theories of, 128-145
    information processing theories of, 137-145
    neo-Piagetian, 137-139
    skill theory, 139-143
    Piagetian, 128-137

Cognition, schooling and literacy, relationships between, 22-26. *See also* Literacy

Cognitive Abilities Test, 202

Cognitive strategies for processing written language, 98, 100-105
  metacognitive strategies, 105
  stages of, 100-105
    confirmation, fluency, ungluing from print, 101
    construction and reconstruction, 102-105
    initial reading or decoding, 100-101
    multiple viewpoints, 101-102
    reading for learning the new, 101

Cohesion in English, 115

Cohesion strategies in written language, developmental data on, 115-116

Communication, intention of, 18-19, 21

Confirmation, fluency, ungluing from print, stage of cognitive development, 101

Conjunctions, use and understanding of, 35-36. *See also* Connectives

Connectives, use and understanding of
  acquisition of, 37
  conjunctions, 35-36
  Connective Reading Test, 36
  development of, 38-39
  understanding of, 36

Connective Reading Test, 36

Construction and reconstruction stage of cognitive development, 102-103, 105

Contexts for language, expanding, 51

Contextual abstraction, 29

Contextualization of written language, 16-18, 21-22
  continuum, terms used, 17(t)

Creole language, as source of identity, 239-240

Cross-sex communication, as example of linguistic socialization, 238-239. *See also* Gender-related talk

Cultural literacy, concept of, 12-13

Decentering, importance of to development of reading, 102

Deductive reasoning, 168-176
  external factors, 170-175
    conditional syllogisms, 174(t)
    syllogisms used, 170, 171(t), 172(t), 173(t)
  internal factors, 169-170
  summary on, 175-176

Description, as category of discourse, 108-109

Descriptive Sequence Story, 254

Developmental perspective, definition of, 24

Developmental schedules, for acquisition of specific syntactic structures, 30-31

Diagram task, 251

Direct teaching, 29

Discourse strategies for processing texts, 98, 105-112
  adolescents, ability of, 107-108
  audience, concept of, 110
  categories of, 108-109

global text organization, 110–111
internalized cognitive structures,
    101–102
narrative structures in stories,
    schema of, 106, 111–112
schema scores, 111–112
written language and, 109–110
Discourse-based approach to syntax,
    77–85
mode, syntactic variation as
    function of, 78
    other genre, 79–80
    planned written language, 79
    unplanned spoken language,
        78–79
text comparisons
    comparisons, 86–87
    narrative, 81–82
    persuasive, 81
    quantitative data, 85(*t*)
Dynamic task, 251

Early language development versus
    later, 2–5. *See also* Language
    development
Elaboration Index, 60
    weights, 61(*t*)
Embeddedness, concept of, 226–227
Endophoric meaning, 17–18. *See also*
    Contextualization
End-weight principle, 70
Exophoric meaning, 17–18. *See also*
    Contextualization
Experiential mode of language, 250
Exploratory talk, 250
Exposition as category of discourse,
    108–109
Expositional mode of language, 250

Figurative language
    conclusions on, 206
    description of, 179
    idioms, 193–200
        comprehension of, 195–196

figurative meaning of, 193–194
interpretation in adolescents,
    196–197
literal meanings of, 194–195
results, 197–199
metaphors and similes, 180–193
    comprehension of, 181–188
    metaphoric productions, 188–193
proverbs, 200–206
summary of, 205–206
studies on, 179–180
Friendship, as example of linguistic
    socialization, 242–243
Fullerton Language Test for
    Adolescents: Second Edition, 8,
    196–197

Gender identity as example of
    linguistic socialization, 235–237
Gender-related talk, awareness of, 260.
    See also Cross-sex
    communication
Global text organization strategies, 106
Growth in Mathematics, 159

High-frequency words, 113–114
Humor, understanding, 216–219
    based on linguistic ambiguity, 217
    jokes, 217–218
    riddles, understanding, 218–219
    summary of, 219
Hypothetical mode of language, 250

Identity crisis as example of linguistic
    socialization, 234–235
Idioms
    children's interpretations of, 198–199
    comprehension of, 195–196
    definition of, 193
    figurative meaning of, 193–195
    interpretation in adolescents, 196–197
    summary of, 199–200
Implicature, rules of, 21

Inductive reasoning problems, 160–168
  external factors, 163–168
    results of studies on, 164–165,
      167–168
  internal factors, 161–163
    CART test, 161, 162–163
    MFFT test, 162–163
  summary of, 168
Information processing theories of
    cognitive development, 137–145
  skill theory, 139–143
    abstractions, development of,
      140–142
    development asynchronies, 142–143
    optimal levels, performing at, 143
    summary of, 143
  triarchic theory, 127, 143–145
Information-related talk, versus chat,
    251
Initial reading or decoding stage of
    reading development, 100–101
Initiation-Response-Evaluation (IRE),
    cycle, 249
Initiation-Response-Followup (IRF)
    cycle, 249
Inner language, written language
    developed from, 109–110
Iowa Tests of Basic Skills, 182
IRE. *See* Initiation-Response-
    Evaluation cycle
IRF. *See* Initiation-Response-Followup
    cycle

Jokes, youngsters' understanding of,
    217–218

Language and cognition, 151–154
Language and socialization. *See*
    Socialization and language
Language development
  early versus later, 2–5
    abstract language and, 4–5
    contrasts between, 3–4
    growth, emphasis on, 3
    metalinguistics, use of, 4
  implications of, 7–8
  research in, 1–2
  standardized tests of later language
    development, 7–8
  themes of, 5–7
Lexical learning and literacy
  conclusions on, 44
  word classes
    adverbs, 34–35
    connectives, 35–39
    summary on, 39
    verbs, 32–34
  word definition, 39–44
    developmental studies of, 40–43
    qualitative classification systems, 41
    summary on, 43–44
    tasks, 40
Lexicalized meaning, 17. *See also*
    Contextualization
Linguistic ambiguity
  advertisements, 219–221
    summary on, 222
  conclusions on, 222
  developmental studies, 211–212
  humor, 216–219
    jokes, understanding, 217–218
    riddles, 218–219
    summary of, 219
  sentences, 212–216
Linguistic determinism, 151. *See also*
    Cognition, language and
Linguistic socialization
  communicative competence,
    developing, 231–232
  constraining nature of language,
    228–229
  examples of
    cross-sex communication, 238–239
    friendship, 241–243
    gender, 235–237
    identity, 234–235
    peer group, 239–241
  language and social power, 232–234
  meaning, 229
  reality, defining, 229
  sociofunctional explanation of
    language use, 230

Literacy and lexical learning. *See*
    Lexical learning and literacy
Literacy, nature of
conclusions on, 26
orality and relationship between
    audience, 18
    communication, intention of,
        18-19, 21
    contextualization, 16-18
    summary on, 21-22
and reading and writing relationship
        among, 11-15
    major feature of, 13-14
    reading and, 12-14
    summary on, 15
    and writing, 14-15
and schooling and cognition,
        relationships among, 22-26
    developmental perspective thesis,
        24-25
    socioeconomic status differences, 23
    summary on, 25-26
    Vai language and, 24-25
Lorge-Thorndike Intelligence Test, 182,
    205

Matching Familiar Figures Test
    (MFFT), 162
Mathetic texts, 19, 21
McCarthy Scales of Children's Abilities,
    40
Mechanisms of change in cognitive
        development, 145-151
    neo-Piagetian approach to, 147-148
    Piagetian approach to, 146-147
    skill theory and, 149-150
    triarchic theory and, 150-151
Metalinguistic awareness, definition of,
    211
Metalinguistic competence, use of, 4
Metaphoric-triads task (MTT), 182
Metaphorically opaque idioms, 193-194
Metaphorically transparent idioms,
    193-194
Metaphors
comprehension of

external factors, 183-188
internal factors, 181-183
definition of, 180
metaphoric productions, 188-193
    formal tasks, 188-190
    informal tasks, 190-192
    summary, 192-193
Metropolitan Achievement Tests,
    182-183
MFFT. *See Matching Familiar Figures
    Test*
Mode-marked language, 250
Monopoly, 71
MTT. *See* Metaphoric-triads task
Multifunctional syntactic structures,
    51-52
Multiple viewpoints stage of cognitive
    development, 101-102
Multistructural index
    elaboration index, 60
    SDS, 60

NAEP. *See* National Assessment of
    Educational Progress
Narrative ability of children, 253-258
    advanced, aspect of, 257
    nonepisodic stories, types of,
        254-255
    in older children, 256-258
    scoring system, 255
    story grammar and story schemata,
        relationship between, 254
    teenage gangs in New York, verbal
        facility of, 256
Narrative structures, schema of, 106,
    108-109, 110-111
National Assessment of Educational
    Progress (NAEP), 108, 121
*National Educational Development
    Test* (NEDT), 197
NEDT. *See National Educational
    Development Test*
Neo-Piagetian theory of cognitive
    development, 137-148
    approach to mechanisms of change,
        147-148

Neo-Piagetian theory of cognitive
        development (*continued*)
    developmental stages of, 137–139
    summary on, 139
The New Yorker, 53
Newsweek, 101
Nominal clauses, 69–70
Nonepisodic stories, types of, 254–255
Noun phrases, 63–65

Opaque message of speakers, 21
Operational mode of language, 250
Orality and literacy, relationship
        between
    audience, 18
    communication, intention of, 18–19,
        21
    contextualization, 16–18
    summary on, 21–22
Orthography, changes in strategies for
        relating, 98, 119–121
Otis-Lennon Mental Ability Test, 182

Particularistic or restricted meaning,
        17. *See also* Contextualization of
        written language
Peer group pressure as example of
        linguistic socialization, 239–241
Phrase level structures
    noun, 63–65
    verb, 65–68
Piagetian theory of cognitive
        development, 127, 128–137
    approach to mechanism of change,
        146–147
    concrete operations of, 128–130
        classification, 128–129
        conservation, 129–130
        seriation, 130
        summary of, 130
    formal operations, 130–137
        combination operations and
            isolation of variables,
            130–132
        conservation of volume, 131–132

hypothetical reasoning, 133–134
opposing evidence, 135–137
proportion, probability, and
        correlation, 134–135
summary of, 137
Pragmatic development
    classroom discourse, 248–251
        information-related talk, 251
        mode-marked language, 250
        process-product approach, 249
        sociolinguistic approach, 249
    conclusions on, 261
    literature on, 248
    narrative ability, 253–258
    peer instruction, 251–253
    special settings, 259–260
Pragmatic texts, 19, 20(*t*)
Process-product approach to classroom
        discourse, 249–251
Pronunciation changes in strategies for
        relating, 98, 119–121
Proverbs
    compared with other types of
            figurative language, 202–203
    definition of, 200
    preadolescents and, 201–202, 203
    sources of difficulty, 203–204
    summary of, 205–206
    task, 204–205
Public Law 94-142, 7
Punctuation, changes in strategies for
        relating, 94, 115–117

Qualitative classification system of
        word definition, 40, 41(*t*)
Quality of Solution domain of scoring
        system, 255
Quantitative data, use of, 60, 62
Quantitative measures of syntactic
        growth
    analysis, unit of, 54
        clause length, 57–58
        index, multistructural, 60
        sentence (T-unit) length, 55–57
        subordination index, 58–59
    use of, 60–62

Reactive Sequence Story, 254-255
The Reader's Digest, 101
Reading, and writing ability
  cognitive strategy development,
      stages of, 100-105
  conclusions on, 121-122
  discourse strategy developments,
      105-112
  literature review, 94-95
  relating, strategies for
    orthography, 120
    pronunciation, 120-121
    punctuation, 121
  semantic strategy developments,
      112-117
  syntactic strategy developments, 117-119
Reading for Learning the New stage of
    reading development, 101
Reading, writing, and literacy,
    relationships among, 12-15
  and literacy, 12-14
  summary on, 15
Relative clauses, 72-73
Riddles, youngsters' understanding of,
    218-219

SALT. *See* Systematic Analysis of
    Language Transcripts
Schemata (internalized cognitive
    structures)
  importance of, 105-106
  of narrative structures, 106
  organizational and global analysis
      strategies, 108
  scores, 111-112
Schooling, cognition and literacy,
    relationships between, 22-26.
    See also Literacy
Scope of Information domain of
    scoring systems, 255
SDS. *See* Syntactic Density Score
Semantic strategies for relating word
    meaning and context, 98,
    112-117
  analysis of variance for TTR
      (ANOVA), 114, 116

developmental data, 115-117
  TTR, 114
  vocabulary measures, 113
  word knowledge and language
      comprehension, correlation
      between, 112-113
Sentence length. *See* T-unit length
Sentential ambiguity, types of, 212-216
  children's understanding of, 212-213
  speed and accuracy in relation to,
      214-215
  psychological bases of, 215-216
  research with adults, 212
  summary of, 216
Sequential Test of Educational Pro-
    gress, 36
Settings, special, youngsters' pragmatic
    behavior in, 259-260
  directive types, 259
  gender-related talk, awareness of, 260
Short-term storage space (STSS), 148
Similes
  comprehension of
    external factors, 183-184
    internal factors, 181-183
  definition of, 180
Situated meaning, 17. *See also*
    Contextualization
Skill theory of cognitive development,
    127, 139-145
  abstractions, development of,
      140-142
  developmental asynchronies, 142-143
  mechanisms of change, 149-150
  optimal levels, performing at, 143
  summary of, 143
Slang expressions, as metaphoric
    production, 191-192
The Social Construction of Reality, 226
Socialization and language
  conclusions on, 243
  definition of, 225-226
  as interaction, 226-228
  linguistic socialization, 228-234
    communicative competence,
        developing, 231-232
    social power, language and, 232-234

Socialization and language (*continued*)
  linguistic socialization examples
    cross-sex communication, 238-239
    friendship, 242-243
    gender, 235-237
    identity, 234-235
    peer group, 239-242
Social power and language, 232-234
Socioeconomic status, reading and
    writing ability associated with, 23
Sociolinguistic approach to classroom
    discourse, 249-251
Sociolinguistic code, concept of,
    232-233. *See also* Social power
    and language
  internalization of, 233
Sounding, as metaphoric production,
    190-191
Spelling. *See* Orthography
Spoken language, unplanned, 78-80
Standardized tests of later language
    development, 7-8
Static Task, 251
Structures, syntactic
  clause level, 68-69
  discourse, syntax of, 73-77
    adverbial conjuncts, 74-76
    word-order variation for theme
        and focus, 76-77
  phrase level, 63-68
    noun, 63-65
    verb, 65-68
  subordination level, 69-73
    adverbial clause, 70-72
    nominal clauses, 69-70
    relative clauses, 72-73
STSS. *See* Short-term storage space
Subordinate clauses
  adverbial, 70-72
  nominal, 69-70
  relative, 72-73
Subordination index, degrees of, 58-59
  average for youngsters in 3rd
        through 12th grades, 59(*t*)
Syllogism tasks, deductive reasoning
    and, 168-176
  conditioning types, 174(*t*)

types used, 170, 171(*t*), 172(*t*), 173(*t*)
Symmetrical discussion, 242
Syntactic Density Score (SDS), 60
Syntactic-paradigmatic shift, 30-31
Syntactic strategies for processing later-
    developing syntactic structures,
    94, 113-115
Syntax, spoken and written
  conclusions on, 87-89
  discourse-based model, 77-87
    syntactic variation as function of,
        78-80
    texts, comparisons of, 80
  issues in study of, 50-53
    adult model, 52-53
    developmental schedules, 50-51
    expanding contexts for language,
        51
    multifunctional structure, 51-52
  qualitative measures in growth of
    data resources, 53-54
    quantitative data, use of, 60-62
    unit of analysis, 54-66
  research, paucity of, 49-50
  structures, development of selected,
        63-77
    at clause level, 68-69
    discourse, syntax of, 73-77
    subordinates, 69-73
Systematic Analysis of Language
    Transcripts (SALT), 99, 117
  use of, 117

Teacher's Word Book of 30,000 Words,
    113
Teenage gangs in New York, verbal
    facility of, 256
Test of Language Competence, 8
Tests of later language, development,
    standardized, 7-8
Time Magazine, 101
Transparent message of speakers, 21
Triarchic theory of cognitive
    development, 127, 143-145
  knowledge-acquisition components,
        145

level of generality, 145
mechanisms of change, 150-151
metacomponents of, 144
performance components, 144-145
summary of, 145
Type-token ratio (TTR)
  ANCOVA for, 114
  ANOVA for, 114
  definition of, 114
Typification, definition of, 227
T-unit, length of as quantitative measure
    of syntactic development, 55-57
  average for 3rd through 12th grades,
      56(*t*)
  increase as function of age, 57
  literature on, 55, 57
T-unit, mean length of, 117-118, 119, 121

Universalistic or elaborated meaning,
    17. *See also* Contextualization

Vai people, language development of,
    24-25
Verb phrases, 65-68
Verbal reasoning
  conclusions on, 176
  deductive reasoning, 160, 168
    external factors, 170-175
    internal factors, 169-170
    summary on, 175-176
  inductive reasoning, 160-168
    external factors, 163-168
    internal factors, 161-163
    summary on, 168
Verbs, comprehension of, 32-34, 114
Vocabulary growth, 31
Vocabulary measures, use of to judge
    children's compositions, 113

Wechsler Adult Intelligence Scale, 40
*Wechsler Intelligence Scale for
    Children—Revised* (WISC-R), 40

*Wechsler Preschool and Primary Scale
    of Intelligence*, 40
Word classes
  adverbs, 34-35
  connectives, 35-39
    acquisition of, 37
    comprehension, development of,
        37-38
    conjunctions, definition of, 35
    Connective Reading Test, 36-37
  verbs, 32-34
    comprehension of and age, 33
    literate, 32
Word definitions
  developmental studies of, 40-43
  interpreting studies of, 43
  qualitative classification system, 41(*t*)
  summary on, 43-44
  tasks, 40
The Word Test, 8
Writing, and reading ability
  cognitive strategy, developmental
      stages of, 100-105
  conclusions on, 121-122
  discourse strategy developments,
      105-112
  literature review, 98-99
  relating, strategies for
    orthography, 120
    pronunciation, 120-121
    punctuation, 121
  semantic strategy developments,
      112-117
  syntactic strategy developments,
      117-119
Writing and reading and literacy,
    relationships among
  definition of writing, 15
  and literacy, 14-15
  summary of, 15
Written language developed from inner
    language, 109-110
Written language, planned, 79-80

Notes

Notes

Notes

Notes

Notes

Notes